JOHN **WESLEY'S**
TEACHINGS

Also by Thomas C. Oden

John Wesley's Teachings, Volume 1

John Wesley's Teachings, Volume 2

John Wesley's Teachings, Volume 3

John Wesley's Teachings, Volume 4

VOLUME 3

PASTORAL THEOLOGY

JOHN WESLEY'S
TEACHINGS

THOMAS C. ODEN

ZONDERVAN®

ZONDERVAN.com/
AUTHORTRACKER
follow your favorite authors

We want to hear from you. Please send your comments about this book to us in care of zreview@zondervan.com. Thank you.

ZONDERVAN

John Wesley's Teachings, Volume 3
Copyright © 2012 by Thomas C. Oden

This title is also available as a Zondervan ebook. Visit www.zondervan.com/ebooks.

Requests for information should be addressed to:

Zondervan, *Grand Rapids, Michigan* 49530

Library of Congress Cataloging-in-Publication Data

Oden, Thomas C.
        John Wesley's teachings / Thomas C. Oden.
            v. cm.
        Rev. ed. of: John Wesley's scriptural Christianity. c1994.
        Includes bibliographical references and indexes.
        Contents: v. 1. God and providence— v. 2. Christ and salvation— v. 3. Pastoral theology—
    v. 4. Issues of ethics and society.
        ISBN 978-0-310-58709-5 (softcover)
        1. Wesley, John, 1703-1791. 2. Theology, Doctrinal. 3. Methodist Church—Doctrines.
    4. Theology, Doctrinal—History—18th century. 5. Methodist Church—Doctrines—History—
    18th century. I. Oden, Thomas C. John Wesley's scriptural Christianity. II. Title.
    BX8331.3.O35   2012
    230'.7092—dc23   2012001655

Cover design: *John Hamilton Design*
Cover image: *Corbis*® *Images*
Interior design: *Beth Shagene*
Edited by *Katya Covrett and Laura Dodge Weller*

Printed in the United States of America

HB 10.08.2024

To my own Wesley mentors:
    Albert Cook Outler
    David Shipley
    William Burt Pope

Contents

VOLUME THREE
Pastoral Theology

C. Baptism and New Birth

1. The Beginning of New Life in the Covenant Community

2. Baptism as a Sign and Seal of Regeneration

3. Begun in Baptism, the New Birth Continues to Grow toward Full Participation in Christ

4. Behavioral Evidences of the Power of Baptism

D. The Meaning of Baptism

1. A Treatise on Baptism

2. What Does It Mean to Be Baptized?

3. An Outward Sign of an Inward Grace

4. Scriptural Accounts of Alternative Modes of Baptism

E. The Benefits of Baptism

1. First Benefit: The Value of Christ's Death Is Applied to Sinners

2. Second Benefit: We Are Welcomed to the New Covenant Community

3. Third Benefit: We Become Members of the Body of Christ

4. Fourth Benefit: We Are Grafted into the Body of Christ and Made Children of God

5. Fifth Benefit: We Are Made Heirs of the New Reign of God

F. Baptism as a Means of Grace Instituted by the Lord

1. A Means of Grace Enduring through Time

2. Saving Effects Conditional upon Reception of Grace

3. Quenching the Spirit

G. Familial Baptism

1. Circumcision and Baptism

2. In Scripture Whole Families Enter the Covenant Together

3. Serious Thoughts Concerning Godfathers and Godmothers

A. At the Lord's Table

1. Duty of Constant Communion

2. Communion Counseling

3. Just Receive the Gift

4. Duty and Emotion

Preface

Tolerance for varied opinions is a prominent feature of Wesley's view of teaching. He wrote:

> Condemn no man for not thinking as you think: Let every one enjoy the full and free liberty of thinking for himself: Let every man use his own judgment, since every man must give an account of himself to God. Abhor every approach, in any kind or degree, to the spirit of persecution. If you cannot reason or persuade a man into the truth, never attempt to force him into it. If love will not compel him to come in, leave him to God, the Judge of all.[1]

The Series

This series provides a reader's guide to John Wesley's teaching. This volume continues the sequence begun in volume 1, Wesley's teaching on God and providence, and volume 2 on Christ and salvation.

In this volume, I focus on the basic tenets of Wesley's evangelical teaching on the church, ministry, and pastoral care. This includes his writings on the call to ministry, discipleship, pastoral leadership, soul care, baptism, and the Lord's Supper. My goal is to convey in the most concise way the core argument of all major and most minor texts of John Wesley.

The method of all four volumes remains the same: close adherence to the primary source texts of John Wesley organized in a systematic sequence. I have tried to hold close to the text itself in Wesley's own plain-spoken writings, and to convey its meaning in contemporary language.

My aim is to introduce Wesley's teaching to evangelical, orthodox, and Catholic readers who have never met him. Many believers in Wesley's connection in the past century have never been given an opportunity to read him in depth or to be intellectually formed by his fertile mind. Nevertheless, millions of believers over the last two and a half centuries have worshiped in faith communities shaped by his remarkable ministry.

---

[1] Advice to the People Called Methodist, B 9:130, sec. 23.

This Volume

With this volume, I seek to deliver to nonprofessional readers the gist of Wesley's teaching on the church and pastoral care. Wesley delved deeply into biblical teachings on the nature of the church, the pastoral office, its ministries of preaching and worship, and outreach to ordinary folk who long to share in life in Christ. His writings on pastoral counsel include teaching homilies on marriage, children, care for families, care for singles, and care for the sick and dying.

While this volume is not comprehensive, it includes core insights from all of these varied types of literature: essays, hymns, homilies, and prayers. My purpose is not to explore every aspect of a given writing or to unpack differences in its interpretation or to try to solve all of the text's implications. Rather, my purpose is to show in each text the heart of Wesley's argument, his intention, and his relevance for today. If we track carefully Wesley's own writings on church, ministry, and pastoral care, we will find ourselves reviewing the full range of issues normally discussed in pastoral theology today.

The Body of Work

Wesley was a relentless writer, an avid diarist, a traveling preacher constantly on the move, and a public figure for six decades. He left behind him a huge body of work. This includes 151 teaching homilies, six decades of daily journals (1735 – 91) and manuscript diaries, and eight volumes of his letters, plus many miscellaneous essays, Scripture studies, doctrinal tracts, and occasional writings.

From this massive literature, I have gleaned Wesley's ideas, thinking, and teaching on the care of souls. And I have sought to condense these for modern readers into understandable and usable segments fit for meditation, preaching, and theological study. Much of Wesley's instruction applies to today's social conditions. The legacy of these writings is immense. The heritage is priceless.

In his address to readers of his collected works of 1771, Wesley sought to organize his teaching homilies into a naturally unfolding sequence: "I wanted to methodize these tracts, *to range them under proper heads*, placing those together which were on similar subjects, and in such order that one might illustrate another."[2] Many of these homilies focused on pastoral theology, challenges in the practice of ministry, and care of souls. This is the systematic design we will build upon.

It is impossible to detach Wesley's pastoral care from his teachings on God, Christ, salvation, and the work of the Spirit. Pastoral care is like an extended footnote to his teaching of salvation. Those who pick up this volume alone and wonder about his view of scriptural authority do well to go back to volume 1 where that

---

[2]"Preface to the Third Edition," J I.3, in a brief address "To the Reader" in the thirty-two duodecima volumes of 1774, italics added.

is fully discussed. Others will consult volume 2 for more detailed expositions on atonement, faith, assurance, grace, election, and predestination.

The Order of Topics

In his "Preface to the Third Edition" of 1771, Wesley concisely stated his desire to serve ordinary readers who sought to grasp an overall perspective on his work: he sought to arrange his writings under proper heads, locate similar subjects together, and allow one to illustrate another. Looking over his whole body of work, Wesley mused that "there is scarce any subject of importance, either in practical or controversial divinity, which is not treated of more or less, either professionally or occasionally" in this body of "practical divinity."[3]

Wesley's works are largely written for laypersons. He deals with issues commonly discussed today on the nature and mission of the church, its laity, and its clergy and their calling and preparation for gospel ministry, counsel, care, and admonition. The homilies on these subjects are supplemented here by the occasional treatises, journal references, and letters on these subjects that are spread widely apart. As far as possible, I have followed Wesley's own pattern in unfolding the logical order of subjects dealing with church and ministry and key topics of pastoral theology.

Defining Pastoral Theology

Pastoral theology is the branch of theology concerned with the study of God within the context of the ministry of the clergy and the ministry of lay believers. Pastoral theology seeks to give practical expression to life with God. It is often considered to be the more down-to-earth part of theology, more pragmatic than speculative, and intended for the equipping of ministers, clergy and lay. Its subtopics ordinarily include all the topics of our table of contents: the church, the office and gifts of ministry, homiletics, pastoral care, liturgics, and church leadership and the applications of doctrinal and moral theology. Pastoral theology teaches the gifts and tasks of "the ministers of Christ, and stewards of the mysteries of God" (1 Cor. 4:1). Systematic theology establishes the Scriptures as the depository of revealed truth and systematizes the deposit of faith that Christ entrusted to his church. Pastoral theology teaches the ministers of Christ how to pass along the wisdom of the Christian tradition of revealed truth to congregations and believers. Moral theology sets forth the basis of moral judgments in the Christian community. Pastoral theology teaches the practical bearing of these forms of wisdom, means of grace, and implications for the daily life of one called to the care of souls. Pastoral theology takes the wisdom of all these forms of theology and makes their results effective for the salvation of souls through the ministry established by Christ.

Though a specific discipline called "pastoral theology" has emerged only fairly

---

[3]"Preface to the Third Edition," J I:3.

recently, the wisdom it conveys is as old as the church itself. The sources of pastoral theology are the Bible, the ancient Christian writers, and the major writers from the medieval and Reformation periods as they portray the pastoral office, the church and ministry, and approaches to the care of souls.

The subject matter of pastoral theology appears in the many instructions Jesus gave to his apostles for the care of souls.[4] The ancient Christian exegetes from the apostolic age onward are replete with pastoral instructions, from Ignatius of Antioch (AD 110) to Gregory the Great's *Regulae pastoralis liber* of AD 590. This defining period of pastoral theology includes the works of Clement of Alexandria, Cyprian, Gregory of Nazianzus, John Chrysostom, Augustine, and Ambrose. From there the great tradition continues from Bede to Thomas Aquinas, to Bonaventure, to Luther, Calvin, Cranmer, and Wesley.

Since the time of Gregory I, classic treatments of pastoral theology have often been framed under the threefold headings of teaching, imparting the sacred mysteries, and shepherding souls. These include catechesis, homiletics, and liturgics. Since pastors have often been mediators of medical wisdom to poor congregations, pastoral care has often imparted medical knowledge requisite for the proper care of souls, sometimes called pastoral medicine. As an academic field in modern universities and seminaries, pastoral theology encompasses the theological foundations of healing and care, pastoral psychology, psychology of religion, and the theories and practices of counsel.

The Method of Inquiry into Pastoral Theology

The Jewish tradition of textual comment on the truth conveyed by the inspired sacred text remains our pattern for this volume. The aim of rabbinic and patristic exegesis was to draw the truth out of the text, adhering closely to each word and phrase and context of the text, and to bring it home to a useful recognition, so as to effect behavioral change. The sacred text here is not that of Wesley, but the Holy Writ that informed every stitch of the fabric of his teaching.

The classic Christian exegetes interpreted Scripture to the faithful text by text. Regrettably few works in pastoral care function today by this method. Wesley's approach to pastoral theology used teaching homilies grounded in Scripture texts. He thus provided a fresh look at pastoral care.

The method of inquiry we find in Wesley is a time-tested comparison of Scripture with Scripture. It works to connect text with text and with the subtexts that reveal Scripture's intent for the church and pastoral care. Here theological and pastoral truth is derived directly from the primary text itself, as distinguished from the contextual history surrounding its development. Wesley unapologetically assumed the internal coherence, unity, and continuity of the prophetic and apostolic witnesses. He constantly employed "the analogy of faith" by comparing texts with texts

---

[4]Matt. 3:12 – 7:28; 10:6 – 10; 25; Mark 6:8 – 11.

in their plain sense, praying for the inspiration of the Spirit. Where a Scripture text appears ambiguous, it is clarified in relation to Scripture texts that are unambiguous. This method is primarily exegetical and secondarily systematic. This means that I will work textually with Wesley's key writings on a given subject, organizing these texts thematically so they present a coherent picture of Wesley's teaching.

I have deliberately focused on primary sources written by John Wesley rather than secondary sources about him. I leave to others, especially those with more historical than pastoral interests, the pursuit of developmental questions concerning Wesley's theological and biographical transformations in their social context. However intriguing the social history, the psychological history, social location issues, and historical critical issues may be, they have not left behind a practical track record of helpful insight for preaching pastors and pastoral counselors.

I appeal to you to go back to the original texts. Check out for yourself the viability of Wesley's teaching by letting him speak for himself. This study is only an invitation to go directly to the primary Wesley text to gain further insight.

Wesley has often been treated as a "folk theologian" or primarily a practitioner of "practical divinity." He has seldom been viewed either as a pastoral counselor or one-on-one caregiver or as a master teacher of pastoral theology. In the first two volumes of this series, I have presented Wesley as a profound systematic theologian covering all the major theological loci from creation to consummation. This volume shows him as a pastoral theologian engaged constantly in the practice of pastoral counseling and leadership in ministry.

My aim is to provide a fair, present-day exposition of Wesley's teaching on pastoral care. This method is inductive and expository. Its order is systematic. If I have intruded my own views inordinately upon Wesley, I have failed in my deeper intention. My aim is not to speculate unnecessarily on the complex social and political circumstances in which he was writing. These I leave to specialists who better know that territory.

Tracking References to the Major Editions

The preferred scholarly edition of *The Works of John Wesley* is the Oxford/Abingdon Bicentennial edition (Oxford: 1975–83; Nashville: 1984–), signified by B.[5]

The most frequently reproduced edition, often still the only one appearing on library and pastoral bookshelves, is the Thomas Jackson edition, first published in 1829–31, signified by J for Jackson. Thus, whenever B or J appears in the footnotes, the reader is being directed to either the Bicentennial edition (B) or the Jackson edition (J). This is necessary because the reader may have access to one but not both editions. Many more copies of the Jackson edition have been distributed than the Bicentennial edition.

---

[5]In rare cases where Sugden's edition of the Standard Sermons (see Abbreviations: *SS*) is quoted, the reader's attention is directed especially to Sugden's annotations.

Here are the key guidelines for the scholarly apparatus:

- Volume references in Arabic numerals refer to the Bicentennial edition. Volume references in uppercase Roman numerals refer to the Jackson edition.
- Both the Bicentennial edition (B) and the Jackson edition (J) are available in searchable CD ROMs or online. In the case of B, the current disk is still incomplete, awaiting print publication of many volumes.
- Distinguishing a B reference from a J reference is easy: If the first digit is an Arabic numeral, the reference is to B. If the first digit is an uppercase Roman numeral, the reference is to J. A reference to B 4:133 indicates the Bicentennial edition, volume 4, page 133. But a reference to J IV:133 indicates the Jackson edition, volume 4 (IV), page 133.
- In cases where a new homily is being introduced in order to be discussed more fully, I have referenced in parentheses the Bicentennial edition (B) in this conventional order: the homily number, the date of the homily, and the volume and page references in the Bicentennial edition. Where the Jackson edition (J) is referenced, I have listed the homily number and the volume and page references in Jackson.
- At times the homily numbers appear in a different order and number in the Bicentennial than in the Jackson edition.[6]

My purpose is to assist those who wish to handily access the proper text in the available edition. Readers will more frequently be working out of either J or B but ordinarily not both. For convenience, we cite both editions. An appendix titled "Alphabetical Correlation of the Sermons in the Jackson and Bicentennial Editions" can be found at the back of all volumes. Those who are doing scholarly research work are advised to work with the Bicentennial edition whenever possible.

On Biblical References

Though Wesley expressed abiding gratitude for the King James Version, especially in its value for common worship, his study text was normally in the original language. In citing the lead text for his homilies, I ordinarily cite the King James Authorized text (KJV) from which Wesley was preaching or writing, unless specified otherwise.

When he published his own translation of the New Testament, many references in the Authorized Version of 1611 were altered to communicate with his plain-speaking audience of the 1700s. There is no reason to think that Wesley regarded his own English rendering of the Greek as definitive for future centuries of English readers for whom the language protocols and usages would have shifted as they normally do over decades.

Those who might assume that Wesley himself was constantly working out of the

---

[6]For example, "The Trouble and Rest of Good Men" appears as Sermon 109 in the Bicentennial edition (B #109), and as Sermon 127 in the Jackson edition (J #127). The numbering is often the same but in some instances is different.

King James Version do well to recall that Wesley read the Greek New Testament fluently. He studied it daily in his early morning and evening meditation.

On Other Editions of Wesley's Works

The only collected edition published during Wesley's lifetime was the thirty-two-volume Bristol edition of *The Works of the Rev. John Wesley* (Bristol, UK: William Pine, 1771 – 74).

The second edition of *The Works of the Rev. John Wesley* was edited by Joseph Benson (17 vols., London: Conference Offices, 1809 – 13; repr. New York and Philadelphia in 10 vols., 1826 – 27).

The most-used third edition of *The Works of the Rev. John Wesley*, edited by Thomas Jackson (14 vols., London, 1829 – 31), has been frequently reprinted in America and is employed here as one of two major available editions of Wesley's Works.[7]

Prior to the Bicentennial edition, the editions that presented an annotated editorial apparatus to the works of Wesley, with scholarly introductions according to modern standards, were Nehemiah Curnock's edition of the Journals (see *JJW* in Abbreviations) in 1916, Edward H. Sugden's edition of the Standard Sermons (see *SS*) in 1921, John Telford's edition of the Letters (see *LJW*) in 1931, and Albert C. Outler's selection of Wesley's key writings (see JWO) in 1964. These are all commended here. The Oxford/Abingdon Bicentennial edition (see B in Abbreviations)[8] will stand for generations to come as the definitive edition.

Wesley's Patrimony

The untold numbers of hymns were mostly written by John's brother Charles but many were edited by John. These were the fruits of their editing and publishing over a very long time span. It is difficult to think of a single figure in the eighteenth century who left behind such a massive body of work as did John Wesley.

This series seeks to deliver to the nonprofessional reader the gist of the whole of Wesley's patrimony in systematic order. It provides a window into the basic wisdom

---

[7]That Telford, Sugden, Curnock, and Jackson (see Abbreviations) are hardly mentioned in the Bicentennial edition of the Sermons remains a puzzle. They all contain useful notes pertinent to this study. The American edition, edited by John Emory, was published in New York in 1831, based on the Jackson edition. In many libraries, the Jackson edition is the only one available.

[8]When "Articles of Religion" (Art.) are indicated, I am referring to Wesley's own recension of the Twenty-Four Articles (to which the 1784 American Methodist Church added a twenty-fifth), derived and edited down from the Anglican Thirty-Nine Articles. The Articles have played a central role in the American Wesleyan doctrinal traditions. They are included in the constitutions of most church bodies of the Wesleyan tradition. When Confession (Confes.) is referenced, I am indicating the summary of Wesleyan faith set forth in the 1962 Confession of the Evangelical United Brethren, which by a constitutionally restrictive rule has become a doctrinal standard of the United Methodist Church. A reference to the first article of the Confession appears as Confes. 1.

of his Christian teaching. While it cannot claim to be comprehensive, it seeks to include core insights from all of these varied genres of literature.

This is why we need multiple volumes to examine this massive range of Wesley's works. A shorter series would threaten to cut off essential parts. For readers who want to investigate only one doctrine or idea, the Further Reading on each section will make these searches more accessible.

On This Edition

Zondervan has a distinguished reputation as a publisher of reference works and classics, many of them bound in multivolume editions. My hope is that this series will become a sufficiently useful resource for lay and professional readers that it will be in due time made available digitally for international readers for decades to come. Nothing like this text-by-text review of the content of Wesley's teaching exists in Wesley studies.

In 1994 Zondervan published my earlier study of Wesley's doctrine under the title *John Wesley's Scriptural Christianity: A Plain Exposition of His Teaching on Christian Doctrine (JWSC)*. In this present edition, much of the content of that single volume is now expanded and extensively revised, quadrupling the information presented in the earlier single volume.

Abbreviations

ACCS	*The Ancient Christian Commentary on Scripture.* Edited by Thomas C. Oden. Downers Grove, IL: InterVarsity, 1997–2010.
art.	article.
AM	*Arminian Magazine.*
AMW	Karen B. Westerfield Tucker. *American Methodist Worship.* New York: Oxford University Press, 2001.
AS	*Asbury Seminarian.*
B	Bicentennial edition of *The Works of John Wesley.* Edited by Frank Baker and Richard Heitzenrater. Oxford, Clarendon, and New York: Oxford University Press, 1975–83; Nashville: Abingdon, 1984–; in print: volumes 1, 2, 3, 4, 7, 18, 19, 20, 21, 22, 23, 24. Vols. 14–16 of the Bicentennial edition, on pastoral, ethical, and instructional writings, and on medicine and many other topics are as yet in preparation.
BCP	Book of Common Prayer.
BEM	Bernard G. Holland. *Baptism in Early Methodism.* London: Epworth, 1970.
Bull.	Bulletin
CCJW	*The Cambridge Companion to John Wesley.* Edited by Randy L. Maddox and Jason E. Vickers. Cambridge: Cambridge University Press, 2009.
CH	*A Collection of Hymns for the Use of the People Called Methodists,* vol. 7 of the Bicentennial edition.
Chr.	Christian.
CL	A Christian Library
Confes.	1962 Confession of the Evangelical United Brethren.
CTA	John Fletcher. *Checks to Antinominism.* New York: J. Collard, 1837.
CWT	Robert W. Burtner and Robert E. Chiles. *A Compend of Wesley's Theology.* Nashville: Abingdon, 1954.
Diss.	Dissertation.

DOS   *The Doctrine of Original Sin according to Scripture, Reason, and Experience.*

DPF   "Dialogue between a Predestinarian and His Friend."

DSF   "The Doctrine of Salvation, Faith and Good Works Extracted from the Homilies of the Church of England."

DSWT   Thomas C. Oden. *Doctrinal Standards in the Wesleyan Tradition.* Grand Rapids: Zondervan, 1988.

EA   "An Earnest Appeal to Men of Reason and Religion."

ENNT   *Explanatory Notes upon the New Testament.*

ENOT   *Explanatory Notes upon the Old Testament.*

ETS   Evangelical Theological Society.

EWT   Paul Mickey. *Essentials of Wesleyan Theology.* Grand Rapids: Zondervan, 1980.

FA   "A Farther Appeal to Men of Reason and Religion."

FAP   Francis Asbury Press, Zondervan.

FB   Howard Slaatte. *Fire in the Brand: Introduction to the Creative Work and Theology of John Wesley.* New York: Exposition, 1963.

FW   Kenneth Collins. *A Faithful Witness: John Wesley's Homiletical Theology.* Wilmore, KY: Wesleyan Heritage, 1993.

FWAT   Mildred Bangs Wynkoop. *Foundations of Wesleyan-Arminian Theology.* Kansas City: Beacon Hill, 1967.

HSP   *Hymns and Sacred Poems.*

J   Jackson edition of Wesley's Works. Edited by Thomas Jackson, 1829–32. 1872 edition reprinted in many 14-volume American editions (Eerdmans, Zondervan, Christian Book Distributors, et al.); portions digitally available on Wesley.nnu.edu.

JBR   *Journal of Bible and Religion.*

JJW   *The Journal of John Wesley.* Edited by Nehemiah Curnock. 8 vols. London: Epworth, 1916.

JWCE   Frank Baker, *John Wesley and the Church of England.* London: Epworth, 2000.

JWO   *John Wesley.* Edited by Albert C. Outler. Library of Protestant Theology. New York: Oxford University Press, 1964.

JWPH   Robert Monk. *John Wesley: His Puritan Heritage.* Nashville: Abingdon, 1966.

JWSC   Thomas C. Oden. *John Wesley's Scriptural Christianity: A Plain Exposition of His Teaching on Christian Doctrine.* Grand Rapids: Zondervan, 1994.

JWTT	Colin Williams. *John Wesley's Theology Today*. Nashville: Abingdon, 1960.
LCM	Letter to the Rev. Dr. Conyers Middleton (January 4, 1749).
LJW	*Letters of John Wesley*. Edited by John Telford. 8 vols. London: Epworth, 1931.
LPC	Letter on Preaching Christ (same as Letter to an Evangelical Layman, December 20, 1751).
LQHR	*London Quarterly and Holborn Review.*
LS	Thomas C. Oden. *Life in the Spirit*. San Francisco: HarperSanFrancisco, 1992.
LW	James H. Rigg. *The Living Wesley*. 3rd ed. London, 1905.
LWM	Henry Moore. *Life of Wesley*. London: n.p., 1824–25.
MH	*Methodist History.*
Minutes	"Minutes of Some Late Conversations between the Rev. Mr. Wesley and Others."
MLS	*Martin Luther: Selections from His Writings*. Edited by John Dillenberger. New York: Doubleday, 1961.
MM	*Methodist Magazine.*
MOB	William M. Arnett. "John Wesley: Man of One Book." PhD dissertation. Drew University, 1954.
MPL	*Patrologia latina (Patrologiae cursus completus: Series latina)*. Edited by J.-P. Migne. 217 vols. Paris: 1844–64.
MQR	*Methodist Quarterly Review.*
MR	*Methodist Review.*
NDM	Reinhold Niebuhr. *The Nature and Destiny of Man*. 2 vols. New York: Scribner, 1941, 1943.
NIV	New International Version.
NT	New Testament.
OED	*Oxford English Dictionary.*
OT	Old Testament.
PACP	*A Plain Account of Christian Perfection.*
PCC	"Predestination Calmly Considered."
PM	*Preacher's Magazine.*
Pref.	Preface.
Publ.	Publishing, Publishers.
PW	*Poetical Works of Charles Wesley and John Wesley*. Edited by George Osborn. 13 vols. London: Wesleyan Methodist Conference, 1868–72.

PWHS	*Proceedings of the Wesley Historical Society.*
Q	Quarterly.
QR	*Quarterly Review.*
RC	Roman Catholic.
RE	Henry D. Rack. *Reasonable Enthusiast.* Philadelphia: Trinity Press International, 1985.
RJW	George Croft Cell. *The Rediscovery of John Wesley.* New York: Henry Holt, 1935.
RL	*Religion in Life.*
RPTK	*Realencyklopädie für protestantische Theologie und Kirche.* Edited by J. J. Herzog and A. Hauck. 24 vols. Leipzig: J. Hinriches, 1896–1913.
SS	*The Standard Sermons of John Wesley.* Edited by Edward H. Sugden. 2 vols. London: Epworth, 1921; 3rd ed., 1951.
SOSO	John Wesley. *Sermons on Several Occasions.* 3 vols. London: W. Strahan, 1746.
SSM	*The Sunday Service of the Methodists in North America, with Other Occasional Services* (1784). Edited by Edward C. Hobbs. Nashville: Methodist Student Movement, 1956.
TIRC	"Thoughts on the Imputation of the Righteousness of Christ."
TJW	William R. Cannon. *Theology of John Wesley: With Special Reference to the Doctrine of Justification.* New York: Abingdon, 1946.
TUN	"Thoughts upon Necessity."
Tyerman	Luke Tyerman. *Life and Times of Rev. John Wesley.* 6th ed., facsimile. Stoke on Trent: n.p., 2000.
UMC	United Methodist Church.
unpubl.	Unpublished.
WC	John Deschner. *Wesley's Christology.* Grand Rapids: Zondervan, 1989.
WHS	Lycurgus M. Starkey. *The Work of the Holy Spirit.* Nashville: Abingdon, 1962.
WMM	*Wesleyan Methodist Magazine.*
WOF	Isaac Ambrose and Samuel Kneeland. *The Well-Ordered Family: Wherein the Duties of Its Various Members Are Described and Urged.* Charleston: Nabu Press/BiblioBazaar, 2010. See digital version available at nnu.edu.
WQ	Donald Thorsen. *The Wesleyan Quadrilateral: Scripture, Tradition, Reason, and Experience as a Model of Evangelical Theology.* Grand Rapids: Zondervan, 1990.
WQR	*Wesleyan Quarterly Review*

WRE	John W. Prince. *Wesley on Religious Education.* New York: Methodist Book Concern, 1926.
WS	Harald G. A. Lindström. *Wesley and Sanctification.* Nashville: Abingdon, 1946.
WTH	Albert C. Outler. *The Wesleyan Theological Heritage: Essays of Albert C. Outler.* Edited by Thomas C. Oden and Leicester R. Longden. Grand Rapids: Zondervan, 1991.
WTJ	*Wesleyan Theological Journal.*
XXV	Twenty-Five Articles. Adapted from the Sunday Service of 1784.
XXXIX	Anglican Thirty-Nine Articles of Religion.

Introduction

A. Biblical Pastoral Care through Wesley's Eyes

The way pastoral care was taught by eighteenth-century Anglican divines was largely through published teaching homilies, quite different from the way we write on pastoral theology today. Teaching by a book of homilies was a familiar pattern of the English church tradition of Thomas Cranmer, John Jewel, and Matthew Parker. These instructional sermons were based on biblical texts. They were designed to guide congregations on commonly received Christian teachings.

Similarly, John Wesley followed this two-hundred-year Anglican tradition by modestly offering his own teaching homilies to those in his direct connection of spiritual formation. My objective is to set forth the inner cohesion of these diverse points of Wesley's pastoral teaching.

To stand "in Wesley's connection" has meant that one voluntarily looks to him for spiritual formation. Millions in the eighteenth and nineteenth centuries have stood within this direct connection (spelled *connexion* in Wesley's day; today regarded as archaic but still used among British Methodists). They may not have read Wesley's writings, but they have been fed by his pastoral instruction, his ways of engendering vital communities of faith, and the productive literary outcome of his powerful ministry.

The most conspicuous feature of Wesley's work on the church and pastoral care is his persistent focus on the church as a work of the Holy Spirit. Everything follows from this premise. The Spirit is bringing into being the communities of faith in Christ. The office of pastor is to guide the flock toward the life that God the Spirit is creating.

The study of Wesley's pastoral care is an exercise in daily practical spiritual maturation. Protestant, Orthodox, and Catholic readers all have found benefit.

1. Wesley as Pastoral Guide

The early evangelical revivals in Great Britain were profoundly shaped and informed by the ministries of George Whitefield, the Countess of Huntingdon, William Wilberforce, and William and Catherine Booth. Earlier than all of these, however, was the evangelical revival initiated by the Spirit through the calling of John and Charles Wesley. All of the above owed a great debt to the Wesleys.[1]

John Wesley showed remarkable gifts and skills as a pastoral guide. Wesley gave himself unreservedly to the soul care of thousands in countless Welsh, English, Colonial Georgian, Native American, Irish, and Scottish villages, traveling incessantly to serve the interests of their spiritual maturation. Much of his pastoral care is revealed in his letters and journals, but most of its grounding appears in his teaching homilies.

Many evangelicals today remain in Wesley's evangelical connection or in remnants of it. Their lives and histories have been shaped by these pastoral instructions, read and reread over two and a half centuries. The roots of the global Pentecostal tradition have been decisively shaped by Wesley's teaching on the work of the Spirit in our hearts and in human history. The Pentecostals alone have a quarter billion evangelical believers. These worldwide communities of Wesleyan, charismatic, Pentecostal, and holiness churches resulting from his ministry are growing exponentially at much faster rates than are the mainline churches in North America and Europe. Today believers in all of these church traditions are asking how they might be formed by Wesley's wisdom and joyful integrity.

A conspicuous array of worldwide church bodies has spun off from the early evangelical Methodist and holiness revival preaching. These include the Wesleyan Church, the Free Methodist Church, the Church of the Nazarene, the Salvation Army, the African Methodist Episcopal and African Methodist Episcopal Zion traditions, and many mission agencies, as well as the United Methodist Church worldwide. These far-flung, fruit-bearing missional spin-offs have been more faithful to Wesley than the institutional giants among these bodies. Christians of widely different traditions who have no connection with Wesley often see in him a godly leader of special spiritual power who has quietly affected their own traditions. The estimated thirty million believers around the world who attend Wesleyan and Methodist churches have doctrinal and disciplinary standards that have deep roots in Wesley's teaching on the care of souls.

Modernity has not outdated Wesley. It is still possible for persons thoroughly immersed in modern consciousness and technology to appropriate Wesley's spiritual counsel. He is not as remote in language and time as the earliest Christian writers, but he is very close to them in spirit. In pastoral care, he was deeply attentive to the historic roots from which he drew strength, especially the patristic writings and the magisterial Reformation texts of Luther and Calvin, as well as Anglican, holiness, and in particular, the Puritan traditions.

What is most powerful in Wesley's pastoral teaching has close affinities with the classic consensual Christian writers of the earliest Christian centuries. Wesley

---

[1] Wesley was a contemporary of Jonathan Edwards and had read Edwards on the religious affections with great appreciation.

offered his teaching in plain speech because the gospel was addressed to ordinary people in plain speech. Diverse audiences, including Reformed, Catholic, pietistic, and charismatic hearers have listened to his teaching or appropriated echoes of his teaching. They intuitively recognize his affinity with the best minds of ancient ecumenical teaching.

In classic Christian teaching, all truth claims are tested in relation to apostolic teaching. That rule applies to Wesley, and he confirms its truth. So do not brace for some sort of disproportionate dogmatic slant on pastoral care. Wesley was an evangelical Anglican who was thoroughly grounded in classic orthodoxy predating modern partisan divisions.

2. A Personal Retrospect

A personal, vocational retrospect may help some readers to get in touch with my motivation for including this volume in this series. My calling for the last forty years[2] has been to assist in recovering classic Christian wisdom. Within classic consensual Christianity, I come from the orthodox and evangelical circle of teaching. Many orthodox and evangelical believers have not had the opportunity to explore Wesley's pastoral teaching.

For thirty-three years, my work has been primarily located in the New York City area. At Drew University, one of Methodism's premier academic institutions, I taught graduate students in the heart of modern, liberal, ecumenical Protestantism. This was during a time when Western society was languishing in a desperate series of social and moral crises.

I have taught and written chiefly on patristic exegesis and systematic theology but without ever losing affectionate interest in pastoral theology. During the more than three decades I had the pleasure of teaching excellent graduate school candidates at Drew, some of my most gratifying classes were those in the Wesley seminar and in the seminar on pastoral theology. In this volume, I take special delight in bringing together these two interests — Wesley and pastoral care.

Wesley was the foremost eighteenth-century evangelical teacher on pastoral theology. The only plausible competitors between the times of Richard Baxter (1615 – 91)[3] and Jean Nicholas Grou (1731 – 1803)[4] for enduring contributions to practical theology would likely be Edmund Gibson (1669 – 1748),[5] Josiah Hort (d. 1751),[6] Jonathan Edwards (1703 – 58),[7] and Johann Frederic Jacoby (1712 – 91).[8] None of these reached the range and depth of Wesley on either pastoral theology

---

[2]Since the early 1970s. See *Agenda for Theology* (Harper, 1979); the revised edition, published a decade later in 1990 by Zondervan, was retitled *After Modernity ... What? Agenda for Theology.*
[3]*Christian Directory: A Body of Practical Divinity.*
[4]*Manual for Interior Souls.*
[5]*Codex juris ecclesiastici Anglicani*, 2 vols., 1713.
[6]*Instructions to the Clergy*, 1742.
[7]*The Religious Affections*, 1754.
[8]*Beitrag zür Pastoral Theologie*, 2 vols., 1774 – 82.

or pastoral practice.[9] His indefatigable energies decisively shaped the earliest stages of the first Great Awakening.

The few books on Wesley's pastoralia have hardly scratched the surface. A full treatment is required. Since writing *Pastoral Theology: Essentials of Ministry* (HarperOne, 1983), I have been focusing most of my research energies on the twenty-nine-volume *Ancient Christian Commentary on Scripture* (IVP, 1996 – 2010) and its derivative projects. Now this series has given me a welcome opportunity to return again to Wesley studies and pastoral care.

These pastoral interests are not merely an incidental part of my vocation, nor are they at odds with my vocation of recent years to focus on postmodern orthodoxy and classical consensual Christianity. This volume is another expression of my ongoing work in classic Christianity, for Wesley is among the best exemplars of classic consensual exegesis in modern Christianity. He was teaching at Oxford during a revival of the study of the ancient Christian writers. The classic consensual teaching found in the *Ancient Christian Commentary on Scripture* is the seedbed of Wesley's pastoral teaching. A veiled providence has brought me to the point of returning to these classic Christian teachings, primarily for my own spiritual formation and the recovery of balance in theological reasoning.

My constant aim is to avoid all pretenses of originality. I seek to be relentlessly attentive not only to Mr. Wesley but to classic consensual texts on Christian pastoral care. I promise nothing innovative. I am intent on not trying to "improve" on classic consensual Christianity. As a theologian dedicated to the rediscovery of classic Christian teaching on behalf of the modern church, I am grateful to be able to spend these sunset years living once again with these Wesley texts and communicating their wisdom to believers today.

3. Serving Nonprofessionals

This volume welcomes lay readers interested in penetrating the teachings of John Wesley on care of souls. A major part of Wesley's work was marshaling the resources of lay ministers and local church believers. My focus is ministry, but not narrowly of clergy alone. The ministry of the laity is the very purpose of the ministry of the clergy in Wesley's view. "Care of souls" is the ministry of the whole laity in the body of Christ. The idea of pastoral care is not modern in origin, but in the modern period it has sometimes come to be superficially narrowed to refer to certain professional disciplines. Not so in Wesley. His audience was mostly ordinary layfolk, not just religious professionals or finely educated thinkers.

For nonprofessionals, my hope is that you will enjoy Wesley's plain speaking — straight talk without airs. To give an ear to Wesley is to risk being uplifted by the power of his spirit and instructed by the integrity of his thinking. What are contemporary believers likely to enjoy most in Wesley? His good sense, practical

---

[9]See the bibliography of Thomas C. Oden, *Pastoral Theology: Essentials of Ministry* (New York: HarperOne, 1983).

wisdom, and biblical depth. If reading the eighteenth-century text sometimes feels like a heavy burden, this series seeks to lighten that burden by making his teaching more accessible without loss of the candor of his plain speaking.

Some will find this volume most useful for quiet spiritual formation. Others will see Wesley's approach as a ready reference work on case studies in pastoral care. Some will be surprised to hear Wesley's views on sexuality, singleness and marriage, parenting, and family life. Others will see him as a profound resource for countering addictive behaviors, permissiveness, and absolute moral relativism. For parents who are homeschooling, I especially commend Wesley's pastoral teaching. If his views cannot always be directly transferred into contemporary language, in most cases their basic instincts and principles still apply.

For professional readers in the teaching and practice of pastoral care, Wesley's writings provide a model for placing pastoral care within the larger framework of classic Christian teachings on the church and ministry, the work of Christ, and the active work of the Spirit in the whole of history and in the body of believers.

My part in this is to relieve the heaviness and empower the teaching itself by making it understandable to modern laity. Wesley's teaching on church and ministry brings to us today a great gift to be joyfully received. So do not think of this gift as a duty. Take a deep breath. Relax. Receive the gift.

Further Reading

Wesley as Pastoral Theologian

Abraham, William J. *Waking from Doctrinal Amnesia: The Healing of Doctrine in the United Methodist Church.* Nashville: Abingdon, 1995.

———. *Wesley for Armchair Theologians.* Louisville: Westminster John Knox, 2005.

Bowmer, John Coates. *Pastor and People: A Study of Church and Ministry in Wesleyan Methodism.* London: Epworth, 1975.

Outler, Albert C. "Pastoral Care in the Wesleyan Spirit." In *The Wesleyan Theological Heritage: Essays of Albert C. Outler,* edited by Thomas C. Oden and Leicester R. Longden, 175–88. Grand Rapids: Zondervan, 1991.

Rivers, Isabel. "Dissenting and Methodist Books of Practical Divinity." In *Books and Their Readers in Eighteenth Century England,* edited by Isabel Rivers, 127–64. New York: St. Martins, 1982.

Shipley, David C. "The Ministry in Methodism in the Eighteenth Century." In *The Ministry in the Methodist Heritage,* edited by Gerald McCulloh, 11–31. Nashville: Department of Ministerial Education, 1960.

Wesley's Theological Method

Abraham, William J. "Inspiration in the Classical Wesleyan Tradition." In *A Celebration of Ministry: Essays in Honor of Frank Bateman Stanger,* edited by Kenneth C. Kinghorn, 33–47. Wilmore, KY: Francis Asbury, 1982.

————. "The Wesleyan Quadrilateral." In *Wesleyan Theology Today*, edited by Theodore H. Runyon, 119–26. Nashville: Kingswood, 1985.

Anderson, Neil D. *A Definitive Study of Evidence Concerning John Wesley's Appropriation of the Thought of Clement of Alexandria*. Lewiston, NY: Edwin Mellen, 2004.

Armistead, M. Kathryn. *Wesleyan Theology and Social Science: The Dance of Practical Divinity and Discovery*. Newcastle, UK: Cambridge Scholars, 2010.

Cheek, H. Lee. *Confronting Modernity: Towards a Theology of Ministry in the Wesleyan Tradition*. Lake Junaluska, NC: Wesley Studies Society, 2010.

JOHN **WESLEY'S** TEACHINGS

CHAPTER 1

The Office and Gifts of Ministry

A. The Call to Ministry

1. An Address to the Clergy

On January 5, 1756, John Wesley wrote in his journal, "This week I wrote An Address to the Clergy, which considering the state of public affairs, I judged would be more seasonable and more easily borne at this time than at any other"[1] Aware that he had hard words for his fellow clergy, Wesley carefully picked this time to convey them. In this essay, he set forth a thoughtful doctrine of the high calling to ministry coupled with an assessment of what sort of theological education is necessary to prepare for it.

a. Gifts and Graces for a Calling to Ministry

The study of the work of ministry begins with the call to ministry. Anyone examining a presumed call to ministry will benefit from "An Address to the Clergy" [J X:480 – 500 (February 6, 1756)]. It is regrettable that this important address is not yet available in the contemporary critical version; hence all references are to the Jackson edition of Wesley's Works.

Wesley first asks what gifts and graces are required for those "who watch over the souls of others as they that must give account."[2] The core idea of "gifts and graces" is ubiquitous in the Wesleyan pastoral tradition. It points to a foundational description of qualities of character and preparation that are required for ministry. Anyone considering the vocation of ministry or who expects to go before an examining board will soon discover that the primary concern of the church is to discern a person's gifts and graces for ministry.

Those given the task of watching over the souls of others stand responsible before God for guiding the final destiny of each one under their care. In the last judgment, shepherds of the people of God will be called on to account for the care they gave to the souls committed to their charge.

---

[1]B, Journals and Diaries 4.
[2]"An Address to the Clergy," J X:481, proem.

b. A Vocation

Soul care is not strictly speaking a job, but a vocation. A job is a paid position of regular employment. A vocation is a calling from on high, transcending the economic, political, and domestic spheres. To receive God's call, Christians must listen for his voice.

Soul care exists as a response to God's concern for whole persons. The ultimate frame of reference for soul care is the eternal destiny of persons in relation to God.[3] Even if accountability for the vocation of soul care is postponed, it will ultimately be required in the final judgment. This is not just serious business, but a grave matter on which the eternal destiny of souls depends.

No one is forced to undertake such a calling. It can only be pursued freely, as a voluntary response to the riches of divine grace. Worldly poverty is no match for these riches. Whoever enters this arena does so voluntarily or not at all.

2. Natural Gifts and Endowments

To discern this calling, Christians must solemnly examine themselves to determine whether they are ready for such a ministry. In his "Address to the Clergy," Wesley asked: What are the characteristics that make for an effective minister? What does the community of faith have a right to look for in and expect from those called to be preachers, liturgists, teachers, caregivers, evangelists, and overseers of the church that Christ has bought with his own blood?[4] In setting forth the desired gifts and graces, Wesley considered first "natural gifts," as distinguished from hard-won, acquired endowments.

Natural gifts shape patterns of personal growth. They are not ordinary skills but are natural gifts of the Creator. They are not given to all. They are given through God's unfathomable providence and preparing grace. They do not work mechanically but require cooperative receptivity. They work through and within the various spheres of natural causality (inorganic, organic, animal, rational laws), not by direct fiat. They give evidence of the work of the Spirit, drawing the person in a beneficial direction by the abundance of a combination of talents. Not everyone has these gifts, even though they are offered by means of natural processes such as judging, thinking, and remembering.[5]

Some natural gifts are essential to ministry. Some can be more easily acquired by some than others, depending on genetics, environmental opportunities, and self-selected patterns of response. If not given in abundance, they may be obtained by hard work and perseverance.

The whole people of God are called into ministry of the laity. Some are called to the distinctive role of ordained ministry. Some are called, others not, to the momentous task of care of souls. Those lacking some acceptable combination and quality of

---

[3]"The Wisdom of Winning Souls," B 4:307, sec. 1.
[4]1 Cor. 1:30; 7:23; Heb. 10:29; 13:12; Rev. 5:9.
[5]"The Imperfection of Human Knowledge," B 2:568 – 77, sec. 1.1 – 13.

natural gifts for soul care do well to pray for grace to listen carefully for discernment of God's calling.

a. Good Judgment, Quick Mind, and Retentive Memory

Among natural gifts essential for the work of ministry are these:

- sound judgment
- lively intellect
- good memory[6]

The first of these natural gifts underscored by Wesley is sound judgment. Wise counsel requires good prudential judgment — the ability to reason closely and lucidly about complicated circumstances. Since our lives and passions are complicated, they call for good judgment, which has the power to penetrate self-deceptions. Good judgment sees through human frailties and dubious voluntary human actions.

These deceptions limit knowing and doing good. Faith is confronted with powerful adversaries, not only in persons' ideas but in their inward struggle for freedom. The adversarial powers would like nothing better than to penetrate and undermine effective ministries. These demonic powers are viewed in the New Testament as a part of the larger cosmic realm of the father of lies, the devil. They move in the arena of twisted and confused reasoning, distorting the capacity for persons to function responsibly. Fools cannot do this work of soul care. It requires battling with the spirits of darkness.[7]

b. A Quick Mind and a Retentive Memory

Hence a second natural gift required for soul care is a quick mind, ready to match wits with the demonic. Those called to shepherd souls must have the capacity to discern situations swiftly in order to respond immediately and fittingly. A good heart does not always overcome the deficit of a sluggish mind. Otherwise, "how will he be able, when need requires, to 'answer a fool according to his folly'?"[8]

The third of these natural gifts underscored by Wesley is a retentive memory. In ministry memory will be put to the test.[9] The minister will be required to "bring out of his treasures things new and old."[10] Persons who cannot readily remember what the Scriptures teach will be disadvantaged in the care of souls. Readiness implies the practical capacity to apply scriptural truth to particular situations instantly when the proper time comes. The Scriptures are the quarries out of which pastoral care brings good tidings. Talking to clergy who lack a good memory is like "pouring water into a leaky vessel."[11] Lack of discernment about these natural gifts has led to

---

[6]"An Address to the Clergy," J X:81–82.
[7]"An Address to the Clergy," J X:482.
[8]Ibid.
[9]"The Good Steward," B 2:290–94.
[10]"An Address to the Clergy," J X:482.
[11]"An Address to the Clergy," J X:489.

an abundance of "dull, heavy, blockish ministers" whose capacity to reason is "low and shallow" and whose apprehension is "muddy and confused."[12]

3. Acquired Endowments for a Sound Calling

In addition to these natural gifts there are acquired habits of mind crucial for the work of ministry. These are gained by study, discipline, and sound forms of knowing — linguistic, biblical, and theological. Hence education is intrinsically a part of readiness for ministry, but not just any form of education. Rather, it requires a properly balanced education for service to the community of faith in preaching, sacramental life, and pastoral care.

Wesley points to four acquired endowments in particular: understanding the pastoral office; inhabiting sacred Scripture text by text; immersing oneself in the Scripture studies of the ancient Christian writers of the first five centuries; and obtaining a broad general education in preparation for ministry.

a. Grasping the Nature of the Pastoral Office and Understanding Scripture

Among acquired endowments, candidates for ministry must clearly grasp the nature of the pastoral office itself. Those who do not know what God the Spirit wants done cannot do it. The Scriptures are necessary and sufficient to define what needs to be done.[13] The office of ministry is a sacred trust. Careful study of the Acts, Paul's letters, especially 1 and 2 Timothy and Titus, and the Johannine writings are fundamentally important.

To grasp the nature of the pastoral office, ministers must study to gain a thorough knowledge of the Scripture that empowers the task. No one can be a good pastor who cannot deal in depth with the sacred text. This cannot be done without a working knowledge of the original Hebrew and Greek languages in which the Scriptures were first conveyed. These linguistic competencies are essential for rightly dividing the Word of Truth. Good pastors must be prepared to grasp "the literal meaning of every word, verse, and chapter, without which there can be no firm foundation on which spiritual meaning can be built."[14]

Pastors having a deep and practiced knowledge of Scripture will be capable of comparing Scripture with Scripture and applying Scripture accurately in real-life situations of human need. Only Scripture can guide pastors in learning how to guide others. Pastors must master the content of each narrative of salvation history separately and the whole synoptically. They must be ready to grasp objections and meet them clearly.[15] Like most clergy in his time, Wesley was grounded in a classical education, able to read the ancient languages easily. He expected every gospel

---

[12]Ibid.
[13]"An Address to the Clergy," J X:482.
[14]Ibid.
[15]"An Address to the Clergy," J X:483.

minister to be competent in language and literary skills. His lay preachers were urged to study to obtain them. He himself began learning Greek at his father's knee.

b. Immersion in the Scriptural Exegesis of the Church Fathers

The study of the sacred text extends to the study of its most reliable interpreters. The most reliable of these are those closest to the apostolic period. Evangelical pastors must therefore gain substantial grasp of the biblical message as understood in its earliest centuries by the early apologists, the patristic sources, the church fathers. Why? They were "the most authentic commentators on Scripture, being nearest the fountain, and eminently endued with that Spirit by whom all Scripture was given."[16] The best foundation for scriptural interpretation is a deep immersion in the earliest commentators and homilists on Scripture, commonly called the ante-Nicene writers. The ancient Christian exegetes are still most pertinent to a grasp of scriptural wisdom. The recent publication of the *Ancient Christian Commentary on Scripture* in twenty-nine volumes provides a sample of the texts of the ancient Christian writers from whom Wesley was deriving his arguments.[17] It should not be surprising that this work was conceived and nurtured and its research work housed in a seminary of the tradition of Wesley's spiritual connection — Drew Theological School.

Among post-Nicene commentators on Scripture whom Wesley most often commended were the great ecumenical teachers — Athanasius, Basil, Gregory Nazianzus, Chrysostom, Jerome, Ambrose, and Augustine. Among hymn writers, Wesley commended especially "above all, the man of a broken heart, Ephraim Syrus."[18] This core list shows the breadth of knowledge of the ancient tradition that comes not only from the Greek East and Latin West but also from the less familiar Syriac tradition.

Well-prepared evangelical pastors will be firmly grounded in ancient Christian doctrine, which Wesley thought was definitively formulated in the ancient church's "Three Creeds" — Apostles', Nicene, and Athanasian (or *Quicunque*) — all based on early baptismal creeds. They provide a concise ordering of basic Christian teaching. To be rightly understood, they must be "firmly believed."[19] When confessed, they must be uttered from the heart (*ex anima*).

Wesley believed that the views of evangelical pastors ought to be consistent with "Scripture, reason and Christian antiquity."[20] By "Christian antiquity," he was referring to "the religion of the primitive church, of the whole church in the purest

---

[16]"An Address to the Clergy," J X:484.

[17] *The Ancient Christian Commentary on Scripture*, ed. Thomas C. Oden (Downers Grove, IL: InterVarsity), 1997 – 2010.

[18]"An Address to the Clergy," J X:484.

[19]"On Laying the Foundation of the New Chapel," B 3:582, sec. 1.3. For various comments on "orthodoxy" see B 1:220, 694; 2:415 – 16, 3:582, 587; 4:50, 57, 146, 175, 398; 11:22, 39, 477 – 78; *LJW* 3:183, 203; 4:347, 364.

[20]Wesley's preface to the 1771 edition of his works, quoted by Jackson in his "Preface to the Third Edition" (March 1771), sec. 4; cf. "On Sin in Believers," sec. 3.1 – 10.

ages." The voice of classic Christianity is best heard through the writings of its most widely received scriptural interpreters. Among these Wesley's favorites were Clement of Rome, Ignatius, Polycarp, Tertullian, Origen, Clement of Alexandria,[21] and Cyprian,[22] as well as Chrysostom,[23] Basil,[24] Ephrem Syrus,[25] and Macarius.[26]

The wisdom of the ancient Christian writers is not ancillary to the work of ministry in the modern world. "No thinking man will condemn the Fathers of the Church." Their views are "indispensably necessary" for the practice of ministry. There is no excuse for "one who has the opportunity, and makes no use of it," and no warrant for "a person who has had a University education" yet remained ignorant of the ancient Christian writers.[27] Wesley had learned from his father, Samuel Wesley, an abiding "reverence to the ancient church" when he was a child at Epworth and a student at Oxford.[28] He often commented on specific patristic references from Irenaeus,[29] Minucius Felix,[30] Origen,[31] Didymus of Alexandria,[32] Eusebius,[33] Athanasius,[34] Epiphanius,[35] Gregory of Nyssa,[36] Gregory Nazianzus,[37] Augustine,[38] Jerome,[39] Pachomius,[40] Theophylact,[41] Pseudo-Dionysius,[42] John of Damascus,[43] and others.[44]

---

[21] See *LJW* 2:327 – 28, 342, 387.

[22] For Wesley's extensive reference to Cyprian see B 2:461 – 62; 3:196 – 97, 450 – 51, 458 – 59, 469 – 70; *LJW* 1:277, 323; 2:320, 333 – 37, 361, 373, 387; B 11:437; JWO 42 – 43, 126, 195, 264, 309, 328; *JJW* 1:416; 2:263; 4:97.

[23] For further references to John Chrysostom, see FA 11:156 – 62, 175; B 11:155 – 59, 381 – 453; 2:113; 3:586; 4:402; JWO 131 – 32, 264, 328.

[24] *LJW* 4:176; B 11:8.

[25] *JJW* 1:276, 279, 284 – 85, 294 – 95, 3:284; 4:457 – 59.

[26] For notes on the identity and view of "Macarius the Egyptian," see JWO 9:9, 31, 119, 252, 274 – 75; *JJW* 1:254; *LJW* 2:387.

[27] "An Address to the Clergy," J X:484, sec. 1.2; see Ted A. Campbell, *John Wesley and Christian Antiquity: Religious Vision and Cultural Changes* (Nashville: Kingswood, 1991).

[28] Thirty years prior to his writing to William Dodd, March 12, 1756, *LJW* 3:172, hence probably around 1726.

[29] For further references to Irenaeus, see *LJW* 2:319, 332, 387; *JJW* 1:356.

[30] *LJW* 2:332, 348.

[31] For further references to Origen, see *LJW* 2:91 – 92, 100, 105, 324, 332, 353, 362, 387; 3:137; 4:176; B 4:33n.

[32] Didymus Alexandrinus (the blind), JWO 129.

[33] *LJW* 2:331.

[34] FA 11:162 – 63, 175; *LJW* 1:367; B 2:397.

[35] *LJW* 2:360.

[36] B 1:75, 188n.; JWO 9 – 10, 31, 119.

[37] JWO 130.

[38] The bulk of Wesley's references to Augustine (St. Austen) are to be found in the letters, *LJW* 1:45; 2:60, 70; 3:171; 4:176; 6:175; 7:58, 33; see also B 2:548, 566; 11:236, 492; JWO 124 – 26, 131 – 32, 409; *JJW* 5:118.

[39] *LJW* 2:353; B 2:113; 3:62n.; FA 11:156, 159.

[40] B 9:354.

[41] B 4:6.

[42] *JJW* 2:365.

[43] B 11:189n.

[44] FA, pt. 1, 11:155 – 63, sec. 5.16 – 22.

c. Broad General Education as Preparation for Ministry

Beyond the knowledge of Scripture and classic Christian tradition, the work of the evangelical pastor requires a broad general education in the sciences and a knowledge of human nature and of the world, as well as common sense and a prudent grasp of the dynamics of human behavior.[45] Therefore they must also have a broad knowledge of history. Since God is revealed in history, ministers cannot fulfill their office without a firm grasp of universal history, philosophy of history, and discrete historical studies, including an understanding of "ancient customs, chronology, and geography,"[46] hence of culture, time, and space.

Since God's revelation is addressed to persons within the limits of human history, freedom, and time, effective ministers will develop a practical knowledge of human nature, of "maxims, tempers, and manners, such as they occur in real life,"[47] where it is necessary to deal with a vast variety of characters and to discern the spirits. The minister must have knowledge of the world we live in, of the real lives people lead.

Since God's revelation is to persons, attesting God's revelation requires knowledge of persons, personality development, and what we would today called psychology. Wesley commended the study of the affective life, interpersonal relations, and the psychosomatic interface between body and soul.

Since God's revelation must be applied to specific situations, effective ministers will acquire by experience a good measure of ethical prudence. This means a situational sense of how to apply knowledge to living contexts. Prudence requires good common sense and a sense of the appropriateness and consequences of particular actions. This comes only by the "habitual consideration of all the circumstances of a thing," along with the "facility of adapting our behavior to the various combinations of them."[48]

Serving in ministry requires the ability to think logically about the data and inferences in the sciences, in natural philosophy, geometry, and in metaphysics, for logic is "the very gate" to all other sciences.

d. The Value of a Wisely Educated Evangelical Clergy

In no way did Wesley intend to make his arguments for lay preachers an apology for a poorly prepared, uneducated, and unsupervised ministry. He acknowledged the importance of education for gospel preaching. In "A Letter to a Clergyman,"[49] he offered these reasons for a wisely educated evangelical clergy:

- Their office is the saving of souls from death.
- Among all human concerns, care of soul is of highest significance.

---

[45]"An Address to the Clergy," J X:484–86.
[46]"An Address to the Clergy," J X:483.
[47]"An Address to the Clergy," J X:484.
[48]"An Address to the Clergy," J X:485.
[49]J VIII:496, sec. 1.5–10.

- Life everlasting and holiness, or health of soul, are at stake in the quality of their care.
- Ministers are physicians of the soul.
- Full trial should be made of them in all respects "and that by the most competent judges before they enter on the public exercise of their office."
- After such trial, they may be authorized to exercise that office by those who are empowered to convey that authority.
- The supervisors (*episkopoi*) of holy orders are empowered to do this and have been so from the apostolic age.

For these reasons, "they should have all advantages of education and learning."[50]

4. A Pastoral Temperament

The character and temperament of gospel ministers must be courteous, caring, and humane. Pastors must have some evidence of a good quality of character. By this Wesley meant "easiness and propriety of behavior ... all the courtesy of a gentleman joined with the correctness of a scholar."[51] Courtesy is not merely an artificial convention but a profound aspect of sensitivity to the neighbor.

Those who preach well will seek to develop "a strong, clear musical voice and a good delivery." Accurate communication requires sentences that can be understood. The public communicator cannot be effective without learning the skills of voice projection, enunciation, and the requirements of public speaking.[52] Those who have a "weak and untunable voice" may by diligence gain a "strong and agreeable" voice. Grace has helped "those who stammered almost at every word" to learn to speak clearly and concisely. Those "ungraceful in their pronunciation and awkward in their gesture have in some time, by art and labor, not only corrected that awkwardness of action and ungracefulness of utterance, but have become excellent in both."[53]

All of these acquired gifts are expedient for ministers, yet it would be presumptive to mandate each one of them as necessary in every instance. Some who have lesser endowments or less access to the study of these disciplines may nonetheless serve well. However, any candidate for ministry who has the opportunity to acquire these disciplines and neglects it will be disadvantaged in soul care. In this way, Wesley lays down "*ex professo* the qualifications, the learning in particular, which (as I apprehend) every clergyman who can have ought to have."[54]

a. Congruence of Intentions, Affections, and Actions

These acquired skills, however, are incomplete if not enabled and blessed by the unmerited grace of God. So in addition to natural and acquired endowments, there are certain excellences of intention and affections of the heart along with moral

---

[50]"A Letter to a Clergyman," J VIII:496, sec. 1.1 – 3.
[51]"An Address to the Clergy," J X:485.
[52]Ibid.
[53]Ibid.
[54]Letter to Dr. Rutherforth, B 9:377, sec. 2.2.

courage that only God can give, and that can only be received by faith through prayer.[55] These intentions and affections lead to behavioral actions that characterize the effective gospel minister.

God assists all who pray for grace to make a sincere effort. God's own Spirit precedes, counsels, and accompanies the pastor in every step along this way. All gifts of ministry come from God, but God's grace calls for a cooperative will and awakens rigorous human effort. This grace is offered at every level of human consciousness, including intent, feeling, and action.

Laity have a right to look toward the guidance of a pastor whose life is characterized by purity of heart. They expect the pastor to have the affections of love along with behaviors that do not lead to reproach. These graces are summarized by Wesley as evidences of good intent, genuine affection, and unsullied behavior.[56]

The undeviating intent of the high calling of ministry is "singly this: to glorify God, and to save souls from death."[57] The soul of the pastor cannot be divided. The heart must be single in intent. The motive when mixed becomes tainted.

This can occur only by grace. Without singleness of eye and purity of heart, "all our sacrifice, our prayers, sermons, and sacraments are an abomination to the Lord."[58] This inward sphere is the arena where outward actions begin to form.[59] If the deeply inward spiritual formation is thorough, then the outward behavioral responses will follow.

b. The Affections of the Gospel Minister

The affections of gospel ministers are like those of loving parents who joyfully and willingly attend to the needs of their families. The emotive life of mature pastors is filled with the love of God, of neighbor, of the community of faith, and of the whole world for whom Christ died. The radical commitment required for ministry flows out of the abundance of this love, enabling one to reach out with "such an earnest concern for the glory of God, and such a thirst after the salvation of souls, that he is ready to do anything, to lose anything, or to suffer anything, rather than one should perish for whom Christ died."[60]

These affections stand in stark contrast to love of the world, money, praise, ambition, sensual pleasure, and diversions.[61] Those who are emotionally intemperate are not ready for ministry, nor are those who are willing to turn aside from the cry of need.

Out of the wellsprings of this overflowing love stream all active behaviors necessary to ministry. All outward actions are an expression of this renewed inward life.

---

[55]"An Address to the Clergy," J X:486 – 88.
[56]"An Address to the Clergy," J X:486 – 87.
[57]"An Address to the Clergy," J X:487.
[58]"An Address to the Clergy," J X:497.
[59]"Sermon on the Mount, 6," B 1:573 – 76, secs. 1 – 4; "A Single Intention," B 4:371 – 76, secs. 1 – 9.
[60]"An Address to the Clergy," J X:487.
[61]"The Image of God," B 4:294 – 95.

Those who teach that grace gives birth to holy living but do not live accordingly will be easily found out. Their teaching will be debased even if logically correct. The words are discredited by the behavior.[62]

The private and public character of pastors is called to exhibit as much as possible "holy and heavenly tempers."[63] The calling is high but the grace of God is higher. Displaying godly character would be impossible without grace. The pastoral office calls for abstaining from every evil word or act insofar as possible. There is no double standard in which the clergy are distinguished from the laity in virtue; rather, preachers are validated by what they practice. They are expected to take seriously what they are saying and commending to others.

c. Pastoral Self-Examination

Self-examination is a regular and continuing requirement of ministry. "An Address to the Clergy" concludes with a model for meditation. Wesley personally confronts the clergy of his time with the simple question: Are we clergy fulfilling this calling?[64] To play loose with this question is to weaken the integrity of ministry. Each one charged with shepherding the flock is called to be honest before God, assess deficiencies, and pray for grace to rectify them.

There follows a series of probing questions for candid self-examination. Among these intensely personal questions, it is fitting to ask: Are my own gifts and natural endowments fit for ministry? Have I acquired a readiness of thought that is prepared to speak out? Have I nurtured a retentive memory? Do I have sound understanding? Have I acquired competent general knowledge?[65] Have I studied the Scriptures in their original languages, or if not, does not that leave me "at the mercy of everyone who does understand or even pretends to understand, the original?"[66] Have I understood the nature of the pastoral office? Do I have sufficient knowledge of history, the sciences, and natural philosophy to match minds with those I am serving? "Have I read over and over the golden remains of Clemens Romans, of Ignatius and Polycarp; and have I given one reading, at least, to the works of Justin Martyr, Tertullian, Origen, Clemens Alexandrinus and Cyprian?"[67] Have I learned to be as wise as a serpent and as harmless as a dove, and to be courteous to all?

The questions continue without relenting. Each one must probe his own spirit by asking himself: How deeply is grace penetrating into my intentions, my affections, and my will? "Do I have this singular intention to serve that unmixed with desire for preferment? Do I walk as Christ walked? Do I seek a comfortable livelihood? Are my affections grounded in grace? What is a minister of Christ, a shepherd of souls, unless he is all devoted to God, unless he abstain, with the utmost

---

[62]"The Repentance of Believers," B 1:338–39.
[63]"An Address to the Clergy," J X:488.
[64]"An Address to the Clergy," J X:488–500.
[65]"An Address to the Clergy," J X:486–93.
[66]"An Address to the Clergy," J X:491.
[67]"An Address to the Clergy," J X:493.

care and diligence, from every evil word and work; from all appearance of evil; yea, from the most innocent things, whereby any might be offended or made weak."[68] Do I practice the life of being wholly devoted to God? Am I an example to believers? "Does the love of God and man not only fill my heart, but shine through my whole conversation?"[69] As a minister of the gospel who has voluntarily responded to the call, I am called not to fall short, and to pray earnestly for grace to press on to the high calling and to be ready to sacrifice for it.

Each hearer is called before the bar of their own inward conscience for rigorous review in readiness for the final judgment. If these questions are asked thoughtlessly or cheaply, it would be "like that of a surgeon who lets his patient be lost because he is too compassionate to probe his wounds. Cruel compassion!... Let me probe that God may heal."[70]

B. The Authority of the Pastoral Office

1. On Obedience to Pastors

a. The Calling of the Church to Soul Care

Laypersons are not left without counsel and guidance. The Spirit has provided the church with pastors, counselors, and shepherds to care for the flock. This is seen in Wesley's homily "On Obedience to Pastors" [Homily #97 (March 18, 1785), B 3:373 – 83; J #97, VII:108 – 16]. Through the sincerity of his own behavior, Wesley came to be regarded as a spiritual guide for those in his connection, who voluntarily came to him for guidance.[71] In God's own mysterious way, God calls pastors to serve the flock and enables them by grace to benefit others. On this premise, the flock is called to follow pastors fitly ordered to give wise counsel.

The text for this homily on pastoral care is Hebrews 13:17: "Obey them that have the rule over you, and submit yourselves; for they watch over your souls, as they that shall give account; that they may do this with joy, and not with grief; for that is unprofitable for you" (Wesley's translation).[72] The same passage in today's plain English reads: "Have confidence in your leaders and submit to their authority, because they keep watch over you as those who must give an account. Do this so that their work will be a joy, not a burden, for that would be of no benefit to you" (NIV). Here ministry is conceived as a divinely constituted order for the benefit of believers. Christ himself calls into being the work of ministry and enables it to bear fruit.

Who are pastors? They are the ones duly appointed to watch over the flock. Appointed according to whose authority? By God the Son attesting to God the

---

[68] "An Address to the Clergy," J X:487.
[69] "An Address to the Clergy," J X:499.
[70] "An Address to the Clergy," J X:489.
[71] "On Obedience to Pastors," B 3:382, J VII:115, sec. 3.9.
[72] "On Obedience to Pastors," B 3:373 – 74, J VII:108.

Father through the Spirit, as testified by the apostles. Private conscience is respected, but pastors are called to instruct and counsel the conscience.[73]

b. The Shepherd of the Flock

The shepherd role is based on empathy. As God engages empathically with broken humanity, so pastors empathize with the flock. On this premise, it is to the interest of the flock to be attentive and responsive to pastoral guidance.[74]

The pastor's task is soul care. That is what the leaders of the church do — protect and watch over the flock. It is to the interest of the flock to be attentive and accountable to the pastor in charge, the local shepherd who is accountable to the Great Shepherd, the living Christ. The flock is sheltered from harm when it listens carefully to the voice of the shepherd.[75]

Regrettably, both Catholics and Protestants are tempted to go overboard on one side or the other: Catholics "believe an implicit faith is due to the doctrines delivered by those that rule over them, and that implicit obedience ought to be paid to whatever commands they give." Meanwhile, Protestants "are apt to run to the other extreme, allowing their pastors no authority at all, but making them both the creatures and the servants of their congregations."[76] Wesley sought a middle way with regard to pastoral authority and leadership. In this homily he defines who it is that guides, who the flock is to follow, and what "obey and submit" means.[77]

2. The Discernment of the High Calling to Guide Souls

The phrase "to rule over you" is better translated as "to guide."[78] Those called to care for souls are the very persons who earlier "spoke the word of God to you" (Heb. 13:7 NIV).[79] Who could be more trustworthy?

Who appoints the spiritual guide? You do. No one enters your community of faith by baptism without giving his or her own consent to guidance. You willingly accept the spiritual leaders in your faith community "to be your guides in the way to heaven."[80] The "you" that voluntarily consents is the baptized you, the born-again you.

To be guides, pastors must be out in front of the flock leading, not pushing from behind. Pastors are called to "guide [the flock] in all the ways of truth and holiness."[81] Pastors "nourish [the sheep] 'with the words of eternal life,' to feed them with 'the pure milk of the word.'" They apply God's Word continually. They teach the flock "all the essential doctrines contained therein; 'for reproof,' warning them if they turn

---

[73]"On Obedience to Pastors," B 3:379, J VII:112 – 13, sec. 3.3.
[74]"On Obedience to Pastors," B 3:376 – 77, J VII:110, sec. 1.5.
[75]Ibid.
[76]"On Obedience to Pastors," B 3:374; J VII:108, pref. 1.
[77]"On Obedience to Pastors," B 3:374, J VII:109, pref. 2.
[78]Wesley trans., "On Obedience to Pastors," B 3:374, sec. 1.2; J VII:109, sec. 1.1.
[79]"On Obedience to Pastors," B 3:375 – 77, J VII:109, sec. 1.2.
[80]"On Obedience to Pastors," B 3:374 – 76, sec. 1.2 – 3; J VII:110, sec. 1.3.
[81]"On Obedience to Pastors," B 3:376, J VII:110, sec. 1.4.

aside from the way to the right hand or to the left; 'for correction,' showing them how to amend what is amiss, and guiding them back into the way of peace; and 'for instruction in righteousness.'" They train them up "in inward and outward holiness, 'until they come to a perfect man, to the measure of the stature of the fullness of Christ.'"[82]

These ordained pastors are called to "watch over your souls as those that shall give account." Awesome words. "May God write them upon the heart of every guide of souls!" They watch while we sleep. They watch "over the flock of Christ; over the souls that he has bought with a price." Accountable to whom? Not just humanity. "They watch 'with deep earnestness,' with uninterrupted seriousness, with unwearied care, patience, and diligence, as they that are about to give an account of every particular soul to him that standeth at the door, to the Judge of quick and dead."[83]

a. The Church's Discernment of an Apparent or Potential Calling

The pastor must first be called by God through a spiritual discipline of self-discernment. Then that self-discernment must be confirmed by the believing church. This confirmation is assessed and adjudicated by a legitimate church judicatory assigned to that purpose. Then the pastor is solemnly ordained to care for the flock.

These elections, confirmations, and consecrations occur through due processes within the church, with all its limitations in history. Pastors perform a representative ministry for the Great Shepherd in the local setting. They lead. They teach. They warn. They admonish. They train. They keep the flock healthy. The sheep is more vulnerable to the extent that he tends to wander away.

b. Ordinal Examination

Ordination does not occur by self-choice but by the choice of the worshiping community by due processes consulting ministers and laity. The church prays that the church leadership's decision to ordain will be fair and discerning of the promise of the one to be ordained. This is not a place for duplicity or deceit but for full candor before God.[84] The examiners are called to be aware of their own limitations and to understand that they are acting on behalf of the whole church of all ages to conscientiously confirm this divine calling.[85]

All humanity since Adam and Eve live within a history of sin. That history of sin is being redeemed by God. The postulant for holy orders must understand God's plan of salvation as it is presented in Holy Scriptures.[86]

c. Holy Orders

The Service of Ordination into the Church of England to which John Wesley was

---

[82]Ibid.
[83]"On Obedience to Pastors," B 3:376–77, J VII:110, sec. 1.5.
[84]"Ought We to Separate?" B 9:571–72.
[85]"Of the Church," B 3:55–56; cf. "Ought We to Separate?" B 9:571–72.
[86]BPC Ordinal; "On Obedience to Pastors," B 3:376–77, J VII:110, sec. 1.5.

ordained is a rite by which duly called and duly examined postulants are brought into the work of ministry of Word and sacrament. A postulant in the Church of England is a person on probation before being admitted as a candidate for holy orders. Ordination occurs by the laying on of hands of the *episkopos*, who stands in spiritual continuity with the apostolic tradition, pledged to guard the apostolic teaching.

Wesley never demeaned his ordination. He always thought of himself as fully obedient from the heart (*ex cardia*) to his ordination vows. This remained so even when he was called into a ministry of missionary witness that his church viewed as an extraordinary ministry.

In the Anglican and Methodist traditions, the rite of ordination prays for God the Spirit to bless and enable the ministry of the person being ordained. That ministry is pledged to maintain the continuity of the apostolic witness as contained in Scripture from generation to generation. Whether viewed as a literal succession or as a symbolic succession, it signals that the person ordained is called to stand in a succession of apostolic witnesses to Jesus Christ from the New Testament apostles to the present. Unresolved issues remain as to whether Wesley was ordained in a literal succession of ministers from the apostles to the present. My own view is that he was, as much as any bishop in the Anglican church. But that view has been challenged throughout the history of Methodism. Nonetheless, the language of the rite of ordination among the American Methodists largely follows the pattern of Anglican ordination. The community of pastors into which a person is ordained is made up of bishops, elders, and deacons.

To take holy orders means to receive the rite of ordination into the set-apart ministry of the one, holy, universal church. Ministers are not ordained into a particular denomination as such but into the one whole church of all times and places. The rite of ordination is the process by which postulants are set apart as clergy to preach the Word, administer the sacraments, and follow the order of the discipline.[87]

d. Clergy and Lay Counsel

The Anglican polity to which Wesley was accountable makes a distinction of function between the priesthood of all believers and the priesthood of those who have been duly called into holy orders. The efficacy of both of these ministries is entire because of the one priesthood of Christ. The ordained priesthood is distinguished in function from the common priesthood, which is the priesthood of all the baptized.

The difference between clergy and lay counseling is not that one offers the pardon of God and the other does not. Both may convey God's pardon if the grace of divine forgiveness is truly given and truly received. The difference is that the clergy are called to holy orders through full-time service in the ministry of the Word and

---

[87]"Of the Church," B 3:55 – 56; cf. "Ought We to Separate?" B 9:571 – 72.

sacraments as mutually discerned by the ordinand and the church, in the service of ordination.[88]

The whole ministry of the laity needs the guidance of the ministry of those specially called to devote their whole lives to the care of souls. Pastors perform a representative ministry for the Great Shepherd, God the Son. Pastors act within the limits of time and space in their own local setting. They lead. They guard. They warn. They admonish. They discipline. In short, they feed the flock. They guide the flock toward a health-giving environment. But when the flock wanders away from the shepherd, it is more exposed to risk.

The food is the Bread of Life. Ordained ministry is here conceived as a divinely called and duly instituted order by means of which Christ himself promises to come to bring life.[89]

3. The Soul Guide

a. Voluntary Entry into Pastoral Guidance

The relationship of believers with a spiritual guide is from the outset voluntary, chosen, trusting, and durable through crises. The faithful are responsible for voluntarily seeking guidance from persons able to give them biblically grounded counseling to help them pray for grace to grow in every dimension of the Christian life. The stress here is on voluntary obedience as an act of freedom, not coercion.[90]

Voluntary obedience means to trust your shepherd's advice about yourself, your soul, your inward life, your emotive life, your deepest affections, and your limitations. Trust one whose judgment is sound. The pastor has been readied for you, providentially prepared by biblical and moral formation to relate to your needs. Instruction addresses conscience. This doesn't imply a blind, uncritical following. It means giving the benefit of the doubt to the counselor's wisdom and trusting the shepherd's judgment because the shepherd is equipped to help you in ways you might not see for yourself. But if this level of trust is not fully present in your local minister of Word and sacraments, you may become responsible for seeking out corrective guidance and care from other friends or professionals. You are not under obligation to trust a pastor whose judgment is not sound.[91]

b. The Pastor Encourages the Voluntary Choice of a Soul Guide

Who is called to voluntary total attentiveness to good spiritual direction? Every believer. You are. You are one of those to whom this apostolic challenge is directed. Listen and follow those God has called to care for your soul.[92] If you are a pastor, the same applies to you.

Wesley did not assume that the spiritual guide must be, strictly speaking, one's

---

[88]"Of the Church," B 3:48–57, secs. 7–30.
[89]"On Obedience to Pastors," B 3:375, J VII:111, sec. 2.3.
[90]"On Obedience to Pastors," B 3:375–76, J VII:111, sec. 2.3.
[91]"On Obedience to Pastors," B 3:376, J VII:111, sec. 2.3.
[92]"On Obedience to Pastors," B 3:377, J VII:111, sec. 2.1.

own local pastor, although that would be in accord with the way the Spirit ordinarily works in the worshiping community. The guidance of the Spirit through the work of a godly pastor is to enter into the hidden arena of motivation and human freedom and there convey the truth of faith.[93] But he asked: "Where is it written that we are bound to obey any minister because we live in what is called his parish?... It is far from being a thing indifferent to me who is the guide of my soul. I dare not receive one as my guide to heaven that is himself in the high road to hell. I dare not take a wolf for my shepherd, that has not so much as sheep's clothing."[94] "I owe all deference to the commands of my parents, and willingly obey them in all things lawful. But it is not lawful to 'call them Rabbi,' that is, to believe or obey them implicitly. Everyone must give an account of himself to God. Therefore every man must judge for himself; especially in a point of so deep importance as this is, the choice of a guide for his soul."[95]

As the faithful, you will receive the guidance of one called by God with joy, gratefully, obediently, and with the awareness that a trustworthy partner is accompanying you on your journey. In the good pastor's walk with you, you will see reflected his walk with God. The premise is that someone is caring for you who understands the infinite caring of God for lost humanity.[96] "The wisdom that comes from heaven is first of all pure; then peace-loving, considerate, submissive, full of mercy and good fruit, impartial and sincere" (James 3:17 NIV).

c. Selecting a Trustable Soul Guide

Those who seek guidance in the Christian life "have voluntarily connected themselves with such a pastor as answers the description given therein; such as do in fact watch over their souls, as they that shall give account.... All who have found and chosen guides of this character, of this spirit and behavior, are undoubtedly required by the Apostle to 'obey and submit themselves' to them."[97]

However, if you should be asked by your ordained minister to do something that you know God does not command or approve, you will obey God rather than man. Your minister is there only to help you follow God's commands as revealed in Scripture, not to invent new commands based on the frailties of human moral insight. We have only one Master. The temporal counselor guides in relation to the heavenly Guide, the Shepherd of souls. Unless proven otherwise, we ought to yield to authorized pastors in parishes as we discern our responsibilities in the presence of God.[98] Those who offer and receive counsel "should be 'easy to be entreated,'" open, accessible, not resistant.[99]

---

[93]"On Obedience to Pastors," B 3:375 – 76, J VII:111, sec. 2.3.
[94]"On Obedience to Pastors," B 3:377, J VII:111, sec. 2.2.
[95]"On Obedience to Pastors," B 3:375 – 76, J VII:111, sec. 2.3.
[96]"God's Love to Fallen Man," B 2:422 – 35.
[97]"On Obedience to Pastors," B 3:379 – 80, J VII:111 – 12, sec. 2.4.
[98]"On Obedience to Pastors," B 3:378, J VII:112, sec. 3.1.
[99]"On Obedience to Pastors," B 3:378, J VII:112, sec. 3.2.

4. Ready to Give Account

a. The Duty of the Believer to the Spiritual Shepherd

In relation to the pastor, it is to the interest of the flock to be "ready to yield" in that "amiable temper every real Christian enjoys." The layperson conveys that temper "in a peculiar manner toward those that watch over his soul." He is willing "to be convinced of anything which he did not know before; lying open to their advice, and being glad to receive admonition," ready to give up his own self-assertive will "whenever he can do it with a clear conscience."[100]

Provided the counsel is not contrary to the Word of God, "it is the duty of every private Christian to obey his spiritual pastor."[101] "How little is this understood in the Protestant world!" Nobody dreams there could be "such a duty as this. And yet there is not a more express command either in the Old or New Testament." Those who willfully disobey this instruction will "grieve the Holy Spirit" and "cannot but hinder the grace of God from having its full effect upon the heart." This defiance is "one cause of the deadness of many souls; one reason of their not receiving those blessings which they seek with some degree of sincerity."[102] With nonjudgmental counseling so in vogue today, it may surprise modern readers that Wesley took so seriously the duty of the believer to submit to the spiritual shepherd.

b. Simply Follow the Guidance of the Godly Pastor

For their own good, Wesley called on believers simply and sincerely to apply this instruction directly to themselves when they are under pastoral guidance. It is simple enough: When your trusted spiritual guide tells you to do something, do it. When your voluntarily chosen spiritual guide warns you not to do something, do not do it. Do not stunt your own growth in grace by ignoring this wise scriptural imperative. Otherwise, "You defraud yourself of many blessings which you might enjoy." Just do it. Do it in a joyful spirit. "Do this so that their work will be a joy, not a burden, for that would be of no benefit to you" (Heb. 13:17 NIV). If the counsel requires self-denial, so be it. If required, take up your cross, without which you cannot be a disciple. Grace will supply the strength.[103]

A countercultural motif was at work in Wesley's classes, bands, and societies. To benefit from pastoral gifts, they guarded against becoming "conformable to the world." Rather, they were to be "patterns of plainness." An example is to give undue attention to physical ornaments. While this might seem conformist today, in Wesley's day it was countercultural. This is why plainness of dress was so often emphasized by Wesley. "If you are still dressed like the generality of people of your own rank and fortune, you declare hereby to all the world that you will not obey

---

[100]"On Obedience to Pastors," B 3:379, J VII:112–13, sec. 3.3.
[101]"On Obedience to Pastors," B 380, J VII:114, sec. 3.6.
[102]"On Obedience to Pastors," B 3:381, J VII:114, sec. 3.7.
[103]"On Obedience to Pastors," B 3:381, J VII:114–15, sec. 3.8.

them that are over you in the Lord."[104] "Seek only to be adorned with good works" as Scripture commends.[105] This is not a mere trifle. It is a visible expression of your inward life. Hence Wesley said, "I bind this upon your consciences in the sight of God: Voluntarily 'submit yourselves' to those who 'watch over your souls, as they that shall give account.'"[106]

Further Reading

Calling and Ordination

George, Raymond A. "Ordination [Eighteenth Century]." In *A History of the Methodist Church in Great Britain*, edited by W. Reginald Ward. London: Epworth, 1965.

Van Noppen, Jean-Pierre. "Beruf, Calling and the Methodist Work Ethic." In *Wahlverwandtschaften in Sprache, Malerei, Literatur, Geschichte*, edited by I. Heidelberger-Leonard and M. Tabah, 69–78. Stuttgart: Verlag Hans-Dieter Heinz, 2000.

Temperament and Pastoral Authority

Berg, Daniel. "The Marks of the Church in the Theology of John Wesley." In *The Church*, edited by Melvin Dieter and Daniel Berg, 319–31. Anderson, IN: Warner, 1984.

Campbell, Ted Allen. "John Wesley on the Mission of Church." In *The Mission of the Church in Methodist Perspective*, edited by Alan Padgett, 45–62. Lewiston, NY: Edwin Mellen, 1992.

Collins, Kenneth J. "A Reconfiguration of Power: The Basic Trajectory in John Wesley's Practical Theology," in *Heart of the Heritage: Core Themes of the Wesleyan/Holiness Tradition*, edited by Barry L. Callen and William C. Kostlevy, 131–50. Salem, OH: Schmul, 2001.

Frank, Thomas Edward. *Polity, Practice, and the Mission of the United Methodist Church*. Nashville: Abingdon, 1997.

---

[104]"On Obedience to Pastors," B 3:382, J VII:115–16, sec. 3.10.
[105]"On Obedience to Pastors," B 3:383, J VII:116, sec. 3.11.
[106]"On Obedience to Pastors," B 3:383, J VII:116, sec. 3.12.

CHAPTER 2

Pastoral Counsel

Introduction: The Ministry of Counseling

After surveying the vast secondary literature on Wesley, I have found very little substantively reported about his most important writings on pastoral counseling. There is slight reference and thin analysis of his most lasting pastoral contributions. There is minimal attempt to even acknowledge, much less spell out, and even less to defend, the discrete arguments of his classic pastoral texts. The most substantive reflection comes from the nineteenth-century Wesleyan tradition, not the twentieth or twenty-first.

To date there is little text-by-text exposition of such crucial writings as "On Visiting the Sick," "On Temptation," "On Dissimulation," "The Duty of Reproof," "Family Religion and the Education of Children," and "On Dissipation." They are seldom even mentioned. Serious inquiries into such important homilies as "On the Wedding Garment," "An Israelite Indeed," "Obedience to Parents," and "On Dissipation" are hard to find. Among themes most important to Wesley in soul care are pastoral admonition, pastoral authority, obedience to parents, and the holy life. But where are these treated in the secondary literature? Where are they expounded as his primary treatises on pastoral care and counseling? These are straight ahead in this volume.

These themes and texts have been explicitly treated as soul care. The enduring contributions of Wesley to these important pastoral challenges have hardly been noticed by today's professionals in pastoral counseling. Some passages are not sufficiently "politically correct" in today's terms. Some are not in accord with modern psychological assumptions. Some do not *seem* to further the modern agendas in interpersonal relations, personal growth, child care, and social diagnosis. Nevertheless, they do.

We will begin with visiting the sick, which is a duty of every layperson and especially of all called to ordained ministry. Wesley offers specific guidance on visiting the sick.

A. Visiting the Sick

1. The Biblical Mandate to Visit the Sick

The text of the homily "On Visiting the Sick" is Matthew 25:36: "I was sick, and you visited me" [Homily #98 (May 23, 1786), B 3:384 – 98; J #98, VI:117 – 27].

The care of souls calls for attending to the sick. Whether the sickness is of body, mind, or soul, visiting the sick is a plain duty. It is a calling that all who "are in health may practice in a higher or lower degree."[1] And it is among the foremost works of mercy commanded by Scripture. Those who neglect the exercise of these mercies risk obscuring the radiance of the grace they have received.

The call to visit the sick is addressed to all reasonable people, to all who have a sense of moral responsibility. But it is most clearly a call to the people of faith. It is both an ordinance of God and a channel through which God offers us blessings and gifts (Matt. 25:36 – 43; Luke 10:31 – 32). These works of mercy are the calling of every believer.

Praying, reading Scripture, and attending the Lord's Supper are the chief means of grace instituted by Christ. "These are the ordinary channels which convey the grace of God to the souls of men."[2] They are ordinary in the sense of orderly in relation to the ordering of time in the Christian life.

a. Works of Mercy in the Parable of Sheep and Goats

One of the works of mercy that Jesus clearly set forth in the parable of the sheep and the goats in Matthew 25 is visiting the sick. By neglecting these duties, Christians tend to grow weak in faith and lose sharp recognition of the grace already given them. "Those that neglect them do not receive the grace which otherwise they might," or tend to lose the grace they had received.[3] Disciples who become active in works of mercy walk by faith. These acts manifest "the continuance of that faith whereby we 'are' already 'saved by grace.'"[4] There is no contradiction between "justification by grace through faith alone" and "faith active in love."[5] Anyone who has been saved by grace through faith is called to walk in that faith by being always ready for works of mercy as need arises.[6]

Wesley's text is the Lord's parable of the sheep and goats:

"Inasmuch as ye have done it unto one of the least of these my brethen, ye have done it unto me." If this does not convince you that the continuance in works of mercy is necessary to salvation, consider what the Judge of all says to those on

---

[1]"On Visiting the Sick," B 3:384, pref. 1.
[2]"On Visiting the Sick," B 3:385, pref. 1 – 2.
[3]"On Visiting the Sick," B 3:386, pref. 1
[4]"On Visiting the Sick," B 3:386, pref. 2.
[5]Martin Luther, *Christian Liberty* (Minneapolis: Augsburg Fortress, 2003); "A Treatise on Good Works" (1520), *Luther's Works*, vol. 44 (Philadelphia: Fortress, 1966), 15 – 114; Augsburg Confession, art. 4.20.
[6]Wesley, Minutes, 1746, May 13, Q3, JWO 159.

the left hand: "Depart, ye cursed, into everlasting fire, prepared for the devil and his angels. For I was hungry, and ye gave me no meat: thirsty, and ye gave me no drink: I was a stranger, and ye took me not in: naked, and ye clothed me not: sick and in prison, and ye visited me not. Inasmuch as ye have not done it unto one of the least of these, neither have ye done it unto me."[7]

b. The Calling to Be There in Times of Trouble

"The sick" refers to all who are suffering — whether they are afflicted in body or mind, whether their affections are good or bad, whether they fear God or not.[8] To manifest this gift of visiting the sick, one must physically visit ailing persons where they live, in the context in which they suffer.

The Greek word for "visit" (*episkeptomai*) implies to "look upon" with your own eyes. In this sense, visiting the sick "cannot be done unless you are present with them. To send them assistance is therefore entirely a different thing from visiting them."[9] If you do not "look upon" the sick with your own eyes and take care of their needs, you are not visiting them in the biblical sense. "If you do not [visit the sick], you lose a means of grace; you lose an excellent means of increasing your thankfulness to God."[10] This duty reaches over class barriers to include persons of any station in life, but especially those who are near. Visitors of the sick do not ask about social status or compensation[11] but only about the need itself and where they can make a difference. "One great reason why the rich in general have so little sympathy for the poor is because they so seldom visit them." This is why "one part of the world does not know what the other suffers. Many of them do not know, because they do not care to know: they keep out of the way of knowing it — and then plead their voluntary ignorance as an excuse for their hardness of heart."[12] By being physically present in person, you are reminded of your own vulnerability.

Wesley commended the example of those privileged Christian women of Paris who "constantly visit the sick, particularly the patients in the Grand Hospital ... attend on their sick-beds, dress their sores, and perform the meanest offices for them."[13] They sought to exercise habits of cleanliness and diligence.[14] Bodily needs are central to this duty, but interwoven spiritual needs must also be tended.[15]

2. The Practice of Visiting the Sick

a. Preparation for Visiting the Sick

How is visiting the sick to be done so as to glorify God and serve the neighbor?

---

[7]"On Visiting the Sick," B 3:387, sec. 1; Matt. 25:31–46.
[8]"On Visiting the Sick," B 3:387, sec. 1.1.
[9]"On Visiting the Sick," B 3:387, sec. 1.2.
[10]Ibid.
[11]"On Visiting the Sick," B 3:387–88, sec. 1.3.
[12]"On Visiting the Sick," B 3:388, sec. 2.3.
[13]"On Visiting the Sick," B 3:388, sec. 1.4.
[14]"On Visiting the Sick," B 3:392, sec. 2.6.
[15]"On Visiting the Sick," B 3:389, sec. 1.4.

Before you come into the presence of the sick, you must stand under the conviction that you as such are not sufficient of yourself to supply any comforting word. You must rely on God for strength, not merely on your own wits or goodwill. Seek God's help in prayer before you enter. Ask for gentleness, patience, meekness, humility, and grace to face any contingency.[16]

There is no particular prescribed method for visiting the sick. The visitor is called to let the needs of the situation cue the response. Inquire about physical and material needs, showing readiness to help the "outward condition" as best you can, especially as to "whether they have sufficient food and raiment."[17] Ask what you can do in the present moment with your own hands.[18] "You will then easily discern whether there is any good office which you can do for them with your own hands."[19] Financial resources may be needed. If so, remember Wesley's rule: While you may be ashamed to beg for yourself, never be ashamed to beg for the poor, and do not be easily put off.[20]

Small labors of love pave your way to things of greater importance. Here "you have scope for exercising all the talents which God has given you."[21] "From the beginning to the end, let your heart wait upon him for a continual supply of meekness and gentleness, of patience and long-suffering, that you may never be angry or discouraged, at whatever treatment, rough or smooth, kind or unkind, you may meet with."[22]

b. Show Forth the Power of Godliness

Soul care in visiting the sick is more than helping out with physical needs alone. Wesley emphasized, after expressing active interest in sick persons' physical, social, and economic conditions, do not neglect ministry to their souls. Assure the sick of God's care. Do not hesitate to make clear the promise of the gospel where this seems fitting.[23]

Wesley advised against asking a general theological question like "Have you ever considered that God governs the world?" Rather, communicate your confidence that God governs the world. Find a way of communicating that God "knows all you suffer; he knows all your pains; he sees all your wants."[24]

Show forth the power of godliness through your life. "When [sick persons] begin to understand the nature of holiness and the necessity of the new birth,"[25] then they may give you the opening to speak of repentance and faith. If initial responses indi-

---

[16]"On Visiting the Sick," B 3:389 – 90, sec. 2.1.
[17]"On Visiting the Sick," B 3:390, sec. 2.2.
[18]"On Visiting the Sick," B 3:390, sec. 2.3.
[19]"On Visiting the Sick," B 3:391, sec. 2.4.
[20]"On Visiting the Sick," B 3:390, sec. 2.2.
[21]Ibid.
[22]"On Visiting the Sick," B 3:390, sec. 2.1.
[23]"On Visiting the Sick," B 3:391, sec. 2.4.
[24]Ibid.
[25]Ibid.

cate that they have a reverence for God, then the visitor's task is to provide them resources for the study of Scripture and practical divinity.

Wesley suggests that the visitor have ready some simple Bible-based reading matter, such as a plain tract on steps to life with God. Later you may talk about it if mutually desired.[26]

Conclude every visit to the sick with prayer. If you can't pray, "Ask of God, and he will soon open your mouth."[27]

c. The Calling of the Laity to Visit the Sick

God's command to visit the sick is for the whole laity, not for clergy only. All who hope to inherit the kingdom and avoid God's displeasure are called to this blessed work. Anyone can do it. Whether you are rich or poor, young or old, man or woman, your presence can be comforting. Perhaps only you can make a difference.

Those who have more available resources of time and money have a proportionally larger duty to visit the sick. "Those who 'are rich in this world,' who have more than the conveniences of life, are peculiarly called of God to this blessed work."[28] Nonetheless, those who are poor in worldly resources can offer to the sick what is more valuable than any material gift by means of prayer. They can offer goodwill and intercession, and attest the grace of God. "If you speak 'in the name of Jesus Christ of Nazareth,' may not the words you speak be health to the soul, and marrow to the bones?"[29]

Those who are older have the advantage of experience and wisdom. They are called to take special interest in visiting the sick.[30] Those who are young and vigorous can add their strength to whatever is needed, assisting with whatever gifts they have. "You are able to take up and carry the crosses which may be expected to lie in the way. Employ then your whole vigor of body and mind in ministering to your afflicted brethren. And bless God that you have them to employ in so honorable a service."[31]

Women especially are gifted in this ministry and called to it, as we see in the case of American holiness evangelist Phoebe Palmer (1807–74), inasmuch as they have unique gifts for empathy. "It is well known that in the primitive church there were women particularly appointed for this work."[32] Strong and able-bodied men will also bring unique gifts of encouragement to the weak and sick. Even children are encouraged to form early the habit of doing their part with sick friends.

d. Face-to-Face

Unless disabled by pain or weakness, visiting the sick is a duty to which all

---

[26]Ibid.
[27]"On Visiting the Sick," B 3:392, sec. 2.5.
[28]"On Visiting the Sick," B 3:392, sec. 3.1.
[29]"On Visiting the Sick," B 3:394, sec. 3.4.
[30]"On Visiting the Sick," B 3:394, sec. 3.5.
[31]"On Visiting the Sick," B 3:395, sec. 3.6.
[32]Rom. 16:1; "On Visiting the Sick," B 3:395, sec. 3.7.

believers are called. It cannot be performed by proxy, but only face-to-face. "While you are as eyes to the blind and feet to the lame, a husband to the widow and a father to the fatherless, see that you still keep a higher end in view."[33] The higher view is the eternal happiness of the soul, the greatest gift you could help in offering.

Begin immediately lest the impression you now feel wears off, instead of hearing the Lord's shocking words: "Depart from me.... I was sick and in prison and you did not look after me" (Matt. 25:41, 43 NIV). How much better to hear, "'Come, ye blessed.... For I was sick and you visited me.'"[34]

B. Mediating Conflict

1. The Cure of Evil Speaking

The text of this teaching homily is Matthew 18:15 – 17: "If your brother or sister sins, go and point out their fault, just between the two of you. If they listen to you, you have won them over. But if they will not listen, take one or two others along, so that 'every matter may be established by the testimony of two or three witnesses.' If they still refuse to listen, tell it to the church; and if they refuse to listen even to the church, treat them as you would a pagan or a tax collector" (NIV).

a. Do Not Speak Evil behind Another's Back

Wesley made an up-front appeal for openness, candor, and mutual accountability within the worshiping community [Homily #49, "The Cure of Evil Speaking" (1760), B 2:251 – 62; J #49, VI:114 – 24]. He showed that the rules for mediating conflict are carefully set forth by Scripture.

The text is divided into three parts: Step 1: "If your brother or sister sins, go and point out their fault, just between the two of you. If they listen to you, you have won them over." So what if they do not listen? Step 2: "But if they will not listen, take one or two others along, so that 'every matter may be established by the testimony of two or three witnesses.'" What if confidential mediation is impossible? In the Christian community, there is a step 3: "If they still refuse to listen, tell it to the church; and if they refuse to listen even to the church, treat them as you would a pagan or a tax collector" (Matt. 18:15 – 17). These are Jesus' words, so they cannot be easily dismissed by the community that calls him Lord.

The premise of this mediation procedure: the faithful are called to speak no evil of any person. Evil speaking means telling something evil of another or relating evil events, even if true, about someone when that person isn't present to defend himself or herself.[35] "Evil speaking is neither more nor less than speaking evil of an absent person."[36]

---

[33]"On Visiting the Sick," B 3:393, sec. 3.3.
[34]"On Visiting the Sick," B 3:395, sec. 3.6.
[35]"The Cure of Evil Speaking," B 2:252 – 53, J VI:114 – 15, proem 1.
[36]"The Cure of Evil Speaking," B 2:251, J VI:114 – 16, proem 2 – 3.

b. Backbiting Games Laid Bare

Backbiting, talebearing, and unkind remarks are closely intertwined with evil speaking. All must be carefully constrained in the Christian life. Such remarks are sometimes spoken in a soft and pious manner, with expressions of goodwill to the person. This is a temptation for those believers who may tend to judge too quickly. It is a problem for the church in maintaining the unity of the body of Christ.

Evil speaking may take the humorous form of comic sarcasm. In the guise of humor, we indulge our self-righteousness by yielding to a temporary feeling of superiority. It is self-serving even while appearing to be nurturing. "It gratifies our pride to relate those faults of others whereof we think ourselves not to be guilty." It attacks in disguise with gestures of indignation. No one is exempt from this temptation of the flesh. This is a common sin in ordinary daily life. It should be especially avoided in the community of Christian believers bound together in love.[37]

But evil speaking can be avoided if we use our mediation skills. A community of believers can be largely free from this sin if they allow Scripture to be their guide. By a three-step method, we are called to avoid all evil speaking. Our Lord "lays down a sure method of avoiding offenses and evil speaking together."[38]

2. Confidential One-on-One Admonition

a. How Do I "Tell Him of His Fault"?

The Lord's first step is as simple as it is difficult: "Tell him of his fault, between thee and him alone."[39] Speak with the neighbor in a meek and lowly spirit. Pray that God will "guard thy heart, enlighten thy mind, and direct thy tongue to such words as he may please to bless."[40] Lacking grace, for which we can always pray, the mediation may face many more problems.[41] "The success of a reproof greatly depends on the spirit wherein it is given.... If love is not conquered, it conquers all things. Confirm then your genuine love toward the neighbor, says Paul, and his heart will be warmed."[42]

Both in heart and speech, "avoid everything in look, gesture, word, and tone of voice that savors of pride or self-righteousness, or anything that appears magisterial or arrogant." Arrogance is fatal to the mediation process. Wesley warned, "Beware of the most distant approach to disdain, overbearing, or contempt.... Let there be no token of any warmth but that of love ... no shadow of hate or ill will, no bitterness or sourness of expression."[43]

---

[37]"The Cure of Evil Speaking," B 2:253–54, J VI:114–16, proem 4.
[38]"The Cure of Evil Speaking," B 2:254, J VI:116, proem 5.
[39]Matt. 18:15; "The Cure of Evil Speaking," B 2:254, J VI:116, proem 5.
[40]"The Cure of Evil Speaking," B 2:251, J VI:116–17, sec. 1.1.
[41]Ibid.
[42]Rom. 12:20; "The Cure of Evil Speaking," B 2:251, J VI:116–17, sec. 1.1.
[43]"The Cure of Evil Speaking," B 2:256, J VI:117–18, sec. 1.2.

b. Face-to-Face Preferred to Circumventions

In some cases where face-to-face personal contact is unfeasible, it may be useful to write out the offense calmly, being sure to sign your name. This may be especially useful in the case of young hotheads who have not learned to solicit constructive criticism. If the person is of "so warm and impetuous a temper as does not easily bear reproof," then it actually may be better to write to him or her. Some can "read the very same words which they could not bear to hear. Suppose it makes little impression at first, they will perhaps give it a second reading, and upon further consideration lay to heart what before they disregarded."[44]

You may find a trusted brother or sister who can help you rightly and accurately express the concerns of your heart on paper.[45] But face-to-face candor is preferred.

This first step is not optional, but necessary. "Our Lord absolutely commands us to take" this first step before we attempt any other.[46] We are not to take any other measure either before or beside this first step.[47] In many cases, this will be sufficient to settle the dispute, provided there is goodwill in the worshiping community.

In an emergency situation, an exception may be needed, for example, when the life or limb or property of another would be harmed. Rational judgment may indicate caution. Wesley stated this exception: "It is our bounden duty to speak evil of an absent person, in order to prevent his doing evil to others and himself at the same time."[48] Even in such a rare case, the exception must be applied as little as possible and "only so much as is necessary for the end proposed. At all other times, 'go and tell him of his fault, between thee and him alone.'" This first step is both a reasonable mandate of good judgment and a requirement of God the Father, spoken through his Son. Do not delay or avoid it.[49]

3. If the Offender Will Not Hear

But what if he will not hear? Our Lord has given us clear and full direction. What is the next step for mediation? "Take one or two others along, so that 'every matter may be established by the testimony of two or three witnesses'" (Matt. 18:16 NIV). These witness should be trustworthy persons of good repute, known and respected by all relevant parties, and especially persons lowly in spirit.[50] Take along only those "whom you know to be of a loving spirit." Take those clothed with humility, who are "meek and gentle, patient and longsuffering; not apt to 'return evil for evil' ... men of understanding, such as are endued with wisdom from above; and men unbiased, free from partiality, free from prejudice of any kind," who are acceptable to the estranged neighbor. "Let them mildly and affectionately declare that they have no

---

[44]"The Cure of Evil Speaking," B 2:256, J VI:118, sec. 1.4.
[45]Ibid.
[46]Ibid.
[47]"The Cure of Evil Speaking," B 2:257, J VI:114–18, sec. 1.5.
[48]"The Cure of Evil Speaking," B 2:257, J VI:119, sec. 1.7.
[49]"The Cure of Evil Speaking," B 2:257, J VI:119, sec. 1.6–7.
[50]"The Cure of Evil Speaking," B 2:258, J VI:119–20, sec. 2.1.

anger or prejudice toward him, and that it is merely from a principle of goodwill that they now come."[51]

Many readers today are familiar with confrontation in family counseling to help those with addictive behaviors. They will immediately see both how difficult and how promising it is to take this second step. But it is mandated in order to move toward reconciliation. "Our Lord gives us no choice, leaves us no alternative, but expressly commands us to do this, and nothing else in the place of it. He likewise directs us when to do this. Neither sooner, nor later: namely, after we have taken the first, and before we have taken the third step."[52]

Let love show the way. Let love determine the demeanor and quality of the interaction. "Love will dictate the manner wherein they should proceed, according to the nature of the case."[53]

4. Accountability to the Community of Faith

a. How Do We "Tell It to the Church"?

The third step in mediation transcends all secular methods. It will be regarded as implausible to anyone who does not take seriously grace in the redeeming community. It is this: "If he will not hear them, tell it to the church."[54]

Those who watch over the souls of persons must give account to God. "Tell it to the elder or elders of the church, to those who are overseers of that flock of Christ to which you both belong."[55] The reference is not to a legislative process but to an interpersonal process. "The elders" are the wise in the community. They have seen many conflicts. They have had extensive experience with grace working amid people. Take it to them. Let the wisest among you mediate. "The church" here refers less to a formal public charge than to a mediation process that occurs within the community of reconciliation.[56]

This third step should be taken "in its order, after the other two; not before the second, much less the first."[57] The wisest in the community of faith then may fairly and clearly consider the conflict from every relevant perspective.[58] Those who are responsible for the welfare of the whole community will see the interpersonal conflict in the context of the continuity and health of the whole community. They will pray for grace to grasp adequate insight. They will seek to illumine the conflict in the light of Scripture. It may belong to their office "to rebuke with all authority ... yet with all the tenderness and love which the nature of the thing will admit."[59] All

---

[51]Ibid.
[52]"The Cure of Evil Speaking," B 2:259, J VI:120–21, sec. 2.4.
[53]"The Cure of Evil Speaking," B 2:258, J VI:120, sec. 1.2.
[54]Matt. 28:17; "The Cure of Evil Speaking," B 2:259, J VI:121, sec. 3.1.
[55]"The Cure of Evil Speaking," B 2:259, J VI:121, sec. 3.1.
[56]Ibid.
[57]Ibid.
[58]Ibid.
[59]"The Cure of Evil Speaking," B 2:259–60, J VI:121–22, sec. 3.1–2.

steps toward reconciliation have thus far been inadequate. The wisest in faith may admonish or reprove, but always gently and with tender affection.

b. Avoid Residual Guilt and Remain Open for New Understandings

The community of faith does not need to feel further responsibility after completing these steps conscientiously. "When therefore you have done this, you have done all which the Word of God or the law of love requireth of you. You are not now partaker of his sin, but if he perish his blood is on his own head."[60]

Remain open for new understandings as they develop, just as you would with any other person. Then at least you will have delivered your own soul.[61]

"Let this be the distinguishing mark" of a believer: "Put ye away evil speaking, talebearing, whispering."[62] Let others say, "See how these Christians love one another!" This mark could serve as an example to corollary communities of accountability.[63]

c. Set a Continual Watch upon Your Mouth

It remains regrettable that so few Christians follow these three steps of mediation commended by the Lord. Believers do not have to be carried away by the torrent of the times. They can obey these three simple steps, for none is impossible and all are commanded by the Lord. Wesley admonished, "From this very hour set a watch, a continual watch before your mouths."[64] Restrain the tongue.

When these three steps are taken in order, there will be very little evil speaking. The love of God will abound more in the world and the ties of fellowship will be strengthened if this process is fully respected.

C. Speaking without Guile

1. Speaking the Truth in Love

a. An Israelite Indeed

Wesley's homily #90 calls believers toward personal openness and plain speaking — hence "without guile" ["An Israelite Indeed" (1785), B 3:278 – 89; J VII:37 – 45]. It describes the character of Nathanael in a revealing phrase used by Jesus: "Behold an Israelite indeed, in whom is no guile" (John 1:47).

Nathanael models speaking the truth in love. He embodies the virtues of veracity, sincerity, and simplicity of speech. In him, human language, which had become broken by sin, is restored to truth-telling. This homily is closely associated with earlier homilies on dissimulation.[65]

---

[60]"The Cure of Evil Speaking," B 2:260, J VI:122, sec. 3.2.
[61]"The Cure of Evil Speaking," B 2:260, J VI:121, sec. 3.3.
[62]"The Cure of Evil Speaking," B 2:262, J VI:123, sec. 3.5.
[63]Ibid.
[64]"The Cure of Evil Speaking," B 2:262, J VI:122 – 23, sec. 3.4.
[65]B appendix, vol. 4:138A and 138B – C; "On Dissimulation" (1728), B 4:255 – 66.

b. We Love as God Loved Us

Long before Carl Rogers, Wesley was arguing that human interpersonal interactions function best when inward motivations are congruent with outward behaviors and when these motivations are flooded with wholehearted love. His biblical model was the guilelessness of Nathanael in John 1:47.

Wesley argued from Scripture and experience that love of God is the first commandment, and the love of neighbor derives from it.[66] Wesley had learned from Scripture that secular benevolence itself alone does not justify sinners unless it springs from the love of God revealed in history.[67]

In this teaching homily on spiritual formation, Wesley was implicitly answering philosopher Francis Hutcheson, who had attacked the Christian premise that the love of God shapes our love of fellow creatures. Ironically Hutcheson himself elsewhere even conceded that Christianity is "unquestionably the most benevolent institution that ever appeared in the world,"[68] but he rejected the idea of a relationship with God as an ethical foundation for good works. Wesley regarded the theories of Hutcheson in this case as a fundamental attack on the whole of the Christian religion. These ethicists "put asunder what God has joined" (see Mark 10:9). Christianity unites the love of God and neighbor into a single twofold command.

Paul calls all to speak "the truth in love" (Eph. 4:15). Truth and love are united in the one who knows the hearts of all. In their union lies the practice of benevolence to all. In those whose hearts are touched by divine love, there is no guile, no need for deception. This is shown in the biblical figure of Nathanael.[69] Showing a healthy hesitation against being deceived, Nathanael was the one who asked, "Can ... any good thing come out of Nazareth?" (John 1:46).

c. Congruence of Talk with Behavior

Wesley viewed Nathanael as the biblical model of one "not hasty of belief, and yet open to conviction, and willing to receive the truth."[70] What is implied by the Lord's characterization of him as "a man in whom is no guile"? The Lord saw in him one who was true to God from the heart, and whose speech was congruent with his heart.

Nathanael's congruent character is revealed early in John's gospel. Just as Jesus was calling his first disciples,[71] he found a man without guile — that is, having no taint of deceit.

After Jesus called Philip of Bethsaida, Philip found Nathanael (John 1:43–45). Wesley is working off of this text: "Philip found Nathanael and told him, 'We have

---

[66]"An Israelite Indeed," B 3:281, J VII:38, pref. 2.
[67]"An Israelite Indeed," B 3:282, J VII:38, pref. 7.
[68]"An Israelite Indeed," B 3:280–81, J VII:38, pref. 2–4.
[69]"An Israelite Indeed," B 3:280–81, J VII:38–39, pref. 4–5.
[70]"An Israelite Indeed," B 3:281, J VII:39, pref. 6.
[71]"An Israelite Indeed," B 3:282, J VII:39, pref. 7.

found the one Moses wrote about in the Law, and about whom the prophets also wrote — Jesus of Nazareth, the son of Joseph" (v. 45 NIV). But wait a minute. Really?

"Nazareth! Can anything good come from there?" Nathanael asked.

"Come and see," said Philip.

When Jesus saw Nathanael approaching, he said of him, "Here truly is an Israelite in whom there is no deceit."

"How do you know me?" Nathanael asked.

Jesus answered, "I saw you while you were still under the fig tree before Philip called you." (John 1:46 – 48 NIV)

Though skeptical, Nathanael knew he was suddenly in the presence of a discerning mind. He was quick to recognize who was speaking to him: "Then Nathanael declared, 'Rabbi, you are the Son of God; you are the king of Israel.'" Jesus was candid and swift to acknowledge Nathanael's immediate insight, and he gave Nathanael a glimpse of what was yet to come: "'You believe because I told you I saw you under the fig tree. You will see greater things than that.' He then added, 'Very truly I tell you, you will see "heaven open, and the angels of God ascending and descending on" the Son of Man'" (John 1:50 – 51). Nathanael was ready for discipleship because he asked salient questions and was ready to believe truthful answers.

2. Being True to God from the Heart

a. Finally, No Lie Can Stand

From this Wesley probed what it means to have our hearts "true to God." He said, "Only is our heart 'true to God' when we give it to him" immediately and completely.[72] Readiness for the truth is an evidence of character. But does it admit of varied degrees? Though this giving of our heart to God may occur in low degree, Scripture speaks of a much higher and complete degree of this volitional act.[73] When we seek our happiness in God rather than in honor, esteem, or applause, the truth is revealed to the inner person. We actually *find* our happiness in God rather than merely *seek* it.

How does this learning occur? By the power of the Spirit: "This happiness undoubtedly begins when we begin to know him by the teaching of his own Spirit ... when it pleases the Father to reveal his Son in our heart ... when the Son is pleased to reveal his Father in us by 'the Spirit of adoption, crying in our hearts, Abba Father,' and 'bearing his testimony to our spirits, that we are the children of God.' Then it is that 'the love of God' also 'is shed abroad in our hearts.'"[74]

But what is to prevent this feeling from being only temporary, from lasting for only a few days? Jude counsels us to "keep yourselves in the love of God."[75] This means that "something is to be done on our part in order to [enable] its continu-

---

[72]"An Israelite Indeed," B 3:282, J VII:40, sec. 1.1.

[73]Ibid.

[74]"An Israelite Indeed," B 3:283, J VII:40, sec. 1.2.

[75]Jude 1:21; "An Israelite Indeed," B 3:282, J VII:41, sec. 1.3.

ance."[76] We do well to respond to grace in order to receive it in greater measure. Here the saying of Jesus applies that "whoever has will be given more, and they will have an abundance. Whoever does not have, even what they have will be taken from them" (Matt. 13:12 NIV).[77] The principle of receptive grace is "whoever improves the grace he has already received, whoever increases in the love of God, will surely retain it." For whoever does not improve this talent cannot possibly retain it.[78]

b. Straight from the Heart to the Lips

One whose heart is true to God will have words that are also true. There will be no guile lodged in his heart, hence none in his lips. He speaks truth from his heart. He puts away willful lying.

A lie is a falsehood "known to be such by the speaker, and uttered with an intention to deceive."[79] The medieval moralists made a distinction between three sorts of lies: malicious, harmless, and officious. An officious lie is a lie with a design to do good. All three sorts of lying were, in Wesley's view, inconsistent with the guileless life.[80] In this he followed Augustine.

A lie supposedly spoken with a design to do some good might seem to some as valid or plausible. They even see it hinted at by Paul in Romans 3:7: "For if the truth of God hath more abounded through my lie unto his glory; why yet am I also judged as a sinner?" (emphasis added). Wesley instead rendered that same passage from the Greek: "Will not that lie be excused from blame, for the good effect of it?" Wesley argued that Scripture does not call us to "do evil, that good may come." For the supposed good effect of a lie can be no excuse to continue lying.[81]

c. Guileless Speech

Guileless speech from the heart true to God is characterized by sincerity, prudence, discretion, and simplicity, with no dissimulation whatever. "As veracity is opposite to lying, so sincerity is to cunning.... Wisdom is the faculty of discerning the best ends, and the fittest means of attaining them. The end of every rational creature is God: the enjoying him in time and in eternity.... The best, indeed the only, means of attaining this end is 'the faith that works by love.'"[82]

The cunning of the father of lies uses two means to deceive: simulation and dissimulation. "Simulation is the seeming to be what we are not; dissimulation, the seeming not to be what we are.... The man of sincerity shuns them both, and always appears exactly what he is."[83] In some cases, it is wise to keep silent.

No one can sincerely speak the truth in order to deceive. The end would

---

[76]"An Israelite Indeed," B 3:283, J VII:41, sec. 1.4.
[77]"An Israelite Indeed," B 3:283–84, J VII:41, sec. 1.4–5.
[78]"An Israelite Indeed," B 3:284, J VII:41, sec. 1.5.
[79]"An Israelite Indeed," B 3:284, J VII:41, sec. 2.1.
[80]"An Israelite Indeed," B 3:284–85, J VII:42, sec. 2:2–3.
[81]"An Israelite Indeed," B 3:285, J VII:42, sec. 2.3.
[82]"An Israelite Indeed," B 3:286, J VII:44, sec. 2.4.
[83]"An Israelite Indeed," B 3:286, J VII:43, sec. 2.5.

contaminate the means. We may honestly "speak with reserve, to say only a part, perhaps a small part, of what we know. But were we to pretend it to be the whole, this would be contrary to sincerity."[84] Wesley cautioned: "Although this is not contrary to veracity, yet it certainly is to sincerity. It is therefore the most excellent way, if we judge it proper to speak at all, to put away both simulation and dissimulation, and to speak the naked truth from our heart."[85]

If I speak with simplicity, I will speak no known falsehood. That would splinter simplicity. I will speak plainly and artlessly to everyone. I will not deceive anyone at any level. Here Wesley revealed his loathing of the term *compliment*, which in its eighteenth-century sense had the implication of saying nice things about someone whether true or not. Such speech tempts toward insincerity.[86] The guilelessness of a soul touches every behavior. "The sincerity and simplicity of him in whom is no guile have likewise an influence on his whole behavior."[87] Speaking truth in love gives a color and tone to one's whole outward conversation. Every word is plain and "free from all disguise, being the very picture of his heart."[88]

Human behavior refracts the image of God when it speaks with sincerity, prudence, discretion, and simplicity, with no dissimulation whatever. "Truth and love united together are the essence of virtue or holiness. God indispensably requires 'truth in the inward parts,' influencing all our words and actions." So "let the humble, gentle, patient love of all mankind be fixed on its right foundation, namely, the love of God, springing from faith, from a full conviction that God hath given his only Son to die for my sins."[89]

Further Reading on Pastoral Counsel

Armistead, M. Kathryn. *Wesleyan Theology and Social Science: The Dance of Practical Divinity and Discovery*. Newcastle, UK: Cambridge Scholars, 2010.

Demaray, Donald E. *Devotions and Prayers of John Wesley*. Grand Rapids: Baker, 1957.

Outler, Albert C. "Pastoral Care in the Wesleyan Spirit." In *The Wesleyan Theological Heritage: Essays of Albert C. Outler*, edited by Thomas C. Oden and Leicester R. Longden, 175–88. Grand Rapids: Zondervan, 1991.

Telford, John, ed. *Letters of John Wesley*. 8 vols. London: Epworth, 1931.

---

[84]"An Israelite Indeed," B 3:287, J VII:43, sec. 2.6.
[85]"An Israelite Indeed," B 3:287, J VII:44, sec. 2.7.
[86]"An Israelite Indeed," B 3:287–88, J VII:44, sec. 2.8.
[87]"An Israelite Indeed," B 3:289, J VII:44, sec. 2.10.
[88]Ibid.
[89]"An Israelite Indeed," B 3:289, J VII:45, sec. 2.11.

CHAPTER 3

Soul Care

One who offers soul care has a duty to speak the truth in love and to enable others to do so. This requires learning how to admonish phoniness, penetrate deceptions, resist defiance, and correct misplaced love. The good shepherd of souls will know how to offer gentle but firm reproof when it is called for.

A. Pastoral Admonition

In what spirit are we to admonish another person who is self-deceptively trapped in behaviors that will harm oneself or others? Client-centered therapies have taught us not to judge. Wesley presented the case for empathic encounter but, when needed, gentle confrontation. This is a correlate of his discussion of dissimulation (see chapter 2).

These admonitions are intrinsic to the pastoral office. Lacking this capacity, the pastor cannot fully function.

1. The Duty of Reproving Our Neighbor

Nothing is further from the Wesleyan approach to counseling than simply listening passively. The aim of Wesley's approach is truth-telling.

a. The Manner, Timing, and Compassion of Counsel and Admonition

The law of Moses provides the key text for Wesley's teaching homily on admonition titled "The Duty of Reproving Our Neighbor" [Homily #65, B 2:511 – 20; J #65 VI:296 – 304 (July 28, 1787)]: "'Do not hate a fellow Israelite in your heart. Rebuke your neighbor frankly so you will not share in their guilt. Do not seek revenge or bear a grudge against anyone among your people, but love your neighbor as yourself. I am the LORD'" (Lev. 19:17 – 18 NIV). This same ethic of honesty in human interactions recurs in the New Testament (Col. 3:16; 1 Thess. 5:14; 2 Tim. 4:2; Titus 1:13 – 16).

The law calls the faithful to "rebuke the neighbor frankly" when honesty requires it. Wesley wanted to teach those in his connection of spiritual formation how to rebuke the neighbor frankly yet sustain the spirit of love.

Neighbor means the next one, the one next door, the next person you meet. The neighbor is the closest one to you, the one into whose eyes you look when face-to-face. Do not hate him when he falls. Rather, on behalf of love, speak clearly about what he most needs to hear. Do not shrivel.[1]

In the worshiping community, each believer is called to help the other get in touch with conscience, the inner citadel of moral judgment.[2] This is a service we render to each other in a trusting community. It requires being ready to listen and to speak the truth.

b. The Pastoral Duty to Warn of Dangers to the Soul

But introverted self-examination is not enough for life together in a Christian fellowship. In this community, love requires believers to admonish each other as needed interpersonally and to actively resist any behaviors that would lead to sin. We are called to reprove in a timely way the misjudgments of fellow believers that will lead to sin as well as mistakes of finite perception that might elicit further evil if continued.

To warn of danger is an act of love. To "reprove" (or "admonish" or "rebuke") means to gently help our fellow believers to see the limitations and faults of their voluntary acts of freedom. Such reproving must stem from motives rooted in the love of God. With this motive of redeeming love, all believers are called to help their neighbors resist unseen temptations. God does not want our neighbors to be abandoned to their own deceptions. They need a special kind of friendship.[3]

Admonition is a duty under both the old covenant of Moses and the new covenant of Christ. The former is based on law, the latter on gospel. Admonition does not, strictly speaking, condemn persons; rather, it warns against behaviors that go against their best interests. It is a duty of candor owed to our neighbors to help them see anything that "would naturally lead to sin."[4] If we love our neighbors as ourselves, we will want them to be as candid with us as we are with them.

c. Rightly Discerning Behaviors That Require Admonition

To be spare in reproof, we should rarely reprove anyone for anything that is morally ambiguous or trivial. Do not reprove another for minor scruples that may lie more in your own mind than in another's wrongdoing. Instead, focus on the unambiguous moral requirements, the clear commands of God as discerned in the light of Scripture. We have a special duty to reprove whatever is "clearly and undeniably evil."[5] Appeal directly to the person's conscience. Be candid. Look the person steadily in the eyes.

---

[1]"The Duty of Reproving Our Neighbor," B 2:511–14, J VI:296–97, proem.
[2]"On Conscience," B 3:479–90.
[3]"The Duty of Reproving Our Neighbor," B 2:514, J VI:297, sec. 1.1.
[4]Ibid.
[5]"The Duty of Reproving Our Neighbor," B 2:513, J VI:297, sec. 1.1.3.

2. Respectful Love as the Basis of Admonition

To whom is the duty of admonition owed? To any person in danger of falling away from life with God. For what should one be warned or admonished? For anything that would detract from a life honoring to God.

Everyone with a soul to be redeemed from sin deserves loving admonition when it is due.[6] Anyone who values another's soul is called to perform this office of love in accord with highly varied circumstances at hand and in the various stages along life's way. Admonition is not called for in the same degree or spirit with everyone or every station or relationship. Children are not admonished as adults would be. For the sake of civil order, those in positions of legitimate authority are to be admonished as needed, but not in the same way as those who do not occupy positions of legitimate authority. The relation of child to parent or citizen to policeman must be taken into account. Our associates or employers or employees may be in a different proximity to our scale of responsibilities. Yet to each of them we owe the duty of admonition when necessary, taking into consideration the differences. We owe the duty of admonition to our fellow citizens, and indeed to all humanity, yet with varying degrees of proximity.[7]

a. Close Proximity Increases the Duty to Admonish

Proximity is the ever-variable factor in neighborliness. The neighbor afar is less pertinent to my responsibility than the neighbor nearby — the spouse, the daily coworker, the neighborhood bully. Loving admonition is particularly due to those of our immediate family, but we should proceed in awareness of the differences between age and gender relationships: spouse with spouse, parents with children, brothers with sisters, and in diminishing intensity with relatives allied to us in nearness or distance, either by blood or marriage.[8]

If the neighbor is not ready to hear, do not be too ready to speak. Jesus himself chose the metaphor of casting pearls before swine as a warning about readiness to hear.[9]

A still different special order of responsibility lies in admonishing those with whom we have special bonds of affection in an evangelical society. Especially in a worshiping community of those born anew who intentionally seek accountability before God and whose purpose is to watch over each other do we owe this duty of not permitting one another to sin without a fit word of warning.

To deny this service of love is to abandon our neighbors in their sin. To refuse admonition is in effect to demean our neighbors' responsible freedom, and in effect to "hate our brother in our heart." For example, the neighbor with whom we are bound is entitled to hear our warning if we see his or her marriage in danger.[10]

---

[6]"The Duty of Reproving Our Neighbor," B 2:514, J VI:297, sec. 1.1 – 2.
[7]"The Duty of Reproving Our Neighbor," B 2:515, J VI:299, sec. 2.4.
[8]Ibid.
[9]Ibid.
[10]"The Duty of Reproving Our Neighbor," B 2:515 – 16, J VI:297, sec. 2.4.

Especially for those charged with the care of souls, admonishing is a duty. Your neighbor may die in his or her sins if you do not perform this office of love. At the final judgment, you yourself will be called to account.[11]

b. The Manner of Admonition

The duty of admonition is easier to state than to accomplish. However great the difficulty, we know that the promises of God, who is revealed as the one most trustworthy, will not fail when we pray for grace. Continue in the fear of God, not man. God will provide strength as needed.[12]

Whatever you do must be done in the spirit of "tender goodwill," for you are dealing with one for whom Christ died. Love him enough to warn him of the untoward consequences of his own freedom, that he might be a partaker of increasing grace.

The genuine affections of a caring person will reach into the heart of the neighbor.[13] Speak with humility, and with no hint of contempt. Disclaim any superiority on your part. Bless God for what is good in the neighbor. Watch out for any signs of pride in yourself. "If you think too highly of yourself, you can scarce avoid despising your brother. And if you show, or even feel, the least contempt of those whom you reprove, it will blast your whole work."[14]

True admonition is a work of the Spirit. Speak in a spirit of meekness, avoiding anger. "Everyone should be quick to listen, slow to speak and slow to become angry, because human anger does not produce the righteousness that God desires."[15]

Do not trust in your own cleverness, but in God's providence, lift up your heart to God in your daily conversation. Trust by grace that love will beget love. "Put no confidence in your own wisdom or address, or ability of any kind. Trust in the great Author of every good and perfect gift," remembering that "whatsoever is spoken in the spirit of prayer will not fall to the ground."[16]

c. Communicating Gentle Admonition

The preceding points deal with the inward spirit of effective admonition. What follows deals with the outward manner of the communication.

Preface an admonition with an honest expression of goodwill.[17] Avoid any hint of flattery. Trust that the flame of disinterested love that God kindles in your heart will penetrate the hardest of hearts.

Reprove with seriousness, using directly the very words of Scripture if possible. Let God the Spirit be the source of reproof.[18] You may have times, however, when "a little well-placed raillery will pierce deeper than solid argument," especially with

[11]Ibid.
[12]"The Duty of Reproving Our Neighbor," B 2:513–14, J VI:299–300, sec. 3.1.
[13]"The Duty of Reproving Our Neighbor," B 2:516, J VI:300–301, sec. 3.2.
[14]"The Duty of Reproving Our Neighbor," B 2:516, J VI:297, sec. 3.3.
[15]James 1:19–20 NIV; "The Duty of Reproving Our Neighbor," B 2:516, J VI:297, sec. 3.4.
[16]"The Duty of Reproving Our Neighbor," B 2:516, J VI:300–301, sec. 3.5.
[17]"The Duty of Reproving Our Neighbor," B 2:517, J VI:301, sec. 3.6.
[18]"The Duty of Reproving Our Neighbor," B 2:517, J VI:301, sec. 3.7.

those who are "strangers to religion."[19] Let the situation shape the tone of the communication, whether with many words or no words at all, as with a sigh or merely a glance.[20] Speak your word seasonably, without inordinate delay, when the person is in an amenable humor. With those you see regularly, you may wait for the right time. Those whom you meet only once, speak in or out of season. "God will both teach you how to speak, and give a blessing to what is spoken."[21]

Do not attempt to communicate a serious admonition to one who does not have his senses about him or is locked into compulsive anger or intoxication.[22] Be compassionate yet firm toward compulsive and addictive behaviors. Allow time for fruit to emerge out of the communication. Do not be quickly discouraged.[23]

In this way, especially in evangelical communities, let every person be free in Christian love to "rebuke his neighbor and not suffer sin upon him."[24] Revival has never taken place without a spirit of admonition.

3. A Case Study of Candid Confrontation

a. Letter to the Moravian Church

In a letter headed "To the Moravian Church" [Letters, B 26:109–12 (June 24, 1744)], Wesley offered a case study in gentle admonition. The background is set forth in his journal of June 1744.

First, Wesley asked for candid admonition from his partners in dialogue. The context was his ongoing clash with his friends and mentors, the Moravians, especially those associated with the Fetter Lane Society. His difficulty with the Moravians was their tendency to quietism, especially when it was tempted toward antinomianism.

b. Smite Me Friendly: The Openness of Believer to Believer

Wesley began the letter empathically. He set forth those aspects of Moravian teaching that he held in high esteem. Then he offered what he called "a naked relation (among other things) of many facts and conversations that passed between us in the same order of time as they occurred." His aim was to clarify "what I cannot approve of, yet, that it may be tried by the Word of God."[25]

By "naked relation" Wesley meant a relation of completely transparent openness with nothing to hide, to elicit the highest level of trust among dear friends in Christ. His key request is the memorable phrase "Smite me friendly." Friendship in the Lord is no reason to be unclear about real differences. It asks for serious admonition and gentle counsel. Wesley famously wrote, "And if any of you will, smite me friendly,

---

[19]"The Duty of Reproving Our Neighbor," B 2:518, J VI:301–2, sec. 3.8.
[20]"The Duty of Reproving Our Neighbor," B 2:518, J VI:302, sec. 3.9.
[21]"The Duty of Reproving Our Neighbor," B 2:518, J VI:302, sec. 3.10.
[22]"The Duty of Reproving Our Neighbor," B 2:519, J VI:302, sec. 3.11.
[23]"The Duty of Reproving Our Neighbor," B 2:520, J VI:303, sec. 1.13.
[24]"The Duty of Reproving Our Neighbor," B 2:520, J VI:303–4, sec. 3.14.
[25]Letters, B 26:111.

and reprove me."[26] He wanted his fellow Christians to show him precisely where he might have erred, either in fact or interpretation, substance or style, in part or whole, within this relation of openness.

B. On Penetrating Resistance

1. The Dynamics of Deception

Care of souls requires punching holes in deceptions. If the deception is massive and diffuse, the punch may need to be tough and precise. To let deceptions stand unchallenged is dangerous to the health of the soul.

That Wesley despised phoniness is evident as early as 1728 in one of his earliest manuscript sermons, "On Dissimulation" [Homily #138A (January 1728), B 4:255 – 61 (not in the Jackson edition)]. His text was John 1:47. This sermon stands sixth in the chronological order of Wesley's Sermons. It is closely associated with two fragments of manuscript sermons, usually called #138B – C, "Two Fragments on Dissimulation" [B 4:262 – 66]. The text of homily #138B is Romans 12:9: "Let love be without dissimulation."

a. Homily "On Dissimulation"

In admonishing the dissembler, it is necessary to help him see why he is deceiving. The counselor's task is to sort out in the situation the connection between self-deception and deceiving others. This is a delicate task of soul care, requiring all the acumen and analytical power the counselor can muster.

This sermon is an early expression of Wesley's lifelong disgust with deceit in any form. He was writing from his father's parsonage in Epworth. He had long been taught by his parents a strict ethic of plain speaking and plain dealing. This is a theme that recurs from his earliest to his latest writings.[27] It was already well-developed in the cradle of his ministry when he was only twenty-three years old.

In *The Grumbling Hive* by Bernard Mandeville, eighteenth-century readers were offered mocking descriptions of a thriving community of bees that flourished until they decided to pursue a strict ethic of honesty and virtue. Lacking the motive of self-interest, the colony dwindled. Mandeville's barbed point is that without private vices there exists no public benefits.

Wesley held the opposite view. He commended complete sincerity and openness and repudiated all forms of deceit. The vicious habit of dissimulation is "directly opposite to that which God recommends." Dissimulation wants to make invisible the consequences of an action.[28] Wesley's purpose in this homily was to "paint in opposite colors the opposite vice, insincerity: to show the baseness, deformity, and folly of it — how mean, odious, and imprudent it is to dissemble."[29]

---

[26]Ibid.

[27]See "Sermon on the Mount, 4," J IV:3, 52, and "The Reformation of Manners," J IV:4 – 5.

[28]"On Dissimulation," Homily #138A, B 4:255, pref. 2.

[29]"On Dissimulation," B 4:255, pref. 3.

b. The Father of Lies

The devil was the first to employ dissembling. Artifice and dissembling have their primitive origin in "the father of lies," even before human freedom chooses to tell a lie. The liar then comes to resemble the father of lies, whose wickedness from the beginning "immediately laid him under a necessity of dissembling, to hide it." "He deceived by seeming better than he was." This is what Satan has been doing "before the world began, and such has he been ever since."[30] He first deceived himself and then the children of men, who were unable to discern his motives, because they were hidden.[31] The baseness of a human act of deception can best be grasped by comparing it to the baseness of its originator. The common human condition resembles the devil in many respects. Both the devil and fallen humanity have been "created upright; both had it in their power to continue so; but both wilfully declined it." To cover their corrupted will, they "sewed fig leaves together to hide their shame."[32] No morally sensitive rational mind can conscientiously defend dissembling, either in oneself or others.[33]

The enemy "smiles in our face while he prepares to wound us."[34] The dissembler conceals "real enmity under the appearance of indifference" and "real indifference under the appearance of love." Either way the dissimulation is infuriating and elicits resentment.[35]

When good counsel smells deception, it is fitting to recall that fallen human history is saturated with the deceptions of the father of lies. For deceivers, Wesley recalled the stinging words of Jesus: "You belong to your father, the devil, and you want to carry out your father's desire. He was a murderer from the beginning, not holding to the truth, for there is no truth in him. When he lies, he speaks his native language, for he is a liar and the father of lies" (John 8:44 NIV).

If human freedom was not restrained by conscience and religion, the harmful consequences of deceit would multiply.[36] But no deceit can end conscience, since it is built into human consciousness.

Those who dissemble do so out of hate, not love. Those who have yielded permanently to dissembling may lose the capacity to love. "The nature of love is sincere, plain, and open."[37]

c. The Folly of Dissembling

When I sin, I lose character. Then I try to guard against the loss of character by attempting to conceal sin A under virtue B. Wesley astutely observed that those who follow this delusion "had rather sin twice against their conscience than once against

---

[30]"On Dissimulation," B 4:256, sec. 1.1.
[31]Ibid.
[32]"On Dissimulation," B 4:256, sec. 1.2.
[33]"On Dissimulation," B 4:257, sec. 1.3.
[34]"On Dissimulation," B 4:257, sec. 1:1.
[35]"On Dissimulation," B 4:257 – 8, sec. 1:1.
[36]Ibid.
[37]Ibid.

their character."[38] Our demonic adversary attempts to "persuade us into one sin to hide another." Deception works like a chain of covert decisions and actions. Regrettably this trick is all too commonly successful. We are up against a dreadful enemy.

"Dissembling is base and odious, and in fact despised and hated by God and man." It proposes to itself "vain, perishable ends, and using difficult, dangerous, sinful means to attain them." Believers are called to "join in David's prayer: 'Save me, O Lord, from lying lips and from deceitful tongues.'"[39]

The dissembler offends not only against God's truth but also against God's mercy — God's truth by lying, God's mercy by presuming on leniency.

The end results of dissembling are always unsatisfactory while they last. Yet they are incapable of lasting long. All lies are subject to being found out.

The means of deceit used to attain supposedly good ends are odious, dangerous, and sinful.[40] The temporal wrong is vulnerable to the eternal right. "The end the dissembler proposes to himself must be some temporal advantage.... But this [temporal] end, whether wealth, honor, power, or sensual pleasure, if ever he should attain it, when attained, will not satisfy his desires, will not make him happy, even while it lasts."[41] Even the best of temporal ends "can only please the sense; but that is not enough to make us happy." The soul breathed in by God seeks durable happiness.[42] What the dissembler seeks is perishable. "He has not only chosen the worse part, but that which soon will be taken away."[43]

d. The Difficulty of Prolonging Sustained Dissembling

It is extremely difficult to prolong sustained dissimulation: "To act in perpetual contradiction to one's own desires and sentiments, to commend him for whom one has no real esteem, to watch over his interests for whom one has no real love, are instances of the most low and abject slavery."[44] The dissembler is forced to try "to perform all the tender offices that naturally flow from real affection, all which nothing but real affection can make pleasing."[45] Deception raises a feeling of contempt in all who witness it occurring. "From professed enemies prudence and caution may secure us; but what will secure us from professing friends?"[46]

"The dissembler has so many parts to play that without the utmost pains and vigilance he can scarce avoid being out in some.... How hard is it to shift the scene so often and never be suspected of shifting it at all!" wrote Wesley. Each part of dissembling grows harder to maintain the longer it persists.[47] The dissembler is

---

[38]"On Dissimulation," B 4:255, pref. 1.
[39]Ps. 120:2 NIV; "On Dissimulation," B 4:260 – 61, sec. 3.5.
[40]"On Dissimulation," B 4:259, sec. 3.
[41]"On Dissimulation," B 4:259, sec. 3.1.
[42]Ibid.
[43]"On Dissimulation," B 4:259, sec. 3.2.
[44]"On Dissimulation," B 4:263, sec. 2.
[45]"On Dissimulation," B 4:264 – 66, sec. 2.
[46]"On Dissimulation," B 4:264, sec. 2.
[47]"On Dissimulation," B 4:259, sec. 3.3.

exposed to continual danger of being found out.[48] The dissembler's "talk is smooth as butter, yet war is in his heart; his words are more soothing than oil, yet they are drawn swords.... But you, God, will bring down the wicked into the pit of decay; the bloodthirsty and deceitful will not live out half their days" (Ps. 55:21–23 NIV).

This is why dissimulation is foolish. Soul care seeks to reduce this foolishness, if possible, to zero. This requires punching holes in pretenses.

2. On Deceit

a. Homily #138B, On Dissimulation: Protecting Love from Deceit

Two other manuscript fragments were found among Wesley's papers. The first of these two fragments, labeled #138B, "On Dissimulation," is based on Romans 12:9: "Let love be without dissimulation." There is no indication of date or provenance, but probably it comes from the same period as above, around 1728. It has been preserved in the Elmer T. Clark Collection of Wesleyana. Wesley contended that love must be protected from deceit. Loving our neighbor as ourselves is the indispensable duty of the believer. No Christian can be and none ever desired to be released from it. "So express and frequently repeated are the precepts that enjoin it, that while their authority is allowed to be divine, their force can never be eluded."[49]

Great and numerous advantages result from this duty to love our neighbors. Love gives the faithful the spirit and vigor to attempt and conquer the most dangerous and difficult parts of our duty. Life without love would be tedious if not painful. "While we are employed in relieving one we love from pain, we ourselves can very hardly be sensible of any: while we bring an addition to his happiness, we can't avoid increasing our own." Hence Paul laid down the caution: "Let love be without dissimulation."

b. Homily #138C, On Dissimulation: Deceit Goes Viral in the Realm of Love

The second fragment [Homily #138C, "On Dissimulation," B 4:263–66] is an incomplete draft of a sermon on the same theme.

Dissembling becomes most viral when it tries to enter the realm of love: "To dissemble love implies either that we really have none, or that we strive to make the love we have appear greater than it is."[50] Dissimulating love is dangerous: "Like a maniac shooting flaming arrows of death is one who deceives their neighbor and says, 'I was only joking!'" (Prov. 26:18–19 NIV).[51] "Every precept that enjoins the love of our neighbor enjoins love without dissimulation."[52] We do not need to

---

[48]"On Dissimulation," B 4:260, sec. 3.4.
[49]"On Dissimulation," a fragment, B 3:262.
[50]"On Dissimulation," B 4:263, sec. 1.
[51]Ibid.
[52]"On Dissimulation," B 4:263, sec. 2.

dissemble in real love of the neighbor. Of all forms of dissimulation, the most inexcusable is that which "counterfeits affection where there is none."[53]

God is able to keep his promise. God promises to supply more love just when we feel the strength of our love is insufficient. God is incomparably abundant in love. God's love does not diminish.[54]

Both of these fragments point to a central feature of Wesley's view of soul care: honest disclosure. He calls for simple truth-telling and openness.

C. Counsel for Those Facing Temptations

1. On Temptation

a. No Temptation Has Overtaken You Alone

We touch the heart of soul care when we counsel persons urgently facing temptation. There we discover, just as promised, that God permits no temptation beyond that which is proportioned to our strength.

Wesley offered counsel for all those who are discouraged because they "once ran well and were afterwards overcome by temptation."[55] He plunged directly into the analysis of the dynamics of temptation in his homily #82, "On Temptation" [B 3:156–68; J VI:475–84 (October 7, 1786)]. He taught that pastoral care must become firm and must penetrate deceit.

Wesley's text is 1 Corinthians 10:13: "No temptation has overtaken you except what is common to mankind. And God is faithful; he will not let you be tempted beyond what you can bear. But when you are tempted, he will also provide a way out so that you can endure it" (NIV).

In counseling those facing temptations, Wesley stressed the power of grace to overcome the weak links in human character, aware of the promise that God will provide "'a way of escape' for those who remain steadily faithful."[56]

b. Why Temptation Is Common to All Humanity: The Body-Soul Composite

Temptation is the ordinary condition of fallen freedom. It is endemic to the fallen nature and circumstances of bodies and souls living in history.

Consider first the nature of your body and soul, their connection, and the history of the fallenness of all things. Amid these distorted historical conditions, we all experience temptation and should not be surprised at any form it may take. It may come anytime. Every hour of every day we are vulnerable to "weakness, sickness, and disorders of a thousand kinds," any of which can bring about temptation.[57]

Think of the awesome and humbling complexity of the body. Every part is com-

---

[53]"On Dissimulation," B 4:263–65, sec. 2.
[54]Ibid.
[55]"On Temptation," B 3:157, J VI:477–78, pref. 3.
[56]"On Temptation," B 3:157, J VI:477, text.
[57]"On Temptation," B 3:158–59, J VI:477, sec. 1.1.

posed of "inconceivably minute fibers" with "circulating juices," any one of which can instantly obstruct the brain, or heart, or lungs. Since "all pain implies temptation, how numberless must the temptations be which will beset every man, more or less, sooner or late, while he dwells in this corruptible body!"[58]

Believers troubled by persistent temptation do well to recall the teaching that no temptation has ever overtaken you "except what is common to mankind" (1 Cor. 10:13 NIV).

2. Why the Faithful Are Tempted

a. The Same Body-Soul Interface Continues in Believers

This is the human body-soul condition that characterizes not only the unrepentant sinner, but also believers in the community of the faithful who have "tasted grace." Our vulnerability to temptation is the persistent "present state of the soul as long as it inhabits the house of clay." This is most evidently seen in those living in the unregenerate state. They lie "in the shadow of death, under the dominion of the prince of darkness, without hope, and without God in the world."[59]

But what of the condition of those born anew? They have been raised up to a new life as children of God's family. Yet even in those who are most faithful we still note "how weak is their understanding!... How liable are the wisest of men to mistake! To form false judgments! How many are the temptations which we have to expect, even from these innocent infirmities!"[60] The faithful "dwell in the ruins of a disordered world, among men that know not God." Think of one unarmed man "surrounded by a thousand armed men! Now this is the case of every good man."[61]

Temptations constantly arise out of social, familial, and economic conditions. But more profoundly they arise from deep within the human will. They are bound to emerge from the essential condition of the variability and vulnerability of freedom itself in its relation to changing time. Born to a heavenly destination, the soul dwells in a fragile body.

b. Are the Most Mature Believers Most Subject to Temptation?

Some may imagine that they would be free from temptations if only they could get away from evil external influences. That fantasy fails to grasp how deeply the heart itself is entwined in ambiguous choices. The heart itself remains vulnerable to temptations from within the sphere of its own willing. The faithful are freed from the dominion of sin but not from the consequences of it. For the faithful sin remains but does not reign.[62] "For even good men in general, though sin has not dominion over them, yet are not freed from the remains of it. They have still the remains of an evil heart, ever prone to 'depart from the living God.' They have the seeds of

---

[58]"On Temptation," B 3:159, J VI:477, sec. 1.2.
[59]Ibid.
[60]"On Temptation," B 3:159 – 60, J VI:477, sec. 1.3.
[61]"On Temptation," B 3:160, J VI:478, sec. 1.4.
[62]See "Sin in Believers," B 1:314 – 34; 2 Cor. 5:17 – 21.

pride, of anger, of foolish desire; indeed of every unholy temper, [which] ... if they do not continually watch and pray, may, and naturally will spring up and trouble not themselves only, but all that are round about them."[63]

But does this same condition of vulnerability to temptation apply even among those who walk in perfect love, those far along in growth in grace? Yes. They, too, "are still encompassed with infirmities. They may be dull of apprehension; they may have a natural heedlessness, or a treacherous memory; they may have too lively an imagination: and any of these may cause little improprieties, either in speech or behavior, which though not sinful in themselves may try all the grace you have." Obviously, you will find every kind of temptation among "those who suppose they are perfected when indeed they are not," and also "from those who once really were so." But less obviously this remains also the condition of "even those who 'stand fast in the liberty wherewith Christ has made them free'" through "defect of memory or weakness of understanding."[64]

"Who is out of the reach of their malice and subtlety? Not the wisest or the best of the children of men. 'The servant is not above his Master.' If then they tempted him, will they not tempt us also?" To the end of our lives God permits evil to challenge the will toward deeper strength of faith.[65]

Temptation counseling thus places the temptation of the individual within the history of sin and redemption. The Bible tells the story of that history.

3. God Permits No Temptation beyond That Which Is Proportioned to Our Strength

a. God's Ways of Helping the Tempted

Counseling amid trials and temptations offers a new opportunity to point to God's faithfulness: "Meantime what a comfort it is to know, with the utmost certainty, that God is faithful, who will not suffer us to be tempted above that we are able." God knows what our ability is. God knows we are made of dust. The biblical promise remains: God will permit "no temptation to befall us but such as is proportioned to our strength."[66]

This unambiguous promise is fitting to God's justice, which would not hold us accountable for resisting temptation if temptation were "so disproportioned to our strength that it was impossible for us to resist it." This promise is also grounded in God's mercy and faithfulness to his Word.[67]

b. God May Make a Way of Escape by Removing the Occasion of Temptation

Scripture promises, "God is faithful; he will not let you be tempted beyond what

---

[63]"On Temptation," B 3:161, J VI:478–79, sec. 1.5.
[64]"On Temptation," B 3:161, J VI:479, sec. 1.6.
[65]"On Temptation," B 3:162, J VI:479–80, sec. 1.7.
[66]"On Temptation," B 3:162–63, J VI:475–84, sec. 2.1.
[67]"On Temptation," B 3:162–63, J VI:480, sec. 2.1.

you can bear. But when you are tempted, he will also provide a way out so that you can endure it." Only God has the wisdom and power to do this.[68] This "making of a way" may occur in two different forms.

First, God may "make a way to escape out of the temptation" by removing the occasion of it.[69] God "removes trouble, or sickness, or pain; and it is as though it never had been."[70]

c. God May Make a Way of Escape by Taking Away the Bitterness of It

Second, even when the temptation cannot be taken away, God is able to deliver out of temptation by "taking away the bitterness of it; so that it shall not be a temptation at all, but only an occasion of thanksgiving. How many proofs of this have the children of God, even in their daily experience!"[71] At these times God "does not make any outward change" in the pain or trouble, "but the consolations of the Holy One so increase as to over-balance them all."[72]

4. Counsel for Those Who Think No One Has Ever Had a Trial Like They Are Having

Wesley turned to Paul's caveat: " 'Let him that most assuredly standeth, take heed lest he fall' into murmuring; lest he say in his heart, 'Surely no one's case is like mine: no one was ever tried like me.' "[73] Remember that there is "no temptation taken you but such as is common to man."[74] Even the Lord faced temptation. He was tempted as we are yet without sin. "For we do not have a high priest who is unable to empathize with our weaknesses, but we have one who has been tempted in every way, just as we are — yet he did not sin" (Heb. 4:15 NIV).

We risk tempting God by imagining in our own case, "This is insupportable; this is too hard; I can never get through it; my burden is heavier than I can bear. Not so; unless something is too hard for God.... He proportions the burden to your strength. If you want more strength, ask and it shall be given you."[75] When your strength is emptied, God will offer a way out, whether through removing the obstacle or making it a means of consolation. "Let us then receive every trial with calm resignation, and with humble confidence that he who hath all power, all wisdom, all mercy, and all faithfulness, will first support us in every temptation, and then deliver us out of all." In the end, we see that "all things shall work together for good, and we shall happily experience that all these things were for our profit, 'that we might be partakers of his holiness.' "[76]

---

[68]"On Temptation," B 3:162 – 63, J VI:475 – 84, sec. 3.1.
[69]"On Temptation," B 3:165, J VI:475 – 84, sec. 3.3.
[70]"On Temptation," B 3:165 – 66, J VI:484, sec. 3.4.
[71]"On Temptation," B 3:165 – 66, J VI:475 – 84, sec. 3.4.
[72]Ibid.
[73]1 Cor. 10:12; "On Temptation," B 3:167, J VI:475 – 84, sec. 3.7.
[74]"On Temptation," B 3:167, J VI:475 – 84, sec. 3.7.
[75]"On Temptation," B 3:167, J VI:475 – 84, sec. 3.8.
[76]"On Temptation," B 3:168, J VI:475 – 84, sec. 3.10.

D. The Wilderness State and Manifold Temptations

1. The Wilderness State

In offering counsel to those facing temptation, we find Wesley at his best in two important homilies: "The Wilderness State" and "Heaviness through Manifold Temptations." They are closely related, describing the difference between the "darkness of mind" and the "heaviness of the soul" under a storm of temptations. They provide counsel for two very different stages of dealing with temptation.

First, the text of "The Wilderness State" [Homily #46 (1754 – 57), B 2:205 – 21; J #46, VI:77 – 91] is John 16:22: "Now you are having pain. But I will see you again, and your hearts will rejoice, and no one will take your joy away from you" (ISV). Wesley first noted that after the exodus the people of Israel "did not immediately enter into the land which he had promised to their fathers, but 'wandered out of the way in the wilderness.' "[77] They were freed but remained in the wilderness.

Similarly in the Christian life, after receiving divine pardon and reconciliation, we are often like the exodus people: God has delivered us from bondage to sin. We have been justified by grace but have not immediately entered the Promised Land. We are somewhere between the land of bondage and the land of milk and honey. We are still wandering in a howling desert (Deut. 32:10).[78] We still face temptations and frustrations. This is the recurrent condition of believers who have experienced and received God's saving grace but have not realized its promised rest of peace and joy.

This paradox calls for tender compassion. The light has shown upon our heads, but we still wander in darkness. This stage is common to the journey of faith but often not well understood. It requires digging deep into the whole sense of Scripture, comparing text with text for a grasp of the integrity of God's saving design. Think of this as if we once had a disease that has been basically cured, yet many lingering complications and symptoms remain. We remain mired in our infirmities and sins.[79]

Using a medical analogy, Wesley taught that we must first identify the symptoms of our disorder, next identify their multiple causes, and only then seek a fitting cure corresponding with the specific symptoms.

a. The Nature of Our Disorder

The problem focuses on the apparent temporary loss of that faith which God once wrought in our hearts but which we have not yet fully laid hold of.[80] At one time we experienced the evidence of things unseen. Now we do not possess the evidence we once saw with our spiritual senses.

---

[77]"The Wilderness State," B 2:205, J VI:77, proem, sec. 1; Ex. 13:3; Ps. 107:40.
[78]"The Wilderness State," B 2:205, J VI:77, proem, sec. 2.
[79]"The Wilderness State," B 2:206, J VI:79, proem, sec. 2.
[80]"The Wilderness State," B 2:206, J VI:78, sec. 1.1.

Once we were able to say, "The life I now live in the body, I live by faith in the Son of God, who loved me and gave himself for me" (Gal. 2:20 NIV). Later we do not experience the Spirit as shining in our hearts. We forget that faith's evidence is invisible. It is "of things not seen" (Heb. 11:1).[81] Once we saw the light, but now we wander in darkness. The Spirit seems no longer to be witnessing with our spirits that we are the children of God. We once said in our hearts, "Abba, Father," but now we lack the liberty of approaching the Father with the boldness of a child. We have not yet learned to say with Job, "Though he slay me, yet will I trust in him" (Job 13:15).

This is what it means to be in the wilderness. We may be on the porch but not in the house of the family of God.[82] This darkness of mind is not a decree of God. It is very common in the Christian life, often at its earliest stages. There is a remedy.

How do we recognize the wilderness state? What are its symptoms? There are six in particular: loss of love, faith, power, joy, zeal, and peace.

b. The Symptoms

Its first sure evidence of the wilderness state is the loss of *love*. Why? Because, rightly understood, the works of love come only out of *faith*. Lacking faith, we lack the love that springs from faith.[83]

Lacking faith and love, we lack *joy*. We are no longer happy in God, as we were when we could sense with all our spiritual senses the evidences of things unseen. We no long savor simply being in the presence of God. We no longer delight in the "smell of the odor of his ointments" in public worship, where we once loved to praise his name. Now our desire is cold.

What else? We are likely to have lost that *zeal* for the souls of men, "that longing after their welfare, that fervent, restless, active desire of their being reconciled to God." In the tender days of the new birth, we were once gentle toward everyone, seeking by encouragement and correction, their benefit. If we saw anyone who was falling, we caught them up. We restored them in the spirit of meekness. But at some point, we may notice that our anger is beginning to regain its power. Peevishness and impatience deaden our sensitivities.[84] Joy is gradually diminished. "If the Spirit does not witness with our spirit that we are the children of God, the joy that flowed from that inward witness must also be at an end.[85] Once we rejoiced "with joy unspeakable ... in hope of the glory of God," but now are blocked from the joy that hope brought. If the cause of our happiness is removed, so is its effect in the loss of joy. The living waters that once refreshed our thirsty souls seem to have been dammed up.[86]

---

[81]Ibid.
[82]Ibid.
[83]"The Wilderness State," B 2:206, J VI:79, sec. 1.2.
[84]Ibid.
[85]"The Wilderness State," B 2:207, J VI:79, sec. 1.3.
[86]Ibid.

With loss of faith, love, zeal, and joy, in due time we begin to feel a "loss of that *peace* which once passed all understanding. That sweet tranquility of mind, that composure of spirit, is gone. Painful doubt returns; doubt, whether we ever did, and perhaps whether we ever shall, believe. We begin to doubt whether we ever did find in our hearts the real testimony of the Spirit; whether we did not rather deceive our own souls, and mistake the voice of nature for the voice of God."[87] We glumly imagine that we will never again hear God's voice or find favor in his presence.

These doubts may elicit a "servile fear" of the anger of God, just as we had before we first believed. We then may "sink again into that fear of death, from which we were before wholly delivered."[88] Loss of faith, love, joy, and peace is experienced as a *loss of power*, a feeling of helplessness. Wesley explained: "We know everyone who has peace with God, through Jesus Christ, has power over all sin. But whenever he loses the peace of God, he loses also the power over sin. While that peace remained, power also remained, even over the besetting sin, whether it were the sin of his nature, his constitution, of his education, or that of his profession; yea, and over those evil tempers and desires."[89] Once sin had no dominion over the believer. Now the self has no dominion over sin. "The crown is fallen from his head. His enemies again prevail over him, and, more or less, bring him into bondage. The glory is departed from him, even the kingdom of God which was in his heart."[90]

This is the wilderness state, in which one is "dispossessed of righteousness, as well as of peace and joy in the Holy Ghost" that had once been enjoyed.[91]

This deterioration is not caused by "the bare, arbitrary, sovereign will of God," since God rejoices in the prosperity of the faithful. It does not delight God to afflict the children of men.[92]

Rather, God wills "peace and joy in the Holy Ghost" (Rom. 14:17). Without coercing our freedom, God wills that we should receive his own free gifts of love, faith, holiness, and that happiness fitting to life in the family of God.

c. Distinguishing Sins of Commission and Sins of Omission in the Wilderness State

It is not God who has deserted us but we who have deserted God. We may desert him by either sins of commission or omission. It is not God who withdraws the gifts he has given but we who withdraw from receiving them.[93]

Face it: "the most usual cause of inward darkness is *sin*, of one kind or another." It is our own failure to receive grace that encumbers our path, leading toward the intertwining of sin and misery.[94]

---

[87]"The Wilderness State," B 2:207, J VI:80, sec. 1.4.
[88]Ibid.
[89]"The Wilderness State," B 2:208, J VI:80, sec. 1.5.
[90]Ibid.
[91]Ibid.
[92]"The Wilderness State," B 2:208, J VI:80, sec. 2.1; cf. Lam. 3:33.
[93]"The Wilderness State," B 2:208, J VI:80, sec. 2.1.
[94]"The Wilderness State," B 2:208, J VI:80, sec. 2.2; note that here begins the first of three points

To move ahead, it is especially useful to grasp the difference between two types of sin: the sin we willfully commit and the sin that results from our omitting some good we might have done. This is the familiar distinction between sins of commission and omission. Sins of commission are less easy to hide from oneself. Anyone who has been "walking in the clear light of God's countenance" who commits a gross and deliberate sin will cause that person immediately to feel a sense of the loss of grace.[95]

Wesley concedes that willful, presumptuous sins are less frequent than sins of neglect or *omission*, where we simply omit doing a known good. We turn away from the good. We close our eyes to consequences.[96] Those who have tasted life in the Spirit are less likely to "grossly and presumptuously rebel" against God than to ignore his promptings.[97] Sins of omission do not immediately quench the Spirit, but gradually and slowly they do. Wesley compares sins willfully *committed* to "pouring water" upon the fire of the enkindling Spirit, as distinguished from sins *omitted*, which are more like "withdrawing the fuel from it."[98]

In omission we neglect the secret notices God gives before we willfully sin. It is usually by a long train of omissions, with which we willfully collude, that we feel the loss of the power over sin. This is the darkness of the wilderness state. But God does not arbitrarily depart from the inward precincts of the soul. The Spirit provides many "inward checks" to prevent our fallenness.[99]

d. Early Signs of Deterioration

Neglect of prayer is a major and typical instance of a sin of omission: "Perhaps no sin of omission more frequently occasions this than the *neglect of private prayer*."[100] Lacking prayer, none of the other ordinances of God (Eucharist, Scripture studies, hearing the Word preached) are deeply nourishing. "Nothing can be more plain than that the life of God in the soul does not continue, much less increase, unless we use all opportunities of communing with God and pouring out our hearts before him." If we do not use the means of grace God has given us in prayer and common worship, we cannot expect the continuance of a healthy life of the soul. If we hurry over our prayers "in a slight and careless manner," or "long or frequently intermit them," the healthy life will cease to grow and may eventually die away.[101]

Another sin of omission that frequently draws the soul toward darkness is the neglect of hearing and receiving *admonition*. It is strongly recommended in both testaments of Scripture: "'Thou shalt, in any wise rebuke thy neighbour, and not

---

oddly numbered in most editions of "The Wilderness State" as I, II, and III, while still retaining the Arabic numerals. Readers will not be lost if they ignore the Roman numerals.

[95]"The Wilderness State," B 2:209, J VI:81, sec. 2.3.
[96]"The Wilderness State," B 2:208, J VI:80, sec. 2.3.
[97]Ibid.
[98]Ibid.
[99]Ibid.
[100]"The Wilderness State," B 2:209, J VI:81, sec. 2.4, italics added.
[101]Ibid.

suffer sin upon him.' 'Thou shalt not hate thy brother in thine heart.' Now, if we do hate our brother in our heart, if we do not rebuke him when we see him in a fault, but suffer sin upon him, this will soon bring leanness to our own soul; seeing hereby we are partakers of his sin. By neglecting to reprove our neighbor, we make his sin our own: We become accountable for it to God. We saw his danger and gave him no warning" (Lev. 19:17; cf. Josh. 22:20; Rev. 18:4).[102] So "if [our neighbor] perish in his iniquity, God may justly require 'his blood at our hands'" (2 Sam. 4:11). We grieve the Holy Spirit when we "lose the light of his countenance."[103]

Other insidious inward sins that cause us to lose the light of his countenance are pride and anger. Those who are proud in their hearts are viewed in Scripture as "an abomination to the LORD" (Prov. 16:5).[104] This is especially so when *pride* is concealed in superficial pleasantness. How easy it is for an egocentric man "to imagine that he has more grace, more wisdom or strength, than he really has to 'think more highly of himself than he ought to think'! How natural to glory in something he has received, as if he had not received it!"[105] But since God always resists the proud and only gives grace to the humble, this in due time destroys the light that had previously shown within his heart.[106]

The equilibrium of grace is thrown off by "giving place to *anger*, whatever the provocation or occasion be," even if it is "colored over with the name of zeal for the truth, or for the glory of God."[107] Regarding zeal mixed with anger, Wesley warns that nothing is a greater enemy to the mild, gentle love of God than a zeal that is not motivated by love.

> In the same proportion as this prevails, love and joy in the Holy Ghost decrease. This is particularly observable in the case of *offense*; I mean, anger at any of our brethren, at any of those who are united with us either by civil or religious ties. If we give way to the spirit of offense but one hour, we lose the sweet influences of the Holy Spirit; so that, instead of amending them, we destroy ourselves, and become an easy prey to any enemy that assaults us.[108]

Even when anger is asleep and love is waking, we may still be tempted into foolish desires and inordinate affections. When we carefully examine our affections, we see how often they are rooted in *idolatry*. This happens when we *make an idol of a creaturely good*, when we

> set our affection on things of the earth, on any person or thing under the sun; if we desire anything but God, and what tends to God; if we seek happiness in any creature; the jealous God will surely contend with us, for he can admit of no rival. And if we will not hear his warning voice, and return to him with our

---

[102]"The Wilderness State," B 2:209, J VI:81, sec. 2.5.
[103]Ibid.; cf. Ezek. 3:18; 33:8. See also the homily "The Duty to Reprove Our Neighbor."
[104]"The Wilderness State," B 2:210, J VI:82, sec. 2.6 (III.1 of sec. 2).
[105]"The Wilderness State," B 2:210, J VI:82, sec. 2.6; cf. Rom. 12:3; 1 Cor. 4:7.
[106]"The Wilderness State," B 2:210, J VI:82, sec. 2.6 (III.1 of sec. 2); cf. 1 Peter 5:5.
[107]"The Wilderness State," B 2:210, J VI:82, sec. 2.7.
[108]Ibid., italics added.

whole soul, we continue to grieve him with our idols, and running after other gods, we shall soon be cold, barren, and dry; and the god of this world will blind and darken our hearts.[109]

If we do not "stir up the gift of God, which is in [us]," we tend to lose it (2 Tim. 1:6). If we fail to enter the straight gate, we tend to go astray (Luke 13:24). Wesley's used this epigram: "There needs no more than not to fight, and we are sure to be conquered."[110] If we are easy and indolent, our natural darkness will soon return and overspread our souls.

We are responsible for our *inattentiveness* toward our own sins of omission. In a brilliant passage, Wesley shows that the cause of our discontent may be far away from our conscious recognition. Our failures of attentiveness

> might be committed days, or weeks, or months before. And that God now withdraws his light and peace on account of what was done so long ago is not (as one might at first imagine) an instance of his severity, but rather a proof of his longsuffering and tender mercy. He waited all this time if haply we would see, acknowledge, and correct what was amiss. And in default of this he at length shows his displeasure, if thus, at last, he may bring us to repentance.[111]

e. Whether This Inattentiveness Is a Necessity Imposed by God

One common form of biblical ignorance is the idea that the darkness of our discontented minds is an eternal necessity imposed directly by God. Those who do not fully grasp the merciful nature of God in the Scriptures might imagine that "all believers without exception *must* sometimes be in darkness."[112] This turns darkness into an absolute necessity and indeed a divine decree. This tempts us to expect darkness. But to expect darkness is already to be overcome by it.

Wesley contended against those theologians, both Catholic and Protestant, who have taught the believer to expect depression. This expectation is based on the assumption that grace is not fully capable of fulfilling God's promises. Others commend toughing it out in the wilderness by "naked faith." By naked faith they sometimes imply faith "stripped both of love, and peace, and joy in the Holy Ghost!"[113] Hence they come to prefer a state of spiritual dryness as if it were natural to the Christian life. If living in light and joy is good, living in darkness and depression is, to them, better.

A similar problem arises when we imagine that faith permanently *relieves us from all temptation.* It is true that those who have experienced divine pardon may at first find a complete reprieve from temptation but later find temptation reappearing.

---

[109]"The Wilderness State," B 2:211, J VI:82–83, sec. 2.8.

[110]"The Wilderness State," B 2:211, J VI:83, sec. 2.9; later a similar thought was attributed to Edmund Burke: "All that is necessary for the triumph of evil is for good men to do nothing" (attribution disputed); cf. "Thoughts on the Causes of Present Discontents" (1770).

[111]"The Wilderness State," B 2:211, J VI:83, sec. 2.10.

[112]Ibid., italics added. Note after sec. 2.10 the section the same as B.II.1; see note above on this numbering anomaly.

[113]"The Wilderness State," B 2:212, J VI:84, sec. 2.2 (i.e., B.II.2).

"It is then very natural to suppose that we shall not see war any more. And there are instances wherein this calm has continued, not only for weeks, but for months or years. But commonly it is otherwise: In a short time 'the winds blow, the rains descend, and the floods arise' anew" (Matt. 7:25 – 27).[114] When God "slackens the bridle in our teeth," we may at first feel relief but soon find temptation returning so as to elicit anger and bitterness that inward sin has not all gone away. If we think the day of evil will never return, we are not ready for the fiery darts that will always be aimed at the faithful. The soul will at some point be called to wrestle with not only its own "flesh and blood, but against principalities, against powers, against the rulers of the darkness of this world, against spiritual wickedness in high places" (Eph. 6:12).

These are all temptations from within. They are not forced upon us. They arise out of the vulnerabilities of our own fallen freedom.[115] We yearn for a stage where temptation is totally gone, never to return. "How naturally do we imagine this during the warmth of our first love! How ready are we to believe that God has 'fulfilled in us the whole work of faith with power'!"[116] in a single blow. When the faithful are tempted to believe that they will never again be tempted, this will lead eventually either to depression ("heaviness of soul") or extended wandering in the "wilderness state."[117]

f. Rigorous Self-Examination

If these are the usual multiple causes of this "second darkness" after receiving divine-human reconciliation, is there one single cure for all of them? Bad theology uses only one medicine. It is a fatal mistake to suppose that all these different causes of depression and spiritlessness can be cured by one single remedy. The cheap tonic Wesley has in mind is too often practiced by clergy. It is simply to "say many soft and tender things concerning the love of God to poor helpless sinners and the efficacy of the blood of Christ. Now this is *quackery* indeed, and that of the worst sort."[118]

What is Wesley so exercised about? Unfortunately, this is standard cliché treatment in much pastoral care in both Wesley's century and ours: "To give comfort is the single point at which they aim,"[119] not to upbuild by gentle admonition. Wesley has tough words for these all-too-easy counselors. They are in the majority among modern hedonically fixated caregivers: "It is hard to speak of these 'daubers with untempered mortar', these promise-mongers, as they deserve.... They vilely prostitute the promises of God by thus applying them to all without distinction.... The cure of spiritual, as of bodily diseases, must be as various as are the causes of them. The first thing, therefore, is to find out the cause; and this will naturally point out the cure."[120]

---

[114]"The Wilderness State," B 2:212, J VI:84, sec. 2.1 (C.III.1).
[115]"The Wilderness State," B 2:213, J VI:84, sec. 2.1 (III.1), end of section B.
[116]"The Wilderness State," B 2:213, J VI:84, sec. 2.2 (III.1).
[117]"The Wilderness State," B 2:213, J VI:85, sec. 2.2 (B.III.1).
[118]"The Wilderness State," B 2:214, J VI:84, sec. 3.1.
[119]"The Wilderness State," B 2:214, J VI:85, sec. 3.1.
[120]Ibid.

We do better to try to find out whether this darkness may be caused by a willful sin. If so, is it outward or inward sin? In either case, is it by omission or commission? This requires listening and the courage to give or receive gentle admonition under the guidance of the Spirit. Each believer owes it to himself to make careful examination of conscience to find which layer of temptation is at work in the heart in his own wilderness wanderings.[121]

Do you want to get out of this wilderness and back on the path of joyous faith? Begin by entering into a much closer self-examination. "If, upon the closest search, you can find no sin of *commission* which causes the cloud upon your soul, inquire next, if there be not some *sin of omission* which separates between God and you."[122] Are you neglecting to admonish your brother when he is walking near a precipice he does not see?

Go deep to search out the hidden causes. "If you habitually neglect any one of these known duties, how can you expect that the light of his countenance should continue to shine upon you?"[123] Grace will supply what is lacking if you earnestly ask for it. "Till the sin, whether of omission or commission, be removed, all comfort is false and deceitful. It is only skinning the wound over, which still festers and rankles beneath. Look for no peace within till you are at peace with God, which cannot be without 'fruits meet for repentance.'"[124]

If after serious examination of conscience you are still "not conscious of even any sin of omission which impairs your peace and joy in the Holy Ghost," probe more deeply whether "some inward sin, which as a root of bitterness, springs up in your heart to trouble you. Is not your dryness, and barrenness of soul, occasioned by your heart's 'departing from the living God'?" (Heb. 3:12).[125] To find the way out of the wilderness, you must plunge deeper into your own imagination, memory, and willing. You are looking for sins of omission or commission.

Here the questions are rigorous: "Have you not boasted of something 'you have received, as though you had not received it?'"[126] If you have fallen by pride, "humble yourself under the mighty hand of God, and he will exalt you in due time."[127] Have you nursed envy or anger? "Then look unto the Lord, that you may renew your strength; that all this sharpness and coldness may be done away; that love and peace and joy may return together."[128] Have you yielded to "foolish desires? To any kind or degree of inordinate affection? How then can the love of God have place in your heart, till you put away your idols?" God "will not dwell in a divided heart.... The Lord being your helper, enter in at the strait gate; take the kingdom of heaven by

[121]"The Wilderness State," B 2:214, J VI:84, sec. 3.2.
[122]"The Wilderness State," B 2:215, J VI:86, sec. 3.3, italics added.
[123]Ibid.
[124]Ibid.
[125]"Heaviness through Manifold Temptations," B 2:23, J VI:101, sec. 3.4.
[126]"The Wilderness State," B 2:216, J VI:87, sec. 3.4; cf. 1 Cor. 4:7.
[127]Cf. 1 Peter 5:6.
[128]"The Wilderness State," B 2:216, J VI:87, sec. 3.4.

violence! Cast out every idol from his sanctuary, and the glory of the Lord shall soon appear."[129]

Spiritual *sloth* may be keeping your soul in darkness.[130] You may be too much at ease, always on the same track of outward duties every day while your soul is dying. "O stir yourself up before the Lord! Arise, and shake yourself from the dust; wrestle with God for the mighty blessing; pour out your soul unto God in prayer, and continue therein with all perseverance! Watch! Awake out of sleep; and keep awake! Otherwise there is nothing to be expected, but that you will be alienated more and more from the light and life of God."[131]

Ask yourself: have your past tempers, words, and actions been right before the Lord? "Commune with him in your chamber, and be still" (see Ps. 4:4).[132] Ask God to probe your heart to recall any time you have offended his glory. "If the guilt of any unrepented sin remain on our soul, it cannot be but you will remain in darkness, till, having been renewed by repentance, you are again washed by faith in the 'fountain opened for sin and uncleanness.'"[133]

g. Compare Scripture with Scripture to Discern God's Promise of Joy

If the cause of your discontent is not perceived sin but something of which you are ignorant, there are remedies. First probe Scripture. Examine and compare text with text for a grasp of the "true meaning of those texts which have been misunderstood."[134] Along with examining your own conscience, let your own conscience be examined by Holy Writ.

This leads Wesley back to the core text of his homily: John 16:22: "Now you are having pain. But I will see you again, and your hearts will rejoice, and no one will take your joy away from you" (ISV). This does not imply that God wills to withdraw himself from all believers no matter what their complicity. The context shows that he is "here speaking personally to the apostles and no others; and that he is speaking concerning those particular events, his own death and resurrection." In the grave, they will not see him, but after the general resurrection they will see him, hence, "your sorrow shall be turned into joy" that no man can take away from you.[135]

The Bible does not teach that darkness is "much more profitable for the soul than light," or that "a believer [is] more swiftly and thoroughly purified by sorrow than by joy," as certain mystics teach. "The Scripture nowhere says that the *absence* of God best perfects his work in the heart!"[136] Rather, a strong consciousness of God's *presence* and Word "will do more in an hour than his absence in an age. Joy in the Holy Ghost will far more effectually purify the soul than the want of that joy;

---

[129]Ibid.
[130]"The Wilderness State," B 2:217, J VI:87, sec. 3.
[131]"The Wilderness State," B 2:217, J VI:87–88, sec. 3.5.
[132]"The Wilderness State," B 2:217, J VI:88, sec. 3.6.
[133]Ibid.; John 16:22.
[134]"The Wilderness State," B 2:217, J VI:88, sec. 3.7.
[135]"The Wilderness State," B 2:218–19, J VI:89, sec. 3.10.
[136]"The Wilderness State," B 2:219, J VI:90, sec. 3.12, italics added.

and the peace of God is the best means of refining the soul from the dross of earthly affections."[137] Get rid of the baggage that says that joy in the Holy Spirit is "obstructive of righteousness; and that we are saved, not by faith, but by unbelief; not by hope, but by despair!"[138] As long as you carry that baggage, you will tend to walk in darkness. Remove the obstacles to darkness, and the light will reappear.

It is unrealistic to assume that temptation will end or that darkness will never return. "Though a wound cannot be healed while the dart is sticking in the flesh, yet neither is it healed as soon as that is drawn out."[139] The well-grounded believer will always be ready to face temptation and always be aware of the vulnerability of human freedom that dwells in a fallen world. Temptation will always challenge human freedom. But the darkness of wandering can be overcome by removing the very obstacles that caused it.

When we first believe, we are like newborn children who need time to gradually grow up. We may face many storms before we come to the full stature of Christ. The whole work of sanctification is not usually done all at once. Amid the storms to come, ask for grace to learn to pray. "Dwell upon the faithfulness of God, whose 'word is tried to the uttermost'" (Ps. 119:140; cf. Ps. 12:6).[140] God will then bear witness to his word and bring our souls out of trouble, saying: "Arise, shine; for thy light is come, and the glory of the LORD is risen upon thee" (Isa. 60:1).[141]

2. Heaviness through Manifold Temptations

The darkness of mind described in "The Wilderness State" bears many similarities with the heaviness of heart described in homily 47 on "Heaviness through Manifold Temptations" [B 2:222–35; J VI:91–103 (1760)]. Yet they are different. This homily hopes to encourage believers to transcend the wilderness state, even amid conditions of heavy temptation. The text is: "Now for a season, if need be, ye are in heaviness through manifold temptations" (1 Peter 1:6).

Wesley asks five questions on the theme of this Scripture text: Who is in heaviness? What kind of heaviness? What are its causes? Why does God permit it? What does it mean?

a. What Is Meant by "Heaviness"?

Those in heaviness to whom the apostle was speaking were faithful disciples who were being "kept by the power of God through faith unto salvation" (1 Peter 1:5) precisely while they were facing "the trial of their faith." The outcome of this trial can be "much more precious than of gold that perisheth"(1 Peter 1:7). Through this trial of faith, they were offered the possibility of "receiving the end of [their] faith, even the salvation of [their] souls" (1 Peter 1:9). Though "'in heaviness,' they

---

137Ibid.
138"The Wilderness State," B 2:219, J VI:90, sec. 3.1.
139"The Wilderness State," B 2:220, J VI:90, sec. 3.13.
140"The Wilderness State," B 2:220, J VI:91, sec. 3.14.
141Ibid.

were possessed of living faith." Their heaviness did not destroy their faith. They still "endured, as seeing him that is invisible."[142]

They were finding precisely amid their trials a "peace that passeth all understanding" (see Phil. 4:7).[143] This peace was "inseparable from true, living faith." They already enjoyed the blessings of pardon and justifying grace. Paul was praying that these blessings be multiplied so as to be "more abundantly bestowed upon them," and through them upon others. Amid their struggles, they were already "full of a living hope" (see 1 Peter 1:3).[144] They were already looking toward an inheritance "incorruptible, and undefiled, and that fadeth not away" (1 Peter 1:4).[145]

Despite their exceedingly great temporal heaviness, they still "rejoiced in hope of the glory of God," looking confidently toward the final revelation of God's judgment and mercy, filled with joy in the Holy Spirit. "Their heaviness, therefore, was not only consistent with living hope, but also with joy unspeakable: At the same time they were thus heavy, they nevertheless rejoiced with joy full of glory" (see 1 Peter 1:8).[146] The love of God was shed abroad in their hearts. They had not seen God face-to-face, yet they loved God, knowing him by faith.[147] They were kept by God from the power of sin. They remained holy in all their words and deeds.

Mark well that their heaviness was consistent with their faith, "with hope, with love of God and man, with the peace of God, with joy in the Holy Ghost, with inward and outward holiness. It did no way impair, much less destroy, any part of the work of God in their hearts. It did not at all interfere with that 'sanctification of the Spirit' which is the root of all true obedience; neither with the happiness which must needs result from grace and peace reigning in the heart."[148]

b. The Heaviness of Sorrow

What kind of heaviness were they experiencing?

The recipients of Peter's letter were grieved. They were sorrowing. This is a feeling that every child knows.[149] The degree of their heaviness was great, and its long continuance made it greater. Their grief had sunk deep into their souls. It was not "a transient sorrow, such as passes away in an hour; but rather, such as, having taken fast hold of the heart, is not presently shaken off, but continues for some time, as a settled temper, rather than a passion, — even in them that have living faith in Christ, and the genuine love of God in their hearts."[150]

The continuing heaviness of the soul under fire may be so deep as to color the soul and all its affections. It is not surprising that such deep grief would have an

---

[142]"Heaviness through Manifold Temptations," B 2:223, J VI:92, sec. 1.1.
[143]"Heaviness through Manifold Temptations," B 2:223, J VI:92, sec. 1.2.
[144]"Heaviness through Manifold Temptations," B 2:223, J VI:93, sec. 1.3.
[145]Ibid.
[146]"Heaviness through Manifold Temptations," B 2:224, J VI:93, sec. 1.4.
[147]"Heaviness through Manifold Temptations," B 2:225, J VI:93, sec. 1.5.
[148]"Heaviness through Manifold Temptations," B 2:224, J VI:93, sec. 1.6.
[149]"Heaviness through Manifold Temptations," B 2:224, J VI:94, sec. 2.1.
[150]"Heaviness through Manifold Temptations," B 2:225, J VI:94, sec. 2.2.

effect on the body. Then in turn "the corruptible body presses down the soul."[151] The body-soul interface is in heavy labor during grief.

This is not the "darkness of mind" of the wandering people (see above), but the "heaviness of heart" of the true faithful under fire (see below). "This may well be termed a 'fiery trial.'"[152] This is not an endless wilderness wandering of the half-hearted, but the wholehearted faith of saints in dire circumstances.

c. What Causes Such Grief in the True Believer?

The cause of this kind of sorrow of the truly faithful is clear in the text: "Ye are in heaviness *through manifold temptations*" (1 Peter 1:6, italics added). Note that the strong in faith were facing temptations just like the weak in faith. Indeed, their temptations were *manifold*, "not only many in number, but of many kinds."[153] Their "very diversity and variety makes it more difficult to guard against them." The forms of temptation even for the most faithful are numberless and unpredictable. "Among these we may rank all bodily disorders; particularly acute diseases, and violent pain of every kind, whether affecting the whole body or the smallest part of it."[154]

"Faith does not overturn the course of nature: Natural causes still produce natural effects. Faith no more hinders the sinking of the spirits (as it is called) in an hysteric illness than the rising of the pulse in a fever."[155]

Some believers may have such strength of constitution that they "have seemed not to regard pain at all,"[156] even of the severest kind, as if they were raised above the state of nature. Even then they "possess their souls in patience."[157] Those weaker in natural constitution may feel more deeply the pain of the body pressing upon the soul. In persistent pain, the soul is sympathizing with the body. "All diseases of long continuance, though less painful, are apt to produce the same effect."[158] The contagious, wasting diseases of tuberculosis and malaria if not treated will not only consume the body but "cause sorrow of heart."[159] So also with what are termed nervous disorders.

It is no small temptation "when calamity overtakes you like a storm, when disaster sweeps over you like a whirlwind, when distress and trouble overwhelm you" (Prov. 1:27 NIV), or when poverty comes to you as if it were "an armed man" (Prov. 24:34). "Although this also may appear but a small thing to those who stand at a distance, or who look and 'pass by on the other side,' yet it is otherwise to them who feel it."[160] What shall they do who have neither food nor a place to live, "who

---

[151]"Heaviness through Manifold Temptations," B 2:224, J VI:94, sec. 2.2; cf. Wisd. Sol. 9:15.
[152]"Heaviness through Manifold Temptations," B 2:225, J VI:94, sec. 2.4.
[153]"Heaviness through Manifold Temptations," B 2:226, J VI:95, sec. 3.1.
[154]Ibid.
[155]"Heaviness through Manifold Temptations," B 2:226, J VI:96, sec. 3.2.
[156]"Heaviness through Manifold Temptations," B 2:226, J VI:95, sec. 3.1.
[157]Cf. Luke 21:19.
[158]"Heaviness through Manifold Temptations," B 2:226, J VI:95, sec. 3.1.
[159]"Heaviness through Manifold Temptations," B 2:226, J VI:95, sec. 3.2.
[160]"Heaviness through Manifold Temptations," B 2:227, J VI:96, sec. 3.3; cf. Luke 10:31–32.

have only the earth to lie upon, and only the sky to cover them, who have not a dry, or warm, much less a clean, abode for themselves and their little ones"?[161]

The worst side of poverty, Juvenal wrote, is exposing men to ridicule[162] (and Juvenal underestimated even that, since he stood at a distance from real poverty). "But how many are there in this Christian country, that toil, and labor, and sweat, and have it not at last, but struggle with weariness and hunger together. Is it not worse for one, after an hard day's labor, to come back to a poor, cold, dirty, uncomfortable lodging, and to find there not even the food which is needful to repair his wasted strength?"[163] Those who are living at ease often do not even bother to see this suffering. "O want of bread! want of bread! Who can tell what this means unless he hath felt it himself?"[164] This poverty in time elicits heaviness of heart.

d. How the Adversary Uses Suffering to Defeat Faith

Wesley paints a series of dramatic pictures of situations that understandably elicit the heavyheartedness of the faithful. Think of the death of a loved one or of "a beloved child, just rising into life, clasping about our heart." Think of a "friend that was as our own soul."[165] Think of the grief parents must feel in seeing their own "child rushing into sin, as an horse into the battle … in spite of all arguments and persuasions," hastening to work out his own destruction.[166] This elicits anguish of spirit. Think of one who "once ran well in the way of life" now on a sure path toward disaster. His suffering becomes more afflictive when his past actions are unnoticed. This is the sort of grief that the disciples were going through at the time 1 Peter 5 was written.[167] Even the most faithful may have to face such situations.

In every case, the adversary will tempt. He who is always walking about, "seeking whom he may devour" (1 Peter 5:8), will use these situations of vulnerability to exercise all his skill "if haply he may gain any advantage over the soul that is already cast down. He will not be sparing of his fiery darts, such as are most likely to find an entrance, and to fix most deeply in the heart, by their suitableness to the temptation that assaults it. He will labor to inject unbelieving, or blasphemous, or repining thoughts. He will suggest that God does not regard, does not govern, the earth; or, at least, that he does not govern it aright, not by the rules of justice and mercy."[168] In temptation we are facing a greater enemy than simply temporal inducements.

Amid such situations, some are too quick to suggest that God is "withdrawing himself from the soul because it is his sovereign will." Solely because of his will? Even from the tested faithful? Not arbitrarily. Not without their turning their back

---

[161]"Heaviness through Manifold Temptations," B 2:227, J VI:96, sec. 3.3.
[162]*Satires*, 3.152 – 53; Loeb Classical Library 91:42.
[163]"Heaviness through Manifold Temptations," B 2:227, J VI:96, sec. 3.3.
[164]Ibid.
[165]"Heaviness through Manifold Temptations," B 2:227 – 28, J VI:97, sec. 3.4.
[166]"Heaviness through Manifold Temptations," B 2:228 – 29, J VI:97, sec. 3.5.
[167]"Heaviness through Manifold Temptations," B 2:229, J VI:97, sec. 3.5.
[168]"Heaviness through Manifold Temptations," B 2:229, J VI:97, sec. 3.6.

on the sufficient grace supplied. Only if they grieve the Holy Spirit do believers put themselves in danger of God's turning his back on them. God never withdraws himself arbitrarily or "merely because it is his good pleasure."[169] That, says Wesley, "I absolutely deny. There is no text in all the Bible which gives any color for such a supposition."[170] It runs against the whole tenor of Scripture. It is repugnant to the very nature of God to say that God arbitrarily, or only due to his absolute eternal decree, withdraws his grace from the faithful. That pernicious idea runs contrary both to Scripture and to "the sound experience of all his children."[171]

Wesley challenges the idea of some mystics that "the knowledge of ourselves ... must, even after we have attained justifying faith, occasion the deepest heaviness."[172] Must? Is "the deepest heaviness" an absolute divinely decreed necessity for those justified by faith? Does every believer have to face deep depression? Wesley thought this was nonsense. He wished to protect his connection of spiritual formation from those who inordinately love suffering and inordinately distrust the scriptural promise of consummate love. The faithful do not seek misery, but "love, and peace, and joy, gradually springing up into everlasting life."[173]

e. Why God Permits Heaviness through Manifold Temptation

There must be some reason why the children of God are at times permitted to fall into heaviness of soul. The apostle gives the plain answer in this same text. The cause of heaviness is temptation. But why are they tempted? *These trials have a redemptive purpose.* "These have come so that the proven genuineness of your faith — of greater worth than gold, which perishes even though refined by fire — may result in praise, glory and honor when Jesus Christ is revealed" (1 Peter 1:7 NIV; cf. Rom. 8:18).[174]

The trials serve to strengthen faith. Without being tested, how would faith be recognizable as faith? "Gold tried in the fire is purified thereby; is separated from its dross. And so is faith in the fire of temptation; the more it is tried, the more it is purified — yea, and not only purified, but also strengthened, confirmed, increased abundantly, by so many more proofs of the wisdom and power, the love and faithfulness, of God. This, then — to increase our faith — is one gracious end of God's permitting those manifold temptations."[175] Many more evidences of God's faithfulness are revealed when tested than when untested.

The trials themselves are permitted to purify and increase the living hope of the sufferers. "Indeed our hope cannot but increase in the same proportion with our faith."[176] As a result, "we have a confident expectation of the glory which shall

[169]"Heaviness through Manifold Temptations," B 2:230, J VI:98, sec. 3.7.
[170]Ibid.
[171]Ibid.
[172]"Heaviness through Manifold Temptations," B 2:230, J VI:98, sec. 3.8.
[173]"Heaviness through Manifold Temptations," B 2:230, J VI:99, sec. 3.9.
[174]"Heaviness through Manifold Temptations," B 2:231, J VI:99, sec. 4.1.
[175]"Heaviness through Manifold Temptations," B 2:232, J VI:100, sec. 4.2.
[176]"Heaviness through Manifold Temptations," B 2:232, J VI:100, sec. 4.3.

be revealed." Increased faith and hope in turn "increase our joy in the Lord, which cannot but attend a hope full of immortality."[177]

This is why we can "rejoice that we are partakers in the sufferings of Christ."[178] On this very account, "happy are you; for the Spirit of glory and of God resteth upon you; and hereby ye are enabled, even in the midst of sufferings, to 'rejoice with joy unspeakable and full of glory'" (1 Peter 1:8).[179] "The clearer and stronger evidence they have of the glory that shall be revealed, the more do they love Him who hath purchased it for them, and 'given them the earnest thereof' in their hearts" (see 2 Cor. 1:22).[180]

By these means they grow in holiness: "holiness of heart and holiness of conversation."[181] The good tree brings forth good fruit. Our sufferings for the cause of Christ draw us through grace toward holiness. "They calm and meeken our turbulent spirit, tame the fierceness of our nature, soften our obstinacy and self-will, crucify us to the world, and bring us to expect all our strength from, and to seek all our happiness in, God."[182]

The final meaning and end of faith, hope, love, and holiness is this: to be found ready to receive God's praise on the last day and the gratitude of beneficiaries in this life. On the last day, "these 'light afflictions, which are but for a moment, work out for us a far more exceeding and eternal weight of glory'" (2 Cor. 4:17, adapted).[183] Our behavior under affliction "makes a deeper impression upon us than precept."[184] It becomes an advantage to others to behold faith at work in patient love. Our actions may have a stronger influence than we know on those "who have not known God," when they behold "a soul calm and serene in the midst of storms; sorrowful, yet always rejoicing; meekly accepting whatever is the will of God, however grievous it may be to nature."[185]

f. How Darkness of Mind Differs from Heaviness of Soul of the Faithful under Affliction

Taking these two homilies together, Wesley draws four conclusions. First, however much these two conditions appear similar, darkness and heaviness differ substantially. The darkness of the wilderness state implies a total *loss of joy* in the Holy Spirit. Heaviness does not. Rather, it still is able to "rejoice with *joy unspeakable*" even under affliction (1 Peter 1:8, italics added). Those wandering in darkness have lost the peace of God. The faithful who experience heaviness through manifold temptation have not. Instead, grace is multiplied through them. In darkness "the

---

[177]Ibid.
[178]Cf. 1 Peter 4:13–14.
[179]"Heaviness through Manifold Temptations," B 2:232, J VI:100, sec. 4.3.
[180]"Heaviness through Manifold Temptations," B 2:232, J VI:100, sec. 4.4.
[181]"Heaviness through Manifold Temptations," B 2:233, J VI:101, sec. 4.5.
[182]Ibid.
[183]"Heaviness through Manifold Temptations," B 2:233, J VI:101, sec. 4.6.
[184]"Heaviness through Manifold Temptations," B 2:233, J VI:101, sec. 4.7.
[185]Ibid.

love of God is waxed cold," but in heaviness that love increases daily.[186] In darkness faith is "grievously decayed," while the faithfulness of believers who are suffering through manifold temptations "yet have a clear, unshaken confidence in God."[187]

Second, "there may be need of heaviness" for a season, "but there can be *no need of darkness*" as an ongoing way of life.[188] "Exceeding joy" under conditions of heaviness of soul is a great gift. It thrives under conditions of " 'manifold temptations' which are needful to try and increase our faith, to confirm and enlarge our hope, to purify our heart from all unholy tempers, and to perfect us in love."[189] While darkness does not add to our eternal weight of glory, joy under conditions of persecution and affliction brightens our crown and prepares us for eternal life with God.

Third, when heaviness comes under many temptations, it is *only for a season*, which measured by eternity is short. And it is purposeful, as seen in the apostle's phrase, "Now for a season, *if need be*" (1 Peter 1:6, italics added).[190] It is "not needful for all persons; nor for any person at all times." God is able to work in the soul by means other than the storms of temptation and affliction which are caused by the fallenness of humanity. God's grace commonly goes on "from strength to strength," even till they "perfect holiness in his fear."[191] Only in rare cases is the holy life sustained "with scarce any heaviness at all." Rather, "God generally sees good to try 'acceptable men in the furnace of affliction.'" Indeed, manifold temptations and heaviness "are usually the portion of his dearest children."[192]

We are called to watch and pray and to avoid falling into darkness and to grow by heaviness, waiting upon the Lord so that even manifold temptations may "fully answer all the design of his love," hoping that they may be *a means of increasing our faith, of confirming our hope, of perfecting us in all holiness.*[193]

E. The Special Work of the Spirit in the Patient Soul

1. So You Have Trials? Count It All Joy

a. On Patience

The apostle James begins his short but powerful epistle with an unusual plea:

> Consider it pure joy, my brothers and sisters, whenever you face trials of many kinds, because you know that the testing of your faith produces perseverance. Let perseverance finish its work so that you may be mature and complete, not lacking anything. If any of you lacks wisdom, you should ask God, who gives

---

[186]"Heaviness through Manifold Temptations," B 2:234, J VI:102, sec. 5.1.
[187]Ibid.
[188]"Heaviness through Manifold Temptations," B 2:234, J VI:101, sec. 5.2, italics added.
[189]Ibid.
[190]"Heaviness through Manifold Temptations," B 2:234, J VI:101, sec. 5.3.
[191]Ibid.
[192]Ibid.
[193]"Heaviness through Manifold Temptations," B 2:234, J VI:103, sec. 5.4, italics added.

generously to all without finding fault, and it will be given to you. But when you ask, you must believe and not doubt, because the one who doubts is like a wave of the sea, blown and tossed by the wind. That person should not expect to receive anything from the Lord. Such a person is double-minded and unstable in all they do. (1:2 – 8 NIV)

It seems counterintuitive to "consider it pure joy whenever you face trials of many kinds," since trials are unpleasant and grievous, and joy is the opposite of displeasure and grief. Yet Wesley had learned from the apostle James and by experience the reason for this seemingly paradoxical language: "The trying of your faith worketh patience. But let patience have her perfect work, that ye may be perfect and entire, wanting nothing" (James 1:4) [Homily #83, "On Patience" (March – April 1784), B 3:169 – 80; J #83, VI:484 – 92].

b. That You May Be Perfect and Entire

The Bible gives this instruction to all who share every day in the life of faith, not just for select people facing occasional trials. Why? Temptation abounds in every cranny of human history. As long as any of us are on earth, we are subject to temptation. Even Jesus faced trials and temptations: "He who came into the world to save his people from their sins did not come to save them from temptation. He himself 'knew no sin'; yet while he was in this vale of tears 'he suffered, being tempted'; and herein also 'left us an example, that we should tread in his steps.'"[194]

In reference to the "perfect work" of patience, Wesley focused on the metaphor of completeness: "Let patience have her perfect work, that ye may be perfect and entire, wanting nothing" (James 1:4). Wesley regarded perfect love as the fitting end toward which every challenging act of the Christian life moves. You want Christian maturity? Discover the perfect work of patience. To dodge this instruction is to miss out on a powerful means of grace in spiritual formation.

The perfect work of patience leads to new strength in the Christian life. Hence, in the examination for approval to preach, every preacher in Wesley's connection was asked: "Are you going on to perfection?" and "Do you expect to be made perfect in love in this life?" Why? How could this be a presupposed condition for ministry? This homily answers.

c. The Need for Patience: The Universality of Conditions Requiring Patience

No human being with the gift of human freedom can avoid being "liable to a thousand temptations from the corruptible body variously affecting the soul."[195] The body-soul relation is "encompassed with infirmities" even among the wisest of human beings. "The most dangerous of our enemies are not those that assault us openly," but secretly, invisibly, from within. The devil is like a roaring lion, seeking

---

[194]"On Patience," B 3:170; J VI:484 – 85, secs. 1 – 2.
[195]"On Patience," B 3:170; J VI:485, sec. 2.

whom he may devour. This is the case not only with all the children of men, but "with all the children of God."[196]

Therefore we do not willfully and carelessly rush into trials. Yet in the course of our journey, we "shall surely fall into divers temptations — temptations innumerable as the stars of heaven." Instead of counting trials a loss, as would human outrage over its fallen condition, the faithful count them as a disguised means of joy that elicits the virtue of patience. Only in this way can we "let patience have its perfect work."[197]

2. What Is Patience?

What is this extraordinary gift of patience? It seems so alien to the typical condition of human freedom. It is not a naturally acquired virtue, but "a gracious temper wrought in the heart of a believer by the power of the Holy Ghost."[198]

Christian patience is grounded in grace. It is a work of the Spirit, a disposition to accept whatever pleases God. This patience is given so that God may test the strength of the freedom for which Christ has set us free. We do not choose the manner and time of our trials. We receive what God permits, like Job, in order to grow stronger in faith. "Naked I came from my mother's womb, and naked I will depart. The LORD gave and the LORD has taken away; may the name of the LORD be praised" (Job 1:21 NIV). We do not despise our sufferings or pretend they are little or pass over them lightly. We do not treat them either as chance events or wooden necessities, but as hidden gifts of grace.[199]

Our trials are given by God for our profit "that we may be partakers of his holiness."[200] Patience is closely akin to meekness, which "teaches not to return evil for evil, or railing for railing; but contrariwise, blessing. Our blessed Lord himself seems to place a peculiar value upon this temper. This he peculiarly calls us to 'learn of him,' if we would 'find rest for our souls.'"[201]

3. The Special Work of the Spirit in the Patient Soul

What does it mean to "let patience have its perfect work"? It means giving grace time to have its "full fruit or effect." Growing fruit requires time. The fruit the Spirit produces in our hearts in due time is "peace — a sweet tranquility of mind, a serenity of spirit, which can never be found unless where patience reigns. And this peace often rises into joy." This is why the faithful, "even in the midst of various temptations ... are enabled 'in patience to possess their souls.'"[202]

Closely akin to the opening paragraph of James's letter is the salutation of

[196]Ibid.
[197]"On Patience," B 3:170; J VI:485, sec. 2.
[198]"On Patience," B 3:171; J VI:485–86, sec. 3.
[199]"On Patience," B 3:171–72; J VI:485–86, sec. 3.
[200]"On Patience," B 3:172; J VI:485–86, sec. 3.
[201]"On Patience," B 3:172; J VI:486, sec. 4.
[202]Luke 21:19; "On Patience," B 3:172–73; J VI:486, sec. 5.

1 Peter 1, where Peter praises God who "in his great mercy ... has given us new birth into a living hope through the resurrection of Jesus Christ from the dead" (v. 3 NIV). This saving act of God ushers us "into an inheritance that can never perish" (v. 4 NIV). This inheritance is "kept in heaven for [us], who through faith are shielded by God's power until the coming of the salvation that is ready to be revealed in the last time" (vv. 4 – 5 NIV). The worshiping community is preserved between the time of present trials and their promised outcome by the grace of persevering. There the gift of patience is exercised amid obstacles that offer human freedom the possibility of growing in faith.

A deep joy comes from looking beyond the present trial to its purpose: to strengthen faith. Within the long history of salvation we are able to rejoice, looking beyond the present suffering. "In all this you greatly rejoice, though now for a little while you may have had to suffer grief in all kinds of trials" (1 Peter 1:6 NIV). What do these trials mean? What is their purpose viewed from the vantage point of the history of God's saving acts? "These have come so that the proven genuineness of your faith — of greater worth than gold, which perishes even though refined by fire — may result in praise, glory and honor when Jesus Christ is revealed" (v. 7 NIV).[203]

Patience is the gift that is given between the trial and the consummation of its hope. In the gift of patience, we are already here and now "receiving the end result of [our] faith" (1 Peter 1:9 NIV).[204] The patient faithful are those gifted by grace to believe in the inheritance promised in the resurrection. Even without seeing the outcome, they know the promise is sealed by the Son through the Holy Spirit. "Though you have not seen him, you love him; and even though you do not see him now, you believe in him and are filled with an inexpressible and glorious joy" (v. 8 NIV).

a. The Desired Outcome: Perfect Patience

"The 'perfect work' of patience" is nothing less than the total love of God. Quite simply, we embody perfect love when we love everyone as Christ loved us.[205] It is having in us "the whole mind which was also in Christ Jesus." It is "the renewal of our soul in the image of God, after the image of him that created us."

Perfect love consists of "entirely giving up all we are, all we have, and all we love, as a holy sacrifice, acceptable unto God through the Son of his love. It seems this is the 'perfect work of patience,' consequent upon the trial of our faith."[206]

Does this life of perfect love differ from the life that follows from receiving justifying grace? No. Perfect love cannot be separated from justifying grace. Wesley cautioned against making the "great and dangerous mistake" of thinking of the work of patience as if it dealt with a subject entirely different "from that which is wrought

---

[203]"On Patience," B 3:173; J VI:487, sec. 6.
[204]1 Peter 1:9; "On Patience," B 3:173; J VI:487, sec. 6.
[205]"On Patience," B 3:173; J VI:484 – 87, sec. 8.
[206]Ibid.

in justification.... The glorious work of God which was wrought in us when we were justified" calls forth a life of patience.[207] Wesley had a warning for those who inordinately distinguish between the justified life and the sanctified life of perfect love. "In that moment when we are justified freely by his grace, when we are accepted through the Beloved, we are born again, born from above, born of the Spirit."[208]

There is as great a change wrought in our souls when we are born of the Spirit as was wrought in our bodies when we were born of a woman. There is in that hour "a new spiritual birth — a general change from inward emptiness to inward fullness.... The love of the creature is changed into the love of the Creator, the love of the world into the love of God" in regeneration.[209] "From the moment we are justified till we give up our spirits to God, love is the fulfilling of the law — of the whole evangelical law, which took [the] place of the Adamic law."[210]

b. Holy Patience

This transition may come in smaller or larger degree, varied according to the circumstances in which the Spirit is doing the Son's transforming work. Anyone born of God, though only a babe in Christ, "has the love of God in his heart, the love of his neighbor, together with lowliness, meekness, and resignation. But all of these are then in a low degree, in proportion to the degree of his faith. The faith of a babe in Christ is weak, generally mingled with doubts or fears; with doubts whether he has not deceived himself; or fear that he shall not endure to the end."[211] "In the same proportion as he grows in faith, he grows in holiness: he increases in love, lowliness, meekness, in every part of the image of God." In such a believer the promise of God is fulfilled that was "made first to his ancient people" to circumcise their hearts "to love the Lord thy God, with all thy heart and with all thy soul."[212]

New birth is like resurrection from the dead.

This is a total change in the direction of the soul, different in every way from the way he had been going before. Until he respond[ed] to the free gift of justifying grace, his love for God was ambiguous, his humility mixed with pride, his meekness interrupted by anger. His love of God was frequently damped by the love of some creature. But with patience which elicits perfect love, he can now say "Lord, not as I will, but as thou wilt." ... His whole soul is now consistent with itself: there is no jarring string. All his passions flow in a continued stream, with an even tenor to God, [since] Jesus now reigns alone in his heart.[213]

When asked whether this occurs gradually or instantaneously, Wesley answered with broad toleration toward both views. "As to whether this change comes gradually,

---

[207]"On Patience," B 3:174; J VI:487–88, sec. 9.
[208]Ibid.
[209]Ibid.
[210]"On Patience," B 3:174–75; J VI:488, sec. 10.
[211]"On Patience," B 3:175–76; J VI:488–90, sec. 10.
[212]"On Patience," B 3:175–76; J VI:489, sec. 10.
[213]Matt. 26:39; "On Patience," B 3:176–77; J VI:488–89, sec. 10.

by slow degrees, or instantaneously, in a moment, the point is not determined — at least, not in express terms — in any part of the oracles of God.... Be the change instantaneous or gradual, see that you never rest till it is wrought in your own soul, if you desire to dwell with God in glory." So let the one who attests to one or the other "abound in his own sense" of what is happening to him in all honesty.[214]

4. Praying for Patience Now

In his homily "On Patience," Wesley recalled the empirical inquiry he had made four decades earlier in which he sought to discern whether the new birth was experienced in a moment or in a lifetime. He made inquiry into the lives of several persons well known to his connection whom he thought were rightly described as "going on to perfection." He started with "two or three persons in London whom I knew to be truly sincere [and who] desired to give me an account of their experience. It appeared exceeding strange, being different from any that I had heard before; but exactly similar to what Scripture calls perfect love."[215]

The experiment continued "a few years" later: "I desired all those in London who made the same profession to come to me all together at the Foundery, that I might be thoroughly satisfied. I desired that man of God, Thomas Walsh, to give us the meeting there. When we met, first one of us and then the other asked them the most searching questions we could devise."[216] Their utter sincerity persuaded Wesley that "they did not deceive themselves. In the years 1759, 1760, 1761, and 1762, their numbers multiplied exceedingly, not only in London and Bristol, but in various parts of Ireland as well as England.... In London alone I found six hundred and fifty-two members of our society who were exceeding clear in their experience."[217] However, in that setting, so many attested that this deliverance was "instantaneous, that the change was wrought in a moment" that Wesley was compelled to view this change as having occurred quite often in a very short space of time.

a. Birth and Resurrection

The prevailing metaphors for this experience of new life are birth and resurrection. A resurrection is not a long, drawn-out process but an event that occurs in a moment. That is also true for the metaphor of birth. The new birth is an event that takes its beginning in a moment in time. While respecting those who take the gradual view, Wesley upon investigation came to the empirical judgment that he could not but believe that this experience of new birth is often "an instantaneous work."[218] Whatever time the Spirit takes, the time is in God's hands.

There is only one thing we are to do in order that this work of God may be wrought in us: "Believe on him whom he hath sent" (John 6:29). "By grace are ye

---

[214]"On Patience," B 3:175 – 76; J VI:490, sec. 10.
[215]"On Patience," B 3:177 – 78; J VI:490 – 91, sec. 12.
[216]Ibid.
[217]Ibid.
[218]"On Patience," B 3:178; J VI:491, sec. 12.

saved through faith ... not of works, lest any man should boast" (Eph. 2:8 – 9). "It is the 'gift of God' ... to be received by plain, simple faith."[219] God has promised to "fill [us] with all holiness" (1 Thess. 3:13; cf. 4:3 – 6 and Eph. 3:14 – 21). Wesley said that from new birth to death, "ye shall enjoy as high a degree of holiness as is consistent with your present state of pilgrimage."[220]

b. God Is Willing

When this faith is put to work, it is tried and tested. Then we learn through a longer stretch of time to "let patience have her perfect work" (James 1:4) in us, that we may through trials become fully tested, fully reliant on sheer grace, thus lacking nothing.[221]

All are called to believe that God is here and now "willing, as well as able, to save you to the uttermost; to purify you from all sin, and fill up all your heart with love." This is offered not just at the point of death, "not tomorrow, but today." It is not beyond the power of God the Spirit to transform us entirely.[222]

What the Spirit desires to give us is a new life "wholly delivered from every evil work, from every evil word, from every sinful thought; yea, from every evil desire, passion, temper, from all inbred corruption, from all remains of the carnal mind, from the whole body of sin: and ye shall be renewed in the spirit of your mind, in every right temper, after the image of him that created you, in righteousness and true holiness."[223]

F. Loss of Soul

1. The Important Question

The one homily most often preached by Wesley (117 times) was on the familiar text of Matthew 16:26: "What is a man profited, if he should gain the whole world, and lose his own soul?" [Homily #84, "The Important Question," B 3:181 – 98; J #84, VI:493 – 505 (September 11, 1775)].

a. The Eternal One Who Asks This Question

In this text, it is the Son of God who is asking a straightforward question. His words are plain and simple: If you gain the whole world and lose your own soul, what is your profit? This is God the Son asking. "If a mere inhabitant of this lower world speaks concerning the great things of the kingdom of God, hardly is he able to find expressions suitable to the greatness of the subject. But when the Son of God speaks of the highest things, which concern his heavenly kingdom, all his language

---

[219]"On Patience," B 3:178; J VI:492, sec. 13.
[220]"On Patience," B 3:179; J VI:492, sec. 14.
[221]"On Patience," B 3:169 – 80; J VI:484 – 92.
[222]"On Patience," B 3:179; J VI:492, sec. 13.
[223]"On Patience," B 3:179; J VI:492, sec. 14.

is easy and unlabored, his words natural and unaffected: inasmuch as known unto him are all these things from all eternity."[224]

We cannot grasp the full implication of this text on gain and loss until we ask the question as if on the last moment of our lives. Our imagination is embedded in time. We can hardly imagine eternity, much less put it into words, because we do not see the whole with the eyes of God. But our Lord makes it possible to imagine from within our finitude a glimpse of the whole, and that glimpse transforms our relation to the whole. It relativizes the whole history of sin in relation to the giver and redeemer of the whole world. To get this glimpse, we are compelled by the text to ask what it means to gain the whole world. And what does it mean to lose one's own soul? Seen in this perspective, what would it profit one who gains the whole world and loses his own soul?

b. Gaining the Whole World of Sensual Pleasure

Some might imagine that "gaining the whole world" means conquering the whole world. But no one ever conquered even a "tenth part of the world." So this could not be the Lord's meaning.[225] Rather, he is referring to gaining "all the pleasures which the world can give." The fantasy is that a person might gain all that the world of senses can offer, "all that will gratify his senses of taste and smell and even touch — all that he can enjoy in common with his fellow-brutes ... all the plenty and all the variety of these objects which the world can afford."[226] This includes

> all that gratifies the desire of the eyes; whatever (by means of the eye chiefly) conveys any pleasure to the imagination. The pleasures of imagination arise from three sources: grandeur, beauty, and novelty. Accordingly we find by experience our own imagination is gratified by surveying either grand, or beautiful, or uncommon objects. Let him be encompassed then with the most grand, the most beautiful, and the newest things that can anywhere be found. For all this is manifestly implied in a man's gaining the whole world.[227]

Or take glory. Some might prefer above all the pleasures of sense and imagination something apparently more valuable: "honor, glory, renown — hardly any principle in the human mind is of greater force than this." Fame "triumphs over the strongest propensities of nature, over all our appetites and affections." Some exalt the love of their country, "but this would never have carried them through had there not been also the *Laudum immensa cupido* — the immense thirst of praise." Suppose "[a person's] name is gone forth into distant lands, as it were to the ends of the earth"; without praise he would still feel empty.[228]

Or take wealth. Suppose a person has gained such an "abundance of wealth;

[224]"The Important Question," B 3:182; J VI:493, pref. 1.
[225]"The Important Question," B 3:183; J VI:493 – 94, sec. 1.1.
[226]"The Important Question," B 3:183; J VI:494, sec. 1.2.
[227]"The Important Question," B 3:183 – 84; J:VI 494, sec. 1.3.
[228]"The Important Question," B 3:184; J VI:494, sec. 1.4.

that there is no end of his treasures; that he has laid up silver as the dust, and gold as the sand of the sea. Now when a man has obtained all these pleasures, all that will gratify either the senses or the imagination; when he has gained an honorable name, and also laid up much treasure for many years; then he may be said, in an easy, natural sense of the word, to have 'gained the whole world.' "[229]

c. Losing One's Own Soul: the Specter of Eternity

These pictures of gaining the whole world are fairly easy to imagine. "But it is not so easy to understand all that is implied in his 'losing his own soul.' Indeed none can fully conceive this until he has passed through time into eternity."[230] You cannot even conceive all the ramifications of losing your own soul until the last day, until the final judgment, since you cannot conceive time except from eternity.

So what is lost in losing one's own soul? More than all we have imagined in the thought of losing all the world.[231]

Any reasonable person can ask: Which is greater, time or eternity?

The present life will soon be at an end. It passes away like a shadow. The hour is at hand when the spirit will be summoned to return to God that gave it. In that awful moment one leaves behind the old world, standing on the threshold of the new, departing time, entering eternity. Only then, looking forward and back, how pleasing is the prospect to him that saves his soul! If he looks back, he has "the calm remembrance of the life well spent." If he looks forward, there is an inheritance incorruptible, undefiled, and that fadeth not away, and he sees the convoy of angels ready to carry him into Abraham's bosom.[232]

But a dreadful outcome may ensue. Wesley related the story of a man "struck down in his mid-career of sin," whose visiting friend prayed: "'Lord, have mercy upon those who are just stepping out of the body, and know not which shall meet them at their entrance into the other world, an angel or a fiend.' The sick man shrieked out with a piercing cry, 'A fiend! a fiend!' and died. Just such an end, unless he die like an ox, may any man expect who loses his own soul."[233]

d. The Eternal Garden

Then Wesley describes "the spirit of a good man at his entrance into eternity. See ... the convoy attends, the minist'ring host of invisible friends ... who conduct him safe into Abraham's bosom, into the delights of paradise, the garden of God, where the light of his countenance perpetually shines."[234] "There the wicked cease from troubling, and there the weary be at rest" (Job 3:17). "They have numberless sources of happiness which they could not have upon earth. There they meet with

[229]"The Important Question," B 3:185; J VI:495, sec. 1.5.
[230]"The Important Question," B 3:185; J VI:494, sec. 2.1.
[231]"The Important Question," B 3:186; J VI:494, sec. 2.2.
[232]"The Important Question," B 3:185–86; J VI:496, sec. 2.3.
[233]"The Important Question," B 3:186; J VI:496, sec. 2.3.
[234]"The Important Question," B 3:186–87; J VI:494–96, sec. 2.4; PW 6:211.

'the glorious dead of ancient days,'" with "the saints of all ages; and above all they 'are with Christ.'"[235]

On the last day "'the dead, small and great, stand before God, and are judged, everyone according to his works.' 'Then shall the King say to them on his right hand' (God grant he may say so to you!): 'Come, ye blessed of my Father, inherit the kingdom prepared for you from the foundation of the world.'"[236] "And the angels shall tune their harps and sing, 'Lift up your heads, O ye gates, and be ye lift up, ye everlasting doors, that the heirs of glory may come in.'"[237]

2. Reasonably Weigh Profit and Loss for Yourself

A choice is set before the rational mind: which is greater — time or eternity? Weigh it carefully for yourself. Here Wesley sounds like a combination of Pascal's Wager and Anselm's ontological argument for the existence of God.

"How different will be the lot of him that loses his own soul! No joyful sentence will be pronounced on him, but one that will pierce him through with unutterable horror (God forbid that ever it should be pronounced on any of you that are here before God!)."[238]

Only at this point can we see in the strongest light the meaning of the question: "What is he profited who gains the whole world, and loses his own soul?" How could it be that a "creature endued with reason, should voluntarily choose (I say choose; for God forces no man into inevitable damnation) to lose his own soul. All the world can give can weigh little if the future with God is lost."[239]

a. False Religion and True Happiness

Those who choose this irrational alternative of false religion may falsely assume that "a life of religion is a life of misery," but in doing so they prove that they know little about what religion really is by assuming that religion means doing no harm. Religion is reduced to moral action and religious rites, rather than simply receiving and responding to God's free gift of pardon from the heart. Yet it is possible that the most religious persons may attend religious services all their life "and still have no religion at all. Religion is an higher and deeper thing than any outward ordinance whatever."[240]

Religion viewed from the gospel story is "the love of God and our neighbor — that is, every man under heaven," by receiving the love of the Father enfleshed in his Son. "This love, ruling the whole life, animating all our tempers and passions, directing all our thoughts, words, and actions, is 'pure religion and undefiled.'"[241]

---

[235]"The Important Question," B 3:187; J VI:497, sec. 2.5.
[236]"The Important Question," B 3:187; J VI:497, sec. 2.6.
[237]Ibid.
[238]"The Important Question," B 3:188; J VI:497, sec. 2.7.
[239]"The Important Question," B 3:188; J VI:498, sec. 3.
[240]"The Important Question," B 3:189; J VI:498, sec. 3.1.
[241]"The Important Question," B 3:189; J VI:498, sec. 3.2.

This love is the truest happiness.[242] Even when it brings us worldly unhappiness, it offers the grace to receive a greater eternal happiness.[243]

"The love of God naturally leads to works of piety, so the love of our neighbor naturally leads all that feel it to works of mercy. It inclines us to feed the hungry, to clothe the naked, to visit them that are sick or in prison; to be as eyes to the blind and feet to the lame; an husband to the widow, a father to the fatherless.... The doing all which religion requires will not lessen, but immensely increase our happiness."[244]

[The Christian] must suffer, more or less, reproach; for "the servant is not above his master"; but so much the more does the Spirit of glory and of Christ rest upon him.... So far then are all these sufferings from either preventing or lessening our happiness, that they greatly contribute thereto, and indeed constitute no inconsiderable part of it. So that upon the whole there cannot be a more false supposition than that a life of religion is a life of misery; seeing true religion, whether considered in its nature or its fruits, is true and solid happiness.[245]

b. If You Lose Your Own Soul

Weigh your happiness. One who loses his soul to gain the world may imagine that "a life of wickedness is a life of happiness." Yet "no wicked man is happy," since he has "no peace of mind; without this there can be no happiness."

What Scripture teaches, reason confirms. Ask what can make a wicked man happy. Gaining the whole world? Even if so, what has he gained? "All that gratifies the senses." Even with a full belly, "will he not groan under many a tedious hour"? "If he is not fully employed, will he not frequently complain of lowness of spirits? —an unmeaning expression, which the miserable physician usually no more understands than his miserable patient." They are often called "nervous disorders" or "depression," but they are likely clues to "a kind of consciousness that we are not in our place; that we are not as God would have us to be; we are unhinged from our proper center."[246]

c. Weighing the Temporal and Eternal Duration of Happiness

Weigh the duration of pleasure. Obtain for yourself palaces, art, gold, gardens. Yet "how long will these give him pleasure? Only as long as they are new. As soon as ever the novelty is gone, the pleasure is gone also. After he has surveyed them a few months, or years, they give him no more satisfaction. The man who is saving his soul has the advantage of him in this very respect."[247] Let him go after glory. But will this make him happy? Think about it: "He cannot be applauded by all." It has

---

[242]"The Important Question," B 3:189; J VI:499, sec. 3.3.
[243]"The Important Question," B 3:190; J VI:499, sec. 3.4.
[244]"The Important Question," B 3:191; J VI:500, sec. 3.5.
[245]"The Important Question," B 3:191–92; J VI:500–501, sec. 3.6.
[246]"The Important Question," B 3:192–93; J VI:501, sec. 3.7.
[247]"The Important Question," B 3:193; J VI:502, sec. 3.8.

never happened. Some perhaps, but not all. "He that is fond of applause will feel more pain from the censure of one than pleasure from the praise of many."[248] All unholy tempers are unhappy tempers.

Ambition, covetousness, vanity, inordinate affection, malice, and revengefulness carry their own punishment with them, and avenge themselves on the soul wherein they dwell. "Lust, foolish desire, envy, malice, or anger, is now tearing thy breast: love of money, or of praise, hatred, or revenge, is now feeding on thy poor spirit. Such happiness is in vice!"[249]

Weigh your years: "Are you sure of living threescore years? Are you sure of living one year? One month? One week? One day? O make haste to live! Surely the man that may die tonight, should live today."[250] What is the choice that God proposes to his creatures? "Will you have a foretaste of heaven now, and then heaven for ever; or will you have a foretaste of hell now and then hell for ever? Will you have two hells, or two heavens?"[251] This is a no-brainer.

d. An Appeal to Decision

Wesley ends with this appeal to decision: "It is the very question which I now propose to you in the name of God. Will you be happy here and hereafter — in the world that now is, and in that which is to come? Or will you be miserable here and hereafter, in time and in eternity? What is your choice? Let there be no delay: now take one or the other. I take heaven and earth to record this day that I set before you life and death, blessing and cursing. O choose life!... Choose that better part, which shall never be taken from you."[252]

Further Reading on Soul Care

Glick, Dan. "The Pastoral Counseling of John Wesley through Written Correspondence: The Years 1777 – 1782," Dan Glick Wordpress. Danglick.wordpress.com/2009/05/05/the-pastoral-counseling-of-john-wesley-through-written-correspondence-the-years-1777-1782/.

Outler, Albert C. "Pastoral Care in the Wesleyan Spirit." In *The Wesleyan Theological Heritage: Essays of Albert C. Outler*, edited by Thomas C. Oden and Leicester R. Longden, 175 – 88. Grand Rapids: Zondervan, 1991.

Telford, John, ed. *Letters of John Wesley*, 8 vols. London: Epworth, 1931.

---

[248]"The Important Question," B 3:194; J VI:502, sec. 3.9.
[249]"The Important Question," B 3:194; J VI:502 – 3, sec. 3.10.
[250]"The Important Question," B 3:195; J VI:503, sec. 3.11.
[251]"The Important Question," B 3:197; J VI:505, sec. 3.14.
[252]"The Important Question," B 3:197 – 98; J VI:505, sec. 3.15.

CHAPTER 4

Pastoral Care for the Family

A. The Happiness of the Family

1. Three Teaching Homilies on Family Happiness

Wesley's teaching on family happiness and mutual accountability is concentrated in three thought-provoking homilies that any parent can read. They were addressed not to theologians but to parents and families. These are short pieces that young people old enough to understand can profitably read. They could be a project for a family retreat or a homeschool assignment.

The first of these three homilies envisions the family as the divinely provided means for ordering human society toward the happy life. "On Family Religion" is based on a memorable text from Joshua, "As for me and my house, we will serve the LORD" (24:15).

The second, homily #95, sets forth a vision of the education of children, based on a text from Proverbs, "Train up a child in the way he should go: and when he is old, he will not depart from it" (22:6).

The third speaks of the child's accountability to parents, based on the divine command in Colossians to "obey your parents" (3:20).

Together these three texts treat the most crucial issues for a family living together: the right ordering of family life under God, the ensuing tasks of parenting, and the duty of children to parents. Together they contend for lifelong learning of tough love. They point to God's way of ordering life for the happiness of children. A reading of these three homilies will give any lay believer, any parent, or any thoughtful young person the core of Wesleyan instruction on family religion and the way to increase family happiness by constraining egocentricity and narcissism.

These three teaching homilies grow out of Wesley's profound conviction that vital religion cannot be separated from family life. Wesley's own family life shaped his convictions. He grew up in the Epworth parsonage with caring, godly parents. John was the fifteenth child of Samuel and Susanna Wesley (nineteen were born, nine died as infants, and only eight survived to adulthood). Though his parents sometimes differed on politics, they were completely committed to the nurture of godly children and a godly family.

2. On Family Religion

John Wesley had high regard for the social importance of the family. Society cannot be healthy without healthy families. The worshiping community has a God-given and Spirit-enabled interest in the care of children. Children are blessed when they learn to be accountable within the family. Wesley therefore wrote on the unity of the family as a system. He encouraged spirited Christian parenting grounded in Scripture teaching, and he provided counsel for educating children toward spiritual, emotional, and physical health.

The text for the homily "On Family Religion" is Joshua 24:15: "As for me and my house, we will serve the LORD" [Homily #94 (May 26, 1783), B 3:333 – 46; J #94, VII:78 – 86].

a. Family Accountability in Biblical Perspective from Moses to Joshua

A great deal is expected of the parental leaders of each family. They are ordained to a profound ministry to each person in the family and to the family system as a whole.

The biblical prototype for family commitment is revealed in Joshua, a generation after Moses. God had raised Israel up out of nothing and had revealed the law to Moses. Moses then led the people of God through the desert wilderness, where God sustained them by supernaturally providing food. Now, in the second generation, Joshua was faced with the deterioration of the new covenant community that had begun only a generation earlier. The trend was toward forgetfulness and idolatry. Joshua's dilemma was how to sustain the powerful memory of the revelation of God into the next generation.[1] So it was with the church in Wesley's day and today.

b. God Deals with Humanity Family by Family

God deals with humanity family by family. It is through the family that we learn who we are. We learn how a family chooses commitment to God prototypically from Joshua. He took responsibility for his family's strength, unity, and spiritual happiness.

Joshua's defining moment was when he called all the families in covenant with God to commit themselves to covenant responsibility to each other. Joshua was challenging the head of each household to embrace responsibility of care for the partner parent and for each child who emerged from the unique covenant between one man and one woman. This responsibility was extended to all who lived under his roof and to all strangers who arrived at his gate with human needs.[2]

Joshua called the families under his charge to "choose for yourselves this day whom you will serve, whether the gods your ancestors served beyond the Euphrates, or the gods of the Amorites, in whose land you are living. But as for me and my household, we will serve the LORD" (Josh. 24:15 NIV). Joshua set a pattern for the people of God by ordering his own house under the command of God.

---

[1]"On Family Religion," B 3:334, J VII:76, pref. 1 – 2.
[2]Ibid.

In making their choice, the family of Joshua anticipated the faith of "all who have tasted that the Lord is gracious, all whom he has brought out of the land of Egypt, out of the bondage of sin; those especially who are united together in Christian fellowship." By his example, he calls all families under the covenant to "adopt this wise resolution! Then would the work of the Lord prosper in our land."[3] Those who are concerned about rightly guiding their children in the fallen world do well to listen to Joshua. The children of the Christian family, if wisely nurtured, will join the parents in saying with Joshua: "I and my household will serve the Lord."

3. The Challenge of Transmitting the Intergenerational Covenant to Children

a. Both Sin and Grace Are Transmitted through Families

How is the intergenerational covenant to be passed on from grandparents to grandchildren? The short answer: By the grace made available in family religion. God raises up people of faith, love, and courage to guide vulnerable families through the hazards of time.[4]

Late in his life (1783), Wesley was pondering the weakening second generation of the evangelical revival with the vitality of the first. He was stunned to realize that all that had been gained in the first generation could be lost in the second.

Today the signs of the same dilemma are rife: youth have contempt for parents, and parents shun parental responsibility. The family disintegrates. The permissive parents are doing an injustice to the most vulnerable members of the family — their own dear children. The evidence is overwhelming. Families not rooted in the love of God and humanity under the guidance of godly parents are vulnerable.[5]

b. Train Up a Child in the Way He Should Go

Scripture calls parents to "train up a child in the way he should go: and when he is old, he will not depart from it."[6] The very life and continuity and future of real religion hinge upon good parenting.

The rising generation will miss the benefits of any "present revival of religion"[7] if those benefits are not transmitted to them. They and their offspring will be "utter strangers to real religion." Wesley recalled the maxim that the transgression of the children generally arises from their neglect by their parents.

The future health of society depends on good parenting. Family leaders are called to engender faith in God grounded in the worshiping community's knowledge of God's work in history. God the Father has come to all humanity through God the Son. Hence believing in the Son of God is what grounds the faith in God that is crucial to the very foundation of the family when that foundation is viewed

---

[3]Ibid.
[4]"On Family Religion," B 3:335, J VII:77, pref. 3–4.
[5]"On Family Religion," B 3:335, J VII:77, pref. 4.
[6]Ibid.
[7]"On Family Religion," B 3:335, J VII:77, pref. 3.

in the light of God's Word revealed in the Son by the power of the Spirit. To serve the Lord is, for Christian believers, to worship the Lord in spirit and in truth. This does not happen accidentally but with high intentionality.[8]

4. The Social Importance of the Family

a. Spreading God's Love through the Family

The new life given with faith spreads through the life of the family and makes happier the life of the world. Faith bears fruit in love. This love springs out of an infinitely larger love that God sheds abroad in our hearts.[9]

The family has huge advantages compared with public policy initiatives in education. In the family, children have the first chance to believe in God.

In the family, we learn how to be kind, gentle, and forgiving. There we learn to "love God, because he first loved us." The first evidence of this is "the love of a pardoning God ... shed abroad in our hearts by the Holy Spirit," which comes to us as a sheer unmerited gift.[10] The family engenders the love of their neighbors when touched by grace from above. Those who love God learn to love others as God loves all. Serving the Lord implies learning to love those with whom we live closest in connection.[11]

However young or old, we believers know we are not made righteous by obeying the rules of the family, but rather by divine grace. We learn how privileged we are to have the immense benefits of the family, where we learn to value the family's intrinsic God-given order and receive God's justifying grace. There we learn to love others far away by first practicing love in regard to those closest to us. "Gratitude to our Creator will surely produce benevolence to our fellow-creatures. If we love him, we cannot but love one another, as Christ loved us. We feel our souls enlarged in love toward every child of man ... forgiving one another, if we have a complaint against any, 'even as God for Christ's sake hath forgiven us.'"[12]

Gratitude for God's gifts leads the faithful to carefully avoid what God has forbidden and actively seek what God commands. God finds joy in beholding his sin-prone creatures keeping his commandments to their benefit. If the family is to rightly serve the Lord, the whole family system must learn obedience to God. This means doing what God commands, not reluctantly, but willingly, joyfully.[13]

b. The Promise of God to the Faithful Family

Love for others is learned in inches. It requires living by the rules that prevail in a loving family, in due time finding these rules grounded in abundant grace.

---

[8]"On Family Religion," B 3:336, J VII:77 – 78, sec. 1.1.
[9]"On Family Religion," B 3:335 – 36, J VII:77 – 78, sec. 1.3.
[10]"On Family Religion," B 3:336, J VII:78, sec. 1.2.
[11]"On Family Religion," B 3:336, J VII:78, sec. 1.3.
[12]Ibid.
[13]"On Family Religion," B 3:337, J VII:78, sec. 1.4.

Obedience to God, to the family leadership, and to divinely implanted conscience is crucial for the family to live together in peace and fruitfulness.

Joshua declared that regardless of what others did, "As for me and my house, we will serve the LORD" (Josh. 24:15). Good families can counter bad cultures. Serving the Lord implies obedience to all the guidelines that the good order of family life requires.

The well-ordered family takes joy in good discipline that benefits all. The whole family learns together to "diligently keep [God's] commandments, carefully avoid whatever he has forbidden, and zealously do whatever he has enjoined."[14] The promise of the family is that its offspring will find passage into adulthood having "always a conscience void of offense toward God, and toward men" (Acts 24:16). Those who have been blessed by growing up this way, with wise parenting and a loving family, are prepared to offer increasing gifts to the society in which they live.

The family covenant reflects the divine human covenant. The promise of God to the families of the people of God is: "I will be the God of all the families of Israel, and they will be my people" (Jer. 31:1 NIV). Under the coming new covenant, God is promising, "I will put my law in their minds and write it on their hearts" (v. 33 NIV).[15]

5. Caring for Everyone under the Roof

To this family system, God may entrust for a time the souls of visitors, extended family, and strangers at the gate — all living at the time under the roof of the family. God may bless this family with strangers. Each comes with a need. Each is to be welcomed without counting merits, but by the same measure, each is expected to dwell in the household under the household rules and requirements and to share their gifts with the family.[16]

To heads of households, Wesley maintains, "Everyone under your roof that has a soul ... is under your care."[17] For whatever time they are there, they are to be treated as a part of the family, even if not of the biological family itself. None of these sojourners should go away from this family without receiving something more valuable than gold: the love of God expressed in human respect and love.[18]

B. Pastoral Counsel of Parents

Wesley's homilies offer explicit pastoral counsel regarding the spiritual formation of children. He is attentive to the growing person at every stage of development, from neonate to young people and on into adulthood, at which time the cycle regenerates and continues.

---

[14]Ibid.

[15]*WOF*, sec. 2.1; "Of the Preparatives to Family Duties," in *SOSO*, 4, 1760 ed.

[16]"On Family Religion," B 3:338, J VII:79, sec. 2.3; cf. "The Use of Money," 3.3.

[17]"On Family Religion," B 3:338, J VII:79, sec. 2.3.

[18]Ibid.; cf. William Law, *Treatise on Christian Perfection*, Works, 9 vols. (Hampshire, UK: J. Richardson, 1753–56), 3:223.

1. A Thought on the Education of Children

a. At What Point Does Education Cripple?

When I first read Wesley's short (and mostly unnoticed) essay "A Thought on the Manner of Educating Children" [J XIII:476–77 (July 1783)], I felt as if he was aiming his criticisms directly at me, for I had been just that kind of parent who "objected strongly to … bringing [children] up too strictly," and who was wary of "giving them more of religion than they liked," and who wanted them to be free to choose the truth for themselves.[19] Wesley took off his kid gloves to challenge permissive parenting.

Wesley was quite aware that these permissive views were "quite agreeable to the sentiments of Rousseau in his 'Emilius.'"[20] Rousseau's ideas of education enthralled many of the most influential modern educators (e.g., John Dewey, Mortimer Adler, and William Heard Kilpatrick). Wesley thought that Émile was frankly "the most empty, silly, injudicious thing that ever a self-conceited infidel wrote."[21] Since I had once been enthralled with Rousseau, I braced myself on first reading for what I thought would be a harangue. Now, looking back, I think much that went wrong in my own education got off track with Rousseau and would have benefited from a dose of Wesley's tough love.

Wesley was a contemporary of Rousseau. Rousseau had been abandoned by his family and had abandoned his children. Wesley had been nurtured by his parents in just the sort of rigor that Rousseau despised. Wesley had the advantage of having before his eyes a magnificent model of an encouraging educator in his mother, Susanna.[22] He had seen this model work in his own home. He also admired those models of excellence in education practiced by Mrs. Bosanquet (later John Fletcher's wife) and in the Kingswood School.[23] He could attest the actual performance of that unusual form of education that did not make children worse but better. He knew that few of these young people had "made shipwreck of the faith." Many had learned to become "holy in heart and in life," praising God "to all eternity that ever they saw those schools."[24]

Wesley argued that "what is commonly called a religious education frequently does more hurt than good," and has caused some to contract "an enmity to religion."[25] Too many teachers of religion do not know what true religion is. They imagine that it is simply "doing no harm, abstaining from outward sin," going to church, or

having a train of right opinions, which is vulgarly called faith. But all these,

---

[19]"A Thought on the Manner of Educating Children," J XIII:474, sec. 1.
[20]Emilius = Émile; "A Thought on the Manner of Educating Children," J XIII:475, secs. 1–3.
[21]"A Thought on the Manner of Educating Children," J XIII:474, sec. 2.
[22]B 19:286–91.
[23]"A Thought on the Manner of Educating Children," J XIII:474, sec. 2.
[24]"A Thought on the Manner of Educating Children," J XIII:475, sec. 3.
[25]"A Thought on the Manner of Educating Children," J XIII:475, sec. 4.

however common in the world, are gross and capital errors. Unless religion be described as consisting in holy tempers; in the love of God and our neighbor; in humility, gentleness, patience, long-suffering, contentedness in every condition; to sum up all, in the image of God, in the mind that was in Christ; it is no wonder if these that are instructed therein are not better, but worse, than other men. For they think they have religion, when, indeed, they have none at all; and so add pride to all their other vices.[26]

Even if they have more balanced judgments with regard to the nature of religion, "they may still be mistaken with regard to the manner of instilling it into children." They may lack the spirit of guidance, "to which some even good men are utter strangers. They may habitually lean to this or that extreme, of remissness or of severity. And if they either give children too much of their own will, or needlessly and churlishly restrain them; if they either use no punishment at all or more than is necessary, the leaning either to one extreme or the other may frustrate all their endeavors."[27]

b. The Secret of an Early Start on Timely Discipline

The teaching of the happy life must begin early, "from the very time that reason dawns, laying line upon line, precept upon precept, as soon and as fast as they are able to bear it ... through Scripture, reason, and experience."[28] Together these three testify of the truth of nature, reason, sin, grace, and life with God.

The best education is designed to set aright the tragic imbalances that have so long prevailed in the dismal story of fallen human freedom. The grace revealed in Scripture, reason, and experience turns the deficits of the history of sin away "from self-will, pride, anger, revenge, and the love of the world" and toward the gentle habits of "lowliness, meekness, and the love of God."[29] If we cannot root out these engrained distortions, at least we can check their growth. This is done as far as possible "by mildness, softness, and gentleness."[30]

Those who love their children are careful to discipline them.[31] The proverbs are insistent on this point: "A rod and a reprimand impart wisdom, but a child left undisciplined disgraces its mother" (Prov. 29:15 NIV). "In the name of God, then, and by the authority of His word, let all that have children, from the time they begin to speak or run alone, begin to train them up in the way wherein they should go; to counterwork the corruption of their nature with all possible assiduity; to do everything in their power to cure their self-will, pride, and every other wrong temper."[32]

---

[26]"A Thought on the Manner of Educating Children," J XIII:476, sec. 5.
[27]"A Thought on the Manner of Educating Children," J XIII:476, sec. 6.
[28]"A Thought on the Manner of Educating Children," J XIII:476, sec. 7.
[29]Ibid.
[30]"A Thought on the Manner of Educating Children," J XIII:477, sec. 7.
[31]Prov. 13:24; Heb. 12:8; "A Thought on the Manner of Educating Children," J XIII:477, sec. 8.
[32]"A Thought on the Manner of Educating Children," J XIII:477, sec. 8.

2. Homily on the Education of Children

a. The Human Will in God's Design

Wesley builds on the brief premise of "A Thought on the Manner of Educating Children" with a crucial teaching homily [Homily #95, "On the Education of Children," B 3:347 – 60; J #95, VII:86 – 98 (July 12, 1783)] whose text was Proverbs 22:6: "Train up a child in the way he should go: and when he is old, he will not depart from it."

Children have wills of their own, given by the Creator. But these wills fall as voluntary choices are made in a fallen world. There is an art in restoring health to the fallen will. It operates by a special grace given to parents and teachers as they pray for it and are receptive to it.

Why, Wesley asked, do "some of the best parents have the worst children"? Because good parents "have often too much easiness of temper."[33] To gain a new foothold, we must look toward the prophets and apostles for wisdom on the education of children.[34]

b. The Original Rational Creation of Humanity Distinguished from Its Fallen Condition

In all phases of the education of children, it is fitting to remember that the human condition, after centuries of poor voluntary choices intergenerationally transmitted, is not the same as it was first created.

The use of the word *natural* occurs in classic Christian literature and in Wesleyan teaching with two different levels of meaning: the created nature is different from the fallen nature. The *created nature* of the will is, as seen in Adam prior to the fall, having a will to obey the Creator, with good intent to glorify God. This is distinguished from the *fallen nature* of the will, which is seen in the devolution following Adam during and after the fall. It is prone to disobey the Creator. The will has ever thereafter been turned into asserting its own misperceived interest in defiance of the glory of God. Human history is the story of this fallenness and its redemption.[35]

The parent's God-given challenge in the education of their children is to keep the will as close as possible to its created nature. When it becomes twisted into its fallen nature, the task is, insofar as possible, to restore it to that original natural desire to love and honor God.

The goal of education is to improve the ability of the will to love God and love humanity even amid the distortions of the fallen world. The battle is a daily task for parents.[36]

---

[33]"On the Education of Children," B 3:347 – 48, J VII:86, sec. 1.
[34]"On the Education of Children," B 3:348, J VII:87, sec. 2.
[35]Ibid.
[36]Ibid.

3. The Goal of Education

a. Forming the Will

Within present history, all persons are born with a will that is shaped by temptations toward fallenness. All too soon this inclines toward a "diseased nature," open to ever more temptation. The purpose of education is to "strengthen all that is right in our nature, and remove all our diseases."[37] Education in this sense seeks to correct the loss of the original perfection of the will given in creation, which is logically prior to the fallen self-will of the person.[38]

As physical or bodily treatment seeks to battle natural diseases of the body, so does education seek to battle the diseases of the soul. Chief among these are idolatry, self-will, pride, coveting, and anger. These lead to deviating from telling the truth and toward unjust actions. A good physician will assist in restoring the body to its original or normal condition. The art of restoring physical health is what Wesley called "physic." The art of restoring health of souls Wesley called "education."[39]

b. Shaping the Whole Person

Education includes the proper shaping of intellect, emotive stability, good temperament, and a heart growing fit for life with God. Education seeks by grace to restore the prefallen will in whatever measure possible. Only God can restore it in the most complete way. God's purpose is to nurture the soul back to its original created nature. Parents are given the treasured unique once-for-all opportunity to nurture this grace in their own children.[40]

Classical education from Pythagoras to Plato began by teaching "upon the nature of man, his true end, and the right use of his faculties; upon the immortality of the soul, its relation to God; the agreeableness of virtue to the divine nature; upon the necessity of temperance, justice, mercy, and truth; and the folly of indulging our passions."[41] Wesley follows in that classic tradition.

4. How Parents Combat the Disorders of the Soul

a. Soul Care of Parents for Children

If the history of humanity had continued as God had intended from Adam and Eve to their progeny, all history would have been entirely different. In that case, the perfection of our nature might have been, with the help of prevening grace, "a sufficient self-instructor for everyone. But as sickness and diseases have created the necessity of medicines and physicians, so the disorders of our rational nature have

---

[37]"On the Education of Children," B 3:349, J VII:88, sec. 3.
[38]Ibid.
[39]"On the Education of Children," B 3:348, J VII:87, sec. 3.
[40]Ibid.
[41]"On the Education of Children," B 3:348–49, J VII:87, sec. 3.

introduced the necessity of education and tutors. And as the only end of a physician is to restore nature to its own state, so the only end of education is to restore our rational nature to its proper state."[42]

Christianity has "introduced a new state of things, and so fully informed us of the nature of man and the end of his creation."[43] The history of salvation has given new birth to the possibilities of a higher education. If so, then we "might naturally suppose that every Christian country abounded with schools" that were seeking these very ends. But such is not the case. Education in the faith has become reduced in Wesley's view to "teaching a few questions and answers of a catechism" instead of "forming, training, and practicing children in such a course of life" as this new state of things requires.[44]

"God, not man, is the Physician of souls."[45] Only God gives medicine to heal our ancient human sickness. "None of all the children of men is able to 'bring a clean thing out of an unclean,'" when the pollution is our voluntary sin. God still works in us "'both to will and to do of his good pleasure.' But it is generally his pleasure to work by his creatures: to help man by man. He honors men to be, in this sense, 'workers together with him.' By this means the reward is ours, while the glory redounds to him."[46]

We are not without help. Our guardian angels "suggest nothing to our minds but what is wise and holy; help us to discover every false judgment of our minds, and to subdue every wrong passion of our hearts."[47] Teachers are called to imitate these rational, celestial mentors.

b. Parents Have the First Opportunity to Overcome the Endemic Tendency to Idolatry

What is the spiritual disease that most deeply characterizes man's fallen condition, which due to the history of sin, "everyone that is born of a woman brings with him into the world"? Above all it is the invasive atheism that pretends that fallen human freedom has adequate knowledge of God without grace. This fuels the imagination that we can pull ourselves up to the calling of perfect love.[48]

Fallen man is a "natural atheist," tempted to become his own god. An inveterate atheism resides in the human heart: "Every man is by nature, as it were, his own god. He worships himself. He is, in his own conception, absolute Lord of himself." "His own will is his only law."[49] In his pride, he is continually prone "to think of himself more highly than he ought to think" (Rom. 12:3). "Every man can discern more or

---

[42]"On the Education of Children," B 3:348, J VII:87, sec. 3.
[43]"On the Education of Children," B 3:349, J VII:88, sec. 3.
[44]Ibid.
[45]"On the Education of Children," B 3:349, J VII:88, sec. 4.
[46]Ibid.
[47]"On the Education of Children," B 3:349, J VII:88, sec. 3.
[48]"On the Education of Children," B 3:350, J VII:89, sec. 5.
[49]"On the Education of Children," B 3:350, J VII:89, sec. 6.

less of this disease in everyone — but himself."[50] It is a trait we can discern more readily in others than in ourselves, due to our endemic egocentricity.

From this myopia follows his insidious egoistic "love of the world. Every man is by [his fallen] nature a lover of the creature instead of the Creator; 'a lover of pleasure' in every kind 'more than a lover of God.'" Human freedom has become captive to "the 'desire of the flesh, the desire of the eyes,' or 'the pride of life' [1 John 2:16]. 'The desire of the flesh' is a propensity to seek happiness in what gratifies one or more of the outward senses. 'The desire of the eyes' is a propensity to seek happiness in what gratifies the internal sense, the imagination, either by things grand, or new, or beautiful. 'The pride of life' seems to mean a propensity to seek happiness in what gratifies the sense of honor."[51]

This threefold form of inordinate madness — desire of the flesh, desire of the eyes, pride of life — is "a real, though short, madness wherever it is,"[52] seen from the perspective of eternity. The educational remedy for this madness is to help put the injury in proportional perspective in the light of the eternal, so that we may seek and find forgiveness and enabling grace.

The result of this deception is all-encompassing, viewed historically: "All natural men will, upon a close temptation, vary from or disguise the truth.... They hang out false colors; they practice either simulation or dissimulation. So that you cannot say truly of any person living, till grace has altered nature, 'Behold an Israelite indeed, in whom is no guile!'"[53] "All human creatures are naturally partial to themselves," having "more regard to their own interest or pleasure than strict justice allows."[54] These are the prevailing diseases of fallen human nature.

It is "the grand end of education" to penetrate these deceptions, layer by layer. "All those to whom God has entrusted the education of children" are called "to take all possible care, first, not to increase ... any of these diseases ... and next, to use every possible means of healing them."[55]

c. Teaching Children to Have "No Other Gods"

Children's moral education from the earliest years must deal with this idolatry — the elevation of finite goods and values to an imagined absolute value. To bow to a non-God is idolatry. It is to confuse the almighty God with some lesser imagined absolute value. Children are no less tempted to idolatry than their parents. The remedy for idolatry is to inculcate a sense of the reality and power of God.[56]

Wesley posed this practical question: "What can parents do, and mothers more especially, to whose care our children are necessarily committed in their tender

[50]"On the Education of Children," B 3:350, J VII:89, sec. 7.
[51]"On the Education of Children," B 3:350–51, J VII:89–90, sec. 8.
[52]"On the Education of Children," B 3:351, J VII:90, sec. 9.
[53]"On the Education of Children," B 3:351, J VII:90, sec. 10.
[54]"On the Education of Children," B 3:352, J VII:90, sec. 11.
[55]"On the Education of Children," B 3:352, J VII:90, sec. 12.
[56]"On the Education of Children," B 3:353, J VII:91, sec. 14.

years, with regard to the atheism that is natural to all the children of men?" The first simple step is that parents can choose to avoid feeding "the atheism of their children by ascribing the works of creation to nature or chance."[57]

We need not feed their disease, but what can we do to cure it? The second positive step is that parents can "from the first dawn of reason continually inculcate, God is in this and every place. God made you, and me, and the earth, and the sun, and the moon, and everything. And everything is his: heaven and earth and all that is therein. God orders all things: he makes the sun shine, and the wind blow, and the trees bear fruit.... As God made the world, so he governs the world, and everything that is in it."[58]

The worst option: leave them to their own devices. "To let them take their own way is the sure method of increasing their self-will sevenfold," if without guidance. "To humor children is, as far as in us lies, to make their disease incurable."[59]

5. Breaking the Self-Assertive Will

a. The Hazard of Soft Parenting

This idolatry forever tempts the will to self-will, as opposed to responding to God's ever-flowing grace, which Scripture calls "obeying God." Self-will appears early in the life of a child. The parent must recognize its appearance, and work to bring it back to its created condition. The will of the parent is to the little child like the first breakthrough of the will of God in the child's life. God has given the parent the extraordinary task of being something like God for the child — reflecting in his or her own behavior the goodness of God.[60]

The most disastrous thing a child can experience is the absence of a guiding hand. To fail to reprove when necessary is to reinforce bad habits in the child. To reward the child for deceitful behavior is to lose an opportunity for growth. When we encourage behaviors that incline the will toward egocentricity, we increase the misery and dig the pit deeper.

A wise parent ... should begin to break their will the first moment it appears. In the whole art of Christian education there is nothing more important than this. The will of the parent is to a little child in the place of the will of God. Therefore studiously teach them to submit to this while they are children, that they may be ready to submit to his will when they are men. But in order to carry this point you will need incredible firmness and resolution. For after you have once begun you must never more give way. You must hold on still in an even course: you must never intermit your attention for one hour; otherwise you lose your labor.[61]

---

[57]"On the Education of Children," B 3:352, J VII:91, sec. 13.
[58]"On the Education of Children," B 3:353, J VII:91, sec. 14.
[59]"On the Education of Children," B 3:353–54, J VII:92, sec. 15.
[60]Ibid.
[61]Ibid.

Though Wesley's marriage never gave him opportunity to raise children, he had many souls in his connection of spiritual formation.

Wesley noted personally, with gratitude, that his own mother had direct responsibility for ten children, yet not one of them was ever heard to cry aloud after it became a year old.[62] On this basis, he offers one firm rule from his mother's regimen: "Never, on any account, give a child anything that it cries for.... If you give a child what he cries for, you pay him for crying; and then he will certainly cry again." If the child screams, "it is in your power effectually to prevent it. For no mother need suffer a child to cry aloud after it is a year old."[63] Grace plays the central role in educating. He added: "But I allow, none but a woman of sense will be able to effect this." It takes "a woman of such patience and resolution as only the grace of God can give."[64]

b. To Overpraise Is to Reinforce an Illusion

Even when children do well, they had best not be inordinately praised. It is better to say with the *non nobis* psalm: "Not unto us! Not unto us! But unto thy name give the praise!"[65] Do not habituate your children to the expectation that they will always be increasingly praised, even when they act dreadfully. Just tell the truth.

Parents are right to convey their happiness when their children do well, just as "our Lord himself frequently commended his own disciples, but use praise exceeding sparely." But they do well to strike at the root of signs of pride. "Teach your children as soon as possibly you can ... that they are fallen short of that glorious image of God wherein they were at first created; that they are not now, as they were once" as if they were in their creation "pictures of the God of glory."[66]

Wesley thought that most parents were prone to reinforce self-will and pride by inordinate praising. This habit spreads a net for your children's feet. Let them eat humble pie when they choose to act disobediently. Do not be afraid of the humility elicited in children when they recognize their own pride.

The cure for loving the world inordinately is never to put before the child temptations to love finite goods more than God or out of relation with God.[67] The remedy for worldliness is to seek and find pleasure in God's goodness, God's truth, so as to put the desire for worldly pleasures in proportional perspective.[68]

The child-parent relation is sometimes a delicate problem in the presence of a grandparent or mother-in-law. Wesley advised parents: "In every other point, obey your mother. Give up your will to hers. But with regard to the management of your children, steadily keep the reins in your own hands."[69] Instill in them as early as

---

[62]Ibid.
[63]"On the Education of Children," B 3:54–355, J VII:93, sec. 16.
[64]"On the Education of Children," B 3:354–56, J VII:92–93, sec. 16.
[65]Ps. 115:1; "On the Education of Children," B 3:56, J VII:94, sec. 18.
[66]"On the Education of Children," B 3:355–56, J VII:93–94, sec. 17.
[67]"On the Education of Children," B 3:350–51, J VII:89–90, sec. 8.
[68]"On the Education of Children," B 3:57, J VII:95, sec. 19.
[69]"On the Education of Children," B 3:358, J VII:95–96, sec. 20.

possible an abhorrence of the love of money and of that dangerous idea that riches can produce happiness. "Habituate them to make God their end in all things."[70] Care for their souls.

c. Small Things Matter

Wesley warned: "When you falsely protect your child and pretend that "it was not my child that did it: say, it was the cat.' What amazing folly.... Do you feel no remorse while you are putting a lie in the mouth of your child?"[71] "Teach them to 'put away all lying,' and both in little things and great, in jest or earnest, speak the very truth from their heart.... Teach them to abhor all equivocating, all cunning and dissimulation. Use every means to give them a love of truth: of veracity, sincerity, and simplicity, and of openness both of spirit and behavior."[72] Small things matter: "He that will steal a penny will steal a pound."[73] Do not let children "vex their brothers or sisters either by word or deed."[74]

Pets provide an opportunity for schooling. Good parents will not allow their children to hurt or give pain to anything that has life. Teach them the Golden Rule: "Do unto others as you would have them do unto you."[75]

The combined voices of Scripture, conscience, and parental guidance provide the soul with its main defenses against these moral ailments and diseases of the soul. "Press upon all your children to 'walk in love, as Christ also loved us, and gave himself for us.'"[76]

C. Good Counsel on Parent-Child Communications

1. On Obedience to Parents

Listen parents: Pluck your children from the lion's teeth. Do not offer up your children to the adversary. This is the serious business of parenting.[77] Turn their wills around early and let their souls come alive to God. He will bless you to all eternity, for in doing so, you do God's will.

In homily #96, "On Obedience to Parents," Wesley explained why Scripture calls children to "obey your parents in all things." All? Yes, all. The text is Colossians 3:20: "Children, obey your parents in all things: for this is well pleasing unto the Lord" [Homily #96, B 3:361 – 72; J VII:98 – 108 (September – October 1784)].

a. The Honor Due to Parents

The letter to the Colossians states an innately constant and universal principle

---

70"On the Education of Children," B 3:358 – 59, J VII:96 – 97, sec. 21.
71"On the Education of Children," B 3:359 – 60, J VII:97, sec. 23.
72Ibid.
73"On the Education of Children," B 3:360, J VII:97 – 98, sec. 24.
74"On the Education of Children," B 3:360, J VII:98, sec. 25.
75Ibid.
76Ibid.
77"On Obedience to Parents," B 3:367, J VII:102 – 3, sec. 1.9.

found in all cultures. It should be recognizable to any reasonable observer. The just and happy ordering of human society hinges on the honoring and respecting of parents. Based on his cross-cultural experience and anthropological study, Wesley argued that there is no culture, not even of Native Americans, where this principle is not found.[78]

Similarly Paul wrote to the Ephesians: "Children, obey your parents in the Lord, for this is right. 'Honor your father and mother' — which is the first commandment with a promise — 'so that it may go well with you and that you may enjoy long life on the earth'" (Eph. 6:1 – 3 NIV). And what he wrote to the Ephesians, he wrote even more specifically to the Colossians: "Children, obey your parents *in all things*" (3:20, italics added).[79]

b. The Command and the Promise

The command to children to obey their parents is both right and beneficial. It is also the first command to include a beneficial promise: good life and long life. Its benefits can be examined rationally. They are confirmed in Scripture. God told King Solomon, "If you walk in obedience to me and keep my decrees and commands as David your father did, I will give you a long life" (1 Kings 3:14 NIV). Those who live in obedience to God will secure life enough in this world that they may be prepared for eternal life (Prov. 10:27). Parents are our first guides to that life.

We all know intuitively that we should obey our parents. Even at times when we find it difficult to do, we do not negate their authority, for they brought us into this life.[80] Reason joins with Scripture in commending this moral command. Obedience to parents is intrinsically in harmony with the nature of righteousness and in line with what we know we ought to do. This is the order of domestic relationships that is repeatedly set forth in Scripture as pleasing to God. Under both the old and new covenants, the plan for families that God has created for our human good is made clear.[81]

The divine imperative for families has hidden within it a wonderful earthly promise: "It may go well with you" (Eph. 6:3 NIV). This promise has a beneficial outcome: your life will be more effective so that it will be more likely that your days will be long in the land the Lord your God gives you.

c. A Command "Written on Our Hearts" from Our Creation

Do children have innate moral ideas embedded in their souls from creation? Whether human minds hold any innate principles is disputed. "But it is allowed on all hands, if there be any practical principles naturally implanted in the soul, that 'we ought to honor our parents' will claim this character almost before any other."[82]

---

[78]"On Obedience to Parents," B 3:361 – 62, J VII:98 – 99, pref. 1.
[79]"On Obedience to Parents," B 3:362, J VII:99, pref. 2.
[80]"On Obedience to Parents," B 3:361 – 62, J VII:98 – 99, pref. 1.
[81]Ibid.
[82]"On Obedience to Parents," B 3:362, J VII:99, pref. 1 – 2.

This moral maxim is found throughout world history on all continents in all known cultures.

Paul made clear that when those who do not have the law "do by nature things required by the law, they are a law for themselves, even though they do not have the law. They show that the requirements of the law are written on their hearts, their consciences also bearing witness, and their thoughts sometimes accusing them and at other times even defending them" (Rom. 2:14 – 15 NIV).[83]

What is written in our hearts is made even clearer through the history of God's revealed love. The ordering of the parent-child relation is a part of God's revelation. Obedience to parents "was one of the laws which our blessed Lord did not come to destroy, but to fulfill."[84]

2. What Is That Special Form of Justice That Children Owe to Their Own Parents?

a. Thou Shalt Honor Thy Father and Thy Mother

"Obey your parents" thus is not only a command of Scripture but of conscience, the internally built-in sense of self that comes through human relationships. It is also a rational duty open for examination by anyone who wants to subject family life to rational analysis. Why is the command eminently rational? Because the command uniquely and plainly combines justice with mercy in a way that reflects God's own justice and mercy.

Obedience is due our parents just because it "is what we owe to them for the very being which we have received from them."[85] Children do not choose to have life. Life comes as a gift of God made possible through parents.

Obedience to our parents is merciful because it promises long-lasting benefits to those who follow it. This is the first of the Ten Commandments to which "a peculiar promise is annexed: that it may be well with thee."[86] To have long days and wellness promised shows God's mercy. So it is good for you to "honor your father and your mother, so that you may live long in the land the LORD your God is giving you" (Ex. 20:12 NIV).[87] Wesley thought that both the Bible and human experience offer "innumerable proofs" of the Bible's beneficial effects.

b. Parental Obedience as a Duty

Is obedience to parents a duty? "Here and there a child obeys the parent out of fear, or perhaps out of natural affection. But how many children can you find that obey their fathers and mothers out of a sense of duty to God?"[88] Is the child accountable to both parents equally? "By 'parents,' the Apostle means both fathers

---

[83]"On Obedience to Parents," B 3:361 – 62, J VII:98 – 99, pref. 1.
[84]"On Obedience to Parents," B 3:362, J VII:99, pref. 2.
[85]"On Obedience to Parents," B 3:363, J VII:99, pref. 3.
[86]Ibid.
[87]Ibid.
[88]"On Obedience to Parents," B 3:363, J VII:100, sec. 1.1.

and mothers."[89] Both parents are equally responsible, and children are responsible to both parents equally. This underscores the need for the two parents to be on the same page in parenting and to remain strong in their lifelong fidelity in covenant with each other.

"It is peculiarly pleasing to the great Father of men and angels that we should pay honor and obedience" to the particular father and mother of our flesh. The command is not to children in general but to a unique child in regard to a unique parent.

> Listen, my son, to your father's instruction
> and do not forsake your mother's teaching.
> They are a garland to grace your head
> and a chain to adorn your neck. (Prov. 1:8 – 9 NIV)

c. The Singular Exception to Obedience "in All Things"

"All things" includes things great and things small. "The first point of obedience is to do nothing which your father or mother forbids, whether it be great or small," but with one exception: unless "the thing prohibited is clearly enjoined of God."[90] "It is surely the more excellent way to do nothing which you know your parents disapprove."[91] Similarly sons and daughters are called to "do everything which your father or mother bids, be it great or small, provided it be not contrary to any command of God."[92]

But how long must we treat our fathers and mothers with honor? "How long are we to obey them? Are children to obey only till they run alone? Till they go to school? Till they can read and write? Or till they are as tall as their parents?"[93] This privilege of honoring parents applies to the whole of life.

"But is a man that is at age, or a woman that is married, under any farther obligation to obey their parents?" In marriage "it is true that a man is to leave father and mother and cleave unto his wife; and by parity of reason, she is to leave father and mother and cleave unto her husband."[94] There are cases in which "conjugal duty must take the place of filial [duty]." But marriage does not either cancel or lessen by our having lived a certain number of years.[95] Wesley said, "When I was between forty and fifty, I judged myself fully as much obliged to obey my mother in everything lawful as I did when I was in my hanging-sleeve coat."[96]

3. The God-Given Power of Parenting

Wesley thought that parents have comparatively more operative power in domestic affairs than does the sovereign ruler in the realm of political affairs: "God

---

[89]"On Obedience to Parents," B 3:363, J VII:100, sec. 1.2.
[90]"On Obedience to Parents," B 3:365, J VII:101, sec. 1.5.
[91]"On Obedience to Parents," B 3:364 – 65, J VII:101, sec. 1.5.
[92]"On Obedience to Parents," B 3:364 – 65, J VII:101, sec. 1.5 – 6.
[93]"On Obedience to Parents," B 3:363, J VII:100, sec. 1.3.
[94]"On Obedience to Parents," B 3:364, J VII:101, sec. 1.4.
[95]Ibid.
[96]Ibid.

has given a power to parents which even sovereign princes have not,"[97] because "the will of the king is no law to the subject. But the will of the parent is a law to the child." This means the child directly experiences the parent as lawgiver even more directly than the citizen experiences the law of the state and even though it is not finally the parent who gives the law that God has written into the heart.

The task of parenting is to guide each child through each particular stage of growth toward the glory of God through the love of humanity. In each phase, the child is being prepared for doing God's will and avoiding evil. "Bow down their wills from the very first dawn of reason; and by habituating them to submit to your will, prepare them for submitting to the will of their Father which is in heaven."[98] "The strength of the parents supplies the want of strength" in the child. The understanding of the parents supplies their lack of understanding. "The will of the parents should guide that of their children till they have wisdom and experience to guide themselves."[99]

As a child learns to surrender to the good will of the parent, he or she will gradually learn to surrender to God.[100] Long before the child understands the reasons for this gracious order of the family, it can be taught by precept and example. "Paul directs all parents to bring up their children 'in the discipline and doctrine of the Lord.'"[101] The neglect of this discipline has ample evidence in the families of believers as well as unbelievers. You have seen the proof with your own eyes.[102]

a. The Well-Ordered Family

Wesley commended to his connection of spiritual formation *The Well-Ordered Family* by Isaac Ambrose (in a separate volume of the Christian Library). This moral exposition includes a section titled "The Duties of Children to Parents."[103] The premise is this: "Children have received their substance from the very substance of their parents, and therefore they are to perform this duty of love and fear to them."[104] Here Ambrose compares the love of the child for the parent to love, which, "like sugar, sweetens fear; and fear, like salt, seasons love."[105] Love and fear are mixed in the relation. The fear of a child is not the fear of a servant. It is a reverence rooted in love.[106] Children are called to offer reverent respect to their parents and are called to obey "the commands, instructions, reproofs and corrections of their parents" because of God, whom the parents represent.[107] "Children must remember, that whatsoever they do to their parents they do it to God; when they disobey them,

---

[97]"On Obedience to Parents," B 3:365, J VII:101, sec. 1.6.
[98]"On Obedience to Parents," B 3:366, J VII:103, sec. 1.7.
[99]Ibid.
[100]"On Obedience to Parents," B 3:366, J VII:102, sec. 1.8.
[101]"On Obedience to Parents," B 3:366, J VII:103, sec. 1.7; cf. Eph. 6:4.
[102]"On Obedience to Parents," B 3:366, J VII:102, sec. 1.8.
[103]*WOF*, sec. 7.
[104]*WOF*, sec. 7.1; CL 8:72–85.
[105]*WOF*, sec. 7.1.
[106]*WOF*, sec. 7.2–2b; CL 8:72–85.
[107]Eph. 6:1; Prov. 1:8–9; *WOF*, sec. 7.2; CL 8:72–85.

they disobey God; when they please them, they please God; when their parents are justly angry with them, GOD is angry with them; nor can they recover GOD's favor … till they have submitted themselves to their parents, with this limitation, that they submit or obey them 'in the Lord.'"[108] This honor is due to the parents not only for their physical being but "for their parents' kindness, care, and cost towards them, in the way of thankfulness. In sickness, they must visit them; in want they must provide for them; in time of danger, they must endeavor to effect their protection."[109]

b. Conquering Fallen Self-Will

The parent has the singular duty of breaking the fallen nature's self-will. It is a task that must proceed through various stages of development of the maturing will in accord with the child's ability to discern and reason and listen to conscience. The example of the parent has far more effect than what the parent says. Neither marriage nor grandparenting causes the command to be suspended or to become entirely irrelevant. The parent may, in the fulfillment of this command, be called upon to resist the grandparents' tendency to indulgence. But at whatever age, the duty remains. It must be attentive to changing circumstances of maturity. It will best be applied through prudent judgment.[110]

Wesley takes the shaping of the will very seriously: "To inform their understanding is a work of time, and must proceed by slow degrees; but the subjecting the will is a thing which must be done at once — and the sooner the better."[111]

"Let none persuade you it is cruelty to do this; it is cruelty not to do it."[112] As self-will is the root of all sin and misery, so whatever cherishes this in children ensures their after-wretchedness…. Whatever checks and mortifies it promotes their future happiness."[113]

When parents neglect timely correction, children are tempted to habituate stubborn wills.[114] This correction is "the only foundation for a religious education. When this is thoroughly done, then a child is capable of being governed by the reason of its parent, till its own understanding comes to maturity."[115] "Religion is nothing else but the doing of the will of God, and not our own."[116] "It is chiefly owing to this that so many religious parents bring up children that have no religion at all."[117]

c. Consequences of Excessive Fondness and Parental Neglect

Every parent has to fight against excessive fondness.[118] Parents are called to

---

[108]Eph. 6:1, 3; *WOF*, sec. 7.2b; CL 8:72 – 85.
[109]*WOF*, sec. 2.2b; CL 8:72 – 85.
[110]"On Obedience to Parents," B 3:365 – 66, J VII:102 – 3, sec. 1.6 – 7.
[111]"On Obedience to Parents," B 3:367 – 68, J VII:104, sec. 1.10.
[112]Ibid.
[113]Ibid.
[114]Ibid.
[115]Ibid.
[116]Ibid.
[117]"On Obedience to Parents," B 3:368, J VII:104, sec. 1.11.
[118]"On Obedience to Parents," B 3:369, J VII:105, sec. 2.3.

discipline their children even when that requires resisting the culture and their own natural desires. Do not be intimidated by the child's resistance. You have a duty: nurture the will of the child to good health in body and spirit. "O never be weary of this labor of love; and your labor will not always be in vain."[119] Do not reward them for disobedience. That teaches them to disobey.[120]

Why do parents avoid this responsibility? Wesley's candid answer may shock some modern parents: "Because you are a coward; because you want resolution. And doubtless it requires no small resolution to begin and persist."[121]

d. Persistence in Parenting

Where does the strength come from to persist in parenting? Not from self or nature alone, but from grace. This "requires no small patience, more than nature ever gave. The grace of God is sufficient to give you diligence as well as resolution: without much pains you cannot conquer. Nothing can be done with a slack hand. 'You can do all things through Christ that strengtheneth you.'"[122]

Laziness can be as great an obstacle as cowardice. "Labor on; never tire; lay line upon line, till patience has its perfect work."[123] Do not let cowardice or a misplaced "fondness" become an obstacle to your love for your child, which requires gentle, patient, tough-minded discipline.[124] The longer you wait to make discipline effective, the harder it will be. Parents must pattern by their own behavior the simple life of humble truth-telling.

An admonition to grandparents: "Never take the part of the children against their parent."[125]

Who is at fault for this widespread neglect of discipline? "Why did not you break their will from their infancy?" What if it is too late? "At least do it now; better late than never. It should have been done before they were two years old. It may be done at eight or ten, though with far more difficulty. However, do it now; and accept that difficulty as the just reward for your past neglect."[126]

4. A Direct Appeal to Children Old Enough to Understand

Wesley ended with a direct appeal to children and youth old enough to understand: "As soon as you come home, as soon as you set foot within the door, begin an entirely new course; look upon your father and mother with new eyes; see them as representing your Father which is in heaven. Endeavour, study, rejoice to please, to help, to obey them in all things."[127]

---

[119]"On Obedience to Parents," B 3:368 – 69, J VII:104, sec. 2.1.
[120]"On Obedience to Parents," B 3:369, J VII:105, sec. 2.2.
[121]Ibid.
[122]Phil. 4:13; "On Obedience to Parents," B 3:369, J VII:105, sec. 2.2.
[123]"On Obedience to Parents," B 3:369, J VII:105, sec. 2.2.
[124]"On Obedience to Parents," B 3:369, J VII:105, sec. 2.3.
[125]"On Obedience to Parents," B 3:370, J VII:106, sec. 2.5.
[126]Ibid.
[127]"On Obedience to Parents," B 3:372, J VII:107 – 8, sec. 2.8.

Ponder the command: "Children, obey your parents in all things."[128] If you really have a desire to please God, you will want to understand God's way of providing guidance. "Deal faithfully with your own souls."[129] "Is your conscience now clear? Do you abstain from everything which they dislike, as far as you can in conscience?" Do you study "to make their lives as easy and pleasant as you can?"[130] If so, the promise is to you: "Honor your father and your mother, so that you may live long in the land the Lord your God is giving you" (Ex. 20:12). Even smaller children can learn to "behave not barely as their child, but as their servant for Christ's sake."[131]

If you are the child of godly parents, express your gratitude. Let it shine forth in your behavior. How can you expect grace from God if you do not receive the grace God gives you through your parents?[132] "But suppose you have, by an uncommon miracle of mercy, tasted of the pardoning love of God, can it be expected, although you hunger and thirst after righteousness, after the perfect love of God, that you should ever attain it ... while you live in the wilful transgression of a known law of God, in disobedience to your parents?"[133] If you obey your parents, you will find "in a manner unknown before, God will bless you to them and them to you."[134]

We have set forth the core line of reasoning of the trio of the major teaching homilies on God's grace, plan, and calling for families, parents, and children. Now we turn to the aesthetic side of Wesley's teaching. These teachings represent the rudiments of what might be called primitive Wesleyan aesthetics.

D. The Power of Music

1. Thoughts on the Power of Music

a. The Power to Lift the Soul

The power of music is "its power to affect the hearers; to raise various passions in the human mind ... to inspire love or hate, joy or sorrow, hope or fear, courage, fury, or despair ... and to vary the passion just according to the variation of the music."[135]

Wesley was intrigued by the question of why "modern music has less power than the ancient" ["Thoughts on the Power of Music," J:XIII 470–74 (Inverness, Scotland, June 9, 1779); cf. JJW 6:238]. By "modern" Wesley meant the 1780s.

Even with its great advantages, Wesley thought that music in his day had lost much of its power to lift the soul.[136] Why? Instruments and technologies were better. So why had the power of music become encumbered?[137]

---

[128]"On Obedience to Parents," B 3:371, J VII:106–7, sec. 2.6.
[129]"On Obedience to Parents," B 3:371, J VII:107, sec. 2.6.
[130]Ibid.
[131]"On Obedience to Parents," B 3:372, J VII:107, sec. 2.8.
[132]"On Obedience to Parents," B 3:371, J VII:107, sec. 2.8.
[133]"On Obedience to Parents," B 3:372, J VII:107–8, sec. 2.8.
[134]Ibid.
[135]"Thoughts on the Power of Music," J XIII:470, sec. 1.
[136]"Thoughts on the Power of Music," J XIII:470, secs. 1–2.
[137]"Thoughts on the Power of Music," J XIII:470, sec. 2.

The power of ancient music has been extolled since 324 BC at Susa in the Court of Alexandria, where the effects of the ancient Greek musician Timotheus were capable of inducing ecstatic experience. He was able through "the power of a single harp, to transport, as it were, the mind out of itself."[138] Wesley thought this had been most "beautifully described by Dryden, in his Ode on St. Cecilia's Day."

b. Modern Deterioration of the Power of Music

What happened to music in its transit from Timotheus to eighteenth-century England? "No such effects attend the modern music."[139] Wesley thought music in his day had lost the capacity of simple melody. With the help of his brother Charles, he sought to recover simple melodies that could be sung by everyone.

Rather, what had occurred in Wesley's day was a superficial baroque attempt at fanciful and made-up chords and musical sequences designed to amaze rather than uplift the soul. Wesley thought that "ever since counterpoint has been invented ... it has altered the grand design of music," so much that "it has well-nigh destroyed its effects."[140]

He contrasted ancient and modern music: "We have many capital pieces of ancient music," he said. But he thought that music had fallen into "the hands of the curious."[141] Modern music is not applied to the uplifting of the soul, but "to a quite different faculty of the mind; not to our joy, or hope, or fear; but merely to the ear, to the imagination, or internal sense."[142] The fixation is on sheer invention.

Much modern music consists "altogether of artificial sounds" that do not lift "judgment, reason, common sense." Music is reduced to "unmeaning sound!"[143] Choral music has been reduced to performance, not heart song. The intention is to amaze, not edify. John and Charles set out to train the revival movement in singable hymns. Those hymns are still sung today throughout the world.

c. Sounds That Lift the Soul

As a corrective, Wesley commended the simplicity of plain "Scotch or Irish airs. They are composed, not according to art, but nature.... They are simple in the highest degree." They are rich in "much melody." "If ever we should return to the simplicity and melody of the ancients, then the effects of our music will be as surprising as any that were wrought by theirs; yea, perhaps they will be as much greater, as modern instruments are more excellent than those of the ancients."[144]

---

[138]"Thoughts on the Power of Music," J XIII:470, sec. 3.
[139]"Thoughts on the Power of Music," J XIII:471, sec. 3.
[140]"Thoughts on the Power of Music," J XIII:470, sec. 5.
[141]"Thoughts on the Power of Music," J XIII:470, sec. 6.
[142]"Thoughts on the Power of Music," J XIII:470, sec. 7.
[143]"Thoughts on the Power of Music," J XIII:470, sec. 8.
[144]"Thoughts on the Power of Music," J XIII:473, sec. 12.

2. A Collection of Hymns for the Use of the People Called Methodist

The Wesley brothers viewed the writing of poetry and hymnody as central to their evangelical ministry. Charles wrote more than five thousand hymns, and John wrote, edited, and published many. Among this massive hymnody, many were prepared for use in family worship, where the Christian family gathered in the evening for prayer, Scripture, and song. This feature of Methodist tradition survived to my childhood in the 1930s and 1940s, when through depression and war our family gathered in the evening to sing these Wesleyan hymns.

E. Some Finer Points of Christian Education: On Taste, Genius, and Memory

In considering the education of young people, Wesley wrote four brief pieces on taste, music, genius, and memory, all published in the 1780s. Since they are germane to the task of educating and parenting, I include them here beside the three lengthier teaching homilies above. They, too, deal with the right ordering of family life and the educating tasks of good parenting.

1. Thoughts upon Taste

a. Defining Taste in Christian Aesthetics

When Wesley, in 1780, read Alexander Gerard's "Essay on Taste,"[145] he found many of its assertions "exceedingly disputable." Lacking a clear definition of taste, he proceeded to provide one in his short note on "Thoughts upon Taste" [J XIII:465–70 (1780)].

Taste is a puzzling word. Its meaning extends beyond simple imagination or brilliance. It has few synonyms and an intentionally ambiguous definition. Few have attempted to define it. Wesley said, "A man of taste is almost the same with a man of genius, a man of sense, or a man of judgment; but none of these mean exactly the same thing."[146] Joseph Addison had argued that taste is a metaphor "to express that faculty of mind which distinguishes the most concealed faults and nicest perfections in writings."[147]

b. A Metaphor for Relishing What Is Good

Wesley partially agreed with Addison but found his definition far too narrow, since taste refers to other gifts beyond writings. He conceded to Addison that taste is a "faculty of the soul which discovers the beauties of an author with pleasure,

---

[145]Alexander Gerard, "Essay on Taste," Edinburgh and London: J. Bell, W. Creech, and T. Cadell, London, 1780.
[146]"Thoughts upon Taste," J XIII:466, sec. 4.
[147]*The Spectator*, no. 409, Thursday, June 19, 1712.

and his imperfections with dislike," yet this was hardly definitive, since taste can be applied to that faculty of mind that applies to many things beyond words.[148]

The metaphor of taste comes from the familiar experience of eating and smelling. But rightly understood it has both an outward and an inward meaning: "By the external sense we relish various foods, and distinguish one from the other. By the internal, we relish and distinguish from each other various foods offered to the mind. Taste is therefore that internal sense which relishes and distinguishes its proper object."[149] Taste cannot be reduced to biological terms. It requires an inward response of mind and soul to the empirical experience.

Taste is an act of relishing what is good. No one relishes what is evil or base. Said Wesley, "By relishes, I mean, perceives with pleasure; for in the common acceptation of the word, we are not said to have a taste for displeasing, but only for pleasing, objects. And as various as those objects are, so various are the species of taste."[150] Taste is a metaphor that extends to music, poetry, and architecture, and even to mathematics and physics, as when we say, "It is a beautiful theory" or "It has exquisite proportions."

When we say that "a man has a taste for the mathematics, we mean by that expression, not only that he is capable of understanding them, but that he takes pleasure therein ... he finds a sweetness in the study of them."[151] The taste for beauty has many species: beauties of nature, of art, of "flowers, meadows, fields, or woods ... for painting or poetry."[152] A species of taste is "that which relates to the objects that gratify the imagination."[153]

2. Engendering a Taste for the Beauty of Holiness

a. Relishing Goodness

The metaphor of taste can also apply to the moral life. For beyond these forms of taste relating to objects, there is a quite different form: an "internal sense, whereby we relish the happiness of our fellow-creatures, even without any reflection on our own interest, without any reference to ourselves ... which interests us in the welfare, not only of our relatives, our friends, and our neighbors, but of those who are at the greatest distance from us, whether in time or place.... The most generous minds have most of this taste for human happiness."[154] This form of taste takes pleasure not just in something that we find pleasurable but in that which is beyond our private interest, beautiful in itself, whether perceived or not.

We relish "a beauty in virtue, in gratitude, and disinterested benevolence." Many discern and relish this beauty wherever they find it. They have a taste for moral

---

[148]"Thoughts upon Taste," J XIII:466, sec. 5.
[149]"Thoughts upon Taste," J XIII:466, sec. 6.
[150]Ibid.
[151]"Thoughts upon Taste," J XIII:467 – 68, sec. 7.
[152]"Thoughts upon Taste," J XIII:467, sec. 8.
[153]Ibid.
[154]"Thoughts upon Taste," J XIII:467, sec. 9.

excellence. "Does it not give them one of the most delicate pleasures whereof the human mind is capable? Is not this taste of infinitely more value, than a taste for any or all the pleasures of imagination? And is not this pleasure infinitely more delicate, than any that ever resulted, yea, or can result, from the utmost refinements of music, poetry, or painting?"[155] A taste for moral excellence has greater capacity for enjoyment than a taste for anything worldly. It transcends what can be seen with the eyes, however beautiful. For it is beautiful of itself.

This taste for moral beauty is a taste that anyone may have, and most do in some form.[156]

b. Low Taste, High Taste for Moral Goodness

Hence taste may have lower and higher forms. In any arena, whether architecture or poetry or music, "a dull taste is properly one that is faint and languid, that has no lively perception of its object."[157] By a man of dull taste, I mean one who relishes dull things, such as unimaginative compositions in music or poetry or coarse and worthless pictures. "But this is more properly termed a bad taste," as when one is "hugely pleased with the daubing of a sign-post." It is bad taste when one "supposes things to be excellent which are not."[158] Wesley was seeing what we are experiencing in our culture today when we speak of the coarsening of modern society, the devolution of taste, such as music's reduction to high decibels, heavy beats, lewd lyrics, and glorified violence — all those heightened passions that are so familiar to contemporary art forms. Wesley's examples in his society were bad poetry ("doggerel verses"), "coarse and worthless pictures," and noisy, piercing music in which every admired sound was turned into the sound of bagpipes.

Dull taste takes pleasure in dull things. Good taste takes pleasure in good things. People have good taste when they discern and relish whatever is "truly excellent in its kind."[159]

Why is the worshiping community interested in cultivating good taste in music, art, literature, philosophy, and the moral life? "Such a taste as this is much to be desired," since it "greatly increases those pleasures of life which are not only innocent, but useful. It qualifies us to be of far greater service to our fellow-creatures. It is more especially desirable for those whose profession calls them to converse with many; seeing it enables them to be more agreeable, and consequently more profitable, in conversation."[160] The cultivation of good taste does not happen without practice.

c. Measuring Good Taste by the Wisdom of the Ancients

How do I find out whether I possess this faculty? Addison had the correct response: "Read over the celebrated works of antiquity." There we find the acquired

---

[155]"Thoughts upon Taste," J XIII:467, sec. 10.
[156]"Thoughts upon Taste," J XIII:468, sec. 11.
[157]"Thoughts upon Taste," J XIII:468, sec. 12.
[158]Ibid.
[159]"Thoughts upon Taste," J XIII:468, sec. 13.
[160]"Thoughts upon Taste," J XIII:469, sec. 14.

tastes of experienced minds. There we see criteria that have stood the test of many times and cultures. "If, upon the perusal of such writings, he does not find himself delighted in an extraordinary manner; or if, upon reading the admired passages in such authors, he finds a coldness and indifference in his thoughts, he ought to conclude, not (as is most common among tasteless readers) that the author wants those perfections which have been admired in them, but that he himself wants [lacks] the faculty of discerning them."[161] If you read Plato and he puts you to sleep, the fault does not lie in Plato but in you. You must work to see what's there, acquire good taste for ideas and sounds, and be ready to grasp a gift when it is given.

This awareness will be heightened as an acquired faculty of mind by becoming "conversant with the writings of the best authors,"[162] by hearing those sounds that have stood the test of time. Conversation with these great minds is a "means of improving our natural taste," which may "furnish us with hints which we did not attend to,"[163] and awaken our senses.

Developing a taste for the good is a social experience. It occurs when we converse freely with persons of good taste as they open a window in our soul. In time "we may learn to correct whatever is yet amiss in our taste."[164] Good taste directs the least of us to "that glorious end, the 'pleasing [of] all men for their good unto edification.'"[165] Paul writes to the Romans: "Each of us should please our neighbors for their good, to build them up" (Rom. 15:2 NIV). A taste for the true and the good is edifying to those nearby.

3. Thoughts on Genius

a. Defining Genius

Some parents may be quite surprised that their child has extraordinary competencies in thinking, imagining, understanding, or exercising taste. Just as the disabled child must be offered forms of education favorable to his development, so must the highly gifted child. Despite intense searching, Wesley could not find "one proper definition" for *genius* in the literature of his time. Though widely used, the term had not been well understood. So he set out to speak plainly on encouraging the highly gifted mind ["Thoughts on Genius," J XIII:477 – 79, written from Lambeth, England, November 8, 1787].

Wesley proposed this definition of *genius*: "An extraordinary capacity for philosophy, oratory, poetry, or any other art or science; the constituent parts whereof are a strong understanding, and a lively imagination; and the essential property, a just taste."[166] More definition was needed to grasp the dynamics of this "extraordinary capacity."

---

[161]"Thoughts upon Taste," J XIII:469, sec. 15.
[162]"Thoughts upon Taste," J XIII:465 – 70, sec. 16.
[163]Ibid.
[164]"Thoughts upon Taste," J XIII:469 – 70, sec. 17.
[165]Ibid.
[166]"Thoughts on Genius," J XIII:479, sec. 9.

Wesley distinguished between two meanings of *genius*: "a quality of the human mind" and "a man endued with that quality." These meanings are exemplified in our saying indifferently, "He has a genius" and "He is a genius." Wesley's main interest is in the first meaning: the quality of mind that we commonly recognize as genius.[167]

b. The Essential Quality of Genius

The quality that we immediately notice in a person of genius is imagination. But the description of genius is not fully expressed by terms such as *inventiveness* or *sensation* or *memory* or *capacity for association of ideas* if any of these are taken alone. Rather, "it seems to be an extraordinary capacity of mind," or "extraordinary talents."[168]

The quality of mind we call "genius" may take one of two forms: the general form of "an extraordinary capacity for many things"; or a particular genius, "an extraordinary capacity for one particular thing." For example, in its particular form, Homer had an extraordinary capacity for poetry, Archimedes for geometry, and Isaac Newton for natural philosophy. But Aristotle and Francis Bacon were exemplars of those few minds who "seem to have had a universal genius, an extraordinary capacity to excel in whatever they took in hand."[169] Genius in philosophy, poetry, and oratory seems to imply a strong and clear understanding connected with an unusually extensive and lively imagination. This endowment comes to some extent "by nature, not by art." Yet "art may exceedingly improve what originally sprung from nature."[170] That which springs from nature appears to have been given from the beginning. That which springs from what Wesley called "art" is acquired by the improvement of taste.

To describe the essential property of genius, Wesley turned again to the metaphor of taste: "Taste is here a figurative word, borrowed from the sense of tasting, whereby we are enabled first to judge of, and then to relish, our food. So the intellectual taste has a twofold office: It judges, and it relishes. In the former respect, it belongs to the understanding; in the latter, to the imagination."[171]

The parents of gifted children do well to recognize and encourage both the natural and acquired aspects of these gifts.

4. Thoughts on Memory

Since the learning process involves excellence of memory, Wesley sought to describe accurately just what memory is. In 1756 Wesley had argued the importance of good memory to the work of ministry ["An Address to the Clergy," J X:481–82; cf. "The Good Steward," B 2:290–94; "On Temptation," B 3:156–68, J VI:479–80, sec. 1.7]. Very late in his life, in 1789, Wesley added a short piece called "Thoughts on

---

[167]"Thoughts on Genius," J XIII:477, sec. 3.
[168]"Thoughts on Genius," J XIII:478, secs. 3–4.
[169]"Thoughts on Genius," J XIII:478, sec. 4.
[170]"Thoughts on Genius," J XIII:479, sec. 6.
[171]"Thoughts on Genius," J XIII:479, secs. 8–9.

Memory" [J XIII:480 (Yarmouth, UK, October 21, 1789)], ending with a doxology on memory in the education of the soul.

Wesley concedes the close relation between "memory, reminiscence, and recollection. But what is the difference between them?" Memory may "exert itself sometimes in simply remembering, sometimes in reminiscence or recollection." These are not precisely the same. "In reminiscence, or recalling what is past, the mind appears to be active." Further, "Recollection seems to imply something more than simple reminiscence; even the studious collecting and gathering up together all the parts of a conversation or transaction, which had occurred before, but had in some measure escaped from the memory."[172]

The most mystifying form of memory, however, occurs when there is "a kind of inward voice ... which, like an echo, not only repeats the same words without the least variation, but with exactly the same accent and the same tone of voice. The same echo repeats any tune you have learned, without the least alteration."[173] Correlated with this form of memory are the gifts of the Spirit, which Wesley discusses elsewhere extensively. Grace makes present to consciousness an "inward voice" that is sustained repeatedly through time. After pronouncing a verse or phrase, "you can repeat, in your mind, the words you spoke or heard, without ever opening your lips, or uttering any articulate sound. Now, how is this done?" It remains unfathomable, yet Wesley said, "[I am] as sure of the fact" of this sort of memory "as I am that I am alive." He had experienced this form of time-transcending memory so much that he could attest it as an experienced reality, a datum of consciousness itself.

"But who is able to account for it? Whether it is a faculty of mind or body or both is unfathomable." Wesley could only exclaim, "O how shall we comprehend the ever-blessed God, when we cannot comprehend ourselves!"[174] This is the memory that brings the one who remembers to doxology.

Further Reading on Pastoral Care for the Family

Coe, Bufford W. *John Wesley and Marriage*. Cranbury, NJ: Lehigh University Press, 1996.

Dallimore, Arnold A. *Susanna Wesley: The Mother of John and Charles Wesley*. Grand Rapids: Baker, 1993.

Edwards, Maldwyn. *Family Circle: A Study of the Epworth Household in Relation to John and Charles Wesley*. London: Epworth, 1961.

Headley, Anthony J. *Family Crucible: The Influence of Family Dynamics in the Life and Ministry of John Wesley*. Eugene, OR: Wipf & Stock, 2010.

---

[172]"Thoughts on Memory," J XIII:480.
[173]Ibid.
[174]Ibid.

CHAPTER 5

Pastoral Care for the Family through Its Life Stages

Introduction: Counseling through the Life Cycle

Spiritual shepherds must be attentive to the particular concerns of each life stage of the flock; from singleness to marriage to child-raising to mature adulthood to facing death. Wesley discussed all five of these stages.

A. Covenant Partnership before God

1. Thoughts on a Single Life

In the pages that follow, we will see how highly Wesley valued marriage and the upbringing of godly children. But before that, we note Wesley's strong affirmation of the single life.

In 1743 Wesley published a short essay titled "Thoughts on a Single Life." It was reprinted in 1784 ["Thoughts on a Single Life," J XI:457 – 63]. He described with affection that special form of the holy life that accompanies singleness.

Scripture teaches that we may be holy in either the single life or the married life.[1] The call to holiness in relation to God-given sexuality applies to both the married and single states in equal measure. But one who is unmarried is remarkably free to offer up his or her whole life to God. Those who are married know all too well that they have responsibilities for providing for their families, pleasing their spouses, and carrying out all that is involved in raising children.

Wesley did not want to be misunderstood on the value of marriage. He began by making it clear that "marriage should be honored by all, and the marriage bed kept pure" (Heb. 13:4 NIV).[2] But in this essay, he focused on a life of greater freedom than may be possible in marriage.

Wesley carefully examined Paul's advice to new believers in 1 Corinthians 7, especially to the unmarried and to widows. He told them that it would be good for them to "stay unmarried, as I do. But if they cannot control themselves, they should marry, for it is better to marry than to burn with passion" (vv. 8 – 9 NIV). If they

---

[1]"Thoughts on a Single Life," J XI:457, sec. 1.
[2]"Thoughts on a Single Life," J XI:457, sec. 4.

marry, they will not have sinned. However, they will have additional responsibilities that come with taking on a spouse and family (1 Cor. 7:28).

a. The Undistracted Life

Paul hoped that new believers would not already be loaded down with unnecessary worldly cares. He hoped that some might feel the calling to choose to "serve the Lord without distraction" (1 Cor. 7:8, 28, 32 – 35).[3] The gift of the holy life is most powerfully given when we are first justified. That is the most promising moment to reflect soberly on marriage and singleness.[4]

Those who freely chose the single life are exempt from "a thousand nameless domestic trials."[5] They are "at liberty from the greatest of all entanglements, the loving one creature above all others."[6] On this basis, Wesley went against all assumptions of narcissism so common in modernity by arguing that it is easier "wholly to conquer our natural desires than to gratify them."[7]

Paul had been asked by the church at Corinth to teach them about Christian sexual morality. He wrote: " 'It is good for a man not to have sexual relations with a woman.' But since sexual immorality is occurring, each man should have sexual relations with his own wife, and each woman with her own husband. The husband should fulfill his marital duty to his wife, and likewise the wife to her husband" (1 Cor 7:1 – 3 NIV). If a man enters into an enduring physical relationship with a woman, each must exercise prudent forethought in order to be responsible for the consequences.

But not all are called to be bound by marital responsibilities. It is a question of vocation: "Each of you has your own gift from God; one has this gift, another has that" (1 Cor. 7:7). Marriage is not a requisite for the holy life. All whose lives are oriented toward eternal happiness will pray for discernment of their calling with respect to singleness and marriage. Singleness is not for everyone; it is only for those who receive a gift for singleness. Jesus said of holy singleness: "Not everyone can accept this word, but only those to whom it has been given" (Matt. 19:11). Let those who are called and enabled to receive the glorious gift of singleness receive it.

2. The Special Freedom of the Single Life

In singleness you are free to have only one care, not many that lead to ambiguity. You can take special joy in being freed from the anxieties and guilt that go along with sexual commitment with its innumerable consequences. For some it is

---

[3]"Thoughts on a Single Life," J XI:457, sec. 3; Luke 10:38 – 42.
[4]"Thoughts on a Single Life," J XI:458, sec. 5.
[5]"Thoughts on a Single Life," J XI:458, sec. 6.
[6]"Thoughts on a Single Life," J XI:459, sec. 6.
[7]"Thoughts on a Single Life," J XI:459, sec. 5.

extremely difficult to give your whole heart to God when another has so large a share of it.[8]

The single person is freer to give all to God — all worldly substance, all time, all resources, gifts, and talents. If single, you can better pray and serve without interruption, for it is not necessary to get the consent of your partner.[9]

a. Only by Grace

But you cannot live the single life in your own strength. Only by grace is this divine gift possible,[10] and only by earnestly praying for grace can you receive the strength required. What is impossible for fallen man becomes possible with God's constant help and companionship. Sharing in a community of singles similarly committed may be a part of God's way of helping.[11] If so, "open your heart without reserve."[12]

By grace you are enabled to "keep your heart with all diligence." Resist the first overtures of temptation. Do not let vain thoughts enter into your house. Pray that God will take every thought captive to the obedience of Christ.[13] Resist the temptation to indolence and sloth. Find your happiness in God, not in the pleasures of the world. Those who care too anxiously and relentlessly for their own comfort and immediate pleasure, for a soft life of feeding their appetites and passions, "shall not inherit the kingdom of God."[14]

Wesley carefully avoided the overstatement of Pascal that we should avoid all pleasure,[15] for God "richly provides us with everything for our enjoyment" (1 Tim. 6:17 NIV).[16] You cannot totally resist pleasure without "destroying the body," which God has made for love in its highest expression.[17] Rather, "avoid all that pleasure which anyway hinders you from enjoying God."[18]

"Make full use of all the leisure you have"[19] while living free from fleshly entanglements. Choosing to stay single is not a choice to deprive yourself of joy. Enjoy all things in relation to the enjoyment of that one who brings the most joy, the eternal God. Any pleasure that stands in the way of happiness in God is not your happiness. If you take up your cross, the Son who took up his cross for you will enable you to bear it. Do God's will, and your own willing will be happily served.[20]

---

[8]"Thoughts on a Single Life," J XI:459–60, secs. 7–11.
[9]"Thoughts on a Single Life," J XI:459, sec. 7.
[10]"Thoughts on a Single Life," J XI:460, sec. 10.
[11]"Thoughts on a Single Life," J XI:460, sec. 11.
[12]"Thoughts on a Single Life," J XI:460, sec. 10.
[13]"Thoughts on a Single Life," J XI:461, sec. 12.
[14]"Thoughts on a Single Life," J XI:461, sec. 13.
[15]Ibid.
[16]Ibid.
[17]Ibid.
[18]"Thoughts on a Single Life," J XI:462, sec. 13.
[19]"Thoughts on a Single Life," J XI:462, sec. 14.
[20]"Thoughts on a Single Life," J XI:463, sec. 15.

B. The Choice to Have a Family

1. Becoming Husband and Wife

a. The First and Nearest Responsibility

As Christian families, "our house" requires order. That order begins with the very nature of gender differences and sexuality. A man and a woman, with all their differences, come together in coital love with the possibility, and more likely the probability, of producing offspring. The family is created out of love. To be in a family is to be asked to grow up within the order established by two people who love each other enough to commit their lives to each other and care for the children of their love.[21]

Toward whom is the husband's "first and nearest attention" to be directed? Wesley answered, "Undoubtedly your wife." The husband is called "to love [his wife] even as Christ loved the Church, when he laid down his life for it,"[22] to "use every possible means that she may be freed from every spot, and may walk unblamable in love."[23]

Toward whom is the wife's "first and nearest attention" to be directed? Undoubtedly to the husband. She is called to use every possible means that her husband may walk blameless in love. The goal is that each may be fulfilled in the other, their differences complementing each other's sufficiencies and insufficiencies. Both parents are leaders, but they lead in different ways according to their created gifts. Love your spouse as Christ loved the church.[24] The husband is called to sacrifice for the benefit of the wife, as is the wife for the husband.

b. The Sexual Ordering of God's Creation

The order of the family is designed to fulfill needs that arise out of the differences between a man and a woman. If a man and a woman were built exactly alike, there would be no family, no children, no sex. But men and women are built very differently. It is that God-given difference that engenders sexuality and love. Each complements the other. It is within the obvious order of these physical differences that different duties arise to complement each other. Children are better provided for if the man, unable to give birth or suckle children, can protect and defend the wife and family. This is not a social convention but an elementary fact showing forth the order implicit in the divine creation of male and female. Each spouse aims to free the other from every blemish, that their family may walk in love. Each wants the other to grow up to full maturity in the grace and love of God, not be stunted.[25]

To this husband and wife, God entrusts the souls of children. These are the "immortal spirits whom God hath for a time entrusted to your care, that you may

---

[21]"On Family Religion," B 3:337, J VII:78 – 79, secs. 1.4 – 2.1.
[22]"On Family Religion," B 3:338, J VII:78 – 79, sec. 2.1.
[23]Ibid.
[24]Ibid.
[25]"On Family Religion," B 3:337 – 38, J VII:78 – 79, sec. 2.1 – 3.

train them up in all holiness and fit them for the enjoyment of God in eternity. This is a glorious and important trust; seeing one soul is of more value than all the world beside." Compare the value of the soul of one child with the value of all worldly pleasures. Wesley thought there was no comparison. If you say you value most highly "my child, my very own flesh and blood," you are on the way to grasping your parental opportunity and challenge. "Every child, therefore, you are to watch over with the utmost care, that when you are called to give an account of each to the Father of spirits, you may give your accounts with joy and not with grief."[26]

2. God's Will in Sexual Complementarity

Children are born out of the sexual differences between a man and woman. Each child born is infinitely valuable, incomparable to any other finite value, because each child is born with a God-breathed soul, born specifically out of these God-given male-female differences. The soul is breathed into the child from conception by God the Spirit. The mystery of sexuality is that God is working through it, both by engendering pleasure and the bonding of man and woman, and in the creation of the enfleshed soul.[27]

Each soul is unique, as every parent knows. Each soul is free to risk decisions that may lead to good or ill. Hence the nurture of the soul is from the outset risk-laden and hazardous. The child is born as God's good creation but born into a history of sin. The child is not responsible for that history. But through parental guidance, the child is called to the fullest level of responsibility possible within a history of sin that constantly tempts to disorder and deceit.[28]

The parents are by their own choice undertaking the role as leaders of the family. They are called to love the children they have by grace brought into being, that those children may grow up in the aura of the love that begat them. Their responsibility is to watch over their children with care and draw them toward the holy life of faith active in love.[29]

C. Raising Children Together

1. How Two Godly Parents Can Raise One Godly Child

All of this leads Wesley toward a realistic assessment of what it takes to sustain healthy families. We are not to imagine that raising a healthy family will be easy, but the resulting gifts will exceed the difficulties because of God's blessing of grace.

The heart of Wesley's teaching homily "On Family Religion" focuses on the process of bending the wills of children in the direction of glorifying God in their daily behavior. How do parents do this?

Wesley had definite ideas that run against the grain of modern permissive

---

[26]"On Family Religion," B 3:339, J VII:79, sec. 2.2.
[27]"On Family Religion," B 3:338–39, J VII:79, sec. 2.2–3; cf. B 4:22–25.
[28]"On Family Religion," B 3:337–38, J VII:78–79, sec. 2.1–3.
[29]"On Family Religion," B 3:338–39, J VII:79, sec. 2.2–3; "On a Single Eye," B 126–30.

parenting. Underlying his teaching was a robust biblical and theological premise: a child's will is created good by God but gradually becomes fallen through the child's own choices amid a history of fallenness. This tendency to voluntarily succumb to temptation is universally observed wherever the free will makes choices in a fallen world. This vulnerability to sin must be resisted strongly, early, and with determination. As soon as the child is making choices, this fallen will must be curbed by persuasion and good judgment.[30]

2. Godly Instruction of Children: A Logical Implication of the Choice to Have Children

Parents have the responsibility of providing godly instruction for their children. No one else can do it. All later voices are too late. Godly instruction has to begin as soon as a child is capable of making decisions, even the simplest. If the parents default in this crucial task, the odds are raised against the child ever being able to glorify God and enjoy him forever. But once the fallen will of the child is effectively challenged by a plausible model of righteousness, which rightly should be embodied in the behavior of the parent, the child can then proceed step by step toward greater readiness to come before the majesty of God and learn obedience from God's revelation itself. Only by learning the law can they understand the benefits of the gospel that transforms it.[31]

Parents are given grace to do their job, but their own deficient habits often prevent them from making use of this special abundant grace offered to young parents.

The marriage bond is an incomparable, enduring gift of God. No spouse can stop the consequences of his or her sexual choices. And neither spouse is justly authorized to abandon the family. But whatever evil does occur in the family can always be overcome by doing good. And even when doing good does not seem to bear fruit, there still is no point at which earnest prayer cannot be made for the temptation or trial to be taken away or to be turned into a blessing.[32]

3. Toward Total Accountability between Husband and Wife

Wesley commended the works of the seldom-read Puritan nonconformist divine Isaac Ambrose (1604 – 64). He thought the work of Pastor Ambrose on the relation of husband and wife was sufficiently important that he published it as a Christian classic for the whole connection of spiritual formation. This work was "The Well-Ordered Family: Wherein the Duties of Its Various Members Are Described and Urged."[33] Since Wesley commended it, we will review it.

---

[30]"On Family Religion," B 3:339 – 40, J VII:80 – 81, sec. 3.4.
[31]"On Family Religion," B 3:338 – 39, J VII:79 – 81, sec. 3.1 – 3.
[32]"On Family Religion," B 3:338, J VII:79 – 80, sec. 3.2.
[33]*WOF.*

D. Marriage in the Lord

For a family to be happy, the husband and wife must share common values. Paul exhorted the Corinthian believers:

> Do not be yoked together with unbelievers. For what do righteousness and wickedness have in common? Or what fellowship can light have with darkness? What harmony is there between Christ and Belial? Or what does a believer have in common with an unbeliever? What agreement is there between the temple of God and idols? For we are the temple of the living God. As God has said: "I will live with them and walk among them, and I will be their God, and they will be my people." (2 Cor. 6:14–16 NIV)

1. The Rules Are Simple

Christian parents are called to "marry in the Lord, and then to live chastely in wedlock, that there may be an holy seed."[34] Those who do not "marry in the Lord" and do not live chastely in wedlock cannot expect to have that blessed family that flows out of holy love. The common duties that man and wife owe to each other are chastity in the relation of covenant fidelity in love, abundant affection of one another, and provident care of one for the other.[35]

The chief characteristic of the husband-wife relationship is the "loving and affectionate pouring out of their hearts, with much dearness into each other's bosom. This mutual melting-heartedness ... will infinitely sweeten and beautify the marriage state."[36] This is about as close as a Puritan divine could come to talking about a good sex life of mutual love. The biblical model of this melting compassion is found as blessed in the Canticles: "My fair one, my love, my dove, my undefiled, my well-beloved, the chief of ten thousand" (Song 5:10, paraphrased). Such a fervent and chaste love as this all married couples should imitate.[37] "When the knot is tied, every man should think his wife the fittest for him, and every wife should think her husband the fittest for her of any other in the world."[38]

2. Equal Partners: Husband and Wife

Two sacred texts are complementary: the command of God in Ephesians 5:25 is "Husbands, love your wives." The balancing command of God in Titus 2:4 is "Wives, love your husbands" (paraphrased). Never imagine that one is given without the other. Both covenant partners owe to each other "a provident care of one for the other; which should extend to the body," in light of the Scripture that teaches that "after all, no one ever hated their own body, but they feed and care for their body,

---

[34] *WOF*, sec. 6.2; CL, 2nd ed. 1819–27, 8:72–85.
[35] *WOF*, sec. 6.1.
[36] Ibid.
[37] Ibid.
[38] *WOF*, sec. 6.1; CL 8.

just as Christ does the church" (Eph. 5:29 NIV). The husband cares for his wife's body; the wife cares for her husband's body.

The husband's first duty is dearly to love "the wife of his bosom, to show that she ought to be as his heart in his bosom. He must love her at all times, he must love her in all things. Love must season and sweeten his speech, carriage, actions towards her. Love must show itself in his commands, reproofs, admonitions, instructions, authority, familiarity with her." She is an inheritor with him in the kingdom of heaven. She bears him children. Any lack of these features may "convert the paradise of marriage into an hell."[39]

3. How Are Spouses Called to Love?
Exactly as Christ Loved the Church

If the husband is to love his wife as Christ loved the church, what will that relationship look like? Christ's love for the church was "in every way free." Christ's love "began before the church could love him." The pattern of Christ's sacrificial love stirs the husband to take the lead in loving his beloved.[40] "Christ, having loved his own, loved them unto the end." His love sees to it that "no provocation shall ever change it. Such must be the love of husbands, firm love, an inviolable love," grounded in God's ordering of the family and based on "an inviolable resolution."[41] This resolution is accompanied by tender respect for the wife, providing for her needs and treating her as his companion and yoke fellow.

The wife is to be "[the husband's] delight, and the desire of his eyes." He will never be bitter against her, and he will never permit his wife "to sleep in displeasure." They will never let the sun go down upon their anger.[42]

If bitterness arises, as sometimes it may, he will "keep his words until a convenient time." Then confidentially, "in the spirit of meekness and love," he will speak to her. And if she is ever wayward, he is "mildly to suffer her, that she may not wax worse" (*WOF*, sec. 2.3b; CL 8). The husband should be "as the wellspring of liveliness, lightsomeness, lightheartedness to his wife: she has forsook all for him, and therefore she should receive from him a continual influence to cheerful walking" with her.[43] This is the duty of the husband to the wife.

The wife is similarly called to be ever attentive to her husband, a "helper to him all her days." She is called to remain "soft, pleasant, and amiable, though she be joined with thorns." She should be "meek, mild, gentle." If her husband requires something contrary to Christ, she will "prefer God before man." She is consoled by the thought that "conscientious wives ... have an husband in heaven, as well as on earth."[44] She will be careful to preserve his person, in sickness or health, in adversity

---

[39] *WOF*, sec. 2.2; CL 8.
[40] *WOF*, sec. 2.2; CL 8:72–85.
[41] *WOF*, sec. 2.4; CL 8.
[42] Ibid.
[43] *WOF*, sec. 2.2b; CL 8.
[44] *WOF*, sec. 2.2c; CL 8.

or prosperity, in youth or old age, "that she may help her husband, in erecting and establishing Christ's glorious kingdom in their house, and especially in their own hearts." Without these qualities "their family is but Satan's seminary, and a nursery for hell."[45]

Having set forth the argument of the well-ordered family that Wesley so highly commended to his connection, we return to Wesley's own writings on family religion.

E. Tough Love in the Changing Family

1. Guiding Children

Wesley believed it was the responsibility of each person in the family system to help the others avoid the temptation to sin.[46] This shared responsibility is for the good of the unity of the family because each one has a stake in the family's health.

a. Early and Often

Parents are called to guide children "early and often," always by reasoned argument, not exercise of sheer power. All correction occurs by gentle persuasion. "Instruct them early, from the first hour that you perceive reason begins to dawn ... far earlier than we are apt to suppose." Watch for "the first openings of the understanding" that you may "little and little supply fit matter" for the soul, turning "the eye of the soul toward good things.... From that time no opportunity should be lost of instilling all such truths as they are capable of receiving."[47]

Actively guide their intellectual and spiritual growth: "Take care that they have some time every day for reading, meditation, and prayer." No day should pass "without family prayer, seriously and solemnly performed."[48]

b. Correction through Gentle Persuasion

Parents are responsible for instructing children from the earliest stages of their capacity to reason.[49] "While they are young, you may restrain from evil not only by advice, persuasion, and reproof, but also by correction; only remembering that this means is to be used last."[50]

All corrections occur best by gentle persuasion. Only as a last resort is the rod used, and even then it should never be unleashed in a fit of anger.[51] "Do not set a bad example for the child to follow, indulging their desires, ignoring the needs of others, acceding to idolatrous loyalties, trivializing the serious business of living life in God. If parents act unjustly, the child will certainly follow."[52]

---

[45] WOF, sec. 2.2d; CL 8.
[46] "On Family Religion," B 3:338, J VII:79–80, sec. 3.1.
[47] "On Family Religion," B 3:340, J VII:81, sec. 3.6.
[48] "On Family Religion," B 3:340, J VII:81, sec. 3.5.
[49] Ibid.
[50] "On Family Religion," B 3:339, J VII:80, sec. 3.3.
[51] "On Family Religion," B 3:339, J VII:80, sec. 3.3–4.
[52] "On Family Religion," B 3:340, J VII:81, sec. 3.5.

Persuasion is preferred to coercion. Effective discipline happens by persuasion. Domestic workers who refuse to cooperate will find that it is in the best interest of all to find another roof under which to dwell.[53] Parents are called to exercise legitimate power to restrain family members from entering into temptation. This restraint is best expressed by gentle persuasion shaped by Christian prudence and conscience.[54]

Some think "a child need not be corrected at all." Wesley counters, "Unless you suppose yourself wiser than Solomon ... resort early to correction. Discipline your son while there is still hope. Do not be the one responsible for his death."[55]

2. Guiding the Child Unapologetically

a. Early, Plainly, Frequently, and Patiently

Four key adverbs describe how godly instruction should be administered: early, plainly, frequently, and patiently.[56] Start early. Speak plainly in a way children can understand. Ask God to open their eyes. Speak often to the child. Feed the soul as often as the body. Persevere in the task of instruction. Do not quit until the results bear fruit. Lacking fruits, keep praying for patience. Remember, you cannot be truly patient without mirroring God's own infinite patience.[57]

"Speak to them plainly. Use words little children can understand — words they would use themselves.[58] Wesley offers an example:

Bid the child look up, and ask, "What do you see there?"
"The sun."
"See, how bright it is! Feel how warm it shines upon your hand! Look, how it makes the grass and the flowers grow, and the trees and everything look green! But God (though you cannot see him) is above the sky, and is a deal brighter than the sun! It is he, it is God, that made the sun, and you and me, and everything. It is he that makes the grass and the flowers grow; that makes the trees green, and the fruit to come upon them! He loves you; he loves to do you good. He loves to make you happy. Should not you then love him! You love me, because I love you and do you good. But it is God that makes me love you. Therefore you should love him. And he will teach you how to love him."[59]

b. The Spirit Takes the Lead

God alone "can apply your words to their hearts; without which all your labor will be in vain. But whenever the Holy Ghost teaches, there is no delay in learning."[60] Let the whole family benefit by public instruction on the Lord's Day. Attend the ordinances of God. "Take care that they have some time every day for reading,

---

[53]"On Family Religion," B 3:338, J VII:79 – 80, sec. 3.1.
[54]Ibid.
[55]Quoting Prov. 19:18; "On Family Religion," B 3:339 – 40, J VII:80 – 81, sec. 3.4.
[56]"On Family Religion," B 3:338, J VII:81 – 82, sec. 3.6 – 10.
[57]"On Family Religion," B 3:339, J VII:81 – 82, sec. 3.7 – 10.
[58]"On Family Religion," B 3:341, J VII:82, sec. 3.7.
[59]Ibid.
[60]"On Family Religion," B 3:341, J VII:82, sec. 3.8.

meditation, and prayer." No day should pass "without family prayer, seriously and solemnly performed."[61]

Suppose you see no fruit. "You must not conclude that there will be none. Possibly the 'bread which you have cast upon the waters' may be 'found after many days.'"[62] If you do well, your "children grow in grace in the same proportion as they grow in years."[63]

It is reasonable for modern parents to ask how they can possibly follow Wesley's guidance in the present social situation of rampant disobedience, generational gaps, and risk-laden social and sexual experimentation. To try to answer those questions would take us far away from the purpose of this series, which is limited to stating precisely what Wesley taught without exaggeration or dilution. Present social vexations are not necessarily any thornier than they were in Wesley's day. Indeed, parents today have many advantages of education and technology that Wesley's era did not have. Contemporary social ills do not necessarily prevent modern parents from attempting to apply these instructions within contemporary social contexts.

3. Choosing the Child's Schooling

When the children of godly families come of age, parents should give thoughtful attention to their schooling. Parents do well to ask the fundamental question: For what purpose do we send our children to school? If the answer is upward mobility in this world, God's purpose in educating has already been lost. The deeper issue is: Do you mean this world or the next? "Otherwise to send them to school (permit me to speak plainly) is little better than sending them to the devil." Wesley was largely homeschooled. He firmly believed that a small school with a godly teacher is better than a large school that lacks the fear of God.[64]

Where should you send your girls? Bring them up yourself. Said Wesley, but "if you cannot breed them up yourself (as my mother did, who bred up seven daughters to years of maturity), send them to some mistress that truly fears God, one whose life is a pattern to her scholars, and who has only so many that she can watch over each as one that must give account to God." Avoid overcrowded classes and social climbing. Avoid schools for girls that teach them "pride, vanity, affectation, intrigue, artifice, and in short everything which a Christian woman ought not to learn."[65]

Likewise, for sons, do not just ask how they can achieve upward social mobility. It is better to ask: "In what employment will my son have the greatest advantage for laying up treasures in heaven?" Consider not "how he may get the most money" but "how he may get the most holiness!"[66] You are overseeing your son's education not just for this world but for eternity.

---

[61]"On Family Religion," B 3:340, J VII:81, sec. 3.5.
[62]"On Family Religion," B 3:342, J VII:83, sec. 3.11.
[63]"On Family Religion," B 3:342, J VII:83, sec. 3.12.
[64]"On Family Religion," B 3:342, J VII:83, sec. 3.13.
[65]"On Family Religion," B 3:343–44, J VII:84, sec. 3.14–15.
[66]"On Family Religion," B 3:344, J VII:84, sec. 3.16.

4. Parental Counsel Concerning Their Grown Children's Selection of a Mate

At some point, Wesley said,

Your son or your daughter is now of age to marry, and desires your advice relative to it. Now you know what the world calls a "good match" — one whereby much money is gained. But money seldom brings happiness, either in this world or the world to come.… If you are wise, you will not seek riches for your children by their marriage. See that your eye be single in this also: aim simply at the glory of God, and the real happiness of your children, both in time and eternity.

You might soon find yourself in the dilemma of "calling hell a 'good lodging' and the devil a 'good master.' "[67] This is where you will have great need of the "wisdom from above."[68] Riches seldom bring happiness. The purpose of marriage is to behold the glory of God shining through your children's humanity.

Those who follow these mandates for family maturity will be abundantly rewarded. As young people approach maturity and marriage, Christian parents will have a single mind and eye for their ultimate welfare.[69] "Whatever others do, let you and your house 'choose the Lord.' "[70]

F. Pastoral Care of the Dying

1. Facing Death

a. Death and Deliverance

From the outset of his ministry, Wesley was engaged in care of souls. Facing death is a key question for anyone's spiritual formation and for all forms of soul care. Everyone faces death, some distantly, some closely. The faithful face death no less than the unfaithful. Death is an intrinsic part of the design of Providence to draw our erratic wills toward steady faith and obedience.[71] Death is our teacher. What does death teach us?[72] That is the subject of Wesley's first sermon.

b. The Focus on Hope

Wesley was ordained as a deacon on September 19, 1725. The first sermon he wrote was on "Death and Deliverance" [Homily #133 (Buckinghamshire, England, September 1725), B 4:206 – 14]. It reveals how deeply he was pondering the relation of death and eternity.

---

[67]"On Family Religion," B 3:345, J VII:85, sec. 3.17.

[68]Ibid.

[69]Ibid.

[70]"On Family Religion," B 3:345 – 46, J VII:86, sec. 3.18.

[71]On physical death, see B 2:287 – 88.

[72]In chapter 11 of volume 2 of *John Wesley's Teaching: Christ and Salvation* (Grand Rapids: Zondervan, 2012), we explored the issues of the soul in death. See homily #132, "On Faith," Hebrews 11:1, B 4:189, sec. 2; cf. B:3:531 – 32; 4:386 – 88. Now we are thinking with Wesley about how the believer is called personally to face death.

Wesley was ever the pastoral teacher, even from this earliest effort. In this case, he was counseling the faithful on facing death with the hope divine grace provides. He already showed signs of being deeply influenced by the medieval tradition of spiritual formation on the art of dying (*ars moriendi*), readiness for death, and preparation for eternal life.

The focus is on the eternal happiness that awaits the faithful after death. This fleeting life is a preparation for eternity. In death we are "freed from the tyranny of sin."[73]

His text is Job 3:17. The consolation in death is that "the wicked cease from troubling." Those who have found that life is filled with troubles are invited to ponder the eternal rest for the weary at the end of life.

Although everyone complains that life is a burden, "it is a burden which very few are willing to lay down." The closer we come to death, the more we are sobered by it. "The thought of present death sets all our faculties in alarm."[74]

c. Insurmountable Happiness

Death is to be neither feared nor desired. For the faithful, it is to be understood as an entryway into the fullest imaginable life with God. At that juncture the people of God "rejoice with joy unspeakable and full of glory when they contemplate the inheritance of which they will one day be made partakers." They will see it no longer "through a glass, darkly" (1 Cor. 13:12).[75]

The lives of the faithful are "already possessed of a partial happiness," but present happiness is only an anticipation of "one more complete and perfect."[76] In that day, "to the absence of all evil shall be added the presence of all the good that a Being of infinite wisdom and power is able to bestow."[77] Then God will allow them to "possess the fullness of joy at his own right hand for evermore, and drink of the rivers of pleasure in the new Jerusalem."[78]

Eternal life "is infinitely superior to any happiness it is possible to arrive at in this world."[79] The faithful dead are "delivered from all those cares, afflictions, and dangers, all that anguish and anxiety, which is unavoidably their portion as long as they remain in this transitory life."[80] They shall no more hunger or thirst. From then on they are entirely "exempted from sorrow, need, and sickness, and from a possibility of any future adversity," enjoying perfect quiet and rest from their labors. "[God] will wipe every tear from their eyes" (Rev. 21:4 NIV). The faithful have "an inheritance incorruptible, and undefiled, and that fadeth not away" (1 Peter 1:4).[81]

---

[73]"Death and Deliverance," B 4:212, sec. 14.
[74]"Death and Deliverance," B 4:207, sec. 4.
[75]"Death and Deliverance," B 4:212, sec. 15.
[76]"Death and Deliverance," B 4:212–13, sec. 15.
[77]"Death and Deliverance," B 4:213, sec. 16.
[78]Ibid.
[79]Ibid.
[80]"Death and Deliverance," B 4:212, sec. 14.
[81]"Death and Deliverance," B 4:213, sec. 16.

d. Death Not to Be Feared

The deeper the faith, the more we are able to recognize that all these trials we face have been for our sake, to strengthen the will for good, and to prepare us for life with God. There we will see that "we have the promise of perfect happiness annexed to our obedience." This present awareness calls us all the more to "all holy conversation and godliness." This eternal vision enables us to "encounter all temporal afflictions" with patience.[82]

Paradoxically Wesley argues that the more sensible we are of our present weakness, the more we reasonably rejoice at our deliverance from it. What satisfaction a good man must have to "perceive [that] the good works he had begun in this life" are perfected in his future life. He will find "every one of those Christian virtues with which he had endeavored to adorn his soul improved and drawn out to its utmost extent."[83]

In only a small part of our lives can we lay any claim to real and durable happiness.[84] Even the wise are miserable if they lack eternal wisdom. "Such is the tax laid on knowledge by nature." Out of this experience, the preacher in Ecclesiastes moaned: "In much wisdom is much grief: and he that increaseth knowledge increaseth sorrow" (1:18).[85]

Death is terrible only to the natural man. We do not fear it "when we are assured that all these things work together for our good.... When we are defamed, reviled, or despitefully treated by men, let us comfort ourselves with the firm persuasion that we shall soon rest where the wicked cease from troubling."[86]

This is especially good news for those who are feeling oppressed with a sense of their inexorable physical limitations. These limitations will shortly be remedied. God will in his own good time reunite us with himself. "This corruptible shall put on incorruption, and this mortal be clothed with immortality."[87]

e. Giving Up the Idolatry of Temporal Values

Insofar as we remain in our idolatrous state, "the number of our faculties is in this respect a great inconvenience, since they afford us so many more capacities of suffering: every sense being an inlet to bodily pain, and every power of the mind [an inlet] to vexation of spirit." If any one part of our body is disordered, it gives discomfort to the whole of our body, and with the anxious imagination, seemingly the whole of the universe.[88]

The apostle Paul was not yearning for natural death when he wrote "to die is gain." Rather, he was looking beyond death to new life, sharing in Christ's resurrec-

---

[82]"Death and Deliverance," B 4:213, sec. 17.
[83]"Death and Deliverance," B 4:212, sec. 14.
[84]"Death and Deliverance," B 4:207, sec. 3.
[85]Ibid.
[86]"Death and Deliverance," B 4:213, sec. 17.
[87]Ibid.
[88]"Death and Deliverance," B 4:206, sec. 2.

tion. Christianity sees death as a prelude to new life. In this sense, death offers "a safe and quiet haven, an object of desire rather than fear; where we shall be secure from all future misfortune and danger, from the gusts of passion and the storms of malice and envy which, while we are fluctuating here, will be more or less continually beating against us."[89]

f. They Cease from Troubling

"We learn from Holy Writ that death is not only a haven, but an entrance into a far more desirable country — a land not flowing with milk and honey like the earthly Canaan, but with joys knowing neither cessation nor end." This enables the faithful to "bear up against the assaults of present evils and the fear of future evils." It is good news that all these sufferings come to an end. Misery passes away like a shadow. God has provided for the believer an eternal mansion "where sorrow and pain shall never know him." There "the wicked cease from troubling, and the weary are at rest."[90]

This side of death we find that even the most exemplary virtues can be despitefully used and distorted.[91] "Vice has always been observed to be of a contagious nature, and its progress is the more sure for being unperceived. The wicked drink iniquity like water, even though insipid and tasteless."[92] "They strive to terrify [their fellow man] by threats, or allure him by promises, and represent integrity as nothing but a dead weight, which only makes it the more difficult for him to rise.... That most of the evils of life are owing to wicked men may be proved both from reason and experience."[93]

Those with deceptive intentions will never cease from troubling in this temporal world. But they do not trouble in death. Death ends their twisted intent and supposed virtue.[94] Even when the wicked seem to have temporarily obtained their objectives, they cannot rob the faithful of their inheritance. "Innumerable are the calamities derived from this fountain, with which we are here obliged to maintain a perpetual conflict, till we are made partakers of that blessed rest the weary will enjoy when the wicked shall cease from troubling."[95]

2. Pastoral Care for the Bereaved

a. On Mourning for the Dead

At the funeral of an Oxford friend, John [Robin] Griffiths [Homily #133, "On Mourning for the Dead" (Worcestershire, England, January 15, 1726 or 1727), B 4:236 – 43], Wesley argued that inordinate grief may fail to grasp the grace that

---

[89]"Death and Deliverance," B 4:207, sec. 4.
[90]"Death and Deliverance," B 4:206, sec. 4.
[91]"Death and Deliverance," B 4:206, sec. 6.
[92]"Death and Deliverance," B 4:206, sec. 7.
[93]"Death and Deliverance," B 4:206, sec. 6.
[94]"Death and Deliverance," B 4:206, sec. 8.
[95]"Death and Deliverance," B 4:206, sec. 9.

God gives in challenging believers to face death with hope. What is to be learned from grief?

The setting of the text of 2 Samuel 12:23 is David's grief for the death of his son following his sin against Uriah. David's grief was ordered in different ways fitting to two different situations in the facing of death. Wesley observed that David was "just recovering the use of his reason and virtue after the bitterness of soul he had tasted from the death of a beloved son. He 'fasted and wept' and 'lay all night upon the earth.'" He refused comfort. Then he "came into his house, and behaved with his usual composure and cheerfulness." Wesley explained this "strange alteration in his proceedings," revealing the principles on which he acted." David said: "But now that he is dead, why should I go on fasting? Can I bring him back again? I will go to him, but he will not return to me" (NIV).[96] David knew how to weep, and he knew how to end weeping.

God knows how to extract good out of evil. God has shown us how the candid and faithful facing of death can be the beginning of increasing virtue and happiness. Facing death "greatly assists our imperfect reason."[97] Faith teaches us that we have nothing to fear of our own death and little to bemoan of the faithful friend who goes on to a heavenly abode.

Sacred bands are being torn asunder in death. But these bands are not forever broken, for they will be reunited in eternity.[98] Those who are not fond of misery will mourn but not let grief take over their lives. It is fitting to weep for a season but not to love the misery of weeping.[99] We must guard against allowing grief to "destroy the health of our bodies and impair the strength of our minds."[100]

God knows what is in man. God the Son has been tempted as we have. God knows our sorrow at temporal loss.[101] Put it in God's hands. All things work together for good for those who love the Lord.[102] "Those who sow with tears will reap with songs of joy" (Ps. 126:5 NIV).

Paul warned, "Brothers and sisters, we do not want you to be uninformed about those who sleep in death, so that you do not grieve like the rest of mankind, who have no hope. For we believe that Jesus died and rose again, and so we believe that God will bring with Jesus those who have fallen asleep in him.... Therefore encourage one another with these words" (1 Thess. 4:13 – 14, 18 NIV).

In death "a weary wanderer has at length come to his wished-for home."[103] "Why should I be so unreasonable, so unkind, as to desire the return of a soul, now in

[96]"On Mourning for the Dead," B 4:238, sec. 2.
[97]"On Mourning for the Dead," B 4:239, sec. 6.
[98]"On Mourning for the Dead," B 4:242, sec. 16.
[99]"On Mourning for the Dead," B 4:239, sec. 8.
[100]"On Mourning for the Dead," B 4:240, sec. 9.
[101]"On Mourning for the Dead," B 4:240, sec. 11.
[102]"On Mourning for the Dead," B 4:239, sec. 7.
[103]"On Mourning for the Dead," B 4:240, sec. 10.

happiness, to me, to this habitation of sin?"[104] A great gulf lies between the living and dead, but there will come a time when this gulf will be spanned.[105] There was no death prior to Adam's fall. If death did not exist before human nature was corrupted by sin, then it will not continue when human nature is restored to its ancient perfection.[106]

Who can blame one who drops a tear when a loved one passes on? "The tender meltings of a heart dissolved with fondness when it reflects on several agreeable moments which have now taken their flight never to return, give an authority to some degree of sorrow."[107] There is no way of describing the feelings and secret workings of the soul of a parent who has lost a child, or of a person who has lost a matchless friend.[108] Even well-fashioned words may be of no value. For one who has the applause of God and the confirmation of his own conscience, our well-formed words do little service to the dead.[109] Better to say "a few, plain, and hearty words, such as were his own, and such as were always most agreeable to him."[110] It is natural at these times to imagine that "the next summons may be our own; and that since death 'is the end of all men' without exception, 'tis high time for 'the living to lay it to heart.'"[111]

The comforter must not add grief to grief. "Have my tears or complaints the power to refix his soul in her decayed, forsaken mansion?... Would he wish to change, though the power were in his hands, the happy regions of which he is now possessed for this land of care, pain, and misery? O vain thought! Never can he, never will he, return to me. Be it my comfort, my constant comfort when my sorrows bear hard upon me, that I shortly, very shortly, shall go to him!"[112]

"I shall behold him again, and behold him with that perfect love, that sincere and elevated softness, to which even the heart of a parent is here a stranger! When the Lord God shall wipe away tears from my eyes, and the least part of my happiness will be that the sorrow of his absence shall flee away!"[113] Profuse sorrowing is unprofitable.[114] God is not the author of inordinate grief.[115] "Recur to the bright side of it, and reflect with cheerfulness and gratitude that our own time passes away like a shadow." Soon "this corruptible shall put on incorruption, and this mortal be clothed with immortality; and then we shall sing with the united choirs of men and angels, O death, where is thy sting? O grave, where is thy victory?"[116]

---

[104]"On Mourning for the Dead," B 4:240–41, sec. 12.
[105]"On Mourning for the Dead," B 4:241, sec. 12.
[106]"On Mourning for the Dead," B 4:239, sec. 5.
[107]"On Mourning for the Dead," B 4:242, sec. 16.
[108]Ibid.
[109]"On Mourning for the Dead," B 4:241, sec. 13.
[110]"On Mourning for the Dead," B 4:236–43, sec. 15.
[111]"On Mourning for the Dead," B 4:242, sec. 18.
[112]"On Mourning for the Dead," B 4:238, sec. 3.
[113]Ibid.
[114]"On Mourning for the Dead," B 4:238, sec. 4.
[115]"On Mourning for the Dead," B 4:238–39, sec. 5.
[116]"On Mourning for the Dead," B 4:243, sec. 19.

Further Reading on Pastoral Care
for the Family through Its Life Stages

Byrne, Herbert W. *John Wesley and Learning*. Salem, OH: Schmul, 1997.

Dunnam, Maxie D. *The Christian Way: A Wesleyan View of Spiritual Journey*. Grand Rapids: Zondervan, 1984.

Hynson, Leon O. *Through Faith to Understanding: Wesleyan Essays on Vital Christianity*. Lexington, KY: Emeth, 2005.

Johnson, Susanne. *Christian Spiritual Formation in the Church and Classroom*. Nashville: Abingdon, 1989.

CHAPTER 6

The Church and the Ministry of the Word

A. The Church

1. Of the Church

What is the church? Wesley answers in his homily #74, "Of the Church" [B 3:45 – 67; J VI:392 – 410 (Bristol, England, September 28, 1785)]. The text is from Ephesians 4:1 – 6: "I ... beseech you that ye walk worthy of the vocation wherewith ye are called, with all lowliness and meekness, with longsuffering, forbearing one another in love; endeavoring to keep the unity of the Spirit in the bond of peace. There is one body, and one Spirit, even as ye are called in one hope of your calling; one Lord, one faith, one baptism, one God and Father of all, who is above all, and through all, and in you all."

This homily is a summary of Wesley's ecclesiology.[1] He explicitly contends that his view is "exactly agreeable" with Anglican article 19 on the church. He again makes clear that at this late date, 1784, he had "no more thought of separating from the Church than I had forty years ago."[2]

Pastoral theology must first grasp what the church is. The scriptural premise is that the church is one body in one Spirit called to one hope. It exists among those who find that the risen Lord is among them. He is the one Lord who was sent by the Father who is above all and through all.

2. More Than a Building

When we talk about the church in ordinary conversation, we often are thinking of a building. This illustrates how thin our grasp is of the nature of the church as the living body of Christ.[3]

We ambiguously use the word *church* as a building on the one hand and as a body of people united together in the service of God on the other. Wesley preferred the plain speech of Matthew, who wrote, "Where two or three believers are met together, there is a church" (Matt. 18:20, Wesley's paraphrase).

Those who gather in Christ's name will find that Christ is in the midst of them.

---

[1]JWO, introduction, B 3:45.
[2]*JJW*, September 4 – 30, 1785.
[3]"Of the Church," B 3:46, J VI:392, pref. 1 – 2.

There and only there do you have a church. Paul, in his letter to Philemon, points to "the church in thy house." This means that "even a Christian family may be termed a church."[4]

The church in a neighborhood or the church in a region are equally the church. "Several of those whom God hath called out of the world (so the original word properly signifies), uniting together in one congregation, formed a larger Church; as the Church at Jerusalem; that is, all those in Jerusalem whom God had so called."[5]

3. Sharing in the One Body of Christ

When the day of Pentecost came, Jesus' followers were all together in one place (Acts 2:1). After Peter proclaimed the good news to the crowd, three thousand people accepted his message (Acts 2:41 – 47). Luke reported what happened next:

> They devoted themselves to the apostles' teaching and to fellowship, to the breaking of bread and to prayer. Everyone was filled with awe at the many wonders and signs performed by the apostles. All the believers were together and had everything in common. They sold property and possessions to give to anyone who had need. Every day they continued to meet together in the temple courts. They broke bread in their homes and ate together with glad and sincere hearts, praising God and enjoying the favor of all the people. And the Lord added to their number daily those who were being saved. (Acts 2:42 – 47 NIV)

Soon there were too many to gather physically in a single location, but in their varied localities they still remained the church.[6]

In most places in the Roman Empire before Constantine, the body of Christ was not even permitted to publicly own or build a church building, even a small one. The local church was united with the whole worldwide body of Christ. They met in separate congregations but as one church united in the present and living Lord. When Paul wrote his letter "to all that be in Rome ... called to be saints" (Rom. 1:7), he wrote to all believers in Rome who had heard the calling of the Lord to the life of faith. So the church is misunderstood if it is reduced to a building. What is clear is that believers are called together in Christ's name, and there they experience Christ's presence, uniting them to all believers around world of all times.[7]

a. The Local Church "at Corinth" and the Universal Church "All Over the World"

Paul addressed his first letter to Corinth "To the church of God in Corinth, to those sanctified in Christ Jesus and called to be his holy people, together with all those everywhere who call on the name of our Lord Jesus Christ — their Lord and ours" (1 Cor. 1:2 NIV). All who "call on the name of our Lord Jesus Christ" refers

---

4"Of the Church," B 3:46 – 47, J VI:392, pref. 2.
5"Of the Church," B 3:47, J VI:392, pref. 3.
6"Of the Church," B 3:46 – 47, J VI:392 – 93, pref. 3.
7"Of the Church," B 3:47, J VI:392, pref. 3.

to the whole body of believers everywhere, and in this case, specifically in Corinth. The church refers to "them that are sanctified in Christ Jesus; with all that, in every place (not Corinth only; so it was a kind of circular letter) 'call upon the name of Jesus Christ our Lord, both theirs and ours.' "[8] The body of believers is "called to be his holy people."

The church can be in a house, or in a family, or in a congregation "of one city, of one province, or nation."[9] "It is the Church in general, the catholic or universal Church, which the Apostle here considers as one body."[10]

Paul addressed his second letter to Corinth still more explicitly, showing the multifaceted use of the term *ecclesia*: " 'Unto the Church of God which is at Corinth, with all the saints that are in all Achaia.' Here he plainly includes all the Churches, or Christian congregations, which were in the whole province" (2 Cor. 1:1; cf. Gal. 1:2).[11] There is one body of Christ with numerous "Christian congregations dispersed throughout that country."[12] *Ecclesia* refers not to buildings but to the people who meet together, and in meeting together, meet the risen Lord.[13]

Sometimes the church refers extensively to "all the Christian congregations that are upon the face of the earth."[14] We pray for "the whole state of Christ's Church militant here on earth."[15] "The Church here, undoubtedly, means the catholic or universal Church; that is, all the Christians under heaven."[16] All members are called to "walk worthy of the vocation wherewith they are called."[17]

b. Defining the Church

Pastoral ministry lives in service to the church and would not exist without the church. Thus, it is essential to any ministry of the church that the minister understand the church in which pastoral ministry occurs.

The church is a worshiping community. In this community, Christ calls the faithful to the holy life of faith active in love: " 'The Church at Ephesus,' as the Apostle himself explains it, means, 'the saints,' the holy persons, that are in Ephesus, and there assemble themselves together to worship God the Father, and his Son Jesus Christ."[18]

Those fitly joined to this community live in "one Spirit" who animates "all the living members of the Church of God."[19] They have received by this Spirit "one hope; a

---

[8]"Of the Church," B 3:47–48, J VI:392, pref. 4.
[9]"Of the Church," B 3:46, J VI:392, sec. 1.7.
[10]Ibid.; Eph. 4:1–6.
[11]"Of the Church," B 3:47–48, J VI:392, pref. 4.
[12]"Of the Church," B 3:48, J VI:392, pref. 5.
[13]"Of the Church," B 3:47–48, J VI:392, pref. 5.
[14]Ibid.
[15]BCP.
[16]Acts 20:28; "Of the Church," B 3:48, J VI:392, pref. 5.
[17]"Of the Church," B 3:48, J VI:392, pref. 6.
[18]"Of the Church," B 3:46, J VI:392, sec. 1.7.
[19]"Of the Church," B 3:49, J VI:392, sec. 1.8.

hope full of immortality. They know, to die is not to be lost: Their prospect extends beyond the grave."[20] "In his great mercy he has given us new birth into a living hope through the resurrection of Jesus Christ from the dead, and into an inheritance that can never perish, spoil or fade. This inheritance is kept in heaven for you, who through faith are shielded by God's power until the coming of the salvation that is ready to be revealed in the last time" (1 Peter 1:3 – 5 NIV).

The one Lord "has set up his kingdom in their hearts, and reigns over all those that are partakers of this hope. To obey him, to run the way of his commandments, is their glory and joy."[21]

c. One Spirit, One Hope, One Faith, One Church, One Baptism

The one faith "is the free gift of God, and is the ground of their hope."[22] This free gift enables the faithful boldly to say with Paul: "The life I now live in the body, I live by faith in the Son of God, who loved me and gave himself for me" (Gal. 2:20 NIV).

In the church "'there is one baptism' which is the outward sign our one Lord has been pleased to appoint, of all that inward and spiritual grace which he is continually bestowing upon his Church."[23] The Spirit continually witnesses with our spirits that we are the children of God who is "above all, through all, and in you all" (Eph. 4:6). This inner witness occurs in a manner peculiar to each member who lives in the one body, "making your souls his loved abode."[24] This is the church.

d. Participating in a Local Congregation of Believers

By analogy with the apostles' usage, we can plainly answer the question, "What is the church?" in Wesley's own English community of faith. "What is the Church of England? It is that part, those members, of the universal church who are inhabitants of England," in whom "there is one Spirit, one hope, one Lord, one faith."[25] "That part of this great body, of the universal Church, which inhabits any one kingdom or nation, we may properly term a national church" or the church of one city or neighborhood. "Two or three Christian believers united together are a Church in the narrowest sense of the word. Such was the Church in the house of Philemon." Whether the number be large or small, "they are one body, and have one Spirit, one Lord, one hope, one faith, one baptism, one God and Father of all."[26] This scriptural account "is exactly agreeable to the nineteenth Article of our Church."[27]

By "congregation of believers" (*coetus credentium* in the original Articles), the church plainly meant a community of those "endued with living faith."[28] This con-

[20]"Of the Church," B 3:49, J VI:392, sec. 1.9.
[21]"Of the Church," B 3:49, J VI:392, sec. 1.10.
[22]"Of the Church," B 3:49, J VI:392, sec. 1.11.
[23]"Of the Church," B 3:49 – 50, J VI:392, sec. 1.12.
[24]"Of the Church," B 3:50, J VI:392, sec. 1.13.
[25]"Of the Church," B 3:52, J VI:392, sec. 1.17.
[26]"Of the Church," B 3:51, J VI:392, sec. 1.15.
[27]"Of the Church," B 3:51, J VI:392, sec. 1.16.
[28]Ibid.

gregation of believers was intended to take in "both the whole church and the several particular churches of which it is composed."[29] The visible acts by which we can see and recognize and know the church are clear. The church is that community "in which the pure Word of God is preached, and the sacraments be duly administered."[30]

This classic Christian definition of the church does not cover all its features, but it does set forth its center. It does not exclude from the church Catholic congregations in which occasionally unscriptural doctrines are imperfectly preached or the sacraments poorly administered, if the risen Lord is present. Wesley appealed to tolerance on "opinions": "I can easily bear with their holding wrong opinions, yea, and superstitious modes of worship. Nor would I, on these accounts, scruple still to include them within the pale of the catholic Church."[31]

4. Walking Worthy of the Vocation to Which We Are Called

The gift to us implies a task for us. We are to walk worthy of the calling in Christ. The term *walk* in Scripture "includes all our inward and outward motions; all our thoughts, and words, and actions." It embraces not only everything we do, but everything we think and speak. It is, therefore, no trivial matter to "walk worthy" in the biblical sense of the word.[32] In walking with Christ, we learn lowliness, meekness, patience, forbearance, peace, holiness, and love.

To "walk worthy" means first "walking 'with all *lowliness*,' to have that mind in us which was also in Christ Jesus; not to think of ourselves more highly than we ought to think." It means "to know ourselves as also we are known by Him to whom all hearts are open; to be deeply sensible of our own unworthiness," to recognize our own spiritual sicknesses, and that without grace we are "dead in trespasses."[33] Even when we have been reborn and new life has been given to our deadness, we are called to remember "how prone is our heart still to depart from the living God! What a tendency to sin remains in our heart, although we know our past sins are forgiven!"[34] Even when God has "thoroughly cleansed our heart, and scattered the last remains of sin; yet how can we be sensible enough of our own helplessness, our utter inability to all good, unless we are every hour, yea, every moment, endued with power from on high.... Otherwise we shall be in perpetual danger of robbing God of his honor, by glorying in something we have received, as though we had not received it."[35]

To "walk worthy" means: "Let all our actions spring from this fountain; let all our words breathe this spirit; that all men may know we have been with Jesus, and

---

[29]"Of the Church," B 3:51, J VI:16.
[30]"Of the Church," B 3:52, J VI:392, sec. 1.18.
[31]Ibid.
[32]"Of the Church," B 3:53, J VI:392, sec. 2.20.
[33]Ibid., italics added.
[34]"Of the Church," B 3:53, J VI:392, sec. 2.21.
[35]"Of the Church," B 3:53 – 54, J VI:392, sec. 2.22.

have learned of him to be lowly in heart."[36] In this walk, we learn how profoundly we are being enabled to "walk with all meekness." *Meekness* "implies not only a power over anger, but over all violent and turbulent passions. It implies having all our passions in due proportion; none of them either too strong or too weak; but all duly balanced with each other; all subordinate to reason; and reason directed by the Spirit of God."[37]

Through humility and meekness, we learn *patience*. In this patience, we will then learn to "possess our souls,"[38] and we will be prepared to "walk with all longsuf-fering."[39] Through this patient forbearance, we carry on "the victory already gained over all [our] turbulent passions ... patiently triumphant over all opposition, and unmoved though all the waves ... never being 'overcome of evil,' but overcoming evil with good."[40] Walking in this way means "*forbearing* one another in love ... not avenging yourselves ... bearing one another's burdens; yea, and lessening them by every means in our power."[41] Where this is happening, there is the church.

5. Keeping the Unity of the Spirit in the Bond of Peace

The members of the church of Christ endeavor with all possible diligence to "keep the unity of the Spirit in the bond of peace ... all these cemented and knit together by that sacred tie — the *peace* of God filling the heart. Thus only can we be and continue living members of that Church which is the body of Christ."[42]

This is why in the ancient creed we confess "the holy catholic Church." It is called holy because its ordinances are designed to promote *holiness* and because "our Lord intended that all the members of the Church should be holy" as we seek to mirror the holiness of God in our behavior. Every member of the church, "though in dif-ferent degrees" is called to be holy and in some measure walks as grace enables in that holy way.[43] So "let all those who are real members of the Church, see that they walk holy and unblamable in all things" as "the light of the world!... a city set upon a hill."[44] "Let all your words and actions evidence the spirit whereby you are animated! Above all things, let your *love* abound. Let it extend to every child of man: Let it overflow to every child of God. By this let all men know whose disciples you are, because you 'love one another.' "[45]

36"Of the Church," B 3:54, J VI:392, sec. 2.23.
37Ibid.
38"Of the Church," B 3:54, J VI:392, sec. 2.24.
39"Of the Church," B 3:54, J VI:392, sec. 2.25.
40Ibid.
41"Of the Church," B 3:54, J VI:392, sec. 2.26, italics added.
42"Of the Church," B 3:55, J VI:392, sec. 3.27, italics added.
43"Of the Church," B 3:55, J VI:400, sec. 3.27.
44"Of the Church," B 3:576, J VI:400 – 401, sec. 3.30.
45Ibid., italics added.

B. Wesley's Article 13 on the Church

Wesley revised the Thirty-Nine Articles of the Church of England in 1784 for the American Methodists. Article 19 on the church from the Anglican Thirty-Nine became Wesley's article 13 with little substantive change. The Methodist form of the article on the church flows directly out of the historical continuity revealed in the texts from the consensual patristic Reformation to the Wesleyan core teaching on the church.

1. Continuity with the Augsburg Confession and the Thirty-Nine Articles: Lutheran, Anglican, and Methodist Teaching on the Church

Here are the closely connected teachings of the Lutheran, Anglican, and Methodist traditions. They reveal the obvious continuity of their common heritage, which is grounded in the apostolic witness as viewed consensually by the early church. I have highlighted their common features:

Augsburg Confession of the Lutheran Church, 1530	Thirty-Nine Articles of the Church of England, 1563	Twenty-Five Articles of the American Methodists, 1784
Article 8. **What the Church Is** The Church properly is the congregation of saints and true believers. **Article 5.** **Of the Ministry** That we may obtain this faith, the Ministry of Teaching the Gospel and administering the Sacraments was instituted. **Article 14.** **Of Ecclesiastical Order** Of Ecclesiastical Order they teach that no one should publicly teach in the Church or administer the Sacraments unless he be regularly called.	**Article 19.** **Of the Church** The visible Church of Christ is a congregation of faithful men, in which the pure Word of God is preached, and the Sacraments be duly ministered according to Christ's ordinance in all those things that of necessity are requisite to the same. As the Church of Jerusalem, Alexandria, and Antioch have erred; so also the Church of Rome hath erred, not only in their living and manner of Ceremonies, but also in matters of Faith.	**Article 13.** **Of the Church** The visible Church of Christ is a congregation of faithful men in which the pure Word of God is preached, and the Sacraments duly administered according to Christ's ordinance, in all those things that of necessity are requisite to the same.

Wesley considered that nothing in Anglican article 19 was inconsistent with the apostolic testimony, the ecumenical councils, or the magisterial Protestant confessions.

2. Why Did Wesley Omit the Anglican Censure of Some Aspects of the Ancient Christian Churches of the East and West?

Wesley omitted from Anglican article 19 the phrase "As the Church of Jerusalem, Alexandria, and Antioch have erred; so also the Church of Rome hath erred, not only in their living and manner of Ceremonies, but also in matters of Faith." There are two plausible hypotheses as to why. The first theory is that his editorial purpose was simply to shorten the received Reformation confessions to their most essential and uncontested phrases with no words off the point.

The second hypothesis is that he did not want to cast any aspersions on the confessions of the ancient church of Antioch, whose teachers had been his mentors, and of Rome, with whom he was in significant dialogue over many decades. Wesley did not disavow the last sentence of Anglican article 19, for he specifically wrote in section 16, "Of the Church," "Perhaps it was intended to take in both [the ancient churches of the East and West]; so to define the universal Church as to keep in view the several particular Churches of which it is composed."[46] My view is that both hypotheses apply.

Wesley wished to carefully interpret the crucial phrase "in which the pure Word of God is preached, and the Sacraments duly administered according to Christ's ordinance" (art. 19). Some would take that to rule out dissenters and Catholics from the universal church, either due to doctrine or sacramental practice. Wesley had a more generous reading of the phrase. He defined its meaning in accord with the premise that both members of the dissenting churches and of Rome who truly believed were members of the one body of Christ.[47] Wesley was a lifelong member of the Church of England and the son of an Anglican pastor. He never cast aspersions on his baptism or ordination in the Anglican tradition, nor did he rule out any true believers, "whether they be Dissenters or Catholics."[48]

C. The Evangelical Pastor

1. Prophets and Priests

a. Dual Traditions of Biblical Guidance for the Ordering of Ministries

Wesley's most important teaching on the pastor as evangelist is found in a robust homily called "The Ministerial Office" in the Jackson edition. The homily appears in the recent Bicentennial edition under the title "Prophets and Priests" [Homily #121 (Cork, Ireland, May 4, 1789), B 4:72 – 84; J #115, "The Ministerial Office," VII:273 – 81]. The focus is on the calling of ministers to proclaim the gospel faithfully to the worshiping community. Wesley's text is Hebrews 5:4: "No man taketh this honour unto himself, but he that is called of God, as was Aaron."

It is important to put this homily in its context. Wesley was struggling to defend

---

[46]"Of the Church," B 3:52, J VI:396, sec. 1.16.
[47]"Of the Church," B 3:51, J VI:392, sec. 1.16.
[48]"Of the Church," B 3:45, secs. 17 – 19, J VI:396, sec. 16.

the special form of the worshiping community that resulted from his preaching. Ministers of the established church were uneasy about this new "extraordinary ministry" of preaching to miners in the fields.

Wesley returned to Scripture to explain the relation between the prophetic and priestly offices of ministry, beginning with Aaron in the Old Testament, through the apostles to the Nicene period, and on through to the evangelical revival he led in England. Wesley did not want his bands and evangelical societies to leave the Church of England. He was trying to renew the church from within rather than leave it.

b. The Struggle over Defining Extraordinary Ministries

By 1789 tension was increasing between the growing Methodist societies and the established Church of England. Wesley warned Methodist preachers not to abuse their ministerial office: "Contain yourselves within your own bounds," meaning the bounds set by church law under the leadership of ordained ministers. "Be content with preaching the gospel. 'Do the work of evangelists.'"[49] He urged Methodist ministers in England to be content with simply and courageously preaching the gospel.

Methodist lay preachers had learned from Wesley to regard themselves as a special ministry within the broader church. They had been taught to understand themselves as "extraordinary" evangelists within the Church of England. To sort out the biblical warrant for these new and experimental "extraordinary ministries," Wesley reviewed the Old and New Testament patterns for the office of ministry and their historical developments up to the evangelical revival.

c. British and American Church Situations Contrasted and Compared

From the outset the traveling Methodist preachers were commissioned not as parish priests but as itinerant preachers. In America during and after the Revolution, a special dilemma arose: many Anglican priests left the American East Coast where both Methodism and the Revolution were spreading rapidly. Many Anglican priests tended to draw away from direct participation in the American Revolution and toward loyalty to the Church of England and to the king.

Meanwhile the Methodist preachers were growing much closer to the frontier people who were increasingly involved in the battle to create a new nation. When the Anglican clergy left for Canada or England or sought safe havens due to military conflict, there were fewer ordained ministers to administer the sacraments. There was growing pressure on the Methodist preachers and leaders of the Methodist bands and societies to offer the sacraments in remote villages under these unusual conditions where no Anglican priests were available.

In England Wesley had devised a deed of declaration that legally secured ownership of the Methodist chapel properties in England for the societies. But in doing

---

[49]"Prophets and Priests," B 4:82, J VII:280, sec. 18.

so, he did not wish for the Methodists to withdraw completely from the established church.

In the American situation, a different approach emerged. Richard Whatcoat and Thomas Vasey were the first to be "set apart" as presbyters, and Thomas Coke and Francis Asbury as superintendents. The Methodists in America became known as the Methodist Episcopal Church. They desired the preaching of the Word and the administration of the sacraments to be joined together in an order of ministry that corresponded with the unique conditions present in America but not in England.

d. Diverse Forms of Ministry

Despite his own strong desire to remain within the Church of England, Wesley was unable to persuade many others in his connection in both Britain and America to "remain content as a religious society [with their own lay preachers] within the Church of England [with her priests and sacraments]."[50] The issue of separation, debated as early as 1756, came to a boil in 1784 with the Constitution of the Irish Methodists, who wished to separate visibly from the Church of England. Wesley explained to the Dublin Methodists in 1789: "The original design of the Methodists ... [is] not to be a distinct party but to stir up [inspire] all parties ... the Church of England in particular, to which they belonged from the beginning.... With this view, I have uniformly gone on for fifty years, never varying from the doctrine of the church at all."[51]

These neuralgic conflicts prompted Wesley finally to publish his definitive views of "the degrees of the ministry" which became sermon 121,[52] which he considered his "final word against separation." But the momentum of separation was by that time virtually irreversible. His firm stance on no separation was a conviction he had held throughout his lifetime. This conviction hinged on a long pattern of biblical witnesses concerning prophets and priests. Wesley provided a historical account of this pattern.

2. Prophet and Priest in Scripture

a. How the New Testament Fulfilled the Promises of the Old

From Old Testament times a distinction was made between priestly and prophetic offices. From Adam to Noah, the firstborn in every family was the priest. But this gave him no right to be a prophet or preacher. God would choose whom he would send.[53]

Wesley's instinctive Anglicanism had taught him the traditional distinction found in Richard Hooker: prophets were called to preach and teach; the priests had sacramental responsibilities. Aaron did not preach. His office was to pray and offer sacrifice. Prophets were those divinely called and endowed with prophetic gifts

---

[50]"Prophets and Priests," B 4:72, JWO, "An Introductory Comment."
[51]Ibid.
[52]B 4:72 – 84; AM, May and June 1790.
[53]"Prophets and Priests," B 4:75, J VII:274, sec. 2.

(e.g., Nathan, Isaiah, Jeremiah, and Amos, upon whom the Holy Spirit came with extraordinary power). Or they were those who were routinely trained in prophetic schools and who emerged later in synagogues to instruct people in the Law.[54]

The New Testament followed many of the Old Testament patterns, but with the decisive difference that Christ the Son of God is viewed as our only High Priest.[55] Jesus and the apostles shaped the church's ministerial office largely around the Jewish patterns that assumed a distinction between prophet and priest. Christ called and empowered evangelists to preach the gospel. They served under the church leaders (*episcopoi*) who presided over the elders who cared for the parish flocks and administered the sacraments.[56] The great High Priest "sent apostles and evangelists to proclaim glad tidings to all the world, and then pastors, preachers, and teachers to build up in the faith the congregations that should be found. But I do not find that ever the office of an evangelist was the same with that of a pastor, frequently called a bishop. He presided over the flock and administered the sacraments: the former assisted him and preached the Word, either in one or more congregations."[57] Wesley did not find precedent either in Scripture or apostolic tradition "that the office of an evangelist gave any man a right to act as a pastor or bishop."[58] "It is never understood that this appointment to preach gives them any right to administer the sacraments."[59] On these biblical premises, Wesley built his case for evangelists within the Church of England without separating from the Church of England.

b. The Evangelist and Prophetic Offices after Nicea

After Nicea the two offices of pastor/priest and the evangelist/prophet were combined and vested to a single person, yet the distinction of the two offices persisted underneath the surface.[60] When Constantine poured honor and wealth on the Christians, each congregation had a pastor accountable to a bishop. From then on "the same person acted as priest and prophet, as pastor and evangelist. And this gradually spread more and more throughout the whole Christian church."[61] To this day "the same person usually discharges both those offices, yet the office of an evangelist or teacher does not imply that of a pastor, to whom peculiarly belongs the administration of the sacraments."[62]

3. Wesleyan Guidelines for an Extraordinary Ministry

a. Prophet and Priest among Those in Wesley's Connection

John and Charles Wesley were both devoted priests of the Church of England

[54]"Prophets and Priests," B 4:75, J VII:282, sec. 2.
[55]"Prophets and Priests," B 4:77–78, J VII:274–75, secs. 3–6.
[56]"Prophets and Priests," B 4:77, J VII:275, sec. 7.
[57]Ibid.
[58]Ibid.
[59]"Prophets and Priests," B 4:77, J VII:276, sec. 8.
[60]Cf. FA 3.3.9; *ENOT* 2:957.
[61]"Prophets and Priests," B 4:77, J VII:276, sec. 8.
[62]Ibid.

when they began to sow the Word of God "not only in the churches, but likewise literally 'by the highway side,' and indeed in every place where they saw an open door, where sinners had ears to hear."[63] They were members of the Church of England and "had no design of separating from it. And they advised all that were of it to continue therein, although they joined the Methodist society."[64] Thus, the Presbyterian, Anabaptist, and Quaker members of the Methodist societies "might still retain their own opinions, and attend their own congregations."[65] The only condition required for coming to the Methodist Society meetings was "a real desire to flee from the wrath to come."[66] Then came Thomas Maxfield and others who offered themselves to serve and were received "as prophets, not as priests." They were authorized "solely to preach; not to administer sacraments.... Those who imagine these offices [prophet and priest] to be inseparably joined are totally ignorant of the constitution of the whole Jewish as well as Christian church," said Wesley.[67]

Within the Church of England, the earliest Methodist lay ministers received sacraments from their local pastor-priests and hence did not need to exercise the sacramental offices in their evangelical societies. They instead were especially called to preach and to make disciples. The intent of Methodist preaching was to serve as "extraordinary messengers," to stir the faith of both clergy and laity.[68] Wesley knew many in his connection who had previously never attended church at all but now duly attended.[69]

The further into the eighteenth century, the more Wesley's view was opposed by a rising majority of preachers in Wesley's own connection.[70] Outler calls Wesley's tenacity against his own preachers' tendency "one of Wesley's more interesting 'failures.'"[71]

b. The Struggle over Separation

Wesley rehearsed the development of this opposition against him: some Methodist preachers who at first were received as preachers, not priests, wanted to expand their function, considering themselves authorized to baptize. In the first conference of 1744, they were instructed by Wesley to do the work to which they were appointed — primarily preaching.[72]

Wesley held to this intent whenever possible, even though its plausibility was already being challenged in the American situation, where Coke and Asbury were

---

[63]"Prophets and Priests," B 4:79, J VII:277, sec. 10.
[64]"Prophets and Priests," B 4:75, J VII:282, sec. 9.
[65]Ibid.
[66]Ibid.
[67]"Prophets and Priests," B 4:79, J VII:277, sec. 10.
[68]"Prophets and Priests," B 4:77, J VII:276, sec. 8.
[69]"Prophets and Priests," B 4:82, J VII:279, sec. 17.
[70]*LWM* 2:339–40; Richard Denny Urlin, *Churchman's Life of Wesley*, 2nd ed. 1880, appendix X; *JWCE* passim.
[71]"Prophets and Priests," B 4:74, J VII:282, sec. 9.
[72]"Prophets and Priests," B 4:79, J VII:277, sec. 11.

charged with making responsible prudential judgments. Wesley wanted the English preachers to retain membership in the Church of England and receive Communion there or elsewhere as frequently as possible. He said, the thought of administering sacraments "never entered into our mind."[73] As in biblical times, God continued to call some to be "extraordinary" ministers of the gospel.

4. No One Takes This Honor upon Himself

The central theme of the homily: "No one takes this honor on himself, but he receives it when called by God, just as Aaron was" (Heb. 5:4 NIV). The implication here for the Methodist preachers is that they should not have presumed to take upon themselves the sacramental office but rather focused on evangelical preaching.

a. A Consistent Appeal to Unity

Throughout this struggle, Wesley was careful to show that he had no intention of separating from the Church of England, even though he had reluctantly given the American preachers a slightly wider berth. He held to classical Anglican doctrines and discipline. "Whenever I have opportunity, I attend the Church [of England] service myself, and advise all our societies so to do."[74]

Wesley held that as long as Methodist preachers held fast to their original calling, there was no need to separate from the established church. He pled, "I hold all the doctrines of the Church of England. I love her Liturgy. I approve her plan of discipline and only wish it could be put in execution.... I do not knowingly vary from any rule of the Church, unless in those few instances where I judge, and as far as I judge, there is an absolute necessity."[75]

Wesley was candid about the ambiguities that emerged in several of these few instances: to preach in the open air, to pray extempore, to form societies within the church so as to encourage deeper discipleship in small and trusting groups, and to accept the assistance of lay preachers.[76] But none of these implies "separating from the Church." All of these things Wesley had been doing for fifty years with full disclosure to his ecclesial superiors. He showed no inconsistency here.[77]

b. The Distinctive Methodist Habit of Refusal to Separate

In the history of the churches of the Reformation, new movements in the church had been all too inclined to separate from the mother church. "But with the Methodists it is quite otherwise.... They do not separate from the religious community to which they at first belonged."[78] Wesley regarded this principle of unity as "our peculiar glory,"[79] saying, "It is new upon the earth" in all church history. Those

[73]Ibid.
[74]"Prophets and Priests," B 4:80–81, J VII:278, sec. 15.
[75]Ibid.
[76]"Prophets and Priests," B 4:80, J VII:278, sec. 15; cf. JJW, March 30 and April 12, 1789.
[77]"Prophets and Priests," B 4:81, J VII:278, sec. 15.
[78]"Prophets and Priests," B 4:90, J VII:278, sec. 14.
[79]Ibid.

separatists who said, "Stand by yourselves, for we are holier than you!" did not find a natural home in the ministry of the Methodists.

Wesley made it clear that Methodists "are not a sect or party. They do not separate from the religious community to which they at first belonged. They are still members of the Church; such they desire to live and to die." He went further, declaring poignantly, "I believe one reason why God is pleased to continue my life so long is to confirm them in their present purpose not to separate from the Church."[80] There was thus a decisive difference between the evangelical Methodist renewal of Anglican life and the dissenting and separating churches.

This is the particular splendor of the Methodists: not to separate but to redeem from within both church and society. They are asked to be grateful for their unique position in a broad church that contained wheat and tares. "Be content with preaching the gospel. 'Do the work of evangelists.'"[81] The Methodists are not out to undermine the established church but to build it up.[82] Wesley said, "[We remain] still members of the Church of England, as we were from the beginning, but receiving all that love God in every church as our brother, and sister, and mother."[83]

c. The Evangelical Revival Is No Sect or Party but Friends to All Parties

Wesley concluded with a passionate plea for unity that still echoes throughout the fragmented Wesleyan connection today: "Abide in your place; keep your own station."[84] The connection remained "still members of the Church of England." It was "thrust out, not to supersede, but to 'provoke to jealousy' the 'ordinary messengers.' In God's name, stop there!" said Wesley.[85]

Wesley's ardent plea continued: "Ye are a new phenomenon in the earth; a body of people who, being of no sect or party, are friends to all parties.... Do not cast away the peculiar glory which God hath put upon you, and frustrate the design of Providence, the very end for which God raised you up."[86]

In my view, this plea still represents the epitome of Methodist ecclesiology. Ministry in the Wesleyan tradition is focused on evangelism, not partisanship.

D. On Unworthy Pastors

1. On Attending the Church Service

a. The Problem of Unworthy Pastors

What is to be done about unworthy ministers who have been duly ordained but lack spiritual gifts? This was a serious problem that confronted the early evangeli-

---

[80]Ibid.
[81]2 Tim. 4:5; "Prophets and Priests," B 4:82, J VII:279, sec. 17.
[82]"Prophets and Priests," B 4:83, J VII:279, sec. 21.
[83]"Prophets and Priests," B 4:82, J VII:281, sec. 21.
[84]"Prophets and Priests," B 4:82, J VII:279, sec. 17.
[85]"Prophets and Priests," B 4:82, J VII:280, sec. 18.
[86]"Prophets and Priests," B 4:83, J VII:282, sec. 19.

cal revival. Should believers distance themselves from the corrupt church and its corrupt clergy?

Tenaciously Wesley argues: Unworthy pastors may yet offer worthy prayers. Unholy pastors may administer holy baptism and Holy Communion. The promises of God overcome the limitations of men. The unity of the body of Christ is more resilient than the outrage of the self-righteous.

b. On Attending a Worthy Communion Service of an Unworthy Minister

On October 7, 1787, in a sermon titled "On Attending the Church Service," Wesley addressed the question of whether Methodists should attend the church services of ministers who had deficient piety [Homily #104, B 3:464–78; J #104, VII:174–85]. His text was 1 Samuel 2:17: "The sin of the young men was very great." Which young men? Those who "abhorred the offering of the LORD."

The context of this verse is the priest Eli and the young Samuel ministering. Under their ministry, the sons of Eli were treating the Lord's offering with contempt. They had been sleeping "with the women who served at the entrance to the tent of meeting" (1 Sam. 2:22 NIV).

Did this disqualify Eli from serving in the offering to the Lord? No, the moral deficit of the father did not invalidate the ordinances of God that he had been chosen to administer.[87] The holiness of the church depends not on the holiness of a particular minister or on the holiness of all ministers, but on the holiness of God's promise and command. Don't give up on the divinely instituted ordinances, for God has not given up on delivering you through the ordinances. The Christian ordinances include a bath and a meal (baptism and Communion), a book (Scripture), and a community of worship. Attendance at worship remains a divine command for Christians.[88]

c. Wheat and Weeds

The wheat grower in Jesus' parable of Matthew 13 sowed good seed, but weeds came up among the wheat because the farmer's enemy had sown weeds among the wheat. When the servant of the wheat farmer asked permission to pull up the weeds, the farmer said, "No, because while you are pulling the weeds, you may uproot the wheat with them. Let both grow together until the harvest. At that time I will tell the harvesters: First collect the weeds and tie them in bundles to be burned; then gather the wheat and bring it into my barn" (Matt. 13:29–30 NIV). This is the nature of God's kingdom. God sows wheat, and the enemy sows weeds. Until harvest time — the final judgment — the saving work of God in history will continue on like this.

Still today we find a church made up of wheat and tares, as Christ taught. We do

---

[87] 1 Sam. 2; "On Attending the Church Service," B 3:467–69, J VII:176–77, secs. 7–11.
[88] "On Attending the Church Service," B 3:467–68, J VII:176, secs. 7–9.

not fully know what God knows fully. We are not wise enough to separate the wheat from the tares, because the tares look like wheat. If we try to separate them without God's omniscient wisdom, we risk damaging the wheat itself. Thus, it is better to leave the separating to God in the final judgment. Wesley did not want the separatist tendency in the Methodist movement to win out over those believers who seek patiently and charitably to manifest the unity of the body of Christ.[89]

In the case of Eli, the people did not stop going to the temple, nor did Samuel tell the people to stop going (1 Sam. 2). In Old Testament history, the prophets did not give up on the unreformed priests, because even as unholy men, the priests were capable of offering due sacrifices to God. God would in the long run judge the bad priests rightly. The people of Israel were called to honor the ordinances, even if the priests were corrupt. It is clear from Scripture that God can work through unholy persons, and he still does.[90]

2. When the Ordained Lack Gifts

What is to be done about unworthy ministers who have been duly ordained but lack spiritual gifts, as did many in Wesley's own church? This was a serious problem that confronted the evangelical revival. Should believers distance themselves from the corrupt church and clergy? That would be the dissenters' habit. Or should they remain within and renew? Wesley's answer was typically Anglican, standing in the consenting tradition of church teaching, as distinguished from the noble tradition of dissent. He told his preachers to be content with preaching the gospel, to do the work of evangelists (2 Tim. 4:5). He said, "Abide in your place; keep your own station."[91]

Wesley provided thoughtful reasons for not separating, and certainly not abruptly or with rancor. Even a partially dysfunctional ministry may be affirmed when we are willing to trust that God's grace will work through it in unexpected ways, even when it is confused about itself. "If God's power does bless the ministry of unholy men, then we ought to continue."[92] Ministers are not to be judged by human judges but by the divine Judge. The criterion for judgment is whether God is blessing the ministry, not whether men do. Wesley was convinced that even though the ministry of unholy persons in the Church of England was a serious obstacle to renewal, God may still work through it.

Wesley's ministry remained within the ministry of Word and sacrament in the Church of England in good conscience. Wesley urged members of his societies to attend regularly upon the ordinances of God, whether of established or dissenting churches. Go to church. Receive Holy Communion. Those things are more important than scrupling over the moral habits of the minister of Word and sacrament.

---

[89]"On Attending the Church Service," B 3:467 – 68, J VII:176 – 77, secs. 7 – 11.
[90]Ibid.
[91]"Prophets and Priests," B 4:82, J VII:279, sec. 17.
[92]"On Attending the Church Service," B 3:465 – 66, J VII:174 – 75, secs. 1 – 5.

The people called Methodists were called to participate not only in the class meetings but in the weekly services of worship of the local church.[93] Some pastors may indeed be unworthy of their office, but that is not sufficient reason to abandon common worship.

a. The Disastrous History of Separation

Christianity has experienced a long and disastrous history of separation. We see it in Corinth, and we see it further developed in the history of some reformist and ascetic movements. As early as the second century, some "who were afraid of being partakers of other men's sins, thought it their duty to separate from them."[94] Even after the Reformation had rejected many aspects of monastic models, there still remained a temptation to trust too much in the virtues of leaving.[95]

History shows that separation seldom achieves the purity it intends. These believers unwisely separated because they thought that "no good was to be expected from the ministration of unworthy men."[96] This belief holds false hopes. Wesley examined this opinion that unworthy ministers justify not attending church. The subject of this sermon is "calmly to inquire, whether God ever did bless the ministry of ungodly men, and whether he does so at this hour."[97]

b. If God Blesses a Ministry, Do Not Separate

Wesley's decisive rule at the end of his ministry was the same as it was at the beginning: "If God *never* did bless it [the church's ministry], we ought to separate from the Church; at least where we have reason to believe that the Minister is an unholy man: If he *ever* did bless it, and does so still, then we ought to continue therein."[98] "Never" and "ever" are the crucial terms.

If "never," go. If "ever," stay. If God really never blesses a ministry, it can be left behind. But if God does show evidence of blessing a church or a ministry, even in small or indirect ways, separation should not be considered.

Separation from the established church has never been what the Methodists were called to do. Rather, they were called to transform the church from within. They were not even to think of separation. Every member of the society was encouraged to attend church and receive the means of grace the church offers.[99]

3. The Perennial Debate

a. From Eli to Cyprian

Evangelical revival has time and again sought to deal with this issue of separation. "For more than twenty years this [thought of separation from the Church of

---

[93]Ibid.
[94]"On Attending the Church Service," B 3:465, J VII:174, sec. 1.
[95]"On Attending the Church Service," B 3:465–66, J VII:175, secs. 2–3.
[96]"On Attending the Church Service," B 3:466, J VII:175, sec. 3.
[97]"On Attending the Church Service," B 3:466, J VII:175, sec. 5.
[98]Ibid.
[99]"On Attending the Church Service," B 3:466, J VII:175, secs. 4–5.

England] never entered into the thoughts of those that were called Methodists."[100] "We were all, at our first setting out, determined members of the Established Church."[101] The minutes of the conference at Leeds became standard discipline within Wesley's connection. There "the reasons were set down at large, and they stand equally good at this day."[102] It was only much later when those from active dissenting traditions entered robustly into the Methodist societies that there was increasing talk of separation. "But as more and more who had been brought up dissenters joined with them, they brought in more and more prejudice against the [Anglican] Church."[103]

In his determination to "put this matter beyond all possible dispute," Wesley in this homily took the biblical case of the sons of Eli who "were wicked to an uncommon degree" in order to speak about "what the dealings of God in his Church have been, even from so early a period."[104] "Many of the people were so deeply offended [at the sexual abuses], that if they did not wholly refrain from the public worship, yet they attended it with pain; abhorring the Priests, while they honored the sacrifice."[105] Even with priestly families who were "wicked to an uncommon degree," as were the sons of Eli, the offering of the priest was to be respected.

From Jeremiah to Malachi, "people and Priests wallowed in all manner of vices," but this did not end the ordinances commanded by God.[106] The abuse of the priestly office continued even until the Son of God appeared. Pentecost provided a new beginning for Spirit-filled ministries that engendered holiness through grace. But even these soon became distorted and corrupted.

Wesley warned against misquoting Paul on separation: When Paul wrote, "Be ye separate" and "touch not the unclean thing," he was referring to the devil, not the minister (2 Cor. 6:17).[107]

The mystery of iniquity among church leaders has continued throughout the church's history.

> When St. Cyprian, about an hundred and fifty years after the death of St. John, describes the spirit and behavior both of laity and Clergy that were round about him, one would be ready to suppose he was giving us a description of the present Clergy and laity of Europe.... The corruption which had been creeping in drop by drop, during the second and third century, in the beginning of the fourth, when Constantine called himself a Christian, poured in upon the Church with a full tide and from then on overflowed.... The Clergy were not a whit more innocent than the laity.[108]

---

[100]"On Attending the Church Service," B 3:467, J VII:175, sec. 6.
[101]"On Attending the Church Service," B 3:466, J VII:175, sec. 4.
[102]"On Attending the Church Service," B 3:467, J VII:175, sec. 6.
[103]Ibid.
[104]"On Attending the Church Service," B 3:467, J VII:176, sec. 7.
[105]"On Attending the Church Service," B 3:468, J VII:176, sec. 9.
[106]"On Attending the Church Service," B 3:468, J VII:176, sec. 11.
[107]"On Attending the Church Service," B 3:474, J VII:177, sec. 11.
[108]"On Attending the Church Service," B 3:469–70, J VII:178, sec. 14.

Tares are endemic to wheat in the history of God's saving work. Let God be the judge.

b. Augustine on Donatism

Augustine faced the same problem with the Donatists, who broke from the universal consensus of the penitential practice accepted throughout the Christian world. Augustine recognized that the wisdom of the universal consensus on penitence was more reliable than a small local group of hotheaded radicals in Numidia. He fought the errors of the Donatists but not the sacraments they had distorted.

In classic Christian teaching, the church is intrinsically one, holy, catholic, and apostolic. When it becomes divided, it is not embodying the body of Christ. God does not bless the church that is needlessly divided.

Wesley did not want the separatist tendency in the evangelical revival to divert those who seek patiently and charitably to manifest the unity of the body of Christ. Even with a strong doctrine of the capacity of the spirit to elicit a full response to grace, he wanted those who sought the life of perfect love to do so within the worshiping community, the community of persons who live out their lives in entire devotion to Christ.[109]

c. From the Reformation to the Evangelical Revival in the Church of England

From the postapostolic age to the Reformation, many have sought refuge in solitary religion and absolute perfectionism that leaves no room for failure. From the monks to the sectarian separatists, they have sought purity and perfection. Yet what has often resulted? Sometimes even more corruption. As a result, the light of those who withdraw from community has become hidden under a bushel. When the righteous separate, they leave the church to further corruption.

But did not Luther and Calvin voluntarily separate from the established medieval Catholic tradition? No, they did not voluntarily abandon the historic church, argued Wesley. They were driven out, were harassed by bulls of excommunication, and became hunted men. When they sought amelioration, they were rebuffed. They did not choose to separate.[110]

Wesley was a dutiful priest of the Church of England who was himself badly treated by his church but did not separate. Rather, he remained patiently irenic: "I am far from desiring to aggravate the defects of my brethren, or to paint them in the strongest colors. Far be it from me to treat others as I have been treated myself; to return evil for evil, or railing for railing."[111]

The pastoral deficiency continued: "Many, if not most, of those that were appointed to minister in holy things, with whom it has been my lot to converse in almost every part of England or Ireland, for forty or fifty years last past, have

---

[109]Ibid.

[110]"On Attending the Church Service," B 3:469–70, J VII:178, secs. 14–15, cf. sec. 25.

[111]"On Attending the Church Service," B 3:471, J VII:179, sec. 17.

not been eminent either for knowledge or piety." Yet Wesley did not take this as an excuse for abandoning the ordinances commanded by God for every minister of the gospel — baptism and Holy Communion. Amid all these deficiencies, Wesley asserted that "there are many Clergymen in these kingdoms, that are not only free from outward sin, but men of eminent learning; and, what is infinitely more, deeply acquainted with God." But most are not. Sadly, most "have not been holy men, not devoted to God, not deeply acquainted either with God or themselves."[112]

Wesley then defended against negative public perceptions of lay leaders in his own connection. He conceded that they had "been taken immediately from low trades, tailors, shoemakers, and the like" and hence had been viewed by some merely as "stupid, illiterate men that scarce know their right hand from their left." Wesley retorted that he would sooner cut off his right hand than allow unprepared people to preach in his connection. He would not approve them without reasonable proof that the proposed person had "more knowledge in the Holy Scriptures, more knowledge of himself, more knowledge of God and of the things of God, than nine in ten of the Clergymen I have conversed with, either at the Universities or elsewhere."[113]

4. Unholy Pastors May Administer Holy Ordinances

The central question that Wesley addressed was, "Ought the children of God to refrain from his ordinances because they that administer them are unholy men?... Is it possible that we should receive any good from the hands of those that know not God?"[114] The prophets provided reliable guidance. They did not command the people of Israel to stop using the ordinances of God just because they had been corrupted by certain persons or practices. "Did Isaiah, or any of the Prophets, exhort them, for that cause, to forsake the ordinances of God?" Neither did "Malachi, or Jeremiah, or any other of the Prophets, exhort the people to separate themselves from these ungodly men."[115]

Did Jesus "refrain from that public service which was performed by these very men" [the Pharisees] who were "full of pride, lust, envy, covetousness, of all ungodliness and unrighteousness?... Or did he direct his Apostles so to do? Nay, just the contrary: In consequence of which, as he constantly attended them himself, so likewise did his disciples."[116] Jesus himself did not despise or neglect the means of grace established by God through the old covenant. Though Jesus well knew the corruption of the temple leadership, he did not forsake the temple or urge others to do so.

Jesus did not forsake the law or the priesthood as such, but through his own body pointed to their fulfillment in the coming kingdom of God. He even viewed Judas as an example of how God could send an unholy person into ministry and

---

[112]"On Attending the Church Service," B 3:471, J VII:179, sec. 18.
[113]"On Attending the Church Service," B 3:471, J VII:179, sec. 17.
[114]"On Attending the Church Service," B 3:472, J VII:180, sec. 19.
[115]Ibid.
[116]Ibid.

yet use him for a greater good than appears on the face of it. God in fact sent Judas as a sign that God can and does offer salvation by means of persons who have not accepted salvation themselves. The Holy Spirit works to overcome barriers to healthy growth, even when we obstruct.[117]

a. God Saves Even by Means of Those Who Will Not Accept It Themselves

Wesley's ironic conclusion: God sends salvation to persons even by means of "those who will not accept it themselves."[118] Though Jesus harshly denounced the scribes for their abuse of their office, Jesus still commanded the people to "attend to their ministrations." Their office as such was not abandoned or derogated simply because of their abuses. We must not think we are wiser than the Lord in this matter.[119] It may seem that those who do not receive the grace of God cannot convey it to others, but there are many biblical examples of God using bad men to accomplish good purposes.

Those who further divide the church by separation often do not improve in justice or faith active in love. "Most of them separated, either because of some opinions, or some modes of worship, which they did not approve of. Few of them assigned the unholiness either of the Clergy or laity as the cause of their separation. And if any did so, it did not appear that they themselves were a jot better than those they separated from."[120] The apostolic intention on penitence was more reliable than a small group who nursed illusions of a perfect church on earth, as Augustine found. This illusion did not leave room for either human freedom to default on God's redemptive intention or for grace to overcome that default.

The limited unworthiness of ministers does not diminish the unlimited promise of the sacraments they administer. The efficacy of the sacraments is derived not from the moral worthiness of the one who ministers them, but from the grace of God. So bad ministers are not an adequate reason to separate from a good church where the people are singing the hymns of the faithful.

b. The Unworthy Minister Does Not Hinder the Efficacy of Sacrament

"The grand reason which many give for separating from the Church, namely, that the Ministers are unholy men, is founded on this assertion, that the ministration of evil men can do no good; that ... men who do not receive the grace of God themselves cannot convey that grace to others. So that we can never expect to receive the blessing of God through the servants of the devil."[121] This sounds plausible, but it ignores the unintended consequences of separation. Wesley answered: "Did the ordinances, administered in the time of our blessed Lord, convey no grace

---

[117]"On Attending the Church Service," B 3:473, J VII:181, sec. 21.
[118]Ibid.
[119]"On Attending the Church Service," B 3:471–73, J VII:179–81, secs. 17–23.
[120]"On Attending the Church Service," B 3:475, J VII:182, sec. 26.
[121]"On Attending the Church Service," B 3:476–77, J VII:183, sec. 27.

to those that attended them? Surely then the Holy Ghost would not have commended Zacharias and Elizabeth for walking in these ordinances!"[122]

Let the words of Jesus settle into the heart: "The teachers of the law and the Pharisees sit in Moses' seat. So you must be careful to do everything they tell you. But do not do what they do, for they do not practice what they preach" (Matt. 23:2 – 3 NIV).[123] If the holiness of believers depends on the holiness of all the clergy, then a conscientious person cannot be a member of any instituted or multigenerational church in the world.[124] "We know by our own happy experience, and by the experience of thousands, that the word of the Lord is not bound, though uttered by an unholy Minister; and the sacraments are not dry breasts, whether he that administers be holy or unholy."[125]

Many Christians over many centuries have had to forbear extremely bad ministries. This is nothing new. But again and again the faithful have found that "unworthiness of the minister doth not hinder the efficacy of God's ordinances. The reason is plain, because the efficacy is derived, not from him that administers, but from Him that ordains it. He does not, will not suffer his grace to be intercepted, though the messenger will not receive it himself."[126]

Wesley urged all to spread the quiet and peaceable gospel and not to become entrapped in divisive temptations. "Let us bear a faithful testimony, in our several stations, against all ungodliness and unrighteousness, and with all our might recommend that inward and outward holiness 'without which no man shall see the Lord!' "[127]

This issue would not go away. Wesley defended his position repeatedly in three other short essays that follow: "Some Thoughts upon an Important Question" (1781), "On Ministers Who Oppose the Truth" (1782), and "Of Attending the Church" (1782).

5. Some Thoughts upon an Important Question

Most in his connection knew that Wesley had advised Methodist laity to attend church regularly, whether they were from the established church or traditions of dissent. But some were still left wondering whether the hearing of confusing doctrine "does not expose us to temptation from those who continually ask, 'How did you like the sermon today?' " At that point, we cannot dissemble. They wondered whether they should go to church where doctrines opposed to Scripture were "continually inculcated."[128] To assist "many who wish to have a conscience void of offense," Wesley finally wrote an irenic answer ["Some Thoughts upon an Important Question," J XIII:244 – 45 (November 19, 1781)].

---

[122]"On Attending the Church Service," B 3:476, J VII:183, sec. 29.
[123]"On Attending the Church Service," B 3:476 – 77, J VII:184, sec. 30.
[124]"On Attending the Church Service," B 3:477, J VII:184 – 85, sec. 31.
[125]"On Attending the Church Service," B 3:478, J VII:185, sec. 33.
[126]Ibid.
[127]Ibid.
[128]"Some Thoughts upon an Important Question," J XIII:244.

Granting that knowing whether to stay and listen to confusing doctrine was "a delicate, as well as important" question, Wesley deliberately decided not to "lay down any general rule. All I can say at present is, If it does not hurt you, hear them; if it does, refrain. Be determined by your own conscience. Let every man in particular act 'as he is fully persuaded in his own mind.'"[129]

a. On Hearing Ministers Who Oppose the Truth

Although the Spirit is willing to help believers overcome all forms of sin in their lives, the people in Wesley's connection were left wondering what to do when their minister preached that grace is powerless to overcome all sin. They were hearing continually the claim that "we cannot be saved from our sins in this life; and that we must not hope to be perfected in love on this side eternity." Wesley wrote that fallen human nature makes us "very willing to receive this; therefore, it is very liable to hurt us" by placing limits on what the Spirit can do in people's lives. "Hence we have a doubt, whether it is our duty to hear this preaching which experience shows to weaken our souls" ["On Hearing Ministers Who Oppose the Truth," J XIII:245–46 (Lewisham, England, January 9, 1782)].

Late in his life (1782), Wesley submitted this question to the conference of preachers. "They unanimously agreed, first, that it was highly expedient, all the Methodists (so called) who had been bred therein should attend the service of the Church as often as possible," even where the Scriptures are interpreted unwisely. But if a minister ridiculed the power of grace to transform freedom, Wesley advised that "they should quietly and silently go out of the church; yet attend it again the next opportunity."[130] He added, "Only I must earnestly caution them not to be critical; not to make a man an offender for a word; no, nor for a few sentences."[131]

6. Of Attending the Church

In the same year, Wesley received a query from an Arminian believer who sought his counsel on three questions. First, "Is it your wish that the people called Methodists should be, or become, a body entirely separate from the Church?" ["Of Attending the Church," J XIII:246–47 (February 13, 1782)]. As before, Wesley answered no.

The second question was, "If so, how often need one go to the established church?" Wesley answered, go to any church where the gospel is preached.

And the final question was, "What if improper biblical teaching is occurring at the church of the parish where they reside. Are they then, in your opinion, bound in conscience to hear, or may they, at their own option, forbear?" Wesley answered, "I do not think they are bound in conscience to attend any particular church." Do they have liberty to "condemn such teachers? No; by no means."[132]

---

[129]Ibid.
[130]"On Hearing Ministers Who Oppose the Truth," J XIII:246, sec. 3.
[131]"On Hearing Ministers Who Oppose the Truth," J XIII:246, sec. 4.
[132]"Of Attending the Church," J XIII:246.

E. Evangelical Worship

1. The Ministry of Word and Sacrament

a. The Pastor of the Worshiping Community

The gospel calls forth a worshiping community. It awakens a community to proclaim the good news and to praise the revealed God. The model for this worshiping community is set forth in Acts 2:41 – 47:

- Those who accepted Peter's preaching were baptized.
- Many believed, and the community grew rapidly.
- They devoted themselves to the apostles' teaching.
- They enjoyed fellowship in the faith.
- They broke bread together.
- The risen Lord was present in their fellowship.
- They prayed and worshiped together.
- They were filled with awe at the many wonders and signs.
- They had everything in common.
- Their numbers grew exponentially.

Just as in the sequence of Acts 2, so in the times of Wesley and today, a worshiping community of believers emerges gratefully out of Christian proclamation. It is intrinsic to evangelical life, and hence to the work of ministry. Those who understand the good news want to hear it proclaimed and celebrated on the Lord's Day and throughout the seasons of the Christian year.

Wesley's pastoral theology explores all of these phases of the life of the worshiping community. The nurture of this community occurs by bonding believers together in praise and service. Therefore, attending regular worship is intrinsic to this fellowship. The pastor is an evangelist serving a singing, praying, studying, and service-oriented community of worship.

b. The Upbuilding of the Christian Life through the Means of Grace God Has Provided

Those who serve as pastoral guides of the worshiping community voluntarily consent to ordering the life of the worshiping community according to the church's historic doctrinal and disciplinary standards.

Central to the life of the community called by Christ is its sacramental life. Without the sacraments, the church and the Christian life lack the means of reawakening faith prescribed and offered by the Lord. The sacraments have the purpose of enlivening, awakening, and quickening our faith. According to Wesley's teaching, a sacrament must have four characteristics. In the language of Wesley's article 16, "they are certain signs of grace, and God's good will toward us, by which he doth work invisibly in us, and doth not only quicken, but also strengthen and confirm, our faith in him." That is bedrock Methodist doctrine. It reflects both the Lutheran and Anglican teaching of the Reformation. The notion that they are nothing more than symbols of subjective faith or tokens of Christian profession falls short of Christ's teaching.

c. By the Lord's Institution

A dominical sacrament is one constituted and commanded by the Lord. Among Protestants, only two sacraments are recognized as dominically instituted: baptism and Holy Communion.

In order to meet the criteria as a dominical sacrament, the rite must be:

- Ordained of Christ
- Certain and reliable signs of grace
- Showing signs of God's good will toward us
- Working invisibly in the faithful
- Birthing faith
- Strengthening faith
- Confirming faith

d. The Other Five "Medieval Sacraments": The Status of Confirmation, Penance, Ordination, Matrimony, and Last Rites

In the late medieval tradition five practices were added that were "commonly called sacraments," but these were not specifically instituted by the Lord to be continuing signs of grace.

The ministries of catechesis, confession, ordination, blessing of marriages, and ministries to the dying are all crucial gospel ministries blessed in the New Testament, in Wesley's view. In the previous chapters we have already shown how these are all basic to the pastoral office. Yet they are not viewed in Scripture or in Anglican, Methodist, or Reformed traditions as dominical commands of the Lord, durable for all time and absolutely essential to the very nature of the worshiping community. They are not sacraments appointed by the Lord, or holy sacraments strictly speaking.

Yet these five practices are not to be set completely aside, either in the Church of England or by pastoral care in Wesley's connection. They are commended and encouraged in Scripture. Scripture call us to confirm our baptism, but not as a rite separable from baptism. Scripture calls for us to repent of our sins, but not as a dominically ordered rite of penance. We are to respect the due process that leads to an ordered ministry, but not to treat it as commensurable with baptism. Holy Scripture blesses holy matrimony, but it is not a dominically instituted sacrament. Scripture calls the faithful to care for the dying and to pray for God's own anointing of those facing death, but not as a rite of extreme unction. The history of their corruptions indicates that they are not to be treated with the same necessity for all believers as are baptism and Eucharist, which are intrinsic to the well-being of the church.

2. Wesley's Article of Religion 16 on the Sacraments

a. Methodist Sacramental Teaching in Continuity with Augsburg and the Thirty-Nine Articles

Wesley revised the Thirty-Nine Articles of the Church of England in 1784 for the American Methodists. The original article 25 on the sacraments became article 16 with minimal change. Among these minimal edits are that he changed "damnation" to "condemnation"; simplified "certain sure witnesses and effectual signs" to "certain signs of grace"; and edited down the phrase "yet have not like nature of sacraments with baptism" to the simpler phrase, without changing the meaning, "the like nature of baptism."

Two sacraments are specifically ordained by Christ in the New Testament: baptism and the Lord's Supper. The Methodist form of the article on the sacraments comes directly down from the ancient church to the Lutheran to the Anglican and then to the Methodist tradition of worship with little change. Below are the analogous teachings of the three traditions.

Augsburg Confession of the Lutheran Church, 1530	Thirty-Nine Articles of the Church of England, 1563	Twenty-Five Articles of the American Methodists, 1784
Article 13. **Of the Use of the Sacraments** Of the Use of the Sacraments they teach that the Sacraments were ordained, not only to be marks of profession among men, but rather to be signs and testimonies of the will of God toward us, instituted to awaken and confirm faith in those who use them. Wherefore we must so use the Sacraments that faith be added to believe the promises which are offered and set forth through the Sacraments. They therefore condemn those who teach that the Sacraments justify by the outward act, and who do not teach that, in the use	**Article 25.** **Of the Sacraments** Sacraments ordained of Christ be not only badges or tokens of Christian men's profession, but rather they be certain sure witnesses, and effectual signs of grace, and God's good will toward us, by the which he doth work invisibly in us, and doth not only quicken, but also strengthen and confirm our faith in him. There are two Sacraments ordained of Christ our Lord in the Gospel; that is to say, Baptism and the Supper of the Lord. Those five commonly called Sacraments, that is to say, Confirmation, Penance, Orders,	**Article 16.** **Of the Sacraments** Sacraments ordained of Christ are not only badges or tokens of Christian men's profession, but rather they are certain signs of grace, and God's good will toward us, by which he doth work invisibly in us, and doth not only quicken, but also strengthen and confirm our faith in him. There are two Sacraments ordained of Christ our Lord in the Gospel; that is to say, Baptism and the Supper of the Lord. Those five commonly called sacraments, that is to say, confirmation, penance, orders, matrimony, and extreme

Augsburg Confession of the Lutheran Church, 1530	Thirty-Nine Articles of the Church of England, 1563	Twenty-Five Articles of the American Methodists, 1784
of the Sacraments, faith which believes that sins are forgiven, is required.	Matrimony, and Extreme Unction, are not to be counted for Sacraments of the Gospel, being such as have grown partly of the corrupt following of the Apostles, partly are states of life allowed in the Scriptures; but yet have not like nature of Sacraments with Baptism, and the Lord's Supper, for that they have not any visible sign or ceremony ordained of God. The Sacraments were not ordained of Christ to be gazed upon, or to be carried about, but that we should duly use them. And in such only as worthily receive the same they have a wholesome effect or operation: but they that receive them unworthily purchase to themselves damnation, as Saint Paul saith.	unction, are not to be counted for Sacraments of the Gospel, being such as have partly grown out of the corrupt following of the apostles, and partly are states of life allowed in the Scriptures, but yet have not the like nature of Baptism and the Lord's Supper, because they have not any visible sign or ceremony ordained of God. The Sacraments were not ordained of Christ to be gazed upon, or to be carried about; but that we should duly use them. And in such only as worthily receive the same, they have a wholesome effect or operation; but they that receive them unworthily purchase to themselves condemnation, as St. Paul saith.

3. Abuse and Worthy Reception of the Means of Grace

According to article 16, several abuses are to be avoided in the administration of the sacraments. The physical elements of the sacrament of the table (bread and wine) are not to be gazed upon or carried about for display. They are not to be lifted up or worshiped as an object of devotion in themselves. They are offered and intended to be received as means of grace.

What constitutes worthy reception of the Lord's Supper? It is to be received according to the Lord's instruction and intention in such a way that it may have a wholesome effect and work toward making the believer whole. By unworthy reception of the Supper, one brings judgment on himself (1 Cor. 11:29). When one receives the Supper without faith or without any believing recognition of or participation in the Lord's death and resurrection, and without being present to the living Lord at his table, one receives in an unworthy way. These points are all stated and encompassed in article 16 in Wesley's modest revision of the Thirty-Nine Articles.

Further Reading

The Church and the Ministry of the Word

Baker, Frank. *John Wesley and the Church of England*. Nashville: Abingdon, 1970.

Bence, Clarence Luther. "Salvation and the Church: The Ecclesiology of John Wesley." In *The Church*, edited by Melvin Dieter and Daniel Berg, 297–317. Anderson, IN: Warner, 1984.

Harnish, John E., ed. *The Orders of Ministry in the United Methodist Church*. Nashville: Abingdon, 2000.

Kimbrough, S. T. Jr. *Orthodox and Wesleyan Ecclesiology*. Crestwood, NY: St. Vladimir's Seminary Press, 2007.

Kirkpatrick, Dow, ed. *The Doctrine of the Church*. Nashville: Abingdon, 1964.

Kissack, Reginald. *Church or No Church? A Study of the Development of the Concept of Church in British Methodism*. London: Epworth, 1964.

Outler, Albert C. "Do Methodists Have a Doctrine of the Church?" In *The Doctrine of the Church*, edited by Dow Kirkpatrick, 11–28. New York: Abingdon, 1964.

The Sacraments

Borgen, Ole E. *John Wesley on the Sacraments*. Grand Rapids: Zondervan, 1985.

Felton, Gayle C. *This Gift of Water: The Practice and Theology of Baptism among Methodists in America*. Nashville: Abingdon, 1992.

Flew, R. Newton. "Methodism and the Catholic Tradition." In *Northern Catholicism*, edited by N. Williams, 515–30. New York: Macmillan, 1933.

Hymns

Berger, Teresa. *Theologie in Hymnen: Zum Verhaltnis von Theologie und Doxologie am Beispiel des "Collection of Hymns for the Use of the People Called Methodists."* Altenberge, Germany: Telos Verlag, 1989.

Bishop, John. *Methodist Worship in Relation to Free Church Worship*. New York: Scholars Studies, 1975.

Watson, J. Richard. "Charles Wesley's Hymns and the Book of Common Prayer." In *Crammer: A Living Influence for 500 Years*, edited by Margot Johnson, 204–28. Durham, UK: Turnstone Ventures, 1990.

The Life of Prayer

Demaray, Donald E. *Devotions and Prayers of John Wesley*. Grand Rapids: Baker, 1957.

Gill, Frederick Cyril. "Introduction." In *John Wesley's Prayers*, edited by Fredrick Cyril Gill, 9–17. London: Epworth, 1951.

Wesley, John. "A Collection of Forms of Prayer for Every Day in the Week." In *The Works of John Wesley*, edited by Thomas Jackson, 11:203–59. Grand Rapids: Baker, 1978.

———. "A Collection of Prayers for Families." In *The Works of John Wesley*, edited by Thomas Jackson, 11:237–59. Grand Rapids: Baker, 1978.

Evangelical Worship

Harnish, John E., ed. *The Orders of Ministry in the United Methodist Church*. Nashville: Abingdon, 2000.

Wesley, John. "A Scheme of Self-Examination Used by the First Methodists in Oxford." In *The Works of John Wesley*, edited by Thomas Jackson, 11:521–23. Grand Rapids: Baker, 1978.

White, James Floyd. "Introduction." In *John Wesley's Sunday Service of the Methodists in North America*, edited by James Floyd White, 9–21. Nashville: United Methodist Publishing House and United Methodist Board of Higher Education and Ministry, 1984.

CHAPTER 7

The Ministry of Baptism

A. Classic Christian Teaching on Baptism

In chapter 6 we covered the article on the sacraments. Now we will look at the article on one of the sacraments in particular: baptism, the rite of initiation into the body of Christ. In chapter 8 we will deal with the Lord's Supper, which sustains the body of Christ.

1. Twenty-Five Articles of Religion: Article 17 on Baptism

a. Wesley's Teaching Article on Baptism

Wesley's original text of the Articles is found in *The Sunday Service of the Methodists in North America, with Other Occasional Services* (1784). When Wesley revised the Thirty-Nine Articles of the Church of England in 1784 for the American Methodists, article 27 of the Thirty-Nine became article 17. This article on baptism remained virtually unchanged (the modest revisions are compared in my *Doctrinal Standards in the Wesleyan Tradition*).[1]

The sacrament of baptism is ordained of Christ as a sign of grace and of God's goodwill toward us, working invisibly among the faithful to enliven faith and holy living. Baptism is not reducible to a badge of subjective faith or token of Christian profession. Rather, baptism is instituted by the Lord to offer and awaken grace in our hearts, and through it further grace is given (Anglican article 27 in Thirty-Nine Articles, Wesley's article 17 in Twenty-Five Articles).

2. Methodist Baptism Stands in Continuity with Augsburg and the Thirty-Nine Articles

The Methodist form of the article on baptism comes directly from the magisterial Reformation to the Anglican and then to the Methodist tradition of worship with little change. Here are the key sentences of the three traditions, showing the obvious continuity of the heritage:

---

[1] Thomas C. Oden, *Doctrinal Standards in the Wesleyan Tradition* (Grand Rapids: Zondervan, 1988).

Augsburg Confession of the Lutheran Church, 1530	Thirty-Nine Articles of the Church of England, 1563	Twenty-Five Articles of the American Methodists, 1784
Article 9. **Of Baptism** Of Baptism they teach that it is necessary to salvation, and that through Baptism is offered the grace of God, and that children are to be baptized who, being offered to God through Baptism are received into God's grace.	**Article 27.** **Of Baptism** Baptism is not only a sign of profession and mark of difference whereby Christian men are discerned from others that be not christened, but it is also a sign of Regeneration or new Birth, whereby, as by an instrument, they that receive Baptism rightly are grafted into the Church; the promises of forgiveness of sin, and of our adoption to be sons of God by the Holy Ghost, are visibly signed and sealed, Faith is confirmed, and Grace increased by virtue of prayer unto God. The Baptism of young Children is in any wise to be retained in the Church, as most agreeable with the institution of Christ.	**Article 17.** **Of Baptism** Baptism is not only a sign of profession and mark of difference whereby Christians are distinguished from others that are not baptized; but it is also a sign of regeneration or the new birth. The Baptism of young children is to be retained in the Church.

Since we have already discussed above the general article dealing with the sacraments, it now is fitting to take a closer look at Wesley's revision of the article on baptism. He made only minor alterations in the article on baptism, not by dilution but by strengthening. He changed "christened" to "baptized," and he changed "Christian men are discerned" to "Christians are distinguished." To "new birth" he added the definite article *the*, "the new birth," omitting the remainder. But these changes do not indicate that Wesley thereby disagreed with what was omitted.[2] Such an assertion can rely only on an ambiguous argument from silence. If he disagreed with what was omitted, he would be disagreeing with his own Anglican baptism as a promise of forgiveness and adoption, and of baptism as a grafting into the church, which he clearly affirmed.

---

[2]*DSWT* 121.

B. The Baptismal Liturgy

1. The Sunday Service of the Methodists in North America: Office of Baptism

a. Interpreting Wesley's Baptismal Liturgy

Wesley prepared a liturgy for the Methodists in North America that included a service of baptism largely identical with Anglican practice. Since Wesley approved it as a normative liturgy for Methodist people, it is pertinent here to review its chief features. The version of the baptismal liturgy that Wesley sent to American Methodists for their services of baptism is included in *The Sunday Service of the Methodists of North America, with Other Occasional Services*.[3]

This landmark document was sent to the growing Methodist societies in the United States at the crucial time of the birth of American Methodism. It shows Wesley's restrained edits of the Book of Common Prayer. He intended it to serve as a guide for the ordering of worship for what was to become the Methodist Church in North America. It included the first appearance of the revised Articles of Religion, which became the virtually unamendable doctrinal centerpiece of the constitution of the American Methodist Church.[4]

In *John Wesley's Prayer Book*, James F. White has provided the fullest textual presentation and guide to this landmark document.[5] Included are the collects for each Sunday of the year, the lectionary, and Wesley's *A Collection of Psalms and Hymns*.[6] Wesley largely retained the 1662 rubrics for baptism in his 1784 revision of the Book of Common Prayer for the American church. Most of what Wesley teaches on baptism is embedded in the Anglican baptismal liturgy, which he commended for use by the American Methodists.

The Wesleyan baptismal liturgy begins with a call to prayer, calling the congregation to come before God penitently, aware that "all are conceived and born in sin." The baptismal service begins with John 3:5: "None can enter into the kingdom of God except he be regenerate and born anew of water and of the Holy Ghost."[7]

b. Water: The Washing, Sanctifying, Delivering Act of God

Water signifies the cleansing power of God. The liturgy calls for prayer that the Father through the Son will grant to the baptized "that thing which by nature he cannot have."[8] If by nature every child is a child of wrath born of Adam, unfit for

---

[3] *The Sunday Service of the Methodists of North America, with Other Occasional Services* (London: W. Strahan, 1784).

[4] *DSWT* 29–43.

[5] *John Wesley's Prayer Book: The Sunday Service of the Methodists in North America*, ed. James F. White (Maryville, TN: OSL Publications, 1991).

[6] See also Edward C. Hobbs, *The Wesley Orders of Common Prayer* (Nashville: National Methodist Student Movement, 1957); Karen Westerfield Tucker, *American Methodist Worship* (New York: Oxford University Press, 2011).

[7] *Sunday Service of the Methodists in North America* (1784), 139.

[8] Ibid.

coming into God's presence that is remedied in baptism. In the baptismal prayer, the church prays that the person may be "received into Christ's holy Church, and be made a lively member" of the body of Christ. Then follows a prayer for the guidance of the baptized, using three biblical narratives of merciful salvation that prefigure baptism: (1) God saved "Noah and his family in the ark." (2) God led the children of Israel "through the Red Sea, figuring thereby thy holy baptism." (3) God then acted to "sanctify water" in the baptism of his only "well-beloved Son Jesus Christ in the river Jordan."[9] The baptismal prayer asks for God to look upon this person, "wash him and sanctify him with the Holy Ghost; that he being delivered from thy wrath, may be received into the ark of Christ's Church."[10] The church prays that this one may be rescued from the seas of sin and brought into the ark of salvation.

The washing, sanctifying, and deliverance all occur in baptism by grace alone, by God's unmerited mercy. When received by the faithful, they are embraced within the covenant community. The church prays that the baptized person, "being steadfast in faith, joyful through hope, and rooted in charity may so pass the waves of this troublesome world that finally he may come to the land of everlasting life."[11] The rite of baptism looks toward its voluntary and confirmed fulfillment in faith, hope, and love throughout the person's life and beyond.

2. The Prayer for New Birth

a. Beseeching the Spirit

The teaching of new birth that was so crucial to Wesley is found already embedded in the baptismal liturgy. There is little doubt that in this baptismal liturgy there is an earnest prayer for new birth: "that he, coming to thy holy Baptism, may receive remission of his sins by spiritual regeneration."[12]

This is a prayer of the covenanted family, which includes the infants in the family. Does this imply that the infant at the moment of baptism is by grace spiritually regenerated? In an anticipative sense, this is the very faith that the church is praying for, that Almighty God may "receive him, O Lord, as thou hast promised by thy well-beloved Son."[13] It is just for this that the Lord commands us, "Ask, and it shall be given you; seek, and ye shall find; knock, and it shall be opened unto you" (Matt. 7:7).

In Wesley's baptismal liturgy for American Methodists, as in the Anglican service, the gospel is read from Mark 10:13 – 16:

> People were bringing little children to Jesus for him to place his hands on them, but the disciples rebuked them. When Jesus saw this, he was indignant. He said to them, "Let the little children come to me, and do not hinder them, for the

---

[9]Ibid.
[10]Ibid., 140.
[11]Ibid.
[12]Ibid.
[13]Ibid., 141.

kingdom of God belongs to such as these. Truly I tell you, anyone who will not receive the kingdom of God like a little child will never enter it." And he took the children in his arms, placed his hands on them and blessed them. (NIV)

The church through its minister is praying that this baptismal faith may be "confirmed in us evermore." When the church prays, "Give thy Holy Spirit to this Infant, that he may be born again," does this mean at that moment he is born again, or that the church prays that in due time he may be born again?[14] It is on that ambiguity that the ongoing debate about the relation between baptism and regeneration continues. Wesley's intention was that the church is praying that in due time grace may be so fully received voluntarily that he would be born again in fact (de facto), even as he is juridically (de jure) already becoming born again in an anticipative sense.

b. The Old Adam Buried, the New Adam Raised

The major prayers in the baptismal liturgy maintain the same developmental premise. The church prays that "the old Adam in this Child may be so buried, that the new man may be raised up in him."[15] Immediately or later? Or both now and later? The liturgy itself does not explain this further. After all, it is a prayer book, not a doctrinal exposition. The church then prays that "the Spirit may live and grow in him." Growth implies a continuing process that must begin at some point with the risk of falling. Yet it clearly has a beginning in baptism, even as the living person has a beginning in conception and childbirth. The whole church throughout the ages is praying that the baptized may have power in the past, present, and future "to triumph against the devil, the world, and the flesh." The guidance of this growth process is then turned over to the nurturing church and family and ministry that the person "may also be imbued with heavenly virtues."[16]

The Son of God who shed his blood for the forgiveness of our sins commanded us to "go ... and teach all nations, baptizing them in the name of the Father, and of the Son, and of the Holy Ghost" (Matt. 28:19). In the liturgy, the worshiping community is doing no less than following Jesus' direct command, praying that God may "sanctify this water to the mystical washing away of sin; and grant that this Child, now to be baptized, may receive the fullness of thy grace."[17]

3. The Christian Name Given in Baptism

In the Sunday Service baptismal liturgy, after the prayer for new birth, the child is personally named. This naming of the person is intended to seal his personal identity as a communicant in the covenant. In the Anglican service, the minister then symbolically makes a cross on the child's forehead, receiving him into Christ's flock, praying that he may not be ashamed later to confess the faith of Christ. The

---

[14]Ibid.
[15]Ibid.
[16]Ibid., 142.
[17]Ibid.

assumption now is that "this Child is grafted into the body of Christ's Church," as the church "with one accord" prays "that this Child may lead the rest of his life according to this beginning," thanking God that it has pleased him to receive this person "for thine own Child by adoption, and to incorporate him into thy holy Church."[18]

C. Baptism and New Birth

1. The Beginning of New Life in the Covenant Community

The attempt to reconcile the sermons on regeneration with the treatise on baptism has left many puzzled. Three major documents must be reconciled: "The Spirit of Bondage and the Spirit of Adoption" (1746), "A Treatise on Baptism" (redacted 1756), and "The New Birth" (1760). Those who focus on only one of these three as if separable from the others are likely to read Wesley's nuanced dialectic in an oversimplified way, leading to tendentious arguments shaped by predisposed commitments.

The new birth accompanying scriptural baptism is the beginning of a new life to be constantly chosen and reappropriated voluntarily. Its continuance depends first and always on God's unmerited grace, and second on our cooperation with it through responsible living as the baptized people of God. Water alone does not save, nor do priestly words without the consent of the responsible parties. The consenting parties are the community, the promise of the parents, and implicitly the anticipated response of the baptized. Some argue that Wesley changed his mind, in that he earlier had a more Anglican stress on the efficacy of baptism, and later a more evangelical stress on the new birth as the renewal of baptism. This view proposes that there was a gradual development or even a substantive change in his doctrine. In my view, there was a gradual development but not a substantive change.

2. Baptism as a Sign and Seal of Regeneration

Those who might imagine, however, that "The New Birth" (1760) transcends and repudiates "A Treatise on Baptism" (redacted 1756) are hard-pressed to explain why Wesley repeatedly republished "A Treatise on Baptism" and never repudiated it. Wesley's teaching of the new birth was never consensually viewed as a repudiation of "A Treatise on Baptism," which viewed baptism as a regenerative act through a real grace given. In the case of infants, baptism offers truly effective regenerative grace that awaits the age of discretion. Then, by cooperating grace, God's gift can be voluntarily confirmed. In my view, there was no substantive change in Wesley's theology of baptism, but he clearly was responding to different challenges at different times with the same unwavering evangelical Anglican teaching of both regeneration and baptism.

James Harrison Rigg has argued that Wesley's omissions of some of the references to baptismal regeneration in the Sunday Service imply that he had decided

---

[18]Ibid.

not to insist on a fixed view of baptismal regeneration apart from the new birth freely chosen.[19] In my view there is little evidence that Wesley rejected his earlier view of an anticipative baptismal regeneration that seeks voluntary consent. The neonate baptism relies on the silent work of grace to bring the growing child step by step toward a personal decision for Christ as that becomes possible. It is clear that Wesley thought that the effective power prayed for in the rite of baptism at any age may be "sinned away." He attested this of himself when he wrote in his journal that he sinned away his baptism at an early age.

Wesley was the prototype figure of Anglican evangelicals. There is admittedly a subtle tension between his high church Anglican assumptions about baptism and his vigorous evangelical preaching of the new birth. But he appears to be less concerned about this subtlety than would his later American interpreters. He preferred to see grace working both in faithful baptism and its behavioral outcomes.

Wesley points out to his already largely baptized audience that even though they had become children of God by baptism, that does not invariably imply that every individual who has ever been baptized is still in fact and in practice living as a child of God. One may fall away from one's baptism by gluttony, lying, evil-speaking, and voluntary wickedness. One may indeed deny one's baptism and even apostatize one's baptismal faith so as to make it voluntarily ineffectual and fruitless. Such a person does not need another baptism according to Anglican and Wesleyan practice, since this has been specifically proscribed under classic Christian canon law since the fourth century. Rather, the fallen faithful pray for a renewal and reappropriation of their earlier baptism in the triune name.

To those who self-righteously claim they are now saved merely because once baptized, Wesley warned: "Lean no more on the staff of that broken reed, that you were born again in baptism. Who denies that you were then [in baptism] made children of God, and heirs of the kingdom of heaven? But notwithstanding this, you are now children of the devil. Therefore, you must be born again."[20] Their present actions demonstrate that their baptism, which of itself was effectual, was then put in question later by their own voluntary consent and accumulation of bad choices. The inward grace given powerfully and efficaciously at baptism is expected to grow through a constant process of embodiment of the death and resurrection of Christ. This life grows and matures through a living relationship with the Living Vine.

Without diminishing the efficacy of the sacrament of baptism, the focus of Wesley's evangelical preaching clearly stressed the reborn and growing personal relationship with the living Lord that is expressed initially in baptism. He did not approve of a diluted form of Anglican teaching that imagined that the water of baptism itself as such is able to save, without faith in justifying grace.

---

[19]James H. Rigg, *The Churchmanship of John Wesley and the Relations of Wesleyan Methodism to the Church of England* (1878); digital ed., General Books LLC; cf. *A Comparative View of Church Organizations, Primitive and Protestant: With a Supplement on Methodist Secessions and Methodist Union*, 3rd ed. (London: Charles H. Kelly, 1897); cf. *LW* and *JWTT*, 120.

[20]"Marks of the New Birth," B 1:320, J V:222, sec. 4.5.

3. Begun in Baptism, the New Birth Continues to Grow toward Full Participation in Christ

Bishop Ole E. Borgen suggested that we compare "A Treatise on Baptism" "(with its mild allowance of the doctrine of baptismal regeneration) with the sermon on 'The New Birth' where the stress falls heavily on conversion as a conscious adult experience of regeneration. The point is that Wesley held to both doctrines." In the evangelical revival, Wesley was dealing mostly with adults who were already baptized, but whose baptism had been in fact set aside or ignored.[21]

In the homily "The New Birth," Wesley made a careful distinction between the two interconnected doctrines: baptism and regeneration: "Baptism is not the new birth; they are not one and the same thing. Many indeed seem to imagine that they are just the same.... What can be more plain, than that one is an external, the other an internal work." Baptism is public and visible; regeneration is a work of the Holy Spirit within.[22] "One is visible, the other an invisible thing, and therefore wholly different from each other ... the one being an act of man, purifying the body; the other a change wrought by God in the soul; so that the former is just as distinguishable from the latter, as the soul from the body, or water from the Holy Ghost."[23] "A man may possibly be 'born of water,' and yet not be 'born of the spirit'; there may sometimes be the outward sign, where there is not the inward grace."[24] The arena of baptism is where the mystery of the way of grace works amid human sin and human freedom. The inward grace that is offered in the rite of baptism may then be neglected so that it requires a new birth. Leading interpreters of Wesley have commented on the tension between baptism and new birth. Rupert E. Davies and Gordon Rupp wrote that Wesley "believed that a child once baptized was cleansed from original sin, and if he did not commit actual sin would go to heaven. But every child who remained alive did commit actual sin, and needed to be born again for the second time."[25] Bernard G. Holland argued that Wesley viewed infant baptism as a means of regeneration for infants, but that actual sin in due time completely obliterates the benefits received, "requiring the further regeneration of conversion."[26] Wesley himself wrote in his journal: "I believe 'till I was about ten years old I had not sinned away that washing of the Holy Ghost' which was given me in baptism."[27] If the grace of regeneration given at baptism can be diluted or misplaced by sin, then it follows that adults who were baptized as infants may still require a new birth because of their intervening sin.[28]

[21]Ole Borgen, *John Wesley on the Sacraments* (Grand Rapids: Zondervan, 1986), 165.

[22]"The New Birth," B 2:196, J V:73–74, sec. 4.1.

[23]Ibid.

[24]"The New Birth," B 2:196, J V:74, sec. 4.1.

[25]Rupert E. Davies and Gordon Rupp, *A History of the Methodist Church in Great Britain*, vol. 1 (London: Epworth, 1963), 161.

[26]Bernard G. Holland, *Baptism in Early Methodism* (London: Epworth, 1970), 72.

[27]*BEM*, 43.

[28]Cf. Wesley's journal on his baptism of John Smith, B 19:32.

4. Behavioral Evidences of the Power of Baptism

Faith, hope, and love are behavioral evidences by which believers are made able to know assuredly that they are born again, born of God, born of the Spirit as children of God. These privileges "by the free mercy of God, are ordinarily annexed to baptism," which is described in John 3:5 as being "born of water and of the Spirit,"[29] Wesley cautioned, "Say not in your heart, "I was once baptized, therefore I am now a child of God." Do not define the new birth simply as the rite of baptism as such, as if to ignore behavioral responsiveness to the grace of baptism.

The power of baptism is the power of the Spirit to work through and beyond the material means of water. The rite of baptism offers the power of grace beyond our willing. Grace precedes our willing. Yet baptism assumes that what is offered in Christ must be responded to in faith. Meanwhile even this response is the work of grace by the Spirit. The correspondence of the sign (*signum*) with the thing signified (*res*) is a mystery drenched by grace and enabled by the Spirit. Inwardly essential to baptism is faith's response to grace. Outwardly essential to baptism is its due administration by one duly ordained, applying the visible matter of water, and performed in the name of the triune God according to the Lord's command.[30]

Baptism offers the grace of regeneration by the means of grace God provides — bathing the soul in the merits of Christ, cleansing it of the corruption to which the human heart is so prone. Baptism not only washes away the corruption of original sin but restores the moral image of God in the soul.[31] Regeneration is the thing signified, and baptism is the sign.[32] The Articles of Religion view baptism as the sign of regeneration.[33] Baptism points to the thing signified, new birth by grace shed abroad in our hearts.[34]

D. The Meaning of Baptism

1. A Treatise on Baptism

The arguments of "A Treatise on Baptism" are structured around the basic argument of the Anglican article 27, "Of Baptism" [see "A Treatise on Baptism," in JWO, 319–32; J X:188–200, sec. 1.1; adapted from Samuel Wesley].

a. A Visible Sign of New Birth into the Covenant Community

Baptism is a sign of profession and a mark of difference, but it is also a sign of new birth. The profession is "Jesus Christ is Lord." The mark of difference is the line between the natural life and the evangelical life. Baptism is the sign of new birth, new life in Christ transcending our old fallen nature. That does not imply a simple

---

[29]"Marks of the New Birth," B 1:420, J V:222, sec. 4.5.
[30]"The New Birth," B 2:196–200.
[31]"The New Birth," J VI:65–69.
[32]FA, J VIII:48–49; B 1:143, 415, 428–30; 2:196–200.
[33]B 2:196–200; 1:428–30; FA 11:107; cf. 11:253; JWO 321–25.
[34]See the previous discussion of the new birth in volume 2 of this series.

equation between a religious rite and an experience of new birth. Rather, by this means we are grafted into the body of Christ's church; we are made the children of God by adoption and grace.

Christ's chosen means of signifying this new birth is baptism. By this act we are welcomed into God's family. We are enabled to enter into a community set aside to help us become "regenerated or born again; whence it is also called by the Apostle, 'the washing of regeneration.' ... This is grounded on the plain words of our Lord: 'Except a man be born again of water and of the Spirit, he cannot enter into the kingdom of God.'"[35]

Such are the "inestimable benefits conferred in baptism, the washing away the guilt of original sin, the engrafting us into Christ, by making us members of his Church, and thereby giving us a right to all the blessings of the gospel."[36]

b. The Anglican Tradition as Received through the Wesleys

John Wesley until his dying day was a faithful priest of the Church of England who believed in its doctrine and submitted to its discipline insofar as conscience allowed. Since baptism was a settled issue in Anglican teaching that he did not challenge, Wesley did not write extensively on baptism, and when he did, he stayed close to Scripture, referencing where necessary the consensual Anglican sources, the catechism and the Articles of Religion. More closely he relied on the work of his own father, Samuel, who was a tested Anglican minister who had in 1700 written an essay titled "The Pious Communicant Rightly Prepared ... to Which Is Added a Short Discourse of Baptism." It was not so short, but it fully and adequately treated baptism in a way that John Wesley thought sufficient that it could be entrusted to the entire connection. So he passed it along in shortened form to the Wesleyan societies.

There is no implication here that John Wesley treated baptism lightly. Wesley was not seeking a major reform in Anglican sacramental doctrine, but rather only a deepened seriousness about its spiritual reception and evangelical significance. He focused on calling Christians to live out their baptism proactively in their daily lives. The formal doctrine of baptism was not his central passion. The life lived in dying and living in Christ was his passion.[37] He concentrated on the life-changing meaning of baptismal teaching as a core subject matter of all Christian doctrine. Nothing is more crucial to the Christian life than embodying what our baptism truly means.

c. Baptism and the Unity of Believers

Since baptism has been a perennial cause for doctrinal dispute and division, it may seem ironic that Wesley set forth baptism as the crucial rite that brings Christians together. These divisions became especially harsh on the American fron-

---

[35]John 3:5; "A Treatise on Baptism," JWO 320; J X:192, sec. 1.1.
[36]"A Treatise on Baptism," JWO 328; J X:197–98, sec. 4.9.
[37]FA, B 11:107–8.

tier, especially over the mode of baptism. But the strains that became corrosive in America were all present in Wesley's own time.

Some argued for or against various interpretations of the presence of grace in baptism. Others argued for or against some specified age of accountability in which the reception of baptism is fitting, or concerning the mode of baptism. These were destined to remain as contested issues of scriptural exegesis long after Wesley's death. For Wesley's part, these opinions are best seen in relation to the more embracing point that baptism in its various modes brings together the whole world of Christian believers of all times and places.

Despite these differences that would become much sorer points in America, John and Charles Wesley preached and sang about the Holy Spirit who was bringing the church to unity through the "one baptism" attested by the apostles. Thus, Christians in distant cultures can come closer to recognizing their common covenant life with believers of all other times and places through their baptism. True believers can enter instantly into a profound awareness of their common unity with all who confess faith.[38]

Wesley's traditional Anglican teaching on baptism was and remains a central feature of his pastoral theology. It is not incidental that believers are baptized. It is not accidental that the solemn act of conveying the gift of baptism is a pastoral duty. By this means the believer participates in Christ's death and resurrection, as well as in the living body of Christ. We here see Wesley as a pastor for lay Christians,[39] teaching them about the daily renewal of their baptism in a simple, straightforward way that leaves little to speculate about but much to live out experientially.

d. Samuel Wesley's Treatise on Baptism Amended by His Son

As I said earlier, Wesley's father, Samuel, had published a tract three years before John's birth titled "The Pious Communicant Rightly Prepared ... to Which Is Added a Short Discourse of Baptism." It was written as a confirmation manual. Wesley abridged by more than half this discourse on baptism and published it as the sixth section of "A Preservative against Unsettled Notions in Religion."[40] The modified version that was published by John Wesley in 1756 under the title "A Treatise on Baptism" is properly viewed as John Wesley's modest revision and abridgement of this longer treatise written by his father. Apparently Wesley thought that his father had already put into plain speech the teaching on baptism that the people called Methodists needed to hear and embrace, for he published and commended it for his entire connection of Methodist societies. It was addressed first to the conference of preachers of 1756 and then published again in 1758.[41] It was made into a pamphlet and offered as a teaching document for general circulation under still another title,

---

[38]"The Marks of the New Birth," B 5:212–23.
[39]JWO 319–32.
[40]JWO 316.
[41]Vivien V. Green, *The Young Mr. Wesley: A Study of John Wesley and Oxford* (New York: St. Martin's, 1961).

"A Preservative against Unsettled Notions in Religion," but it is commonly known as "A Treatise on Baptism." It is found in the Jackson edition, X:188–201, and in Outler's *John Wesley*.[42]

Speaking of "A Treatise on Baptism," Outler wrote, "Such importance as it had lay in its square-toed summary of what was already essentially commonplace in central Anglican sacramental theology and in its stubborn patience in dealing with any and all objections."[43] Hence it is fitting to treat its contents in effect as Wesley's own view, since Wesley clearly embraced its teaching, took full ownership of its argument, and took initiative to publish it for his entire connection. Outler rightly took this view by including it in his collection of John Wesley's writings. Those who wish to contrast John Wesley's baptismal teaching with that of his father are hard put to explain why he edited, published, praised, and republished it. Relatively little heated scholarly debate has occurred about whether John Wesley's revision of Samuel Wesley's treatise on baptism corresponds with John Wesley's own opinion. Since Wesley's classic consensual teaching on baptism did not have a long history of controversy, he was content to let his father's treatise speak for him. Nonetheless, since I am disinclined to rest on the work of Samuel Wesley alone to represent John Wesley's view of baptism, I will corroborate each of its major points with amplified references to John Wesley's explicit and uncontested writings.

2. What Does It Mean to Be Baptized?

a. The Grace of Baptism

On baptism Wesley stands virtually in total conformity to traditional Anglican teaching, yet with one noticeable shift of emphasis: an intensified evangelical focus on receiving the grace of baptism in the heart.[44] Wesley was seeking to keep baptism and regeneration in proper correlation, in accord with Scripture, as we will see. "A Treatise on Baptism" pursues four basic questions that reveal Christ's command for initiating us into the worshiping community: (1) What is baptism? (2) What are its benefits? (3) Did Christ intend that baptism remain a permanent institution in the church? (4) Are children to be baptized? Whether one agrees with Wesley or not, every evangelical pastor does well to be able to reason from Scripture about baptism on these crucial questions, for they come up repeatedly in the work of ministry and in the care of souls.

b. What Is Baptism?

Baptism is defined as "the initiatory sacrament which enters us into covenant with God."[45] Baptism is instituted by Christ himself under the new covenant in correspondence with circumcision in the old.

---

[42]JWO 319–32.
[43]JWO 317.
[44]"The Means of Grace," J X:187–88.
[45]"A Treatise on Baptism," JWO 319; J X:188, sec. 1.1.

As circumcision was a "sign and seal of God's covenant" under the old dispensation of the law, so is baptism under the new covenant. Baptism is a "sign, seal, pledge, and means of grace, perpetually obligatory on all Christians."[46]

Christ alone "has power to institute a proper sacrament." It is not a matter of legislative votes in a conference of church leaders. It is already settled by the Lord himself and confirmed in canonical Scriptures.[47]

3. An Outward Sign of an Inward Grace

Baptism consists of an outward sign (water), signifying an inward grace (forgiveness). The outward sign is the divinely appointed means by which God the Father in his sovereign wisdom draws us into his new kingdom. By this means the Lord has provided grace for the inward reception of the forgiving grace of the Son, that it may enter into the human heart through the power of the Spirit.[48] This is why baptism is always administered in the name of the one triune God — God the Father, God the Son, God the Spirit. The Lord explicitly commanded the faithful to "go and make disciples of all nations, baptizing them in the name of the Father and of the Son and of the Holy Spirit" (Matt. 28:19 NIV).

a. Water as the Outward Sign and Material Means of Baptism

The material and visible means chosen by the Lord through which to enable and bless the new birth is the least pretentious of all physical creation: simply water. Water is present wherever life is present. Its natural power of cleansing is a visible sign of the transcendent power of grace to cleanse sin and wash away ungodliness.[49] Water is divinely appointed as the sole material or visible element in the sacrament of baptism.[50]

Viewed merely as a physical entity, the water has no power of itself to effect a spiritual change in the soul. It is the Spirit who cleanses the soul through the blood of Christ.[51] "Baptism is performed by washing, dipping, or sprinkling the person in the name of the Father, Son, and Holy Ghost."[52]

b. Essential to Baptism

Following simple Anglican practice, "A Treatise on Baptism" taught that "three things are essential to Christian baptism": (1) a qualified episcopal administrator standing in the tradition of the apostles, (2) the application of water, and (3) administration in the name of the Trinity.[53]

---

[46]Ibid.
[47]Ibid.
[48]"The New Birth," B 2:196–200.
[49]"A Treatise on Baptism," JWO 319; J X:188, sec. 1.2.
[50]"The New Birth," J VI:73.
[51]"A Treatise on Baptism," JWO 319; J X:188, sec. 1.2.
[52]Ibid.
[53]"A Treatise on Baptism," JWO 318; J X:188, proem.

c. Not by Water Alone, and Not without Water

We are not saved by water as such, yet we are not saved without the water of baptism that signifies the inward grace of regeneration. Water is God's own chosen means of offering the grace of initiation. Yet the means do not operate without grace. We are to use all means as means. They are sacramental instruments, not ends in themselves. The means are ordained "not for their own sake, but for the renewal of your soul in righteousness and true holiness."[54]

Wesley sets himself apart from medieval scholastic sacramental teaching in one particular way: "The grace does not spring merely *ex opere operato*" — from merely working the work, saying the words, doing the deed. It does not proceed from the mere elements, or the words spoken, but from the blessing of God in consequence of his promise to such as are qualified for it" ("Popery Calmly Considered," J X:149). It proceeds from the work of the Spirit in both its outward and inward forms. Wesley distinguished evangelical baptismal teaching from medieval sacramental teaching.

4. Scriptural Accounts of Alternative Modes of Baptism

a. Immersion

Accounts of baptisms are sufficiently varied in the New Testament to allow the conclusion that various modes of administering baptism are permissible. Its mode of administration is less crucial than the grace that it conveys and signifies.

On behalf of baptism by immersion, John Wesley commented on the phrase from Colossians 2:12, "buried with him in baptism." He argued that "the ancient manner of baptizing by immersion is manifestly alluded to here, as the other manner of baptizing by sprinkling or pouring of water is, Heb. 10:22."[55]

Scripture reports baptisms by immersion, pouring, and sprinkling without insisting that a single mode is absolutely required. Wesley thought it likely that any and all three of these modes were practiced in the early church. This is set forth in his careful exegesis of Colossians 2, Matthew 3, and Hebrews 10:22.[56] Sprinkling and washing are implied in Hebrews: "having our hearts sprinkled to cleanse us from a guilty conscience and having our bodies washed with pure water" (Heb. 10:22 NIV).

While immersion symbolizes dying and rising with Christ (Rom. 6), pouring and sprinkling symbolize the outpouring of the Holy Spirit at Pentecost.[57] These are not in conflict but are corollary metaphors.

> That there is no express precept, all calm men allow. Neither is there any conclusive example. John's baptism in some things agreed with Christ's, in others differed from it. But it cannot be certainly proved from Scripture, that even John's was performed by dipping. It is true he baptized in Enon, near Salim, where there was "much water." But this might refer to breadth rather than depth, since

---

[54]"The Means of Grace," B 1:376 – 98, J V:185 – 202.
[55]*ENNT* 2, Col. 2:12, italics added; cf. Rom. 6.
[56]"A Treatise on Baptism," JWO 319; J X:190, sec. 1.2.
[57]"A Treatise on Baptism," J X:190, sec. 1.2.

a narrow place would not have been sufficient for so great a multitude. Nor can it be proved that the baptism of our Savior, or that administered by his disciples, was by immersion. No, nor that of the eunuch baptized by Philip, though "they both went down to the water": For that going down may relate to the chariot and implies no determinate depth of water.[58]

b. Apostolic Practice: Multiple Modes of Conveying Water to Prodigious Numbers

Wesley considered it highly probable that "the Apostles themselves baptized great numbers, not by dipping, but by washing, sprinkling, or pouring water," which is clearly represented as "the cleansing from sin, which is figured by baptism. And the quantity of water used was not material." "Three thousand at one time, and five thousand at another, were converted and baptized by St. Peter at Jerusalem; where they had none but the gentle waters of Siloam."[59]

In his notes on the New Testament on Matthew 3:6, Wesley comments on John's baptizing in the Jordan:

> Such prodigious numbers could hardly be baptized by immerging their whole bodies under water; nor can we think they were provided with change of raiment for it, which was scarce practicable for such vast multitudes. And yet they could not be immersed naked with modesty, nor in their wearing apparel with safety. It seems, therefore, that they stood in ranks on the edge of the river; and that John, passing along before them, cast water on their heads or faces; by which means he might baptize many thousands in a day. And this way most naturally signified Christ's baptizing them "with the Holy Ghost and with fire," which John spoke of, as prefigured by his baptizing with water; and which was eminently fulfilled when the Holy Ghost sat upon the disciples in the appearance of tongues, or flames of fire.[60]

As a loyal Anglican priest, Wesley obediently followed his church's typical preference for sprinkling, based on the likelihood that the apostles had employed sprinkling more often due to the great numbers baptized in the first days after Pentecost, and where they were baptized — away from abundant water. Like most Anglicans, Wesley was unconvinced that only adult baptism by immersion is taught in the New Testament.[61] But the mode of baptism was a secondary matter in relation to the benefits of baptism.

E. The Benefits of Baptism

Wesley cites five sure benefits to be found in baptism. (1) In baptism the value of Christ's death is applied to us and to our sins personally. (2) In baptism we are

---

[58]"A Treatise on Baptism," J X:188 – 89, sec. 1.3.
[59]"A Treatise on Baptism," JWO 320; J X:192, sec. 1.1.
[60]ENNT 1; Matt. 3:6.
[61]"A Treatise on Baptism," JWO 319 – 20; J X:191 – 92, sec. 1.3 – 5.

welcomed into the new covenant community. (3) In baptism we become members of the body of Christ. (4) In baptism we are grafted into the body of Christ and made children of God. (5) In baptism we are made heirs of the new reign of God.

1. First Benefit: The Value of Christ's Death Is Applied to Sinners

a. Washing Away the Guilt of Sin

The first benefit of baptism is "the washing away of the guilt of original sin by the application of the merits of Christ's death."[62] In baptism the value of Christ's death is applied to us. Baptism is God's way of communicating to us our forgiveness.

Adam's sin regrettably has caused a chain reaction in the rest of human history. As with Adam, all human acts of freedom cause consequences that cannot be erased by their own willing. Adam's choice to disobey God thus set a pattern for all subsequent human choice. Sin has been transmitted to the whole human race. Each generation adds its own stamp to the history of sin. Every human person following Adam is corrupted and stained and in need of spiritual cleansing.

Everyone in human history therefore needs what God alone can give: a new start in which from God's point of view all the guilt of original sin is washed away by "the application of the merits of Christ's death."[63] The rite of baptism is a sign of that cleansing being applied to the person baptized.

Justification is God's work on the cross for us. It is a completed work that makes an objective change in our relationship to God, and it seeks a full response from us: to freely accept God's gift. The gift is not contingent on our decision, but it calls for our decision. God's gift is unmerited; it does not depend on anything we do (see the chapters on justification and grace in volume 2 of this series).

b. The Redeemed Relation with God Makes Real Change in Us Possible

Being redeemed gives our personal history a new starting point, and as we begin our new relationship with God, the way we live our lives begins to change in response to God's gift of salvation.

The gospel calls for a new vocabulary to speak of new life in Christ: God's justifying pardon is termed by Wesley as a "relational change." Justification means that our relationship with God is objectively changed. Justification is therefore a relational change (or in eighteenth-century English, a "relative" change). What follows after justification (new birth and growth in grace) calls for real, substantive behavioral change.[64] Wesley wrote, "But though it be allowed, that justification and the new birth are, in point of time, inseparable from each other, yet are they easily distinguished, as being not the same, but things of a widely different nature."[65]

---

[62]"A Treatise on Baptism," JWO 321; J X:190, sec. 2.1.
[63]Ibid.
[64]"The Great Privilege," B 1:431–43, J V:223–33.
[65]Ibid.

God creates a new relation with humanity by his pardoning gift, which calls for its reception in a new birth of freedom, a real change in us.

> God in justifying us does something *for* us; in begetting us again, he does the work *in* us. The former changes our *outward* relation to God, so that of enemies we become children; by the latter our *inmost* souls are changed, so that of sinners we become saints. The one restores us to the *favor*, the other to the *image*, of God. The one is the taking away the *guilt*, the other the taking away the *power*, of sin: so that, although they are joined together in point of time, yet are they of wholly distinct natures.[66]

Pastoral counsel of persons is constantly conveying this good news on a one-to-one basis: Our relation with God has been changed by the cross. Our inner life is being changed by the hearing and rehearing of this good news. The cross restores us to the favor of God. The new life begun in baptism calls us to make choices that reflect the image of God. The gift of justification takes away the guilt of sin. The gift of sanctifying grace takes away the power of sin.[67]

Faithful baptism intends to effect a real change in us based on God's will to relate to humanity in a new way, transforming the history of sin. In the death and resurrection of Christ, a new relation comes into being between the sinner and God. In this new relation there is no condemnation. This relational change in the presence of the forgiving God then calls for a real change in behavior in the personal life of the believer.[68]

2. Second Benefit: We Are Welcomed to the New Covenant Community

Wesley thoughtfully developed the analogy between circumcision and baptism: "As circumcision was then the way of entering into this covenant, so baptism is now." Just as the Jews were admitted into the worshiping community through circumcision, Christians are initiated through baptism.[69] This is the second benefit of baptism.

Baptism benefits us by welcoming us into a covenant with God similar to that between God and Abraham, which is a covenant of *promise*. But Christian baptism is a covenant of *fulfillment* in which "sins and iniquities are no more."[70] We enter into the covenant with God through baptism just as the Israelites did through circumcision. This is a covenant entered with a new heart enlivened by the good news. It is everlasting, since it is a covenant by and with the eternal God. Baptism in the gospel dispensation has replaced circumcision as a sign of admittance into Christ's family. In baptism we "put on Christ," and are "mystically 'united to Christ' and

---

[66]"The Great Privilege," B 1:431–43, J V:223, proem 2, italics added.
[67]"A Treatise on Baptism," JWO 321; J X:190, sec. 2.1.
[68]"A Treatise on Baptism," JWO 321–22; J X:189–90, sec. 2.1.
[69]Ps. 111:9; Gen. 17:7–8; "A Treatise on Baptism," JWO 322; J X:188–90, sec. 2.2.
[70]"A Treatise on Baptism," JWO 322; J X:189, sec. 2.2.

made one with him." From this "spiritual, vital union with him proceeds the influence of his grace on those who are baptized.[71] It is due to this union that we share in all the privileges and promises Christ made to us.

a. The Old Man in Adam and the New Man in Christ

"We are all born under the guilt of Adam's sin." That is "the unanimous sense of the ancient Church."[72]

How could it have happened that this was the unanimous sense of the Scripture and the ancient church when so few in the modern world take it seriously? My view is that modernity lacks historical awareness and a sense of how one generation affects another. But my task here is simply to set forth Wesley's teaching, which is saturated with Scripture references: "We were 'shapen in iniquity, and in sin did my mother conceive us'" (Ps. 51:5). We were all "'by nature the children of wrath' [cf. Eph. 2:3], and dead in trespasses and sins; that 'in Adam all die'; that 'by one man's disobedience all were made sinners'; that 'by one man sin entered into the world, and death by sin'; which came upon all men, because all had sinned [cf. Rom. 5:12].... 'Death reigned from Adam to Moses' [Rom. 5:14]."[73]

The good news: "But 'as by the offence of one, judgment came upon all men to condemnation; even so by the righteousness of one the free gift came upon all men unto justification of life'" (Rom. 5:18).[74]

b. Why Scripture Views Baptism as Ordinary Christian Practice

Why baptize? "The virtue of this free gift, the merits of Christ's life and death, are applied to us in baptism. 'He gave himself for the church, that he might sanctify and cleanse it with the washing of water by the word,' namely, in baptism, the ordinary instrument of our justification."[75] The "ordinary instrument" indicates the prescribed means by which we enter into the covenant of grace and are admitted to the church and made members of Christ's body.[76] "Ordinary" points toward the means ordained by God, ordered according to the command of God the Son, the way God has ordered our initiation into the believing community. If infants are irreversibly entangled in the history of sin, then they are proper subjects of the sacrament of cleansing.[77]

c. The Cleansing Work of the Spirit in Baptism

The Holy Spirit, by virtue of the atoning work of Christ on the cross, washes the soul in the blood of Christ so as to pardon sin and remove guilt. This washing should not be treated either as merely a metaphor or as a literal washing of blood.

---

[71]"A Treatise on Baptism," JWO 322; J X:191, sec. 2.2.
[72]Ibid.
[73]"A Treatise on Baptism," JWO 321; J X:188, sec. 2.1.
[74]"A Treatise on Baptism," JWO 322; J X:191, sec. 2.2.
[75]Eph. 5:25–26; "A Treatise on Baptism," JWO 322; J X:189, sec. 2.2.
[76]1 Cor. 12:13; Gal. 3:27; Eph. 4:12.
[77]"A Treatise on Baptism," JWO 324–25; J X:193–95, sec. 4.1–5.

The blood of Christ was real. The washing by water is real. The congregation prays for the Spirit to make the connection. There is no longer any condemnation. Christian parents who do not know how to teach this to their children have deprived them of a great gift.

In the initiatory rite, the church prays to God the Spirit that the believer will "receive remission of sins."[78] The baptized are "washed and sanctified by the Holy Ghost, and, being delivered from God's wrath, receive remission of sins, and enjoy the everlasting benediction of his heavenly washing."[79] Formerly children of wrath by our sin nature and dead in our sins, we are now forgiven and regenerated. The outward washing has no effect unless combined with inward grace, which makes the waters of baptism a means by which "we are regenerated or born again."[80]

3. Third Benefit: We Become Members of the Body of Christ

The third benefit of baptism is this: "By baptism we are admitted into the Church, and consequently made members of Christ, its Head." From this "vital union" with Christ proceeds "the influence of his grace on those that are baptized."[81]

Believers are "mystically united to Christ, and made one with him. For 'by one Spirit are we all baptized into one body'" (1 Cor. 12:13), the church, "the body of Christ" (Eph. 4:12). As a consequence of our inclusion in the covenant community and the family of God, we are through the grace of baptism made inheritors of God's kingdom. We are joint heirs with Christ by participating in the gift of his holiness.

4. Fourth Benefit: We Are Grafted into the Body of Christ and Made Children of God

When a shoot or bud of one plant or tree is inserted into the stem or trunk of another, that is called a graft. So by baptism we "who were 'by nature children of wrath' are made the children of God" (Eph. 2:3). We are "grafted into the body of Christ's Church, made the children of God by adoption and grace."[82]

This is the fourth benefit of baptism. The analogy here is the new Israel being grafted into the old Israel. The children of the Son of God are being grafted into the covenant of promise. There is only one who by nature is the Son of God, but we by faith participate in his sonship and are thereby adopted into the family of God. In baptism we, by God's ordinance, are given the gift of the complete washing away of sins through Christ. By water we are cleansed of our transgressions and drawn into the realm of his incomparable holiness.

The debate over whether Wesley affirmed baptismal regeneration hinges on what is meant by Paul's phrase "the washing of regeneration" (Titus 3:5; cf. Eph. 5:26). This assumes that the water of baptism is the appointed means to the end of

---

[78]"A Treatise on Baptism," JWO 319; J X:188, sec. 2.2.
[79]Eph. 5:25–26; "A Treatise on Baptism," JWO 322; J X:191, sec. 2.2.
[80]"A Treatise on Baptism," JWO 322; J X:191, sec. 2.2.
[81]"A Treatise on Baptism," JWO 322; J X:191, sec. 2.3.
[82]"A Treatise on Baptism," JWO 322; J X:191–92, sec. 2.4.

spiritual regeneration. Wesley made it clear that this regeneration was not ascribed to an "outward washing, but to the inward grace, which, added thereto, makes it a sacrament." It is an inward washing conveyed by water as God's chosen sign of complete cleansing. Once this grace is given and voluntarily received in baptism, it "will not be wholly taken away, unless we quench the Holy Spirit of God."[83]

Only in Jesus' cross and resurrection is the meaning of baptism made completely clear. By it we share in the dying and risen Christ. There we see how Christ gave his life for the church just as a husband is ready to give up his life to protect his beloved. This is the unexpected metaphor used in Ephesians. The question is: How did Christ give himself for the church? Answer: Like a husband willing to give up everything for his beloved. In this word picture, the husband is standing up and, when necessary, sacrificing for his wife, based on the analogy of God the Son standing up and sacrificing himself for the sons and daughters of men: "Husbands, love your wives, just as Christ loved the church and gave himself up for her to make her holy, cleansing her by the washing with water through the word, and to present her to himself as a radiant church, without stain or wrinkle or any other blemish, but holy and blameless" (Eph. 5:25 – 27 NIV).

This "washing with water through the word" draws the covenant community into the realm of holiness. We dwell in the realm of God's holiness where God's will reigns in our lives. What God does for us on the cross and in the resurrection is "without stain or wrinkle or any other blemish."[84]

5. Fifth Benefit: We Are Made Heirs of the New Reign of God

a. In Baptism We Are Made Heirs of the Kingdom

The fifth benefit of baptism is a consequence of all the above benefits: Because we are children of God, we are made heirs of God. We are children of his kingdom, his reign — "heirs of God, and joint-heirs with Christ" (Rom. 8:17). We share in the present and future riches of his life with us as Son of Man and Son of God. Insofar as we live answerable to our baptism, repenting and believing, we are admitted into this covenant as heirs of the coming kingdom.[85]

b. Summing Up

Summing up, these are the five benefits of baptism set forth in Scripture by the apostle Paul, as taught by John Wesley:

1. In baptism the value of Christ's death is applied to us.
2. In baptism we are welcomed into the new covenant community.
3. In baptism we become members of the body of Christ.
4. In baptism we are grafted into the body of Christ and made children of God.
5. In baptism we are made heirs of the new reign of God.

[83] A Treatise on Baptism," JWO 322; J X:191, sec. 2.2.
[84] A Treatise on Baptism," JWO 322; J X:191, sec. 2.3 – 4.
[85] A Treatise on Baptism," JWO 323; J X:191, sec. 2.5.

F. Baptism as a Means of Grace Instituted by the Lord

1. A Means of Grace Enduring through Time

Did Christ intend that baptism remain as a permanent rite in the church? Yes. Baptism is "intended to last as long as the Church into which it is the appointed means of entering."[86] There is no other "ordinary way" to enter the church or the kingdom of heaven. Throughout the ages, baptism remains a permanent rite in the church. Why? Because God has ordained this simple means of grace that anyone can understand. He takes plain water and makes of it a means of grace.

But couldn't I receive new birth in the worshiping community without outward baptism? No. "The outward baptism is a means of the inward." Analogous to circumcision, baptism happens only once. It initiates the believer into the believing community. By analogy, no Jew would say: "I have the inward circumcision and therefore do not bother with giving me its sign and seal."[87] That soul would be cut off from his people "by despising the seal of it."[88] Arguments on the indelibility of baptism hinge on the irremovability of that seal. As once circumcised, a Jew will always be circumcised, so as once sealed by baptism, a Christian will always be baptized.

By means of this visible seal, Jesus promises to be "with you always, even unto the end of the world."[89] All who obey the Christ of all ages will voluntarily follow the Lord's instruction to be baptized. By baptism we receive the promises of the forgiveness of sin. Our adoption as God's children by the Holy Spirit is visibly signed and sealed. Faith is confirmed and grace increased.

"In all ages, the outward baptism is a means of the inward, as outward circumcision was of the circumcision of the heart."[90] As circumcision was necessary for inclusion in the old covenant, so is baptism for the new covenant. Just as outward circumcision signified an "inward circumcision of the heart,"[91] so does the outward sign of baptism signify an inward change from the old sin nature to new birth of the redeemed person. We are called to repent and be baptized, there being no other way to enter the kingdom of God. "Therefore go and make disciples of all nations, baptizing them in the name of the Father and of the Son and of the Holy Spirit" (Matt. 28:19 NIV). How far do we go? "You will receive power when the Holy Spirit comes on you; and you will be my witnesses in Jerusalem, and in all Judea and Samaria, and to the ends of the earth" (Acts 1:8 NIV).

Scripture makes it clear that baptism is an enduring means of grace intended to

---

[86]"A Treatise on Baptism," JWO 323; J X:192, sec. 3.1.
[87]"A Treatise on Baptism," JWO 323; J X:192, sec. 3.2.
[88]Gen. 17:14; "A Treatise on Baptism," JWO 323; J X:192, sec. 3.2.
[89]"A Treatise on Baptism," JWO 323; J X:192, sec. 3.3.
[90]"A Treatise on Baptism," JWO 323; J X:192, sec. 3.2.
[91]Ibid.

remain in effect until Christ's return.[92] Baptism is an abiding feature forever secured by Christ's command in the whole design of Christ's great commission.[93]

2. Saving Effects Conditional upon Reception of Grace

There is, however, a condition, an "if": "Baptism doth now save us if we live answerable thereto — if we repent, believe, and obey the gospel — supposing this, as it admits us into the Church here, so into glory hereafter."[94]

This is a decisive "if." We are saved by the grace communicated in baptism provided we repent, believe, and obey. Lacking those conditions, the act of water baptism as such, if wrongly understood and inadequately received, does not save.

God's love is unconditional. It does not place conditions of worthiness upon its reception. Faith is the simple reception of this unconditional love. Faith is not a new work that serves as a condition for pardon; rather, it is the very act of choice to receive that pardon.

3. Quenching the Spirit

Those who are lapsed, having once been baptized, may become acutely aware of their need for a new birth of spirit.[95]

Ordinarily in Christian teaching, the seal of regeneration comes through the water of baptism, in which the grace of baptism is communicated to the believer.[96] This regeneration has a lasting inward benefit, which completes the outward act of washing, and it is removed only by renouncing or blaspheming the Holy Spirit or persistently living a degenerate life. "Herein a principle of grace is infused, which will not be wholly taken away unless we quench the Holy Spirit of God by long-continued wickedness," wrote Wesley.[97] By our foolish choices, we may quench the Spirit. But this does not make our foolish freedom more powerful than the Spirit. The Spirit can reignite what we have quenched.

Among baptized persons whose baptism had been quenched by their foolish choices, Wesley preached a new birth of the baptism they had once received. Baptism without faith does not save, but neither are we saved without baptism. The grace of baptism must, at some level, be received in faith sooner or later in order to remain in effect. Does this diminish the grace of baptism? No. The infinite grace of God can never be diminished. By our foolish choices, we only appear to diminish it. Baptism is not effected by water alone, nor is it effected without the water of regeneration. This water is both an outward act of cleansing and an inward reception of that cleansing.

---

[92]"A Treatise on Baptism," JWO 323; J X:192, sec. 3.1.
[93]"A Treatise on Baptism," JWO 323; J X:192, sec. 3.3.
[94]"A Treatise on Baptism," JWO 323; J X:192, sec. 2.5.
[95]Ibid.
[96]"A Treatise on Baptism," JWO 323; J X:192, sec. 2.4.
[97]Ibid.

At this point, Wesley's essay turns toward a more vexing issue, hinging on the point just made.

G. Familial Baptism

1. Circumcision and Baptism

a. The Ancient Church Grasped the Sense of Scripture

As children are admitted into the family of Israel by circumcision, so are children admitted into the body of Christ by baptism.[98] But should children be baptized? Wesley grasped the dangers of a doctrine of baptismal regeneration that did not call for its voluntary reception.

Wesley appealed to "Scripture, reason, and primitive, universal practice" in answering the question of who in the covenant community is old enough to be baptized. Those who look for a concise expression of the quadrilateral method find it in these four terms: *Scripture, reason, early Christian tradition*, and *experiential practice*. All of these levels are argued in "A Treatise on Baptism." Only a judicious application of all four criteria will yield a sufficient answer. Only this balance will provide adequate direction for ordinary pastoral practice.

Using these criteria, Wesley argued that there is a reliable answer to the contested issue of infant baptism: if infants are capable of being entered into covenants by their parents, as they were in circumcision, this assumption is sustained and transmuted similarly in the gospel dispensation. Thus, children need not be barred from Christian baptism, as Jewish children were not barred from the old covenant. Christian baptism is the seal of one's entry into evangelical faith and its community. This seal is chosen by the Lord himself, not by subsequent interpreters.[99] Therefore, the new covenant of the gospel should be open to children of faithful parents in a fitting way through baptism, taking into account the children's admittedly limited capacities to respond.[100]

In "A Farther Appeal," Wesley argued that infants are justified in baptism even when they cannot, through no fault of their own, of themselves believe. They are anticipatively believing through their parents and the surrounding congregation and already sharing in the covenant community. Infants are not barred from the promise of believing just because they are newborns. Through the faith of believing parents who must under these conditions speak for their children, the infants already are sharing in that believing community.[101] The case with adults is obviously different. They must in baptism repent and believe if the new birth is to be effectively received in them.[102]

---

[98]"A Treatise on Baptism," JWO 324; J X:193–95, sec. 4.1–5.
[99]"A Treatise on Baptism," JWO 325; J X:193–95, sec. 4.1–5.
[100]"A Treatise on Baptism," JWO 324; J X:194–95, sec. 4.3.
[101]FA, pt. 1, B 3:107–11.
[102]"A Treatise on Baptism," JWO 324; J X:194–95, sec. 4.3.

The history of debate over baptism indicates that faithful believers may differ on the questions of its modes and conditions. The passages of Scripture that must be reconciled are diverse and complex. Since Scripture alone does not decisively settle some questions on the mode of administration and age of baptism, the faithful look to the best historical and contemporary exegetes of these passages to help them better grasp the intent of the sacred text. Hence the church has a history of debate on these passages, praying for the Spirit to guide their reading of the written Word.

Wesley again followed settled Anglican teaching in appealing not only to reason and experience but also to "primitive, universal practice," that is, early ecumenical teaching and its experiential expressions today. Use your good sense to reason with the consensual practice of the ancient church and to the "universal practice" of the multigenerational ecumenical tradition. These criteria provide a significant glimpse into Wesleyan pastoral method.[103] Appeal to the experience not merely of the individual but of the historical Christian community. But first you must submit your own opinions and judgments to the text of Scripture itself.

b. The Family of Abraham

That children and whole families are capable of entering into covenant is evident from scriptural covenant history, for example, the accounts of Abraham's family and of New Testament families being saved together in the gospel dispensation. It is common throughout biblical history for infants to enter into covenants through their parents.

This pattern is found in Deuteronomy 29:10–13:

All of you are standing today in the presence of the LORD your God — your leaders and chief men, your elders and officials, and all the other men of Israel, together with your children and your wives, and the foreigners living in your camps who chop your wood and carry your water. You are standing here in order to enter into a covenant with the LORD your God, a covenant the LORD is making with you this day and sealing with an oath, to confirm you this day as his people, that he may be your God as he promised you and as he swore to your fathers, Abraham, Isaac and Jacob. (NIV)[104]

Scripture makes it evident that God makes covenant with little ones. "God would never have made a covenant with little ones if they had not been capable of it."[105] Can children be entered into covenant? "The custom of nations and common reason of mankind prove that infants may enter into a covenant, and may be obliged by compacts made by others in their name."[106]

The children of Abraham were always anticipatively included in Abraham's cov-

---

[103]"A Treatise on Baptism," JWO 324; J X:193–95, sec. 4.1–5.
[104]See "A Treatise on Baptism," JWO 324–25; J X:194, sec. 4.3.
[105]"A Treatise on Baptism," JWO 326–31; J X:195–200, sec. 4.3.
[106]Ibid.

enant, even before they had or could have made any conscious or informed decision to confirm it. Abraham's covenant of faith anticipates the evangelical dispensation. This is signified by a scriptural type of anticipation: Christ himself receiving the children. Christ invited the children to come to him, and he accepted them as they were brought by their parents.[107]

It is a principle of both law and Scripture that children are bound by covenants made by their parents in their name.[108] If infants can be bound by legal contracts made in their name, they can be baptized and raised according to the promises their parents made in their name. If infants are capable of being embraced under a legal contract, then they are, in an anticipative sense, capable of entering into a covenant with God. If children enter into the sinful realm of fallen history not through their own will but through their parents' actions, then to leave those children without a remedy is to deny them the justice of grace.[109]

2. In Scripture Whole Families Enter the Covenant Together

a. The Intergenerational Covenant

The key to familial covenants such as baptism lies in the intergenerational character of the whole body of Christ in time. It hinges on the analogy between circumcision and baptism: Scripture reveals two complementary covenants, one before, the other after Christ's coming. It is clear that infants of the faithful were circumcised under the old covenant. So, similarly, infants of the faithful new people of God are baptized under the new covenant.[110] During childhood, a child's parents are by God's design stand-in representatives for the interests of the child. This does not relieve the child of taking responsibility for his own baptism when he reaches an age of accountability.

Infants under the old covenant were capable of receiving circumcision and were thus obliged when they came of age to take responsibility for their own actions. They could defy the covenant and give up the benefits of the covenant, but not without consequences. The prophets tell story after story of these consequences. By analogy, it is possible that some anticipatory form of repentance and faith is known to God even for infants. God's knowledge is not limited to present time. God alone is capable of seeing into, without determining unilaterally, the future of the child. Similarly the child of believing parents is capable of entering into the new covenant by faithful Christian baptism. The parents pray for the Spirit to enable the child's future responsible response to the terms of the covenant.[111]

The Lord commanded the apostles to make disciples of all nations by baptizing them. Infants surely were included in "all nations," since the nations include infants.

---

[107]Matt. 19:13 – 14; "A Treatise on Baptism," JWO 324 – 25; J X:195, sec. 4.6.
[108]"A Treatise on Baptism," JWO 324 – 25; J X:194, sec. 4.4.
[109]"A Treatise on Baptism," JWO 324 – 25; J X:193 – 95, sec. 4.1 – 5.
[110]"A Treatise on Baptism," JWO 324; J X:193, sec. 4.1.
[111]"A Treatise on Baptism," JWO 326 – 31; J X:195 – 200, sec. 4.10.

If infants are ruled out of valid baptism, wouldn't it have been the case that infants also on the same grounds would be ruled out of circumcision?[112]

b. Family Baptism

The New Testament repeatedly records that often when a believer was baptized, the believer's whole household was baptized (Acts 16:33; 18:8). Paul wrote that he "baptized the household of Stephanas" (1 Cor 1:16 NIV). Similarly, Luke recorded in Acts: "At that hour of the night the jailer took them and washed their wounds; then immediately he and all his household were baptized. The jailer brought them into his house and set a meal before them; he was filled with joy because he had come to believe in God — he and his whole household" (16:33 – 34 NIV). Speaking of Lydia, Luke recalled, "When she and the members of her household were baptized, she invited us to her home" (Acts 16:14 – 15 NIV). It is clear that whole families were baptized by the apostles. The household was baptized together, regardless of age. A household included all members of the family.[113] Although infants are not specifically mentioned in Scripture as subjects of baptism, neither are women, yet no one questions that women were baptized.[114]

It is a reasonable assumption that in the households baptized there often must have been children. In Acts 2:38 – 39 Peter made the assumption explicit: "Repent and be baptized, every one of you, in the name of Jesus Christ for the forgiveness of your sins. And you will receive the gift of the Holy Spirit. The promise is for you and your children" (NIV).[115] Infants, too, are called in due time to come to Christ. "People brought little children to Jesus for him to place his hands on them and pray for them. But the disciples rebuked them. Jesus said, 'Let the little children come to me, and do not hinder them, for the kingdom of heaven belongs to such as these'" (Matt. 19:13 – 14 NIV). Luke's testimony agrees: "People were also bringing babies to Jesus for him to place his hands on them" (Luke 18:15 NIV).[116]

Wesley had no way to anticipate the extent to which neonate baptism would become a devisive nineteenth-century interdenominational issue on the American frontier. Nor was he able to anticipate how fiercely the battle would rage over the proper biblical definition of baptismal regeneration.

c. The Consensus of the Experience of Historic Christianity on Baptism

To clarify these scriptural evidences, Wesley examined ancient ecumenical and patristic testimony from Origen, Cyprian, Athanasius, Chrysostom, and Augustine to demonstrate this consensual view. Wesley thought that there was compelling historical evidence that the same tradition was found worldwide, not only in the churches of Europe, but also of Africa, Asia, and India, "even those of St. Thomas

[112]"A Treatise on Baptism," JWO 326 – 31; J X:195 – 200, sec. 4.3.
[113]"A Treatise on Baptism," JWO 326 – 31; J X:195 – 200, sec. 4.5 – 10.
[114]"A Treatise on Baptism," JWO 326 – 31; J X:195 – 200, sec. 4.8.
[115]"A Treatise on Baptism," JWO 326 – 31; J X:195 – 200, sec. 4.8 – 9.
[116]"A Treatise on Baptism," JWO 326 – 31; J X:195 – 200, sec. 4.6.

in the Indies."[117] In his "Thoughts on Infant Baptism," Wesley provided for his connection a fuller account of patristic sources on baptism by extracting from William Wall's *History of Infant Baptism*.[118]

Wesley trusted the ancient ecumenical consensus: "If to baptize infants has been the general practice of the Christian Church in all places and in all ages, then this must have been the practice of the Apostles, and, consequently, the mind of Christ."[119] He could not find any instance among the ancient Christian writers that children were refused baptism or that it was held unlawful. He warned against weak arguments based on scriptural word order and overextended etymological arguments.[120]

The ancient Christian writers, with near unanimity, argued that if the apostles baptized infants, so should the apostolic church today. If outward baptism is generally, in ordinary church practice, a command of Christ necessary to salvation, then children should not be arbitrarily ruled out from the way of salvation. Jesus said, "Let the little children come to me, and do not hinder them, for the kingdom of heaven belongs to such as these" (Matt. 19:14 NIV). He also said, "Truly I tell you, unless you change and become like little children, you will never enter the kingdom of heaven" (Matt. 18:3 NIV). The terms of salvation — repentance, faith, and baptism — involve becoming like a little child again, trusting in God and receiving a new birth.

On the basis of these rational, historical, exegetical, and experiential arguments, Wesley concluded that the apostles baptized infants, even as Jesus himself had been circumcised as an infant. He thought this practice stands "in conformity to the uninterrupted practice of the whole Church of Christ from the earliest ages, to consecrate our children to God by baptism, as the Jewish Church were commanded to do by circumcision."[121] Hence Samuel and John Wesley and the whole Wesleyan connection have largely held steadfast to the consensual voices of the intergenerational worldwide church. Accordingly, it is not only lawful and innocent, but right and the pastor's binding duty to follow the continuous practice of the ancient church by bringing children of faithful families to Christ to receive the grace of baptism.

3. Serious Thoughts Concerning Godfathers and Godmothers

a. Surrogate Parents

We get a glimpse of Wesley as a counselor to parents upon the birth of a child regarding the child's growth in faith and holiness in his brief work "Serious Thoughts Concerning Godfathers and Godmothers" (1752).[122] Wesley took for granted the standard Anglican practice whereby parents select godparents who are to guide

[117]"A Treatise on Baptism," JWO 326–31; J X:195–200, sec. 4.9.
[118]William Wall, *History of Infant Baptism* (London: R. Hawes, 1780).
[119]"A Treatise on Baptism," JWO 326–31; J X:195–200, sec. 4.9.
[120]"A Treatise on Baptism," JWO 326–31; J X:195–200, sec. 4.1.
[121]"A Treatise on Baptism," JWO 326–31; J X:195–200, sec. 4.10.3.
[122]J X:506–9.

children when necessary amid any contingencies or deficiencies ahead.[123] Everyone baptized should have three godparents, he thought, two of the same gender as the child. Their task is to encourage the child in the faith in the role of "a kind of spiritual parents." They are specifically called to be attentive to "whatever spiritual helps were wanting" in the natural parents responsible.[124] They may seek to fill in gaps they see in catechesis, confirmation, or moral development. Minimally the child is expected to learn the Lord's Prayer, the Ten Commandments, and the Apostles' Creed.

b. Teaching Children the Meaning of Their Baptism

The duty of godparents is to see to it that the child, as early as possible, is taught the meaning of his or her baptism.[125] It is a solemn duty of parents to teach "what a solemn vow, promise, and profession" has been made or will be made in baptism.[126]

Godparents are responsible, along with parents, pastor, and congregation, for overseeing the spiritual growth of the baptized, to provide a solid foundation for holiness and happiness. Some take this office without ever considering what it implies. Others refuse it because it seems impossible. Only those who "truly fear God" should be chosen as godparents.[127]

Those who take on this responsibility should not fear it, since God intends and provides grace to enable its fulfillment. Ultimately, it is the child who is accountable before God. Parents and godparents do what they can to teach the faith. Godparents are not imperatively required by Scripture, thus they are not "absolutely necessary." But having them is "highly expedient." Godparents are intended to serve as a comfort to parents that their child will be cared for spiritually in their absence. In cases where those chosen as godparents remain lax and inattentive to the baptized child, the parents are responsible.[128]

c. Confirming the Meaning of Baptism

When Wesley formed the Methodist societies, they were part of the Church of England. Later they would embrace many non-Anglicans who had varied baptismal and confirmation practices. When early Methodists were baptized, confirmed, married, or received Communion, they usually did so in the context of a local church under the direction of the local minister. However, if they wanted to be Methodists, they engaged in a rigorous period of doctrinal education, moral reformation, and discipleship training. Here they heard homilies preached in the tradition of Wesley's teaching homilies. The societies took seriously the faith and practice of the Methodist faithful. They looked for behavior to match their confession.

---

[123]*LJW*, Letter to Zachariah Yewdall, 7:64, 271.
[124]"Serious Thoughts Concerning Godfathers and Godmothers," J X:508.
[125]"Serious Thoughts Concerning Godfathers and Godmothers," J X:507.
[126]Ibid.
[127]Ibid.
[128]Ibid.

When Wesley sent a book of worship services to the United States for the Methodists in North America, he did not feel called upon to include in it a formal service of confirmation since the societies were already functioning in the role of traditional catechesis. But that did not imply that the public confession of the heartfelt meaning of one's baptism was unimportant. Wesley's teaching homilies and the intense engagement in the Methodist societies served to instruct persons on the fundamentals of Christian faith. This corresponded with the purpose of catechetical instruction in other traditions. Wesley believed that people should be thoroughly instructed in Christian doctrine and should make a public confession of their beliefs.

Wesley was engaged in an extraordinary ministry that assumed classic Christian teachings on baptism and Communion but did not attempt to change classic Anglican practice or teaching. While not focused on the rite of confirmation, he was focused on the decision a person makes to respond to God's grace with intentional commitment. Wesley's preaching sought public affirmation of the grace of God in one's baptism and the acknowledgment of one's acceptance of that grace by faith. To confirm one's baptism is to take responsibility for living as a member of the body of Christ. Thus, the process of confirming faith in the Methodist societies did not diminish the deeper intent of the practice of confirmation but expanded and intensified it.

Further Reading on the Ministry of Baptism

Cushman, Robert Earl. "Baptism and the Family of God." In *The Doctrine of the Church*, edited by Dow Kirkpatrick, 79–102. New York: Abingdon, 1964.

Davies, Rupert, and Gordon Rupp. *A History of the Methodist Church in Great Britain*. London: Epworth, 1965.

Felton, Gayle C. *This Gift of Water: The Practice and Theology of Baptism among Methodists in America*. Nashville: Abingdon, 1992.

Fisher, Orceneth, *The Christian Sacraments*. San Francisco: Whitton, Towne, and Co., 1858.

Holland, Bernard G. *Baptism in Early Methodism*. London: Epworth, 1970.

Rupp, E. Gordon. "Son to Samuel: John Wesley, Church of England Man." In *The Place of Wesley in the Christian Tradition*, edited by Kenneth E. Rowe, 39–66. Metuchen, NJ: Scarecrow, 1976.

Summers, T. O. *Baptism: A Treatise on the Nature, Perpetuity, Subjects, Administrator, Mode, and Use of the Initiating Ordinance of the Christian Church*. Richmond: John Early, 1853.

CHAPTER 8

The Ministry of the Lord's Supper

A. At the Lord's Table

1. Duty of Constant Communion

In this teaching homily, Wesley offered his "most explicit statement of his Eucharistic doctrine and praxis," according to Albert Cook Outler[1] [Homily #101, "The Duty of Constant Communion," B 3:427, J VII:147, introduction by Outler]. He appealed to the classical Christian writers and to the "catholic tradition throughout."

Wesley's Scripture text was Luke 22:19: "This do in remembrance of me." Earlier, during his days as an Oxford don, Wesley had offered his students a primitive version of the devout teaching of "constant communion." That early draft was the basis for this still further revised homily much later. In 1787 Wesley again abridged, rewrote, revised, and republished that extract (first written in Oxford, February 19, 1732).[2] In a preface "To the Reader," he noted in 1787, "I have added very little, but retrenched much.... I thank God I have not yet seen cause to alter my sentiments in any point."[3]

The most frequent problem the laity have with taking Holy Communion is the unreasonable fear of eating and drinking unworthily (see 1 Cor. 11:29). This homily seeks to heal unwarranted fears by showing "that it is the duty of every Christian to receive the Lord's Supper as often as he can" ("The Duty of Constant Communion," B 3:428, J VII:147, pref.).

a. Christ Commanded: Do This in Remembrance of Me

As the apostles were called to "bless, break, and give the bread to all that joined with them in those holy things, so were all Christians obliged to receive those signs of Christ's body and blood."[4] To be obliged means that this is an obligation of those who being baptized are grafted into the body of Christ.

The signs are bread and wine. The thing signified is the body and blood of

---

[1]Albert C. Outler and Richard P. Heitzenrater, eds., *John Wesley's Sermons: An Anthology* (Nashville: Abingdon), 501.

[2]Revised for *AM*, May–June 1787, J X:229–36, 290–95.

[3]"The Duty of Constant Communion," B 3:427, J VII:147–57, sec. 1.1.

[4]"The Duty of Constant Communion," B 3:428–29, J VII:147, sec. 1.1.

Christ. "The bread and wine are commanded to be received." These were not just any words, but the Lord's own words, indeed his dying words: "This command was given by our Lord when he was just laying down his life for our sakes ... as it were, his dying words to all his followers ... in remembrance of his death, to the end of the world."[5] "When he had given thanks, he broke it and said, "This is my body, which is for you; do this in remembrance of me" (1 Cor. 11:24 NIV).

This is not an ancillary command or one without benefits. It is an absolute command with eternal benefits, chiefly "the forgiveness of our past sins and the present strengthening and refreshing of our souls."[6]

b. Food for the Soul

Since human freedom is never completely free from temptations, and since Satan daily seeks to turn us aside from divine grace, we need frequent reminders of God's providence in our Christian walk. Christ himself makes provision for those reminders. *Providence, provision,* and *provide* all have the same Latin root verb, *provideo* — "to look out for us, to provide, to foresee, to plan in advance for our provision." Only God is able to do this completely, for only God can see everything. This provision is what God palpably offers at the Lord's Table.[7]

Our bodies require food and drink in this life journey. God offers bread and wine as the necessary provisions for our spiritual journey. "As our bodies are strengthened by bread and wine, so are our souls by these tokens of the body and blood of Christ. This is the food of our souls: this gives strength to perform our duty."[8]

Therefore it is to our benefit to "never turn our backs on the feast which our Lord has prepared for us."[9] How could it be reasonable to be given a great and undeserved gift and simply walk away from it? God's grace "confirms to us the pardon of our sins by enabling us to leave them."[10] As for our sins, "what surer way have we of procuring pardon from him than the 'showing forth the Lord's death,' and beseeching him, for the sake of his Son's sufferings, to blot out all our sins?"[11] God's way of feeding our souls is more reliable than our self-invented ways.

c. Receive Eternal Pardon as Often as God Gives the Opportunity in Time

Because God knows how best to feed our souls, "we must neglect no occasion which the good providence of God affords us for this purpose." We are to receive his provision "so often as God gives us opportunity."[12]

God's command is for us to receive what is good for us at all times, not sporadi-

---

[5]Ibid.
[6]"The Duty of Constant Communion," B 3:429, J VII:148, sec. 1.2.
[7]"The Duty of Constant Communion," B 3:429, J VII:148, sec. 1.3.
[8]Ibid.
[9]Ibid.
[10]Ibid.
[11]"The Duty of Constant Communion," B 3:429, J VII:148, sec. 1.2.
[12]"The Duty of Constant Communion," B 3:429, J VII:147 – 48, sec. 1.3.

cally. It is not meant in a legal sense as an obligation or in a calendar sense as every day or every week, but in an evangelical sense as the perpetual reception of the divine gift.

To turn away is simply to misunderstand the benefit offered. "Whoever therefore does not receive, but goes from the holy table when all things are prepared, either does not understand his duty or does not care for the dying command of his Savior, the forgiveness of his sins, the strengthening of his soul, and the refreshing it with the hope of glory."[13]

All who desire to please God will respond to this call. Consult the good of your own soul. Do not refuse the gift whenever a reminder of it is offered.[14] In a moment of time, it offers us a promise of eternal benefit. Paul's letters to Corinth make it clear that "the design of this sacrament is the continual remembrance of the death of Christ."[15]

Does "continual" mean that you do nothing but continually remember the death of Christ or that you do everything out of remembering his death? Communion is not physically offered incessantly, but in time with an eye toward eternity. Does "constant" mean frequent, recurrent, or perpetual? The scriptural answer is that the whole of the Christian life, every moment, is a participation in the body of Christ. The outward answer is not to be looked upon as if it were a bill to be paid, but as an offer of an invitation to banquet on the final day. The table is full of energy-restoring food and drink. To receive such a gift, the faithful "prepare themselves for this solemn ordinance by self-examination and prayer."[16]

d. The Constant Intent to Receive All His Promises

"Constant" carries an unremitting intention to "receive all his promises."[17] Since God's holy love is constant, we are called to be constant in our reception of it. God cannot be selectively obeyed according to the convenience of the believer.[18] If it is what God calls us to do, it is not to be obeyed occasionally, but with our constant intent to live out of the divine intention. One who "when he may obey it, if he will not, will have no place in the kingdom of heaven."[19]

This is a logical argument: If I ought to do it now either by act or intent, I ought to do it without interruption, since "now" flows through every moment.[20] Now is the moving image of eternity in time. I would not be regarding it as a divine command of the Eternal One if I selectively responded to it as I wished, as if its reception were purely according to my pleasure.

[13]Ibid.
[14]"The Duty of Constant Communion," B 3:430, J VII:148, sec. 1.4.
[15]"The Duty of Constant Communion," B 3:430, J VII:149, sec. 1.5.
[16]"The Duty of Constant Communion," B 3:430, J VII:149, sec. 1.6.
[17]"The Duty of Constant Communion," B 3:431, J VII:149, sec. 2.1.
[18]"The Duty of Constant Communion," B 3:431, J VII:149, sec. 2.2.
[19]"The Duty of Constant Communion," B 3:431, J VII:150, sec. 2.3.
[20]"The Duty of Constant Communion," B 3:432, J VII:150, sec. 2.4.

2. Communion Counseling

a. Measuring Time and Eternity: How Happy Do I Want to Be?

Human happiness is a refraction of divine holiness. God's purpose in the history of salvation is to make humanity as happy as possible. To do this, God takes into account the distortions of inveterate human willing in the history of sin.

Our level of happiness hinges on how thoroughly our happiness corresponds with God's happiness. God is infinitely happy. God desires human beings to be infinitely happy, not intermittently, but at all times. God knew that "there was but one way for man to be happy like himself, namely, by being like him in holiness."[21] But we cannot refract this divine holiness by ourselves, on our own initiative alone, without grace. We need God's help. Since God knew that "we could do nothing toward this of ourselves, he has given us certain means of obtaining his help. One of these is the Lord's Supper ... that through this means we may be assisted to attain those blessings which he hath prepared for us; that we may obtain holiness on earth and everlasting glory in heaven."[22]

b. The Invitation Is an Act of Divine Mercy

"Do this in remembrance of me" is not a frightful command without a promise, but a divine gift that asks to be received. It is more an act of divine mercy than a tedious obligation.

In light of this truth, the question becomes: Why do you not accept of his mercy as often as ever you can? Why do you refuse it? "You have an opportunity of receiving his mercy: why do you not receive it? ... Why do not you seize upon every opportunity of increasing your strength?"[23]

The pastor as both liturgist and counselor has the constant opportunity to communicate good news to the weary, guilty, and depressed. This news is effectually offered through the means of bread and wine.

What follows are case studies dealing with misunderstandings of the gift given at the Lord's Table.

c. The Charade of Refusal

It is irrational to refuse our own good. Those who treat the command of God selectively do not rightly know the God with whom they are dealing. Those who refuse to receive mercy or to receive it only occasionally or when it is perceived as beneficial have not rightly grasped that the mercy of God is upon them constantly, not intermittently.[24]

What reason can you give for not wanting to receive what is good for you, indeed eternally good for you, and receiving it as constantly as possible? You are being given the opportunity to increase your happiness by sharing in God's happiness.[25]

---

[21]"The Duty of Constant Communion," B 3:432, J VII:150, sec. 2.5.
[22]Ibid.
[23]Ibid.
[24]Ibid.
[25]"The Duty of Constant Communion," B 3:433, J VII:151, sec. 2.6.

d. Why the Claim That "I am Unworthy to Receive Pardon" Is Absurd

The most common objection to receiving the gift of remembering Christ in Communion is "I am unworthy.... Therefore I dare not communicate, lest I should eat and drink my own damnation."[26] When a person says this, he or she is refusing the gift and treating it as if it is an obligation. Wesley pled for a more rational response:

> God offers you one of the greatest mercies on this side of heaven, and commands you to accept it. Why do not you accept this mercy in obedience to his command? You say, "I am unworthy to receive it." And what then? You are unworthy to receive any mercy from God. But is that a reason for refusing all mercy? God offers you a pardon for all your sins. You are unworthy of it, 'tis sure, and he knows it: but since he is pleased to offer it nevertheless, will not you accept of it?[27]

No sinner is worthy of pardon, but God pardons sinners nonetheless. In Jesus' death and resurrection, we see that pardon lived out in an actual history.

God's pardon is his purposely ordered gift transcending your feeling of unworthiness. So if you answer, "I am still too unworthy to receive a gift that transcends my unworthiness," is this not absurd? How could you be unworthy to receive a gift designed to transcend your feeling of unworthiness?[28]

e. Eating Unworthily Meant Rude and Disorderly Conduct

Paul did not say a word about our "being unworthy" to eat and drink. We are all unworthy to receive a gift that transcends our unworthiness. "Being unworthy" is different from receiving the gift in an unworthy manner: "Indeed he does speak of eating and drinking 'unworthily'; but that is quite a different thing." Consult Paul's text to grasp the difference. Note the context of the text: by "eating and drinking unworthily," Paul clearly was referring to "taking the holy sacrament in such a rude and disorderly way that one was 'hungry and another drunken'!"[29] The unworthiness of which Paul spoke was unworthy behavior demeaning the divine gift.

However unworthy we may be to receive this merciful gift of pardon, there can be no unworthiness in following the command of God and receiving its benefits, which rise above our unworthiness.[30]

At the Lord's Table, we are called and enabled to get out of the fear syndrome: "You fear where no fear is." You would do better to fear not communing at all. You make yourself more unworthy by turning away from God's plan for overcoming your unworthiness.[31]

Wesley conceded, "It is true our Church forbids those 'who have done any grievous crime' to receive without repentance. But all that follows from this is that we

---

[26] 1 Cor. 11:29; "The Duty of Constant Communion," B 3:433, J VII:151, sec. 2.7.
[27] "The Duty of Constant Communion," B 3:433, J VII:151, sec. 2.7.
[28] "The Duty of Constant Communion," B 3:433, J VII:152, sec. 2.8.
[29] Ibid.
[30] Ibid.
[31] "The Duty of Constant Communion," B 3:433–34, J VII:152, sec. 2.9.

should repent before we come; not that we should neglect to come at all."[32] Receiving without repentance is not to receive at all. The Lord did not command us to "commit a new act of disobedience, and God will more easily forgive the past!"[33]

3. Just Receive the Gift

a. Time to Receive

Others out of fear avoid Holy Communion because they think that they "cannot live up to it; they cannot pretend to lead so holy a life as constantly communicating would oblige them to do."[34] But the whole purpose of the Lord's Supper is to give sinners an opportunity to receive pardon freely without works of the law. Those who think they cannot live up to the gift have not understood it as sheer unmerited gift.

Penitent believers come to the table to receive the gift, not to give the Lord a reminder of their previous good works. At the table we receive pardon precisely for our misdeeds. This is not a place to refuse God's pardon or assert our own worthiness. There is no room at the table for claims of self-achieved righteousness. The Lord's righteousness in taking our sins upon himself is enough of a good deed to cover all our misdeeds. "Think then what you say, before you say you cannot live up to what is required of constant communicants."[35]

Others manage to come up with an even more absurd evasion: "We dare not do it, because it requires so perfect an obedience afterwards as we cannot promise to perform." The intent to follow God's command continuously is what we do at the Lord's Table. Constant communion is that constant intent.

Baptism and the Lord's Supper are different expressions of the intent to receive God's pardon. Baptism occurs only once as a new birth of freedom. Constant communion occurs in intent at all moments subsequent to baptism. We come to baptism once, but we come to the Lord's Table again and again. In both sacraments the constant intent is to receive God's pardon.

Communion "requires neither more nor less perfect obedience than you promised in your baptism." Hence it amounts to a repudiation of your baptism if you withhold consent to the promise made at your baptism.[36] This evasion "is not so properly an objection against constantly communicating as against communicating at all. For if we are not to receive the Lord's Supper till we are worthy of it" implies that we never will receive it.[37]

God gives grace to fulfill the command to those who profess the intent to follow the command and receive its benefits.[38] Believers are called to "a full purpose of

---

[32]"The Duty of Constant Communion," B 3:434, J VII:152 – 53, sec. 2.10.
[33]"The Duty of Constant Communion," B 3:434, J VII:153 – 54, sec. 2.10.
[34]Ibid.
[35]"The Duty of Constant Communion," B 3:435, J VII:153, sec. 2.11.
[36]"The Duty of Constant Communion," B 3:435 – 36, J VII:153 – 54, sec. 2.13.
[37]"The Duty of Constant Communion," B 3:436, J VII:153, sec. 2.13.
[38]"The Duty of Constant Communion," B 3:435, J VII:153, sec. 2.12.

heart to keep all the commandments of God, and ... a sincere desire to receive all his promises."[39] Inward intent and sincere desire are not a replacement for the Lord's Supper, but a continuation of it.

b. The Absurdity of Having No Time to Receive God's Pardon

What if you have no time to be pardoned by God? That would be like a condemned prisoner who receives a reprieve but says, "I'm too busy; don't bother me."

Do you have no time to prepare for Communion? "All the preparation that is absolutely necessary is contained in those words, 'Repent you truly of your sins past; have faith in Christ our Savior.' "[40] This requires you to "amend your lives, and be in charity with all men; so shall ye be meet partakers of these holy mysteries."[41] All those who consent to their baptism are thus prepared to "draw near without fear, and receive the sacrament to their comfort."[42]

Do you have some business that prevents you "from believing that Christ died to save sinners"? Put your own time in its eternal context: "No business can hinder you from this, unless it be such as hinders you from being in a state of salvation.... If you resolve and design to follow Christ, you are fit to approach the Lord's Table."[43] If temporal business trumps eternal business, you above all need what Communion offers. "Indeed every prudent man will, when he has time, examine himself before he receives the Lord's Supper" in the simplest way, so as to show "whether he believes the promises of God; whether he fully designs to walk in his ways."

So do not "make reverence to God's command a pretense for breaking it."[44]

4. Duty and Emotion

a. The Absence of Immediate Benefit Does Not Invalidate the Divine Command

Some complain, "If I take Communion frequently, it becomes less meaningful." They say the experience feels less holy, diminished by repetition. Does the uninterrupted intent to receive God's pardon tend to diminish our reverence for the here-and-now provision of bread and wine? Does it make us wearier or less aware of the happiness God is willing to offer us?

Wesley answered, "Suppose it did. Has God ever told you that when the obeying his command abates your reverence to it, then you may disobey it?"[45] "He who gave the command, 'Do this,' nowhere adds, 'unless it abates your reverence.' "[46] True reverence flows out of our receptivity to God, not out of our concentration on our feelings.

[39]"The Duty of Constant Communion," B 3:430, J VII:149, sec. 1.6.
[40]"The Duty of Constant Communion," B 3:436, J VII:154, sec. 2.14.
[41]BCP, Exhortation to Holy Communion.
[42]BCP; "The Duty of Constant Communion," B 3:436, J VII:154, sec. 2.14.
[43]"The Duty of Constant Communion," B 3:436, J VII:154, sec. 2.14.
[44]"The Duty of Constant Communion," B 3:436–37, J VII:154, sec. 2.15.
[45]"The Duty of Constant Communion," B 3:437, J VII:155, sec. 2.16.
[46]"The Duty of Constant Communion," B 3:439, J VII:157, sec. 2.22.

Constant readiness to receive God's pardon will "not lessen the true religious reverence, but rather confirm and increase it."[47] To persist in refusing the gift of the Lord's Table is irrational and imprudent, and especially so for those who consider the institution of the Lord's Supper as a mercy to ourselves.[48]

b. The Divine Gift of Pardon Is Not Contingent on Its Emotive Affect

The absence of emotive affect may indicate simply that "he was not rightly prepared ... to receive all the promises of God."[49] It is not God's fault that we do not properly prepare for receiving the gift. "Our not profiting by it is no excuse, since it is our own fault in neglecting that necessary preparation which is in our own power."[50]

In the Church of England, there is a canonical obligation to receive Communion no less than three times a year.[51] This prompts some to think that this minimum constitutes full and complete obedience to the command, "Do this in remembrance of me." This evasion becomes for the Communion counselor an opportunity to convey the once-for-all good news. It is not a requirement but a gift. The means of grace for the reception of that gift has been conveyed directly to us by God the Son in the flesh.[52]

Some well-meaning persons may report, "[I] have communicated constantly so long, but I have not found the benefit I expected." Wesley shifted the focus away from looking for immediate emotive benefits. Better to simply do what God asks and let the Spirit do the rest: "Whatever God commands us to do we are to do because he commands, whether we feel any benefit thereby or no."[53]

By following God's command, we put a barrier in the way of temptation: "Do this in remembrance of me" is a direct divine command to receive the benefits of baptism every day. To follow this command is to be "preserved from many sins and temptations. And surely this should be enough to make us receive this food as often as we can; though we do not presently feel the happy effects of it," which will become evident to believers in God's due time.[54]

B. Readiness for the End-Time Banquet

1. The Wedding Garment

What is the fit wedding garment for meeting the Lord? Wesley's homily #127, "On the Wedding Garment," answers that the proper wedding garment for the Lord's banquet is the holiness of heart and life that lives out of the righteousness of

---

[47]"The Duty of Constant Communion," B 3:437, J VII:155, sec. 2.17.
[48]"The Duty of Constant Communion," B 3:438, J VII:156, sec. 2.21.
[49]"The Duty of Constant Communion," B 3:438, J VII:156, sec. 2.19.
[50]"The Duty of Constant Communion," B 3:439, J VII:157, sec. 2.22.
[51]BCP, Communion Rubrics.
[52]"The Duty of Constant Communion," B 3:438, J VII:156, sec. 2.20.
[53]"The Duty of Constant Communion," B 3:437, J VII:155, sec. 2.18.
[54]Ibid.

Christ shown in his cross and resurrection [(March 26, 1790) B 4:139 – 48; J #127, VII:311 – 17].

a. The Parable of the Wedding Feast

In Matthew 22 Jesus told the parable of a king who planned a great wedding feast for his son. He sent out invitations, but the people he invited refused to come. He told them about the wonderful dinner prepared, but they paid no attention and went about their business. They were too busy.

At last the wedding banquet was ready, and the king sent messengers to tell those he had invited to come to the feast. They were angry. They even killed the messengers. The king retorted that they did not deserve to come. This was a gift prepared by the king, and the invited guests turned away. Then the king ordered his messengers to go to the street corners and invite anyone they could find, whether bad or good. The guests filled the wedding hall. "When the king came in to see the guests, he noticed a man there who was not wearing wedding clothes. He asked, 'How did you get in here without wedding clothes, friend?' The man was speechless." Annoyed, the king immediately had his attendants throw the man out, saying, "Many are invited, but few are chosen" (Matt. 22:11 – 12, 14 NIV).

b. The Meaning of the Parable

This parable became the basis on which Wesley taught a lesson about being ready for a wonderful occasion: the end-time feast, where the Lord brings broken human history to a fitting conclusion. The end-time banquet is anticipated in the Lord's Supper.

The first to be invited were the people of the covenant. They did not show up. They were too busy doing good works. Then everyone was invited, including the worst. The only thing required was to be ready for the occasion. The symbol of readiness was simply having the proper wedding garment. How could anyone come to such a fabulous banquet without wearing a garment to celebrate the occasion! The man who was unprepared for the end-time celebration was thrown out. He was not ready to receive the king's gifts. He did not come fit for the occasion.

2. Fitness for the Kingdom

Jesus' parable of the wedding banquet calls for fitness for living in the presence of God's eternal holiness. That fitness is grounded not in our righteousness but in Christ's righteousness. It is the sole required garment for fitness. It nurtures the here-and-now church in the hope of eternal life with the Lord. It calls disciples within the constraints of time to be ready to receive everlasting life.

The parable does not speak of readiness for the Lord's Supper alone, but readiness for that revealed righteousness to which the Supper points: God's pardon in the end-time judgment for those who repent and believe.[55]

---

[55]"On the Wedding Garment," B 4:141 – 43, J VII:311 – 13, secs. 2 – 6.

"Without the righteousness of Christ we could have no claim to glory; without holiness we could have no fitness for it."[56] The wedding supper of the Lamb of Revelation 19:7–8 looks toward the righteousness of Christ received in time by the church militant.[57] The supper of the parable is the righteousness of Christ ultimately received by the church triumphant. The banquet is the incomparable event to occur at the end of history. It is at the Lord's Table that we are reminded of that future event. The scene is the last day, not the last Sunday.[58]

If the wedding garment is the righteousness of Christ by which we are covered on the last day (Rev. 19:8), then to be clothed in the righteousness of Christ is to be ready for the banquet table. The garment refers to that holiness based on the righteousness of Christ "without which no man shall see the Lord" (Heb. 12:14).[59] One of Satan's devices (see homily #42) is that we can imagine readiness for the last day without this garment — the holiness of heart and life without which we are unfit to enter the kingdom of God. That subversion has spelled disaster for many and has been palmed off within the church as works righteousness. Only one thing is required to enter the banquet: to hear the call to the holy life that reflects the holiness of God.[60]

The garment required is not good deeds such as clothing the naked, feeding the hungry, giving alms, or performing merciful acts of compassion. The lone garment required for this occasion is the righteousness of Christ, by whose merit alone we enter his glory. That glory may be reflected in our own behavior. By his righteousness alone we are justified (saved from the guilt of sin), sanctified (saved from sin itself), and glorified (lifted up to heaven). The wedding garment of which the Scripture speaks is not simply readiness for eucharistic Communion, but readiness for eternal glory in the presence of the Lord. No one without the fitting wedding garment is admitted to this banquet.[61]

a. A Holiness Not Our Own

The wedding garment is not a holiness of our own, but the Lord's own righteousness enacted and embodied on the cross. Without the righteousness of Christ, we would have no readiness to receive eternal glory. Without the personal holiness that God the Spirit is enabling in us, we are unfit for glory. But by the righteousness of Christ, we become members of Christ, children of God, and heirs of the kingdom. By personal holiness through participation in God's own holiness by faith, we are made fit to be "partakers of the inheritance of the saints in light" (Col. 1:12).

[56]"On the Wedding Garment," B 4:141–43, J VII:314, sec. 10.
[57]"On the Wedding Garment," B 4:143, J VII:314, sec. 8.
[58]"On the Wedding Garment," B 4:141, J VII:314, sec. 4.
[59]"On the Wedding Garment," B 4:144, J VII:314, sec. 10.
[60]"On the Wedding Garment," B 4:141–43, J VII:315, sec. 13.
[61]"On the Wedding Garment," B 4:147–48, J VII:316–17, secs. 17–18.

Here we see the crucial linkage between Christ's righteousness on our behalf and our personal holiness as a fitting response to it.[62]

The garment is not simply attending church or living a moral life or holding to right opinions, but actually having that mind which is in Christ. We wear this garment when we become a new creature in Christ, reborn to our original purpose. By grace you are saved through that faith which calls all who hear it to the holy life. The wedding garment is that "holiness without which no man shall see the Lord" (Heb. 12:14) — namely, the Lord's own righteousness.[63] Without the righteousness of Christ, no sinner will be ready to be received into the kingdom. God the Spirit is ready to avail us with this garment whenever the Word is preached. By the righteousness of Christ, we become members of Christ, children of God, and heirs of the kingdom. By the grace of the Spirit, we are made to partake in the inheritance of the saints.

By justifying faith, we are being saved from sin in order to be made holy. We now see that we are intended to have the mind of Christ and walk as Christ walked. We are called to become a new creation, a new person, born anew. The idea that faith makes personal holiness irrelevant is the core idea of antinomianism, which is the false teaching that the gospel ends all obligation. Rather, faith works by love (Gal. 5:6) — love for God and for humanity. "By faith we are saved from sin, and made holy."[64]

b. Salvation and the Holy Life

The giver of life is willing to save every life given, every soul fallen into the misery of sin. But God will not force any soul to accept the gift of new birth. It is only received by choice. Salvation comes not by divine coercion but by grace enabling our self-determined choice.

Those clothed in the only wedding garment fit for the end-time wedding celebration have already been cleansed by Christ's blood, hence made ready for the banquet. Those who do not have this garment are unready and therefore, by their own negligence, will be turned away from God's banquet.[65] The true wedding garment is the righteousness of Christ by which we are covered on the last day.[66]

In his journal entry for March 26, 1790, on the day he wrote this sermon, Wesley wrote: "I have finished my sermon on the Wedding Garment; perhaps the last that I shall write. My eyes are now waxed dim; my natural force is abated. However, while I can, I would do a little for God before I drop into the dust."

---

[62] "On the Wedding Garment," B 4:146 – 47, J VII:314, secs. 16 – 17.
[63] "On the Wedding Garment," B 4:147, J VII:317, sec. 18.
[64] Ibid.
[65] "On the Wedding Garment," B 4:148, J VII:314, sec. 10.
[66] "On the Wedding Garment," B 4:148, J VII:316, sec. 17.

Further Reading on the Ministry of the Lord's Supper

Baker, Frank. *Methodism and the Love Feast*. London: Epworth, 1957.

Barratt, Thomas H. "The Lord's Supper in Early Methodism." In *Methodism: Its Present Responsibilities, The Proceedings of the Methodist Church Conference, Bristol*, 71–81. London: Epworth, 1929.

George, Raymond A. "The Lord's Supper." In *The Doctrine of the Church*, edited by Dow Kirkpatrick, 140–60. New York: Abingdon, 1964.

Johnson, Susanne. "John Wesley on the Duty of Constant Communion: The Eucharist as a Means of Grace for Today." In *Wesleyan Spirituality in Contemporary Theological Education*, 25–46. Nashville: General Board of Higher Education and Ministry, United Methodist Church, 1987.

Jones, Scott J. *Staying at the Table: The Gift of Unity for United Methodists*. Nashville: Abingdon, 2008.

CHAPTER 9

The Unity of the Body of Christ

A. One Body in Christ

1. On Schism

a. That There Might Be No Schism in the Body of Christ

John Wesley, at age eighty-two, preached a crucial homily titled "On Schism," in which he pleaded, "Do not rashly tear asunder the sacred ties which unite you to any Christian society." His text was 1 Corinthians 12:25: "That there should be no schism in the body [of Christ]." Schism opens the door to destructive tempers, both in ourselves and others, that elicit evil surmisings and uncharitable judgments, "bitterness, malice, and settled hatred," which in turn become "a grievous stumbling-block" to the church's unity and mission [Homily #75 (March 30, 1786, Newcastle, England), B 3:59 – 69; J #75, VI:401 – 10]. Wesley thought little good would come from these temperaments and controversies within the body of Christ.[1] His purpose in this sermon was to resist quarrelsome separationist tendencies within the Methodist societies and to reassure the Church of England that his intentions were not schismatic.

The verb *schisma* means "to cut, tear, or split." When Wesley was charged with splitting the church, he turned to the New Testament understanding of *schisma*. In Paul's letters, a schism is "a disunion in mind and judgment, (perhaps also in affection) among those who, notwithstanding this, continued outward united as before."[2] A schism is a cutting or splitting within the body of Christ.[3] Some in his connection wanted separation from the established church, but he did not, and he steadfastly resisted it.

b. The Nature of Schism

Wesley defined schism as "a causeless separation from a body of living Christians."[4] Where the word *schism* occurs, it refers to "not a separation from any church

---

[1]"On Schism," B 3:59 – 60, J VI:401 – 2, pref. 2.
[2]"On Schism," B 3:60 – 61, J VI:403, sec. 1.2.
[3]Ibid.
[4]"On Schism," B 3:64, J VI:406, sec. 2.10.

(whether general or particular, whether the Catholic or any national church) but a separation in a church."[5]

About what were the schismatics in Corinth skirmishing? The divisive issue in Corinth was quite specific to that congregation: negligent and uncharitable attitudes at the Lord's Table. We can read about it in 1 Corinthians: "When you are eating, some of you go ahead with your own private suppers" (11:21 NIV). This was occurring "in such a shocking manner that while one was hungry, another was drunken."[6] This was bad, but was it bad enough to prompt splitting the one body of Christ?

The Greek word for "heresy" differs in tone from schism, though they are closely related. The original meaning of the word *heresy* has been "strangely distorted for many centuries, as if it meant erroneous opinions." Heresy means the pretense of transcending apostolic truth, the proud imagination that we can improve on the gospel. Schism refers instead to tearing the fabric of the unity that we have in the one body of Christ.[7] Picture a living organism able to function as a unified whole until someone tears away a member so as to distort the unity of the body.

Paul grasped the providential and corrective purposes of heresy in the history of the church: to correct distortions and awaken faith. "For there must be also heresies among you, that they which are approved may be made manifest among you" (1 Cor. 11:19 ERV). "The wisdom of God permits it so to be for this end, for the clearer manifestation of those whose heart is right with him."[8]

Schism is a matter of the heart. It does not necessarily imply "a separation from any church or body of Christians."[9] Rather, in 1 Corinthians 12:25 schism means "an alienation of affection in any of them toward their brethren, a division of heart, and parties springing therefrom."[10]

c. The Evil of Schism

Schism is an evil in itself, and it leads to circumstances that create greater evil.[11] "It is evil in itself ... to separate ourselves from a body of living Christians with whom we were before united."[12] If we love as Christ loved, we do not separate from the unity we have in Christ. "It is the nature of love to unite us together." By their love for one another, even their willingness to die for one another, the ancient Christians showed their love and unity in Christ.[13] "It is only when our love grows cold

---

[5]"On Schism," B 3:60, J VI:402, sec. 1.1.

[6]"On Schism," B 3:61 – 62, J VI:403, sec. 1.5.

[7]Ibid. In this passage, Paul used the words *heresy* and *schism* as functionally equivalent, since upon raising the question of schism, he immediately turned to remarks about heresy.

[8]"On Schism," B 3:62, J VI:404, sec. 1.6.

[9]"On Schism," B 3:63, J VI:405, sec. 1.9.

[10]"On Schism," B 3:63, J VI:405 – 6, sec. 1.7.

[11]"On Schism," B 3:64, J VI:405 – 6, sec. 2.10.

[12]"On Schism," B 3:64, J VI:405 – 6, sec. 2.11.

[13]Tertullian, *Apologia* 30.

that we can think of separating from our brethren.... Want of love is always the real cause" of separation among believers.[14]

Schism is not only evil in itself, but it produces the fruits of evil. Schism "brings forth evil fruit; it is naturally productive of the most mischievous consequences," including "severe and uncharitable judging of each other. It gives occasion to offense, to anger, and resentment."

Evil in the heart brings forth appalling fruits in practice. "He whose heart is full of prejudice, anger, suspicion, or any unkind temper, will surely open his mouth in a manner corresponding with the disposition of his mind." From this will arise "bitter words, talebearing, backbiting, and evil-speaking of every kind."[15] "How mightily does all this altercation grieve the Holy Spirit of God!" Such strife will cause those who are "promoting the work of God in the souls of their brethren [to] grow languid ... to the utter destruction, first of the power, and then of the very form of religion. These consequences are not imaginary, are not built on mere conjectures."[16] The schismatic heart leaves behind it a path of destruction.

To "those who are strangers to religion," this pettiness becomes a stumbling block to mission. The consequence: "Thousands of souls, and not a few of those who once walked in the light of God's countenance, may be turned from the way of peace." The consequences of the schismatic heart reverberate in the social order: "Such is the complicated mischief which persons separating from a Christian church or society do, not only to themselves, but to that whole society, and to the world in general."[17]

2. The Perennial Issue

a. Do Not Countenance the Partisan Spirit

The last part of Wesley's homily "On Schism" (secs. 17–21) has particular application to all those in the Wesleyan connection of churches today, especially those troubled about a failing church that forgets its own core teaching.

All modern Wesleyan traditions today are facing similar questions of inward schism and outward separation, especially regarding sexuality, even more clearly now in connection with the ordained minister officiating at weddings that neglect the classic Christian teaching of covenant fidelity in marriage between one man and one woman.

Some members argue for "amicable separation" from a failed church, just as did those in Wesley's day who said, "[We were] constrained to separate from that society [the Church of England] because we could not continue therein with a clear conscience."[18] Wesley was talking about the separation of Methodism from the Church of England, but today the issue still visits us with talk of separation.

[14]"On Schism," B 3:64, J VI:405–6, sec. 2.11.
[15]"On Schism," B 3:65, J VI:407, sec. 2.13.
[16]"On Schism," B 3:66, J VI:407, sec. 2.15.
[17]"On Schism," B 3:66, J VI:408, sec. 2.16.
[18]"On Schism," B 3:67, J VI:408, sec. 2.17.

Though the separation is usually portrayed as the splitting off of evangelicals from liberally dominated churches, the more accurate way of portraying it is the splitting off of liberal clergy from their roots. The threatening schism is not fueled by laity who are faithful to the classic Christian tradition but clergy who are unfaithful to it. Talk of separation arises from those who demand that the church must disavow its classic teaching on enduring covenant responsibility in the marriage of a man and a woman, and its consequences for their children and their society. It is the pretended improvers of this settled doctrine that have spawned the enmity.

The evangelicals have not created a breach of settled doctrine and pastoral practice. But should they leave the corrupted church or stay to reform the erring minority leadership? Every evangelical church today faces the same basic dilemma that troubled the early Methodist societies: stay or leave. Thus, I am prompted to speak on the relevance of Wesley's homily on schism for Wesleyan bodies today. Doing so requires precise language and a conscience attuned to fairness.

b. A Question of Conscience

After lengthy reservations, Wesley argued that the conscience-stricken separatists "could not be blamed for separating." But his heart was with the unity of the body of Christ.

In his determination to maintain the unity of the church, Wesley conceded that there is one crucial exception: "Suppose, for instance ... you could not remain in the Church of England without doing something which the Word of God forbids, or omitting something which the Word of God positively commands; if this were the case (but blessed be God it is not), you ought to separate from the Church of England."[19]

If the erring church requires you to do that which Scripture forbids, you must leave. But if it does not require you to do what God forbids, you must stay. He thought the Church of England was in the latter category, since it did not require him to do what God forbids. So he stayed.

The problem of conscience narrows to whether the church commands you to do something wrong. Is this the case in the present controversy over sexual ethics? I can say with good conscience for myself that I have not been commanded by my church to do something contrary to God's command. I speak personally because Wesley spoke personally on what constitutes grounds for separation from the church. I respect those who feel otherwise.

Wesley candidly revealed his own personal struggle of conscience in regard to the purity of the church into which he was baptized and received ordination: "I will make the case my own. I am now, and have been from my youth, a member and a minister of the Church of England. And I have no desire nor design to separate from it till my soul separates from my body. Yet if I was not permitted to remain therein

---

[19]Ibid.

without omitting what God requires me to do, it would then become meet, and right, and my bounden duty to separate from it without delay."[20]

Activist dissenters do well to listen carefully to that last sentence. The question: Is the modern liberal church not permitting you to remain within it by "omitting what God requires"? To this point, I do not think that the failing liberal church is requiring me to do something that God requires me not to do. As an ordained minister, I pronounce the wedding vows, but only to those I have in good conscience come to regard as fit for marriage. That duty is embedded in my ordination vows and in church discipline.

The analogy between Wesley's Church of England and my own United Methodist Church is illuminating. If my church might wrongfully require an action causing me to sin or commanding idolatry, then it would be my "bounden duty to separate," according to Wesley. This would be "separation with cause" and not a needless schism. But Wesley did not think that a sufficient cause existed for his connection to leave the Church of England. He thought his own fallen church was reformable. He called for its renewal and worked within it to make renewal happen.

Wesley sought precision in his homily on schism:

> To be more particular, I know God has committed to me a dispensation of the gospel. If I were unable to preach the gospel, I should be under a necessity of separating from it, or losing my own soul. In like manner, if I could not continue united to any smaller society, church, or body of Christians, without committing sin, without lying and hypocrisy, without preaching to others doctrines which I did not myself believe, I should be under an absolute necessity of separating from that society. And in all these cases the sin of separation, with all the evils consequent upon it, would not lie upon me, but upon those who constrained me to make that separation by requiring of me such terms of communion as I could not in conscience comply with.[21]

With Wesley I say, so long as "the church to which I am now united does not require me to do anything which the Scripture forbids, or to omit anything the Scripture enjoins, it is my indispensable duty to continue therein."[22]

Whether this analogy applies to the tragic divisions within the Wesleyan connection today remains a question of conscience to be settled inwardly rather than a question of policy or legislation. Wesley carefully summarized the precise alternative to be addressed to conscience: "Suppose the church or society to which I am now united does not require me to do anything which the Scripture forbids, or to omit anything which the Scripture enjoins, it is then my indispensable duty to continue therein. And if I separate from it without any such necessity I am justly chargeable (whether I foresaw them or no) with all the evils consequent upon that

[20]Ibid.
[21]Ibid.
[22]Ibid.

separation."[23] This is a strong caution to those who too quickly assume separation is preferred. It remains a problem of conscience and should not be answered too quickly.

Some might imagine that far from being a sin, separation is a requirement. Wesley admonished them: "They leave a Christian society with as much unconcern as they go out of one room into another. They ... wipe their mouth, and say they have done no evil!" They may be "justly chargeable before God and man both with an action that is evil in itself, and with all the evil consequences which may be expected to follow."[24]

c. Do Not Rashly Tear Asunder

Wesley reveals his heart when he pleads fervently in the final paragraphs: "Do not rashly tear asunder the sacred ties which unite you to any Christian society.... Take care how you rend the body of Christ by separating.... Separation is a thing evil in itself. It is a sore evil in its consequences.... Do not lay more stumbling-blocks in the way of these for whom Christ died."[25] Do not break further the unity of the body of Christ by your petulance: "O beware, I will not say of forming, but of countenancing or abetting any parties in a Christian society! Never encourage, much less cause either by word or action, any division therein."[26] Do not fuel disruption: "Meddle not with them that are given to dispute, with them that love contention. I never knew that remark to fail, 'He that loves dispute does not love God.' "[27]

Instead, be a peacemaker: "Happy is he that attains the character of a peacemaker in the church of God."[28] "Indeed it is far easier to prevent the flame from breaking out than to quench it afterwards." Do your part in nurturing the body, "and God will be present and bring thy good desires to good effect. Never be weary of well-doing."[29]

d. A Personal Note

As a founder of the confessing movement within the United Methodist Church, I know its purpose: to restore unity in the body of Christ through doctrinal renewal. The schismatic forces have been those who have insisted on repudiating classical Christian doctrine and forcing these revisions on all others in the church through legislation and direct political action. They are the ones who have left the church. Whether they are bishops or laity, they have conspicuously left the church by leaving the church's teachings.

My own decision about whether to leave the United Methodist Church hinges on this steady and clear conviction: as long as the classic Wesleyan doctrinal stan-

[23]Ibid.
[24]"On Schism," B 3:68, J VI:409, sec. 2.18.
[25]"On Schism," B 3:68, J VI:409–10, sec. 2.19.
[26]"On Schism," B 3:68–69, J VI:410, sec. 2.20.
[27]Ibid.
[28]"On Schism," B 3:69, J VI:410, sec. 2.21.
[29]Ibid.; see also "Farther Thoughts on Separation" and "Reasons against Separation."

dards (Wesley's Standard Sermons, Notes, and Doctrinal Minutes) are in place and constitutionally guaranteed, my intention is not to leave the church that baptized me and ordained me. Nothing that the political activists do will cause me to think that either my baptism or my ordination is deficient. But if the church requires of me some act to which I cannot in good conscience consent, I will, like Mr. Wesley, consider it "my bounden duty to separate from it without delay." I hope and pray that such will not be required. For now I appeal to classic Wesleyan doctrinal standards on those matters of sexuality that are rending the body of Christ.

Wesley remained steadfast during his lifetime in his conviction to remain in the church that baptized him until either he was forced out or compelled by unavoidable conscience to depart. He never left, and neither have I, nor do I intend to. I find myself ironically in a position analogous to Wesley's in 1784: after a lifetime of fighting schism and seeking to renew the church from within, I will have to deal with my conscience now and in the future.

"Within" is the decisive word for me and for the movement I helped initiate at Easter of 1994—the confessing movement within the United Methodist Church, which has sought to renew the church from within. I have steadily resisted the well-intentioned voices that wish, sadly, to separate. The morality of separation is not as wrenching for believers in other Reformation traditions who were born with the élan of separation. For Wesley and for me, the very thought of leaving or threatening to leave the church that baptized and ordained me is unconscionable. It would be for me like a tragic divorce from a solemn covenant.

The burning questions of our time are often perceived as legislative decisions to be settled by vote. But Wesley frames the issue of separation not as a question of passing laws or voting, but as a matter of conscience to settle in the presence of God. The civil law on marriage rights is quite different from the minister's liturgical responsibility in the rite of holy matrimony. The judge has the task of rightly seeing that just laws are obeyed. The minister is called to the care of souls in the body of Christ. In marriage the minister is voluntarily asked by a man and a woman to bless their union, their love, and their future children in a way that does not demean the will of God in the creation of man and woman. If church legislative bodies in the Wesleyan connection ignore or reject the settled Christian teaching of holy matrimony, every layperson in the connection will face a question of conscience: Am I being coerced by such legislation in a way that would require me to do what God forbids?

3. Ought We to Separate?

In "Ought We to Separate?" [Appendix C of B 9:567–80, 1755 Conference], Wesley argued that the societies of the evangelical revival had taken great care to follow church law and orderly practice within the Church of England.

a. Follow Church Law

Wesley did not regard himself as a dissenter against Anglican practice or canon law. Far from it. He viewed himself as scrupulously compliant with church law.

The church is the faithful company of believers in which the pure Word of God is preached and the sacraments duly administered. Wesley thought that the Church of England had rightly defined the church as such in accord with Scripture. This gains expression in the Book of Common Prayer that orders this community in worship and in the Articles of Religion that guide it in consensually receiving scriptural doctrine. Wesley taught that the efficacy of the sacraments does not lie in the character of the officiating minister, but in God's grace, for which the sacraments teach us to pray. Thus, there is no compelling reason for Methodists to stay away from Communion just because they see laxity in the one ministering it.

Wesley warned against becoming trapped in a syndrome of impatience, anger, and resentment against the received historic church. He called for obedience and submission within the church and argued for decency and order in the church and its worship. Whatever occasional blemishes the Book of Common Prayer might have, it does not justify separation.

b. Do Not Circumvent the Received Means of Offering Holy Communion under Duly Ordained Ministers

With this high ecclesiology, Wesley had to answer questions frequently about whether unordained Methodist preachers might offer the Lord's Supper and baptize. This question was debated among the preachers in the Methodist Conference of 1755 and many times later.

Though Wesley understood and empathized with some pragmatic reasons for allowing Methodist preachers in America to serve the Lord's Supper, he steadily argued that the focal mission of the Methodist preachers and societies has always been gospel preaching for conversion, new birth, and holy living. Members were instructed to receive Holy Communion from a believing community of faith without inordinate attention to labels. If a traveling preacher was unordained, his ministry should be under the supervision of an ordained ministry accountable to the historic *episkopoi*. Wesley thought that the supervision of the societies under his guidance stood in the apostolic tradition of the old religion.

c. Receive Bread and Wine through Ordinary Means

On the basis of the Old Testament distinction between priests and prophets, Wesley called Methodist preachers in 1755 to hold fast to the New Testament distinction between evangelists and presiding elders. But there was no need for unordained Methodist preachers to seek to administer the sacraments when their people could receive Communion at Anglican or other churches. This did not change his view, however, that it was of the very nature of the church both to preach the Word and administer the sacraments. Methodism's calling was preaching, without any diminution of the sacramental life. Rather, the sacramental life would be strengthened by gospel preaching.

The Methodist preachers in North America would later face an entirely different situation, where the Anglican priests were few and far between. It was not until very late that Wesley permitted those preachers in his connection to administer the sacraments. It was even then only with ambivalence and sadness, and under emergency conditions where the Lord's Supper could not otherwise have been properly received by the laity. Under these pressing conditions, Wesley acceded to blessing the Americans in their determination to preach the Word and administer the sacraments.

Despite varying situational challenges, Wesley's view on ministry, ordination, and separation were remarkably consistent over his long life span.[30] In 1745 Wesley wrote "A Farther Appeal to Men of Reason and Religion."[31] For those who wish to pursue this in more detail, three additional writings carry the same teaching from different periods: "Ought We to Separate from the Church of England?" for the 1755 annual conference of ministers (see B 9:567–80, app. C); "Reasons against Separation from the Church of England" (by John Wesley, printed in 1758 with "Hymns for the Preachers among the Methodists" by Charles Wesley; B 9:332–47); and much later "Farther Thoughts on Separation" in 1789 (J XIII:272–74), but to deal with them intensively would be largely repetitive. We turn instead to Wesley's thoughts on how to achieve intergenerational continuity in the flourishing work of the revival.

4. Address to the Travelling Preachers

After a serious bout with grave illness, Wesley made explicit preparations for the ongoing continuity of his connection in the event of his death. For this purpose he wrote out a brief plan ["Address to the Travelling Preachers" (August 4, 1769), J XIII:242–44]. His desire was "that all those Ministers of our Church who believe and preach salvation by faith might cordially agree between themselves, and not hinder but help one another."[32]

a. A Method to Preserve the Unity of the Connection

He addressed his beloved core of "Travelling Preachers" under his direction: "You are at present one body. You act in concert with each other, and by united counsels. And now is the time to consider what can be done in order to continue this union. Indeed, as long as I live, there will be no great difficulty. I am, under God, a centre of union to all our Travelling as well as Local Preachers."[33] He was pondering "by what means may this connexion be preserved when God removes me from you?"[34] He was concerned with the possible devolution of Methodist discipline. He warned that this transition would require a "single eye among" those who aim at anything but the glory of God, and the salvation of men. It is not likely that those

---

[30]Not in every detail, and not without development, but on the whole Wesley's views were consistent amid changing circumstances.
[31]Previously discussed in volume 1 of this series; see B 9:95–327.
[32]"Address to the Travelling Preachers," J XIII:242, sec. 1.
[33]"Address to the Travelling Preachers," J XIII:242, sec. 2.
[34]Ibid.

"who desire or seek any earthly thing, whether honor, profit, or ease" will continue through thick and thin.[35]

Wesley recommended a method "to preserve a firm union between those who choose to remain together."[36] He proposed: "Let them draw up articles of agreement, to be signed by those who choose to act in concert. Let those be dismissed who do not choose it in the most friendly manner possible. Let them choose a Moderator, who with a committee [does] what I do now: propose Preachers to be tried, admitted, or excluded; fix the place of each Preacher for the ensuing year, and the time of the next Conference ... [and] sign some articles of agreement" under which they would devote themselves entirely to God.[37]

To remain in this union, they must pledge "to preach the old Methodist doctrines, and no other, contained in the Minutes of the Conferences."[38] This sentence became a milestone in the history of Wesleyan doctrinal standards.[39]

b. The Core of the Old Methodist Doctrine

These minutes contained the core of Methodist doctrine and discipline that would continue robustly for the next twenty-five decades, and promises to continue for many more. These minutes set forth clearly the core teaching of "the old Methodist doctrines" to which Wesley and the preachers in his connection held fast — scriptural Christianity, the witness of the Spirit, salvation, faith, regeneration, and sanctification — as spelled out in the conference minutes. These minutes would be called "The Doctrine and Discipline of the Methodist Church." They still remain at the core of what is commonly known in the Wesleyan connection as "The Discipline." This enduring doctrinal definition took firm shape in 1769 with the "Address to the Travelling Preachers." Along with Wesley's Notes upon the New Testament, this classic Methodist doctrine was forever embedded in the constitution of the churches of the Wesleyan connection.

B. Thoughts Concerning Gospel Ministers

In "Thoughts Concerning Gospel Ministers" [J X:455–57], Wesley shows that one can preach with formal intellectual accuracy on the sovereignty of God, providence, and the human condition and never truly become a gospel minister.

The gospel minister cannot be defined without a life corresponding to his teaching. A gospel minister "of whatever denomination" is one who not only declares "the whole counsel of God," but who walks in that counsel himself. He knows how practically to apply all that he teaches to the hearts of his hearers and to himself.[40] The whole counsel includes teaching on the judgment of God against sin, not merely on

[35]"Address to the Travelling Preachers," J XIII:242, sec. 3.
[36]Ibid.
[37]"Address to the Travelling Preachers," J XIII:243, sec. 4.
[38]"Address to the Travelling Preachers," J XIII 243, sec. 5.
[39]DSWT, 61, 64.
[40]"Thoughts Concerning Gospel Ministers," J X:455–56, secs. 1–4.

the promises. The whole counsel of God includes the scriptural teachings of justification and sanctification, that Christ died for us and lives in us.

No one becomes a gospel minister by words alone. Only by a life lived. Nor does anyone become a gospel minister simply by ecclesial election or by divine decree. One becomes a gospel minister only by living the gospel and making direct appeal to the conscience of the hearer to hear it, repent, and believe. One does not become a gospel minister by preaching simply grace and divine sovereignty without also enabling disciples to come to faith that is active in love. The gospel minister does not only talk of righteousness in the blood of Christ, but lives out of its promises, embodying its truth.[41]

1. A Letter to a Friend

a. On Legitimate Authority to Authorize Preaching

In "A Letter to a Friend," Wesley discussed legitimate authority to authorize preaching and the abuse of that authority ["A Letter to a Friend" (April 10, 1761), J XIII:232 – 33].

Soon after the Methodist societies began, a "huge offense was taken at their 'gathering congregations' in so irregular a manner."[42] The complaints: Only the established church has legitimate authority to authorize preaching. Wesley answered, "If a dispensation of the Gospel is committed to me, no Church has power to enjoin me [to] silence."[43]

Suppose the law of the church is abused so as to prevent a minister of Christ from preaching the gospel in the church. Suppose he is further prohibited under any circumstances to preach it elsewhere. Wesley considered such a law illicit and void. If a law "forbids Christian people to hear the Gospel of Christ out[side] of their parish church ... it would be sinful for them to obey it."[44]

b. When Church Law Becomes an Obstacle to Integrity in Preaching

Preaching the gospel is not subversive to good public order. It is only subversive of the "vile abuse of the good order of our Church, whereby men who neither preach nor live the Gospel are suffered publicly to overturn it from the foundation; and ... to palm upon their congregations a wretched mixture of dead form and maimed morality."[45] Wesley was loyal to his church but resistant to abuses in the church.

He faced complaints against his field preaching and his organization of societies of prayer, Scripture study, and discipline. Some argued: "You are born under this Establishment. Your ancestors supported it, and were ennobled on that account.... You have, by deliberate and repeated acts of your own, engaged yourself to defend it. Your very rank and station constitute you a formal and eminent guardian of it."

---

[41]"Thoughts Concerning Gospel Ministers," J X:455 – 57, secs. 4 – 6.
[42]"A Letter to a Friend," J XIII:232 – 33, sec. 1, pref.
[43]"A Letter to a Friend," J XIII:232 – 33, sec. 1.1 – 2.
[44]"A Letter to a Friend," J XIII:237 – 38, sec. 4.1.
[45]"A Letter to a Friend," J XIII:232 – 34, sec. 2.4.

Wesley replied: "Surely no. Your rank, your station, your honor, your conscience, all engage you to oppose this," insofar as the leaders acted to destroy the church's constitution.[46] He argued that the "fundamental principles" of the preachers in his connection were indeed "the very principles of the Established Church."[47] He could not be described as a dissenter, but rather as one who gave full assent to the high calling and teaching of the established church.

c. When the Church Itself Subverts Established Church Order and Discipline

Detractors said that these preachers woo away congregations "and exercise their ministerial office therein, in every part of this kingdom, directly contrary to the restraint laid on them at their ordination."[48] Wesley responded that to preach the gospel "is not contrary to any restraint which was laid upon them at their ordination; for they were not ordained to serve any particular parish" but the whole body of Christ.[49] Anyone could see that thousands of laypersons hungered for the gospel. Many were rushing to hear the Word of God from those who were truly called. Meanwhile, said Wesley, parish priests "who are ordained, and appointed to watch over them, neither care for nor know how to help them."[50] These preachers did not contradict the Articles of Religion to which they had subscribed "in the simplicity of their hearts, when they firmly believed none but Episcopal ordination valid."[51]

They remained "determined never to renounce communion with the Church, unless they [were] cast out headlong."[52] They did not profess to be dissenters when they did not dissent from the established church teachings. "They love the Church, and therefore keep to all her doctrine and rules, as far as possibly they can: And if they vary at all, it shall not be a hair's breadth farther than they cannot help."[53]

d. The Real Subverters of Church Law

Restrictions on preaching the gospel cannot be viewed as valid for a church ordained to preach it on the highways and byways. These restrictions are not valid church order any more "than the tiles are the most fundamental principles of a house."[54] Wrote Wesley:

Perhaps the doors may be essentially constituent parts of the building we call a church. Yet, if it were on fire, we might innocently break them open, or even throw them for a time off the hinges. Now this is really the case. The timber is rotten, yea, the main beams of the house; and they want to place that firm

---

[46]"A Letter to a Friend," J XIII:234–36, sec. 3.4.
[47]"A Letter to a Friend," J XIII:234–36, sec. 3.5.
[48]"A Letter to a Friend," J XIII:234–36, sec. 3.6.
[49]Ibid.
[50]Ibid.
[51]"A Letter to a Friend," J XIII:236, sec. 3.6.
[52]"A Letter to a Friend," J XIII:234–36, sec. 3.6.
[53]Ibid.
[54]Ibid.

beam, salvation by faith, in the room of salvation by works. A fire is kindled in the Church, the house of the living God; the fire of love of the world, ambition, covetousness, envy, anger, malice.... O who will come and help to quench it? Under disadvantages and discouragements of every kind, a little handful of men have made a beginning; and I trust they will not leave off till the building is saved, or they sink in the ruins of it.[55]

Here is what was happening in this revival: "A few irregular men openly witness those truths of God which the regular Clergy (a few excepted) either suppress or wholly deny. Their word is accompanied with the power of God, convincing and converting sinners."[56] That they were a bit irregular was not their choice.[57]

These "irregular men" were compelled to irregularity by the irascibility and defensiveness of the establishment.[58]

The doctrine of the Established Church, which is far the most essential part of her constitution, these Preachers manifestly confirm, in opposition to those who subvert it. And it is the opposition made to them by those subverters which constrains them, in some respects, to deviate from her discipline; to which, in all others, they conform for conscience. O what pity, that any who preach the same doctrine, and whom those subverters have not yet been able to thrust out, should join with them against their brethren in the common faith, and fellow-witnesses of the common salvation![59]

2. A Letter to a Clergyman

Wesley set forth a simple pragmatic text for effective ministry: Look for fruits ["A Letter to a Clergyman," J VIII:496, sec. 1.5 – 10]. He was often under attack from ordained clergy for his decision to supervise lay ministers for field preaching. To answer this question of territoriality, he drew the following telling analogy.

a. Should I Cling to a Physician Who Has No Record of Healing?

Suppose a physician has been well educated, has passed examinations and been credentialed, and has practiced for several years but nevertheless has had no patients who have been cured. Some patients have languished under his "care." Some have died. Wesley asked, how much, then, would his credentials count? A physician who works for decades without any actual record of cures is not indeed rightly called (except in name only) a physician.[60]

Suppose someone else comes into his village who is less educated and not as well credentialed but quickly shows evidence of the ability to provide actual healing and curative medical treatment. Do you condemn that person for exercising his skills?

---

[55]"A Letter to a Friend," J XIII:234 – 36, sec. 3.7.
[56]"A Letter to a Friend," J XIII:237, sec. 4.
[57]"A Letter to a Friend," J XIII:237, sec. 4.1.
[58]"Letter to a Clergyman," J VIII:496, sec. 1.5 – 10.
[59]"A Letter to a Friend," J XIII:237 – 38, sec. 4.1.
[60]"Letter to a Clergyman," J VIII:496, sec. 1.5 – 10.

Suppose that out of tender compassion he even gives counsel and treatment for free. Do you condemn him for not charging fees?[61]

b. The Effectiveness of Lay Preachers

The analogy is similar between supposedly professional but in fact unblessed ordained clergy as distinguished from effective lay ministers. Some lay ministries God has blessed with marvelous conversions. It does not count against the cure that no credentials are shown, no fees paid. What matters is the actual outcome. "Will you condemn a man who, having compassion on dying souls and some knowledge of the gospel of Christ, without any temporal reward, saves many from their sins whom the minister could not save?"[62]

It is by this practical outcome criterion that physicians of the soul are to be assessed. Having both credentials and a record of converting and blessing souls is best. But ministry is never simply a matter of formal credentials. The proper legitimizing authority of physicians of the body is not what credentials they have on their walls but their actual record of cure. So the proper authority of physicians of the soul is their actual effectiveness in the changing of lives.[63]

3. A Letter to the Rev. Mr. Fleury

a. Resisting False Charges on Church Teaching

The eighteenth-century evangelical revival was sometimes charged with lacking a sound doctrine of the church (neglecting apostolic continuity, lacking oversight, working against established church law). Wesley's evangelical doctrine of the church was often attacked by settled Anglican bishops and priests who did not want their diocesan boundaries disturbed. One of the most furious attacks came from George Lewis Fleury of Waterford, Ireland. Wesley wrote a long letter to the Rev. Mr. Fleury answering calmly his questions on ministry, alleged private revelation, ordinal offenses, apostolicity, lay preachers, and church order.[64]

Common charges against the evangelicals were divisive disruptiveness, ecstatic enthusiasm, lay preaching outside the walls of the established parish church, supposed claims of extraordinary individual inspiration, and teaching perfect love. Wesley answered calmly with Scripture and long-established church practice.

Fleury charged that the ministers claimed "the same holy undefiled nature as Christ himself." Wesley showed that Fleury had found those very words not in his own teachings, but in William Law's "An Earnest and Serious Answer to Dr. Trapp."[65] Law had applied these words inaccurately and maliciously to Wesley himself.[66] In

---

[61]"Letter to a Clergyman," J VIII:497, sec. 1.10–14.
[62]"Letter to a Clergyman," J VIII:497, sec. 2.7.
[63]"Letter to a Clergyman," J VIII:497, sec. 2.1–12.
[64]A Letter to the Rev. Mr. Fleury, May 18, 1771, B 9:389–401, J IX:179–91.
[65]William Law, "An Earnest and Serious Answer to Dr. Trapp" (London: W. Innis and R. Manby, 1740).
[66]A Letter to the Rev. Mr. Fleury, B 9:397, sec. 14.

response, Wesley quoted the canonical text of 2 Peter that we are called to become "partakers of the divine nature" (2 Peter 1:4). Those in his connection did not claim any form of inspiration that defied apostolic hopes and testimonies. They followed that scriptural doctrine that was shared by all genuine believers in all times and places.[67] The charge of claiming freedom of sin was answered by the apostle Paul, who wrote, "It is for freedom that Christ has set us free. Stand firm, then, and do not let yourselves be burdened again by a yoke of slavery" (Gal. 5:1 NIV). God has given us "not the spirit of enthusiasm, but of love and of a sound mind" (2 Tim. 1:7, Wesley's translation).[68]

b. The Fury against Lay Preaching

Reverend Fleury's outburst hinged on his fury at lay preaching. Wesley countered by comparing the rigorous criteria for approving lay preachers with commonly loose and careless Anglican ordinal expectations. Among his connection of leaders, wrote Wesley, "none are allowed to be stated preachers but such as (1) are truly alive to God; such as experience the 'faith that worketh by love' for God and all mankind; (2) such as have a competent knowledge of the word of God, and the work of God in the souls of men; (3) such as have given proof that they are called of God by converting sinners from the error of their ways."[69] Those who "convert no sinners to God" are hardly worthy pastors.

Wesley pleaded for fair and honest speech rather than ignorant attacks. "We wish all the same happiness to you which we wish to our own souls. We desire no worse for you than that you may 'present' yourself 'a living sacrifice, holy, acceptable to God.'"[70]

Further Reading on the Unity of the Body of Christ

Couture, Pamela D. "Sexuality, Economics, and the Wesleyan Alternative." In *Blessed Are the Poor? Women's Poverty, Family Policy, and Practical Theology*, 119–34. Nashville: Abingdon, 1991.

Cubie, David Livingstone. "Separation or Unity? Sanctification and Love in Wesley's Doctrine of the Church." In *The Church*, edited by Melvin Dieter and Daniel Berg, 333–95. Anderson, IN: Warner, 1984.

Harrison, A. H. *The Separation of Methodism from the Church of England*. London: Epworth, 1945.

Wainwright, Geoffrey. "Schisms, Heresies, and the Gospel: Wesleyan Reflections on Evangelical Truth and Ecclesial Unity." In *Ancient and Postmodern Christianity*, 183–98. Downers Grove, IL: InterVarsity, 2002.

---

[67] A Letter to the Rev. Mr. Fleury, B 9:397, sec. 13.
[68] A Letter to the Rev. Mr. Fleury, B 9:398, sec. 15.
[69] A Letter to the Rev. Mr. Fleury, B 9:398–99, sec. 16.
[70] A Letter to the Rev. Mr. Fleury, B 9:401, sec. 21.

CHAPTER 10

Effective Church Leadership

A. Assessing Evangelical Effectiveness

Surveying his life work, Wesley published a poignant homily titled "On God's Vineyard" in 1787, asking the question framed by Isaiah 5:4: "What could have been done more to my vineyard, that I have not done in it? wherefore, when I looked that it should bring forth grapes, brought it forth wild grapes?" [Homily #107 (Whitney, England, October 17, 1787), B 3:502–17; J #107, VII:202–13; JWO 104–16].

1. On God's Vineyard

God's vineyard is a biblical metaphor for the people of God. In this vineyard the planted grapes are cultivated carefully, while the wild grapes are pruned. Although in a broader sense the vineyard is the church around the world, it is in its more personal and narrower sense assumed in this homily, the very vineyard of the evangelical revival to which Wesley had dedicated his entire life. It was the people called Methodists.[1] Wesley was aware that God had designed that the evangelical revival "should put forth great branches and spread over the earth."[2] Now he was looking over his own vineyard and reassessing its effectiveness.

Wesley had recently "completed an intensive survey of the entire scope and spread of British Methodism."[3] At this point in 1787, late in his life work, the eighty-four-year-old evangelist was retrospectively reflecting on what he had accomplished in his fifty intense years of traveling and preaching and pastoral ministry, and especially on what still remained to be done. It is touching to read his personal reflection on providence and the continuing vulnerabilities of his long and arduous ministry.

Pensively he asks, echoing the text from Isaiah: "What more?" What more could have been done than has been done? In the Isaiah text, it is God who is bemoaning his disappointment at Israel's bad fruit. In this homily, Wesley is asking himself, "What did we do or fail to do?" He reviews four arenas:

1. doctrinal teaching

---

[1] JWO 105, proem.
[2] JWO 106, proem.
[3] JWO 104; Tyerman, 3:496–99.

2. spiritual formation
3. disciplinary action
4. protection of this great work of God from opposition and persecution

2. The Vineyard Has Been Guarded with Sound Doctrine

With respect to the pastoral effectiveness of doctrinal teaching, Wesley argued that the evangelical communities within the larger church have been seriously exposed to solid biblical, orthodox, classic Christian teaching. This is because from the outset the evangelists and preachers had been "men of one book." The written Word of God had been the constant lamp for their journey. They had sought simply and unpretentiously to be mere biblical Christians, neither more nor less. They had indeed benefited from the wise tradition of divinity of the English church tradition, with its Book of Common Prayer, Elizabethan homilies, and other wonderful works of practical divinity. All these stood up under the judgment of Scripture, the one reliable rule of the Christian life.[4]

In this sermon, Wesley located the revival as doctrinally consonant with patristic and Reformation Christianity. It held to the dialectical balance of justification and sanctification without falling into exaggerations on either side.[5] From the Scriptures, the evangelical preachers had consistently taught justification by grace through faith active in love. They had closely joined God's justifying grace with God's sanctifying grace. In Wesley's view, Luther grasped the former better than the latter. Medieval scholasticism grasped the latter while losing sight almost entirely of the former.[6] The medieval neglect of justification required a corrective.

The preaching of justification sets forth the once-for-all verdict of God by which sinners are forgiven in the light of the cross. Both justification and sanctification are placed in the context of the history of the revelation of grace. They both begin in the new birth enabled by the Spirit. Sanctification is typically a process of growth analogous to humans growing after new birth, whereas the justification is instantaneous upon faith, more analogous to a birth that happens on a particular day in time.[7]

a. Gifts Bestowed through Sound Doctrinal and Biblical Preaching

This balanced scriptural doctrine of Reformation teaching had been firmly linked with serious discipline in the revival. The gospel of unmerited grace calls for fruits worthy of its gift. A Christian, according to Scripture, is one justified by faith, whose new birth is being sanctified by the Spirit both inwardly and outwardly. Thus, however wild some of the grapes in the revival vineyard, they were not due basically to doctrinal error, in Wesley's view.[8]

---

[4]"On God's Vineyard," B 3:505, J VII:204, sec. 1.4.
[5]See volume 2 of this series on justification and sanctification.
[6]"On God's Vineyard," B 3:505, J VII:202 – 6, sec. 1.4.
[7]"On God's Vineyard," B 3:505, J VII:204, sec. 1.5.
[8]"On God's Vineyard," B 3:505, J VII:205, sec. 1.6 – 9.

3. How the Spirit Has Generated New Forms of Lay-Oriented Spiritual Helps

Second, Wesley observed the special helps the Spirit had provided the revival. He said, God has been doing his part in the renewing of gospel ministry. How have the people been responsive? This required a descriptive answer, a brief history of the movement of the Spirit.[9]

Building on this sound ancient apostolic teaching, the evangelical revival was being providentially supplied with grace in practical spiritual formation. This was occurring through small Bible study and prayer groups of those who, having experienced new birth in God, were seeking to live it out in daily life and actively supporting each other in doing so. They were learning to hold each other to evangelical accountability so that they might be worthy of their calling. And they were also learning how to settle contested issues among them by prayer, Bible study, mutual admonition, and consultation by means of regular conferences.[10] What happened when this was grasped?

The first challenge that arose immediately in the earliest period of the revival was that the hearers so packed the churches that the parishioners could hardly squeeze in.[11] They were preaching old doctrines that were perceived as new: "that we are saved by faith, and, that 'without holiness no man could see the Lord.'"[12] "The fruit of their preaching quickly appeared. Many sinners were changed both in heart and life. But it seemed this could not continue long, for everyone clearly saw that these preachers would quickly wear themselves out, and no clergyman dared to assist them. But soon one and another, though not ordained, offered to assist them."[13] God blessed these young men, whether learned or unlearned.

a. The Spiritual Helps God Has Bestowed on His Vineyard

The leaders of this revival did not start with a plan. They simply followed the Spirit.[14] The success of the revival forced them to ask how they should proceed. They wondered how the regenerated people of God could be kept together for their benefit as they sought to discern whether they "walked worthy of their profession."[15] The Holy Spirit took a hand: "They were providentially led ... to divide all the people into little companies, or classes, according to their places of abode, and appoint one person in each class to see all the rest weekly. By this means it was quickly discovered if any of them lived in any known sin. If they did, they were first admonished; and, when judged incorrigible, excluded from the Society."[16] This did not happen by clever administrative planning by Wesley as is often portrayed.

[9]"On God's Vineyard," B 3:505, J VII:204, sec. 2.1.
[10]"On God's Vineyard," B 3:509–11, J VII:207–8, sec. 2.2–8.
[11]Ibid.
[12]Heb 12:14; "On God's Vineyard," B 3:509, J VII:208, sec. 2.1–2.
[13]"On God's Vineyard," B 3:509, J VII:207–8, sec. 2.1.
[14]"On God's Vineyard," B 3:509, J VII:207–8, sec. 2.2.
[15]"On God's Vineyard," B 3:509, J VII:209, sec. 2.3.
[16]Ibid.

Rather, it happened by listening to what the Spirit was saying. "This division of the people, and exclusion of those that walked disorderly, without any respect of persons, were helps which few other communities had."[17]

As the societies increased, stewards were needed to "meet the preachers once a quarter, in some central place, to give an account of the spiritual and temporal state of their several societies."[18] The conferences were the key to their evolving polity: "They soon found that what St. Paul observes of the whole church may be in a measure applied to every part of it: 'The whole body being fitly framed together, and compacted by that which every joint supplieth, maketh increase of the body, to the edifying of itself in love.' "[19]

Since "the people profit[ed] less by any one person than by a variety of preachers," their experience showed them that the preachers did well to itinerate from society to society.[20]

These special helps of the Spirit kindled the rapid spread of the revival. Compared to the ordinary forms of the Church of England, they were perceived as unique to the Methodist societies even though they largely followed the Church of England's canon law.

These societies were blessed with many fruits. When tempted to separate from the Church of England, they determined that "they cannot, they dare not, they will not separate.... It is true, if any sinful terms of communion were imposed upon them, then they would be constrained to separate; but as this is not the case at present, we rejoice to continue therein."[21] Wesley said, if asked whether a Methodist should have become "a separate people like the Moravian Brethren, I answer, This would have been a direct contradiction to [God's] whole design in raising them up; namely, to spread scriptural religion throughout the land, among people of every denomination, leaving everyone to hold his own opinions and to follow his own mode of worship."[22] The vineyard was not planted for those who wanted to form an alternative schismatic church, but rather to revitalize the ongoing visible and historically received church. They simply sought to embody its holy discipline and love of scriptural truth. What more could God the Spirit do than that which has been done for us?

b. The Revival of Gentle and Firm Discipline

Compassionate discipline is one of the gifts the Spirit has provided for cultivating the vineyard. "Nothing can be more simple, nothing more rational, than the Methodist discipline: it is entirely founded on common sense, particularly applying the general rules of Scripture. Any person determined to save his soul may be united

[17]"On God's Vineyard," B 3:509, J VII:207–8, sec. 2.4.
[18]"On God's Vineyard," B 3:509–10, J VII:207, sec. 2.4.
[19]Eph. 4:16; "On God's Vineyard," B 3:509, J VII:207–8, sec. 2.5.
[20]"On God's Vineyard," B 3:509, J VII:207–8, sec. 2.6.
[21]"On God's Vineyard," B 3:509, J VII:207–8, sec. 2.7.
[22]"On God's Vineyard," B 3:505, J VII:204, sec. 2.8.

(this is the only condition required) with them. But this desire must be evidenced by three marks: avoiding all known sin, doing good after his power, and attending all the ordinances of God."[23]

This is a community in which all who join do so voluntarily. No one has ever been forced to come to this vineyard. But if they do come, they must earnestly commit to these three commitments: avoid sin, do good according to the grace given, and use the means of grace God provides in prayer, Scripture reading, and church attendance. In Wesley's societies, those who joined were "placed in a class" once a week and reviewed quarterly. Wesley wrote, "If nothing is objected to him, he is admitted into the Society" and continues as long as he "walks according to his profession."[24] If not, "either the offense or the offender [is] removed in time."[25] Those who refused or neglected correction were not continued in the societies. Every quarter each member of the society would be reviewed and given a validation (sometimes called a "ticket") that entitled them to remain in the fellowship. Morning prayer was observed at 5:00 a.m. The Lord's Supper was provided on Sunday. Wesley explained, "On Sunday evening the Society meets; but care is taken to dismiss them early, that all the heads of families may have time to instruct their several households."[26]

c. The Revival Vineyard Has Been Providentially Protected

The elderly Wesley was pondering how it could have happened that the vineyard would be protected by the Spirit from so much opposition and persecution. For their outward protection amid the hazards of a corrupt social order that sent mobs out to harass them, they had learned simply to trust in God alone. At the time Wesley wrote this homily, persecutions of those in the evangelical revival were continuing, but Wesley urged that they be borne with patience as a part of the privilege of cross-bearing.

Such a movement could not occur "without a flood of opposition." The adversary never sleeps. The accuser works constantly "against a poor, defenseless, despised people, without any visible help, without money, without power, without friends."[27] The people of the vineyard learned from Scripture that "all that will live godly in Christ Jesus shall suffer persecution" (2 Tim. 3:12). "The god of this world was not asleep. Neither was he idle. He did fight, and that with all his power" by stirring up the most brutish forces of the most beastly of bad people. "They roared like lions."[28]

These rioters and hooligans had "encompassed the little and defenseless flock on every side. And the storm rose higher and higher till deliverance came, in a way that

---

[23]"On God's Vineyard," B 3:511, J VII:208–9, sec. 3.1. The one condition: readiness to "flee from the wrath to come."

[24]Ibid.

[25]"On God's Vineyard," B 3:512, J VII:209, sec. 3.2–3.

[26]"On God's Vineyard," B 3:512, J VII:209, sec. 3.3.

[27]"On God's Vineyard," B 3:512, J VII:209, sec. 4.1.

[28]"On God's Vineyard," B 3:512, J VII:209, sec. 4.2; Isa. 5:29.

none expected."[29] The unanticipated calm came through civil order. Wesley thought it was an unprecedented mercy that "God stirred up the heart of our late gracious Sovereign," George II, to order that the persecution be quelled. In response to the appeal by the elder William Pitt, the king declared in open court: "I tell you, while I sit on the throne, no man shall be persecuted for conscience' sake."[30] From that time forward, the Methodists were largely "permitted to worship God according to their own conscience."[31]

4. God Has Done His Part— What Have We Been Doing?

a. Unexpected Outcomes

This is the vineyard in which Wesley had been working fruitfully for more than five decades. "What indeed could God have done more for this his vineyard which he hath not done in it? This having been largely showed," Wesley then proceeded to a "strong and tender expostulation." He thought these fifty years of evidence gave them every reason to expect "a general increase of faith and love, of righteousness and true holiness. Yea, and of the fruit of the Spirit — love, joy, peace, long-suffering, meekness, gentleness, fidelity, goodness, temperance."[32] "Truly, when I saw what God had done among his people between forty and fifty years ago, when I saw them, warm in their first love, magnifying the Lord and rejoicing in God their Savior, I could expect nothing less." He thought this revival would continue, "having constant communion with the Father and the Son."[33]

What happened instead was that "it brought forth wild grapes.... It brought forth error in ten thousand shapes."[34]

[The revival turned] many of the simple out of the way. It brought forth enthusiasm, imaginary inspiration, ascribing to the all-wise God all the wild, absurd, self-inconsistent dreams of an heated imagination.... It brought forth pride, robbing the Giver of every good gift of the honor due to his name. It brought forth prejudice, evil surmising, censoriousness, judging, and condemning one another — all totally subversive of that brotherly love which is the very badge of the Christian profession.... It brought forth anger, hatred, malice, revenge, and every evil word and work — all direful fruits, not of the Holy Spirit.[35]

b. A Warning against the Abuse of Wealth

In this vineyard, Wesley noted pensively, where many of the faithful had worked long and hard side by side, still, sadly, many wild grapes began to grow up unat-

---

[29]"On God's Vineyard," B 3:513, J VII:210, sec. 4.2.
[30]Ibid.
[31]"On God's Vineyard," B 3:513–14, J VII:210, sec. 4.3–4.
[32]"On God's Vineyard," B 3:514, J VII:211, sec. 5.1.
[33]Ibid.
[34]Ibid.
[35]"On God's Vineyard," B 3:515, J VII:211, sec. 5.2.

tended. Against all these the faithful continue to struggle.[36] Against all expectations, the vineyard brought forth "that grand poison of souls, the love of the world, and that in all branches: 'the desire of the flesh,' that is, the seeking happiness in the pleasures of sense; 'the desire of the eyes,' that is, seeking happiness in dress, or any of the pleasures of imagination; and 'the pride of life,' that is, seeking happiness in the praise of men."[37] "It brought forth self-indulgence of every kind, delicacy, effeminacy, softness; but not softness of the right kind, that melts at human woe. It brought [forth] such base, groveling affections."[38]

Wesley had a special warning for the rich: "Are you sensible of your danger? Do you feel, 'How hardly will they that have riches enter into the kingdom of heaven?' Do you continue unburnt in the midst of the fire?"[39] "Do you 'put a knife to your throat' when you sit down to meat, lest your 'table' should 'be a snare to you'? ... Is not eating and drinking, or any other pleasure of sense, the greatest pleasure you enjoy?"[40] "Do not you grow soft and delicate? Unable to bear cold, heat, the wind, or the rain, as you did when you were poor? Are you not increasing in goods, laying up treasures on earth; instead of restoring to God in the poor?"[41]

c. Causes of Deterioration

God had not been lacking on his part. Wesley warned, "Have ye not been fed with the sincere milk of the word? Hath not the whole word of God been delivered to you?"[42] "Was not every branch both of inward and outward holiness clearly opened and earnestly applied?"[43]

Wesley pleaded with the people not to despise the helps that God had prepared for them. Because they wanted to hear no one but "men of learning," Wesley said, "Will you not then give God leave to choose his own messengers?" Wesley's own lay preaching had been very effective. He wondered if supposed "men of learning" might be "one cause of [their] 'bringing forth wild grapes.'"[44]

Others resisted the constraints of accountability to a small group. Wesley countered, "Do you think you can make your own way without a Christian society?"[45] "Have you not read, 'How can one be warm alone?'"[46]

The vineyard people need to come with a "thirst for God" and to desire companions to "watch over your soul as they that must give account." They do well to come "expecting that when you are met together in his name your Lord will be in the midst of you." They are "truly thankful for the amazing liberty of conscience

[36]Ibid.
[37]"On God's Vineyard," B 3:515, J VII:212, sec. 5.3.
[38]"On God's Vineyard," B 3:515, J VII:211 – 12, sec. 5.3.
[39]"On God's Vineyard," B 3:516, J VII:212, sec. 5.4.
[40]Ibid.
[41]Ibid.
[42]"On God's Vineyard," B 3:515, J VII:212 – 13, sec. 5.5.
[43]Ibid.
[44]Ibid.
[45]"On God's Vineyard," B 3:517, J VII:213, sec. 5.6.
[46]Ibid.

which is vouchsafed to them and for 'the Giver of every good gift' for the general spread of true religion."[47]

The eminent Wesley scholar, and my teacher, Albert Outler, commented on this homily, "Save for the hortatory ending, it is an exercise in autobiographical retrospect, aimed at describing and assessing the Revival after fifty years, with a view to its further renewal by recalling it to its origins and essentials — and this by the one man who could speak of both with definite authority."[48]

B. What Hath God Wrought?

The headquarters location for the Methodist societies in the early decades was The Foundery in London where the societies began. Upon the founding of a new headquarters at City Road on April 21, 1777, Wesley preached a sermon that provided a retrospect of the people called Methodist. He again sought to confirm the long relation of his connection of believers within the Church of England.

1. On Laying the Foundation of the New Chapel, City Road

For the memorable occasion of laying a foundation for the new headquarters, Wesley took as his text Numbers 23:23: "According to this time it shall be said..., What hath God wrought!" [Homily #112, "On Laying the Foundation of the New Chapel, City Road," B 3:577 – 93; J #112, VII:419 – 30]. What is the context of the phrase "according to this time"? It is the oracle spoken on the top of Mount Pisgah at the time of the building of an altar to God who "brought [God's people] out of Egypt" (Num. 23:22). In modern terms, this is a proclamation with a promise: "It will now be said of Jacob and of Israel, 'See what God has done!'" (Num. 23:23 NIV). The analogy here is that no curse can touch Jacob. The spell has been broken. And if God can do this for Israel, he can do it for the faithful of the New Israel. The evangelical revival had broken a spell of lethargy that had hung over the sleeping Reformation for generations.

Wesley showed the applicability of this promise for the people called Methodists. In effect he was saying, if you consider factually and descriptively what these societies have done, the people of England and the Church of England will have reason to exclaim: "Look what God has done!"[49]

The homily is not simply addressed to revival insiders. It is boldly intended as an address to the nation. The nation had benefited by the teaching, discipline, and ethic of love of the evangelical revival. Sooner or later the people of England would discover this.

The question of whether God allows extraordinary revivals of religion was contested by the Anglican leadership. Regrettably the bishop of London, Edmund

---

[47]"On God's Vineyard," B 3:517, J VII:213, sec. 5.7.
[48]JWO 105.
[49]"On Laying the Foundation of the New Chapel," B 3:579, J VII:419, pref. 1.

Gibson, had denied even the possibility of such an extraordinary work of God. He refused to allow "that God has wrought any 'extraordinary work' in our nation" in this unauthorized populist revival. Even to imagine such a special work of God was in the bishop's view "downright enthusiasm."[50]

Wesley generously remarked that the bishop was correct if God had not in fact done an extraordinary work in the English evangelical revival. But if God really was doing such a work, "then we may believe and assert it without incurring any such imputation."[51] Wesley regarded his bishop as a "great man" who is "now in a better world."

Yet a still greater man was J. A. Bengel, a man of eminent piety and learning, who had in 1741 prophesied a great revival soon to come.[52] But when asked why he thought it would come by 1836, and why so late a date, he answered: "I acknowledge all the prophecies would incline me to place it a century sooner," which would have been the beginning of the English evangelical revival in 1738 if only Bengel had been aware of it.[53] Wesley was amazed that so few were aware of this anomaly (Bengel's intuition of a coming revival) and how it so obviously correlated with the rise of the Methodist societies. Wesley then appealed to his audience to put a favorable construction on his motives in even introducing this point, lest it be viewed as an ostentation on his part to point out what really happened. He knew that the Wesleys alone had intimate knowledge of this revival from its very beginnings. So it was left to the elder brother to tell this story, and he now had the proper occasion and the obligation to tell it accurately.[54]

a. The Rise and Progress of the Evangelical Revival in England

Wesley then recounted the rise of the revival as he experienced it. It emerged gradually out of the previous period of single-minded devotion to obedience to the law of Christ in 1725. This phase was rooted in the strong effect that Thomas à Kempis and Jeremy Taylor had on Wesley and his students at Oxford. This was not revival but the preparation for it. The earliest glimpse of the coming revival was first seen in the keen awareness felt by several young Oxford students of their need to "flee from the wrath to come" (Matt. 3:7). They had an earnest desire to live according to the rules proposed by Bishop Taylor in his *Rules of Holy Living and Dying*. Between 1729 and 1735, Wesley searched both alone and with other companions who were reading Scripture and encouraging each other to constant faith and good works.[55] A young gentleman of the college noted the regularity of their behavior and remarked, "I think we have got a new set of Methodists" — a name that stuck.[56]

---

[50]"The Signs of the Times," sec. 2.2.
[51]"On Laying the Foundation of the New Chapel," B 3:579, J VII:420, pref. 2.
[52]J. A. Bengel, *Ordo temporium a principio per periedos oeconomiae divinae* (1741), a scriptural chronology on the ordering of times in the divine economy.
[53]"On Laying the Foundation of the New Chapel," B 3:579–80, J VII:420, pref. 3.
[54]"On Laying the Foundation of the New Chapel," B 3:579–80, J VII:420, pref. 4.
[55]"On Laying the Foundation of the New Chapel," B 3:585, J VII:421, sec. 1.1.
[56]"On Laying the Foundation of the New Chapel," B 3:581, J VII:421, sec. 1.2.

This small group was "observant, for conscience' sake, of every rule of the church, and every statute both of the university and of their respective colleges. They were all orthodox in every point, firmly believing not only the three creeds, but whatsoever they judged to be the doctrine of the Church of England, as contained in her Articles and Homilies."[57] They held all things in common, not by duty but by the desire to share. "This was the infancy of the work." Like babies they had no conception of what would follow. They took "'no thought for the morrow,' desiring only to live today."[58] Here were the embryonic "rudiments of a Methodist Society."[59]

b. How the Mission Learned from Failures

The next step in the early preparation for the revival occurred when Wesley served as a missionary to Native American tribes in Georgia. "Our design was to preach to the Indian nations bordering upon that province." Still having a rigorous view of the sacraments and ordination, when a Lutheran in colonial Savannah requested of him the Lord's Supper, Wesley refused: "I told him I did not dare to administer it to him, because I looked upon him as unbaptized, as I judged baptism by laymen to be invalid; and such I counted all that were not episcopally ordained."[60] This shows Wesley's rigor in obedience to canon law. It was this rigor for the law that drove him into a court in Georgia that charged him with excesses in the administration of admission to the sacraments.

With his zeal for rigor questioned, Wesley returned to England in 1738. "I was now in haste to retire to Oxford, and bury myself in my beloved obscurity." But he was "continually importuned to preach in one and another church, and that not only morning, afternoon, and night, on Sunday, but on weekdays also. As I was lately come from a far country, vast multitudes flocked together."[61]

Finally, Wesley was shut out of preaching in Anglican pulpits due to his extraordinary ministry. "Not daring to be silent, after a short struggle between honor and conscience, I made a virtue of necessity, and preached in the middle of Moorfields. Here were thousands upon thousands, abundantly more than any church could contain, and numbers among them who never went to any church or place of public worship at all."[62]

When those cut to the heart came to Wesley for pastoral counsel, he agreed to meet with a few. Soon those few became too many for him alone to counsel. "Thus, without any previous plan or design, began the Methodist Society in England — a company of people associating together to help each other to work out their own salvation,"[63] even when obstructed by church policies.

---

[57]"On Laying the Foundation of the New Chapel," B 3:586, J VII:421, sec. 1.3.
[58]Ibid.
[59]"On Laying the Foundation of the New Chapel," B 3:586, J VII:422, sec. 1.4.
[60]Ibid.
[61]"On Laying the Foundation of the New Chapel," B 3:586–87, J VII:422–23, sec. 1.5.
[62]Ibid. Here begins Wesley's ministry outside of and beyond Anglican parishes.
[63]Ibid.

It is ironic that the need for pastoral counsel of increasing numbers of seekers became the occasion for the founding of the Methodist Society.

As a priest of the Church of England, Wesley was highly qualified for this counsel. "The next spring we were invited to Bristol and Kingswood, where likewise Societies were quickly formed. The year following we went to Newcastle upon Tyne, and preached to all the colliers and keelmen round it. In 1744 we went through Cornwall" and within "two or three years more to almost every part of England." After that came Ireland and finally Scotland. There "we saw the greatest fruit of our labor."[64]

2. The Old Religion

a. Whether the Revival Is a "New Religion"

What was meant by this strange word *Methodism*? Some thought it was a new religion. Though widely supposed, "nothing can be more remote from the truth. It is a mistake all over. Methodism, so called, is the old religion, the religion of the Bible, the religion of the primitive church, the religion of the Church of England."[65]

The "old religion" is the religion of the prophets and apostles. The "primitive church" is the religion of the postapostolic writers and ancient ecumenical teaching. The religion of the prophets and apostles and patristic writers was expressed historically in England in "the religion of the Church of England."[66] Wesley was extending it to a new audience who yearned for the preaching of faith active in love.

"This 'old religion' ... is no other than love: the love of God and of all mankind; the loving God with all our heart, and soul, and strength, as having first loved us, as the fountain of all the good we have received, and of all we ever hope to enjoy; and the loving every soul which God hath made, every man on earth, as our own soul."[67] This love is medicine for the soul. "This love is the great medicine of life, the never-failing remedy for all the evils of a disordered world."[68]

From this love come works of love. "This religion of love, and joy, and peace, has its seat in the inmost soul, but is ever showing itself by its fruits."[69] "This is the religion of the Bible, as no one can deny who reads it with any attention ... so that whoever allows the Scripture to be the Word of God must allow this to be true religion."[70]

b. The Religion of the Whole Church in the Purest Ages

Wesley said, "This is the religion of the primitive church, of the whole church in the purest ages. It is clearly expressed even in the small remains of Clemens

---

[64]"On Laying the Foundation of the New Chapel," B 3:587–88, J VII:423, sec. 1.6–11; FA, pt. 3, sec. 1.4–5.
[65]"On Laying the Foundation of the New Chapel," B 3:585, J VII:422–23, sec. 2.5.
[66]Ibid.
[67]"On Laying the Foundation of the New Chapel," B 3:585, J VII:423, sec. 2.1.
[68]Ibid.
[69]Ibid.
[70]"On Laying the Foundation of the New Chapel," B 3:585, J VII:424, sec. 2.2.

Romanus, Ignatius, and Polycarp. It is seen more at large in the writings of Tertullian, Origen, Clemens Alexandrinus, and Cyprian. And even in the fourth century it was found in the works of Chrysostom, Basil, Ephrem Syrus, and Macarius," which "no one will contest who has the least acquaintance with Christian antiquity."[71]

It was this religion that had been conveyed in the Church of England and which Wesley had been taught by his pastor-father, a priest of the Church of England. The attestation of this religion as the religion of the Church of England is proved textually by the church's liturgy, homilies, and Book of Common Prayer. All this is "beautifully summed up in that one, comprehensive petition, 'Cleanse the thoughts of our hearts by the inspiration of thy Holy Spirit, that we may perfectly love thee, and worthily magnify thy holy name.'"[72] The old religion should not be an offense to faithful Anglicans, since they pray it in every Eucharist.

It is this ancient classic Christian religion that has been recently heard and received by vast numbers of people in the eighteenth-century revival. It is not some new religion. When preached in plain language, this religion finds hungry hearers everywhere. "From this repentance sprung 'fruits meet for repentance': the whole form of their life was changed" not only in an outward behavioral change but by the inward renewal of the gospel in their hearts.[73] When the love of God was shed abroad in their hearts, they quickly came to love God and love humanity because they learned how God first loved us. God's love "constrain[ed] them to love all mankind ... with the mind which was in Christ."[74] This was the revival of religion that spread from town to town throughout the nation.

c. The Old Religion Made New

Wesley could not find an example in Protestant history to match the evidences of the power of the Spirit working among so many souls. On a vast scale, a reversal of hearts in those who repented and believed was occurring before their eyes. Perhaps not since the time of Constantine had so large a progress in any nation been made within so short a time.[75] Wesley reported what he saw:

Multitudes have been thoroughly "convinced of sin"; and shortly after, so filled with joy and love that whether they were in the body, or out of the body, they could hardly tell. And in the power of this love they have trampled underfoot whatever the world accounts either terrible or desirable, having evidenced in the severest trials an invariable and tender goodwill to mankind, and all the fruits of holiness. Now so deep a repentance, so strong a faith, so fervent love, and so unblemished holiness, wrought in so many persons in so short a time, the world has not seen for many ages.[76]

---

[71]"On Laying the Foundation of the New Chapel," B 3:586, J VII:424, sec. 2.3.
[72]"On Laying the Foundation of the New Chapel," B 3:586, J VII:424, sec. 2.4; cf. BCP.
[73]"On Laying the Foundation of the New Chapel," B 3:586, J VII:425, sec. 2.5.
[74]Ibid.
[75]"On Laying the Foundation of the New Chapel," B 3:586 – 87, J VII:425 – 26, sec. 2.6.
[76]"On Laying the Foundation of the New Chapel," B 3:586 – 87, J VII:426, sec. 2.7.

This was the evangelical revival the whole nation was experiencing. Personal conversion was affecting its larger social environment. It was the old religion and not to be feared. Wesley commented, "Nor is their religion more pure from heresy than it is from superstition. In former times, wherever any unusual religious concern has appeared, there has sprung up with it a zeal for things that were no part of religion. But it has not been so in the present case," where the fruits of faith were affecting the whole society. "So pure both from superstition and error is the religion which has lately spread in this nation."[77]

Even if you do not accept the work of the Spirit in such reports, at least see that the outcomes were "sober, manly, rational."[78] Changes were manifested in the moral behavior of those whose lives were touched by God in the revival. Their religion was remarkably pure from bigotry, and they were not overly concerned with holding right opinions. "They have no such overgrown fondness for any opinions as to think those alone will make them Christians, or to confine their affection or esteem to those that agree with them therein."[79] We all have reason to "dread that bitter zeal, that spirit of persecution, which has so often accompanied the spirit of reformation." This return to the "old religion" especially cherished respect for conscience, reason, persuasion, and "practice consistent with their profession."[80]

There have been several revivals of religion in England since the Reformation. "But the generality of the English nation were little profited thereby; because they that were the subjects of those revivals, preachers as well as people, soon separated from the Established Church, and formed themselves into a distinct sect."[81] So it was with the Presbyterians, Independents, Anabaptists, and Quakers. The unity of the body of Christ again and again suffered losses. Not so with the Methodist societies. They emerged precisely as societies of the Church of England and up to the time of this writing have continued on that path.

3. The Peculiar Glory of the Methodists

The Methodist revival weighed the matter of separation very early and "upon mature deliberation determined to continue" in the national church.[82] God has blessed this commitment to affirm the unity of the body of Christ and not separate. "Their fixed purpose is — let the clergy or laity use them well or ill — by the grace of God to endure all things, to hold on their even course, and to continue in the Church ... unless God permits them to be thrust out."[83] And even when they are thrown out, they continue as far as conscience allows to be faithful to the church that baptized them.

---

[77]"On Laying the Foundation of the New Chapel," B 3:587 – 88, J VII:426, sec. 2.8.
[78]"On Laying the Foundation of the New Chapel," B 3:588, J VII:426, sec. 2.9.
[79]"On Laying the Foundation of the New Chapel," B 3:588, J VII:427, sec. 2.10.
[80]"On Laying the Foundation of the New Chapel," B 3:587 – 88, J VII:427, sec. 2.11.
[81]"On Laying the Foundation of the New Chapel," B 3:588, J VII:427, sec. 2.12.
[82]"On Laying the Foundation of the New Chapel," B 3:589, J VII:428, sec. 2.13.
[83]Ibid.

Four of Wesley's strongest pieces of advice on church unity follow:

1. "We do not, will not, form any separate sect, but from principle remain what we always have been, true members of the Church of England."[84]
2. "This is the peculiar glory of the Methodists" — their ancient ecumenism based on the "old religion" of the apostles.
3. "Whenever the Methodists leave the Church, God will leave them," since schism is repugnant to the unity of the body.
4. "If they break from the Church also, we are not accountable for it," since we have consistently resisted separation.[85]

Wesley said these things in 1777. Due to the special conditions that later prevailed in America where Anglican ministers had largely left the former colonies and where the sacraments were less available on the frontier, by 1784 this commitment required partial revision, but only with great reluctance on Wesley's part.

If we consider how swiftly and extensively this renewal of the depth of the "old religion" unfolded, faithful to the historic church in England, we must acknowledge that this revival "cannot easily be paralleled in all these concurrent circumstances by anything that is found in the English annals since Christianity was first planted in this island."[86]

"If these things are so, may we not well say, 'What hath God wrought!' "[87] It is more than trivia that 106 years later that same phrase — "What hath God wrought!" — famously became the text of the first telegraph message ever transmitted. For on May 24, 1844, the 106th anniversary of Wesley's life-changing Aldersgate experience, Samuel F. B. Morse typed, "What hath God wrought!" for the first telegraph line from Washington to Baltimore. At that moment, the theme of the message on laying the foundation of the new chapel became entered into history, stamped on the memory of modern consciousness.

4. An Appeal for Scriptural Primitive Religion

Wesley was appealing to Anglicans to become true Anglicans. Most in Wesley's audience at City Road were, as he said, "members of the Church of England. So at least you are called; but you are not so indeed unless you are witnesses of the religion above described"[88] — namely, the old religion of the prophets and apostles and the earliest exegetes of their texts.

So the appeal to the heart follows: "How stands the matter in your own breast?"[89] "Examine your conscience before God." Wesley's habit as a preacher was often to leave his hearers with a flurry of questions, and so he does here: "Does your heart glow with gratitude to the Giver of every good and perfect gift?... Is your soul

---

[84]"On Laying the Foundation of the New Chapel," B 3:591, J VII:429, sec. 2.16.
[85]"On Laying the Foundation of the New Chapel," B 3:589 – 91, J VII:428 – 29, sec. 2.14 – 16.
[86]Ibid.
[87]"On Laying the Foundation of the New Chapel," B 3:587 – 88, J VII:427, sec. 2.11.
[88]"On Laying the Foundation of the New Chapel," B 3:591 – 92, J VII:430, sec. 2.17.
[89]Ibid.

warm with benevolence to all mankind?... Does the constant tenor of your life and conversation bear witness of this? Do you 'love, not in word only, but in deed and in truth'? If your heart is as my heart, give me your hand."[90]

If so, Wesley said, "Come and let us magnify the Lord together.... Let us join hearts and hands in this blessed work, in striving to bring glory to God in the highest, by establishing peace and goodwill among men to the uttermost of our power."[91] "Let our whole soul pant after a general revival of pure religion and undefiled, of the restoration of the image of God, pure love, in every child of man. Then let us endeavor to promote in our several stations this scriptural, primitive religion."[92]

C. Realistically Assessing the Revival

1. Causes of the Inefficacy of Christianity

a. Avoiding Self-Defeating Habits

Twelve years after the City Road address, Wesley took another look at the same subject: assessing the revival. Under weakened health conditions, with failing eyesight, decreased mobility, and diminishing energy, at eighty-six Wesley reflected on the ironic disparity between promises and performance in the revival. He wondered if the evangelical revival in his time was already tending toward potentially self-defeating behaviors.

He toyed with an unusual economic hypothesis: "Wherever true Christianity spreads, it must cause diligence and frugality, which, in the natural course of things, must beget riches — and riches naturally beget pride, love of the world, and every temper that is destructive of Christianity."[93] Economics became known in the nineteenth century as the dismal science. Wesley may have been its eighteenth-century antecedent.

Wesley's text for this homily, later titled "The Causes of the Inefficacy of Christianity" by Wesley's American editor of Wesley's Works, Joseph Benson, was Jeremiah 8:22: "Is there no balm in Gilead; is there no physician there? why then is not the health of the daughter of my people recovered?" [Homily #122 (July 2, 1789), B 4:85 – 96; J #116, VII:281 – 90].

b. Is There No Balm in Gilead?

Gilead provided healing for Israel, just as Israel was intended to provide healing for the whole world and just as the Methodist societies were intended to become a balm for the healing of the British isles.

Balm from Gilead was used for physical healing in ancient Israel, while God provided priests and prophets to soothe Israel's spiritual wounds. Amid the history

---

[90]"On Laying the Foundation of the New Chapel," B 3:592, J VII:430, sec. 2.17.
[91]"On Laying the Foundation of the New Chapel," B 3:591 – 92, J VII:430, sec. 2.17.
[92]Ibid.
[93]"The Causes of the Inefficacy of Christianity," B 4:95 – 96, J VII:290, sec. 2.17.

of the Babylonian captivity, Jeremiah was puzzled with the hidden purpose of God: how could it be that God was not providing a balm for Israel? Why was the daughter of God's people not recovering?

Wesley was similarly puzzled. Why does genuine Christianity have short spurts followed by long declines? Is there a hidden strain in the evangelical genes that tends toward self-defeat? This required a careful analysis that would plunge Wesley into a broad-ranging reflection on the endemic nature of sin.

c. Universal Corruption of Human Nature

In this sober homily, Wesley wondered with Jeremiah whether God might have forgotten the world he had made, which he created for his own glory.[94] The light created for God's glory had become darkened: "Darkness covers the earth and thick darkness is over the peoples" (Isa. 60:2 NIV).[95] While the mystery of the depth of wickedness remains deeply embedded in the human heart, Wesley argued that some of the causes of the ineffectiveness are able to be remedied.[96]

He narrowed his solemn question: Why has the Christian community had relatively little effect on spiritual vitality and health of the larger world — its cultural, moral, political, and economic order? If you say that it is because of the universal corruption of human nature, then can we not answer that Christianity was itself intended to be the remedy for that corruption? Yet the malaise still remains recurrently in full strength. Why does dysfunction and wickedness of every kind still cover the face of the earth?[97] Still today we wonder why God has not hindered temptation and suffering. Yet with hope we sing the poignant African-American spiritual:

> There is a balm in Gilead
> To make the wounded whole;
> There is a balm in Gilead
> To heal the sin sick soul.

The balm is the gospel. The sick soul is turning away from the best news humanity has ever heard.

2. Why True Christianity Remains So Largely Unknown

a. A Sober Review of Evangelical World Mission Outreach

One chief reason why it seems that Christianity has had little world-historical effect is that it remains so little known in so much of the world. At this point in his message, Wesley launched into a speculative analysis on world population that had great importance for the history of world missions. He estimated that roughly five-sixths of all humanity in his day had never heard of Christianity.

---

[94]"The Causes of the Inefficacy of Christianity," B 4:87, J VII:282, sec. 2.
[95]Ibid.
[96]Ibid.
[97]"The Causes of the Inefficacy of Christianity," B 4:86 – 87, J VII:281 – 82, sec. 1.

Wesley tried to calculate the number of people in the world who had never had a chance to hear the Good News: "I suppose mankind to be divided into thirty parts of which nineteen have no knowledge of Christianity." Then there are the Muslims who "utterly scorn Christianity." Sadly, "twenty-five parts of thirty of mankind are not so much as nominally Christians." The result is that "five parts of mankind out of six are totally ignorant of Christianity. It is therefore no wonder that five in six of mankind, perhaps nine in ten, have no advantage from it."[98] Christianity "can do no good where it is not known."[99]

Wesley then proceeded to survey what was known of the populations of his day, asking about the extent of the knowledge of true Christianity, from the Eastern Orthodox to Roman Catholicism to Protestantism in Europe. He began with Eastern Christianity. He thought that although its constituents had once been faithful, it had lost much of its ancient pre-Constantinian glory. It endured the ravages of the Ottoman Turks and the czars, and even its Christian brothers, the non-Chalcedonians.[100] What do the Christians of the Eastern Church, dispersed throughout the Turkish dominions, know of genuine Christianity? Wesley pondered. Most showed few signs of having even heard of genuine evangelical revival. He thought that the form of Christianity traditionally received in Russia was deeply corrupted.[101] And he viewed the Church of Rome as still stuck in medieval scholastic impediments. He thought that both Orthodox and Catholics were "perishing by thousands 'for lack of knowledge'" of justification by grace through faith.[102]

b. True Christianity Remains Still Largely Unknown in Protestantism

Although Protestants had ample opportunity to hear the Good News, Wesley calculated that on the continent of Europe no more than 2 percent of the population were true believers vitally living out the Christian life. Nine out of ten Protestants in Britain could hardly say what they believed. They knew little of justifying grace, the person and work of Christ, and the inward work of the Holy Spirit. In Germany, Holland, Denmark, and Sweden there were "many knowing Christians. But," said Wesley, "I fear we must not think that one in ten, if one in fifty" are believers in the full sense.[103]

Wesley then shifted the focus of his message from where Christianity is unknown to where it is has had a fair chance of being well known, for example, in England:

Let us see how matters stand at our own door. Do the people of England in general (not the highest or the lowest, for these usually know nothing of the matter, but people of the middle rank) understand Christianity? Do they conceive what it is? Can they give an intelligible account either of the speculative or practical

[98]"The Causes of the Inefficacy of Christianity," B 4:87, J VII:281–82, sec. 3.
[99]Ibid.
[100]"The Causes of the Inefficacy of Christianity," B 4:88, J VII:283, sec. 4.
[101]Ibid.
[102]"The Causes of the Inefficacy of Christianity," B 4:88–89, J VII:283–84, sec. 5.
[103]"The Causes of the Inefficacy of Christianity," B 4:89, J VII:284, sec. 6.

part of it? What know they of the very first principles of it? Of the natural and moral attributes of God? Of his particular providence? Of the redemption of man? Of the offices of Christ? Of the operations of the Holy Ghost? Of justification? Of the new birth? Of inward and outward sanctification? Speak of any of these things to the first ten persons you are in company with, and will you not find nine out of the ten ignorant of the whole affair?[104]

Take, for example, a key premise of classic Christian teaching: the crucial principle of the analogy of faith. Wesley exclaimed, "How small a number will you find that have any conception of the analogy of faith! Of the connected chain of Scripture truths, and their relation to each other!"[105]

c. The Ambiguous Record of the Evangelical Revival: Good Doctrine, Weak Discipline

Next Wesley examined those quarters where "scriptural Christianity is well known," where "Christianity is openly and largely declared, and thousands upon thousands continually hear and receive 'the truth as it is in Jesus.' Why is it then that even in these parts Christianity has had so little effect?"[106] The main reason: "Wherever doctrine is preached, where there is no discipline, it cannot have its full effect on the hearers."[107] No matter how sound the doctrine, if not joined with good discipline, it produces little of lasting effect.

It was to this special vocation that the evangelical revival was called: to preach the truth of Christian teaching so it could be fully embodied by every believer. But even where true doctrine had been preached, it had minimal effect on the culture, its moral behavior, its national spirit, and its intellectual life.[108] This amounted to a massive failure in its later stages.[109]

d. Ineffective Christianity Remaining among the Methodists

Worse. Amid his free-swinging critique of both non-Christians and Christians, Wesley was determined to "bring the matter closer still. Is not scriptural Christianity preached and generally known among the people commonly called Methodists?"[110] Many are "almost Christians." But "why then are not these altogether

---

[104]"The Causes of the Inefficacy of Christianity," B 4:89, J VII:283–84, sec. 6.

[105]Ibid. The analogy of faith is the principle that Scripture interprets Scripture, so that if a particular text is unclear, it is made clear by other Scriptures or by the whole sense of Scripture. This Reformed teaching is expressed in the Westminster Confession (1.9) in this way: "The infallible rule of interpretation of Scripture is the Scripture itself: and therefore, when there is a question about the true and full sense of any Scripture (which is not manifold, but one), it must be searched and known by other places that speak more clearly."

[106]"The Causes of the Inefficacy of Christianity," B 4:90, J VII:284, sec. 7.

[107]Ibid.

[108]"The Causes of the Inefficacy of Christianity," B 4:86, J VII:285, sec. 8.

[109]For an account of this decline, see Andrew Goodhead, *A Crown and a Cross: The Rise, Development and Decline of the Methodist Class Meeting in Eighteenth Century England* (Eugene, OR: Wipf & Stock, 2010).

[110]"The Causes of the Inefficacy of Christianity," B 4:90–91, J VII:285–86, sec. 8.

Christians?" They had heard of both good doctrine and a full life with God. Wesley therefore asked, "Why have we not learned of our very first lesson, to be meek and lowly of heart? To say with him, in all circumstances of life, 'Not as I will, but as thou wilt'? 'I come not to do my own will, but the will of him that sent me'?"[111] Where were the fruits of faith?

Then Wesley came closer to home in questioning the most genuine believers among the Methodists about how they were spending their money. How believers use their income is telling evidence.

The three rules on the use of money laid down among Methodists had been long ago made clear: gain all you can; save all you can; give all you can.[112] Many observe the first, a few observe the second, "but how many have you found that observe the third rule, 'Give all you can'? Have you reason to believe that five hundred of these are to be found among fifty thousand Methodists? And yet nothing can be more plain than that all who observe the two first rules without the third" are falling short.[113]

e. A Weakened Imperative to Self-Denial

Wesley's main theme at last surfaced: the primary reason why there is so little healing of both persons and societies — no balm in Gilead — is the lack of self-denial among the faithful who should know better. "Never was there before a people in the Christian Church who had so much of the power of God among them, with so little self-denial."[114]

Wesley said that God had given the Methodists so much, yet they "continually grieve the Holy Spirit of God, and in a great measure stop his gracious influence from descending on our assemblies." His evidence: "Many of your brethren, beloved of God, have not food to eat; they have not raiment to put on; they have not a place where to lay their head."[115] Wesley's questions became sharp: "Why do you not deal your bread to the hungry?... Did he entrust you with his (not your) goods for this end? And does he now say, 'Servant of God, well done'? You well know he does not. This idle expense has no approbation, either from God or your own conscience. But, you say, you cannot 'afford' it! O be ashamed to take such miserable nonsense into your mouths."[116] How believers spend their earnings reveals how seriously they are taking the Sermon on the Mount. Too many apparently reborn souls have not yet learned to say, "Not as I will, but as thou wilt." Not yet crucified to the world, they are still dead in the flesh. Not living a life that is hid with Christ in God, they remain hidden in themselves.[117]

---

[111]See Matt. 26:39; John 6:38; "The Causes of the Inefficacy of Christianity," B 4:90–91, J VII:285–86, sec. 8.

[112]"The Use of Money," sec. 1.1.

[113]"The Causes of the Inefficacy of Christianity," B 4:90–91, J VII:285–86, sec. 8.

[114]"The Causes of the Inefficacy of Christianity," B 4:86, J VII:291–92, sec. 9.

[115]Ibid.

[116]"The Causes of the Inefficacy of Christianity," B: 4:92, J VII 291–92, sec. 9.

[117]"The Causes of the Inefficacy of Christianity," B 4:86, J VII:291–92, sec. 9.

3. The Self-Destructive Cycle from Faith to Diligence to Riches to Pride

a. An Economic Analysis of Revival Moral Deteriorations

The rest of Wesley's homily spotlights rich but uncharitable and coddled church people who had not yet learned any real form of self-denial.

All believers are called to accountability but especially the rich. Within the evangelical revival, many had through diligence become wealthy, yet they remained tightfisted. They held back from the poor the good that God had entrusted to them.

Some objected that it would not be possible to supply all the poor with what they needed. But Wesley argued that these resources would be entirely within the abilities of evangelical circles if Christians brought their faith to active love. Many of their poor remained sick and weak because they had been neglected by their fellow Christians. Quakers and Moravians had done better.[118]

The Jerusalem church, though poor, cared for the widows, the fatherless, and the hungry. That great church in apostolic times remains the model for evangelical caregiving. "There was not any among them that lacked, but distribution was made to everyone according as he had need" (Acts 4:34 – 35, paraphrased).[119] This distribution was voluntarily offered, not coerced by state power.

Taking care of one's own family is a biblical mandate. But the children of the faithful would be just as well off spiritually with a little less materially. Evangelical Christians are called by God to "give all they can" to the poor. This needs to be far more intentionally taught.

Pastors collude with this negligence by not exercising the duty of admonition. They do no favor to wealthy laity by allowing them to go unchallenged regarding their responsibilities to the poor. The ministerial office is given in order that this teaching discipline be constantly exercised and the faithful protected from the moral dangers of laxity and hedonism.[120]

Wesley jested in prosecuting his case:

> I will not talk of giving to God, or leaving half your fortune. You might think this to be too high a price for heaven. I will come to lower terms. Are there not a few among you that could give a hundred pounds, perhaps some that could give a thousand, and yet leave your children as much as would help them to work out their own salvation? With two thousand pounds, and not much less, we could supply the present wants of all our poor, and put them in a way of supplying their own wants for the time to come.[121]

---

[118]"The Causes of the Inefficacy of Christianity," B 4:92, J VII:286 – 87, sec. 10.
[119]"The Causes of the Inefficacy of Christianity," B 4:92, J VII:287, sec. 10.
[120]"The Causes of the Inefficacy of Christianity," B 4:93, J VII:287, sec. 11.
[121]Ibid.

b. Voluntary Sacrificial Giving

The final turn of this line of argument: Wesley's thoughts turned to the poor. He called for greater sacrifice from those well-off.[122]

God is allowing time for repentance, but that time will eventually run out. Poignantly Wesley observed: "Indeed the work of God does go on, and in a surprising manner, notwithstanding this capital defect; but it cannot go on in the same degree as it otherwise would: neither can the word of God have its full effect unless the hearers of it 'deny themselves, and take up their cross daily.'"[123]

Wesley urged a return to the ancient practice of humble fasting with intercession for the needy. Many have ceased the practice of fasting, but it remains a fitting act of penitent response to God's innumerable gifts.[124] Wesley quoted the patristic writer Epiphanius, who recalled that "this practice of the primitive church is universally allowed. 'Who does not know,' says Epiphanius ... 'that the fasts of the fourth and sixth days of the week (Wednesday and Friday) are observed by the Christians throughout the whole world?'"[125] How did that universal practice fall into neglect?

For several years, the Methodists had observed fasting two days per week. But then it was allegedly carried to excess so as to impair health and increase pretense. Wesley said that in his day, far from fasting twice a week, most "do not fast twice in the month."[126] The only remnant of that tradition of fasting is Lent. What happened? Why did this ancient spiritual discipline fall into disuse?

Sadly, the search for wealth and ease replaced self-denial, already in the second and third generations of the evangelical revival. Nine of ten, Wesley thought, were decreasing in grace as they were increasing in wealth.[127]

4. The Dismal Cycle

a. From Faith to Diligence to Riches to Pride

Wesley became an astute socioeconomic observer with a high sense of realism. Nevertheless, his thought on cyclical patterns has seldom been recognized. He was among the first to note a profound irony in Protestant ethics that later writers like Max Weber and R. H. Tawney would describe more fully: wherever evangelical teaching is rightly heard, Wesley noted, it elicits diligence and self-responsibility. Good so far. Next step: These habits of prudence in turn are prone to beget riches. That should increase charity. But rather than increasing gratitude and generosity, the more likely tendency is that riches lead to more pride, worldliness, and bad tempers.

There is a deep contradiction here: the more serious one becomes about Christian faith, the more frugal one becomes; the more frugal, the richer; the richer,

---

[122]"The Causes of the Inefficacy of Christianity," B 4:93, J VII:287–88, sec. 12.
[123]"The Causes of the Inefficacy of Christianity," B 4:94, J VII:288, sec. 13.
[124]"The Causes of the Inefficacy of Christianity," B 4:86, J VII:282, sec. 14.
[125]"The Causes of the Inefficacy of Christianity," B 4:94, J VII:288, sec. 14.
[126]Ibid.
[127]"The Causes of the Inefficacy of Christianity," B 4:95, J VII:289, sec. 16.

the prouder. The more pride, the less charity? Wesley thought so and presented evidence.[128]

Why is there no balm in Israel? How can it be "that Christianity, true scriptural Christianity, has a tendency in process of time to undermine and destroy itself? For wherever true Christianity spreads, it must cause diligence and frugality, which, in the natural course of things, must beget riches. And riches naturally beget pride, love of the world, and every temper that is destructive of Christianity." Wherever true Christianity prevails, it tends to "sap its own foundation."[129] Each generation of evangelical revivals has regrettably proven this dismal argument from the first to the second to the third generation.

b. The Way Back to Evangelical Economic Accountability

"But is there no way to prevent this?" Is there no hope for continuity and durability of the community of self-denial? Wesley thought the most viable answers were self-evident. The spell is broken by repentance, discipline, and sacrifice. This is just as Jesus taught (Matt. 16:24 – 26).

The rule on money remains so simple a child can grasp it: gain, save, and give all you can.[130] It should be taught to children by parents and to laity by pastors.

Wesley was not advising for others a standard that he did not apply to himself. He gained, saved, and gave away to the fullest during his entire life. But Wesley knew well that nothing he gained, saved, or gave away was the source of his salvation, which hinged on what Christ had already done.[131] We are made wealthy by receiving our divine inheritance where moth and rust do not corrupt.

D. Against Idealizing the Past

Wesley was intensely interested in the course of universal history. He had strong faith in the providence of God, and he was also aware of the mystery of iniquity in all human history. He was wary of superficial theories of progress. He commended the truth of the "old religion," but not so as to idealize it inordinately.

1. Of Former Times

Wesley thought that Christianity had made a decisive contribution to human history, especially in its rare periods of intense spiritual renewal, that showed outward effects on the social order. This is one of the earliest essays by a Protestant theologian that attempts to connect the idea of progress with providence.[132]

a. Comparing Earlier Times with These Times

Those who realistically seek to assess whether the former times were superior

---

[128]"The Causes of the Inefficacy of Christianity," B 4:95 – 96, J VII:290, sec. 17.
[129]"The Causes of the Inefficacy of Christianity," B 4:96, J VII:290, sec. 17.
[130]"The Causes of the Inefficacy of Christianity," B 4:96, J VII:290, sec. 18.
[131]Ibid.
[132]"Of Former Times," B 3:440 – 42, J VII:157 – 58, secs. 1 – 4; JWO, intro.

to present times will delight in this homily. On June 27, 1787, in Dublin, Wesley preached a message titled "Of Former Times" based on Ecclesiastes 7:10: "Say not thou, What is the cause that the former days were better than these? for thou dost not enquire wisely concerning this" [Homily #102, B 3:440–53; J #102, VII:157–66 (*AM* November–December, 1787); J X:566–72, 620–25, 1787]. What does it mean to "enquire wisely" of former times in comparison to these times?

In this homily, Wesley was responding to those who posited an idyllic golden age long gone, so great as to lead to despair over the present. Countering pessimism, Wesley sought to set forth evidences that the spiritual opportunities offered by God today are as great or greater than the spiritual opportunities of former times.[133]

Wesley was aware of Jean Bodin, who in 1566 proposed a dialectical theory of historical oscillations that refuted both extreme pessimism and optimism.[134] In 1668 Joseph Glanvill had expounded the thesis of scientific progress in "The Progress and Advancement of Knowledge Since the Days of Aristotle."[135] Wesley wanted to see how an evangelical interpretation of universal history would stand up against these theories.

b. How Great Were Former Times Really?

Wesley urged caution against romantically idealizing the past while failing to recognize what God was doing in the present. Distance in time makes the former days seem more golden than they were. But to what extent were they actually idyllic? Did the love of God and man fill people's hearts and govern their lives more than now? Wesley was not convinced. He thought the revivals in England showed that "true religion has in no wise decreased, but greatly increased in the present century."[136]

In Homer's time, people foolishly imagined that their ancestors were greater, taller, and stronger than any since. Wesley reviewed this literary history of glorifying the past:

It is generally supposed that we now live in the dregs of time, when the world is as it were grown old, and consequently that everything therein is in a declining state. It is supposed, in particular, that men were, some ages ago, of a far taller stature than now; that they likewise had far greater abilities and enjoyed a deeper and stronger understanding, in consequence of which their writings of every kind are far preferable to those of later times. Above all it is supposed that the former generations of men excelled the present in virtue; that mankind in every age and in every nation have degenerated more and more, so that at length they have fallen from the golden into the iron age, and now justice is fled from the earth.[137]

---

[133]"Of Former Times," B 3:453, J VII:166, sec. 23.
[134]*Method for the Easy Comprehension of History.* Bodin was a Carmelite lawyer and economist.
[135]Joseph Glanvill, "The Progress and Advancement of Knowledge Since the Days of Aristotle" (1668; repr., Hildesheim, Germany: Georg Olms Verlag, 1979); Wesley, "Of Former Times," B 3:441, J VII:157; JWO, intro.
[136]"Of Former Times," B 3:440–43, J VII:157–58.
[137]"Of Former Times," B 3:442, J VII:158, sec. 2.

The weight of empirical evidence is clearly to the contrary: the human race has not diminished in stature. Nor were humans mentally wiser. Nor did they excel in moral virtue.[138]

2. Illusions Remembered

a. The Literary Testimony

Homer wrote of one of his heroes as one who was capable of throwing a stone "which hardly ten men could lift." But from available evidence, "it does not appear that in any age or nation men in general were larger than they are now." Wesley's empirically inquisitive mind sought out evidence. He found it in the size of tombs and coffins of ancient times. None of the mummies of ancient Egypt and none of the catacomb niches carved in rock in third-century Rome were more than six feet long.[139]

There are many wicked and demoralizing aspects of present history, but benevolence and compassion are also increasing in some quarters. Wesley believed that divine grace works with human freedom not to coerce it but to bring it to fulfillment. The classic Christian teaching underlying this is called providence. To fail to see these positive developments in the ongoing history of Christianity is a defect of empirical observation.[140] The preacher in Ecclesiastes was right to question the all-too-easy assumption that "the former days were better." God has not ceased working in history. Wesley thought the evangelical revival itself was powerful evidence.[141]

b. The Search for Evidence

Wesley was looking for evidence that would confirm or deny this common idea of the glory of former times and the intractability of his times. He began his message by sounding like an Oxford don: "It is not wise to inquire into the cause of a supposition unless the supposition itself be not only true but clearly proved so to be. Therefore it is not wise to inquire into the cause of this supposition that 'the former days were better than these,' because, common as it is, it was never yet proved, nor indeed ever can be."[142] The common assumption that former times were better has never been demonstrated, and Wesley was asking whether the assumption was even subject to reasonable proof. The weight of evidence is that times change, and sometimes, but not always, for the better.

c. The Dismal Assumption of Inevitable Deterioration after Adam

The Bible compares Adam before the fall with Adam after the fall. Were things getting worse from the beginning?

---

[138]Ibid.

[139]"Of Former Times," B 3:443 – 44, J VII:157 – 58, sec. 4.

[140]"Of Former Times," B 3:442, J VII:158, sec. 2.

[141]"Of Former Times," B 3:442 – 43, J VII:156, secs. 1 – 4.

[142]"Of Former Times," B 3:442, J VII:157, sec. 1. Note that this method of inquiry places Wesley as a precursor of modern logical analysis as seen in the analytic philosophy of A. J. Ayer and R. B. Braithwaite, wherein assertions or hypotheses that cannot be subjected to validation are futile.

From one perspective, it is certain that "the days which Adam and Eve spent in paradise were far better than any which have been spent by their descendants, or ever will be till Christ returns to reign upon the earth."[143] But from within the frame of the history of humanity following Adam, there is little evidence that early times were superior either in intelligence or virtue. The only ones speaking of Adam's fall are those who also remember that God has transcended and redeemed it.

But just how great were former times really? "Great and little are relative terms"[144] in relation to the greatness of God. As evidence Wesley offered this psychological explanation: "All men judge of greatness and littleness by comparing things with themselves. Therefore it is not strange if we think men are larger now than they were when we were children."[145] What is large to a child is different from what is large to an adult. Similarly, what is great to a spiritual novice is not what is great to one living constantly out of grace.

Wesley conceded that "many of the ancient writers, both philosophers, poets, and historians, will not easily be excelled, if equaled, by those of later ages."[146] "But that the generality of men were not one jot wiser in ancient times than they are at the present time, we may easily gather from the most authentic records," whether of history or literature or studies of ancient tombs. Wesley thought the Egyptians had "no deeper meaning in worshipping cats" than our schoolboys today have in playing with them. "I apprehend the common Egyptians were just as wise three thousand years ago as the common ploughmen in England and Wales are at this day."[147] The structure of the brain has not changed, but the history of consciousness has expanded the functional competencies of the brain.

The history of classic Western literature shows how often and passionately it has been assumed that "every age grows worse and worse." Homer thought that "the age of our parents was more vicious than that of our grandfathers. Our age is more vicious than that of our fathers. We are worse than our fathers were, and our children will be worse than us."[148] It is a typical human habit to think, as did Horace, that humans in every age are all prone to imagine their boyhood to be better than the present.[149] How did this idea of inevitable degeneration arise? Wesley was prepared with a simple empirical answer.

d. A Psycho-Social Explanation of the Premise of Historical Degeneration

Wesley proposed an intriguing explanation based on the psychological analysis of the child's relation to time:

---

[143]"Of Former Times," B 3:443, J VII:158, sec. 3.
[144]"Of Former Times," B 3:444, J VII:159, sec. 5.
[145]Ibid.
[146]"Of Former Times," B 3:445, J VII:160, sec. 6.
[147]"Of Former Times," B 3:445–46, J VII:160, sec. 6.
[148]"Of Former Times," B 3:446, J VII:161, sec. 8.
[149]Horace, Art of Poetry 2.173–74; "Of Former Times," B 3:446, J VII:161, sec. 8.

When those that have more experience than us — and therefore, we are apt to think, more wisdom — are almost continually harping upon this, the degeneracy of the world; [when] those who are accustomed from their infancy to hear how much better the world was formerly than it is now (and so it really seemed to them when they were young, and just come into the world, and when the cheerfulness of youth gave a pleasing air to all that was round about them), the idea of the world's being worse and worse would naturally grow up with them.[150]

Wesley wondered, *Does the idea of inevitable worsening come from the transition of a pleasant childhood to a troubled adulthood?* He thought that a "cool and impartial consideration shows that the former days were not better than these; yea, on the contrary, that these are, in many respects, beyond comparison better than them." So the community of faith "ought to acknowledge, with deep thankfulness to the Giver of every good gift, that the former days were not to be compared to these wherein we live."[151] To idealize former days may cause us to miss what God is doing today.

3. Assessing the Evangelical Revival

a. How Far Did the Reformation Elicit Durable Behavioral Change?

Beyond literary and psychological arguments, Wesley pressed toward the heart of the question: "But the principal inquiry still remains. Were not 'the former days better than these'" in the more consequential realms of virtue and religion? He said, "By religion I mean the love of God and man, filling the heart and governing the life. The sure effect of this is the uniform practice of justice, mercy, and truth." He pointed to modern exemplars of virtue and religion from France, England, and Ireland in both the Catholic and Protestant traditions. He asked, "Which of the former times were better than these with regard to this, to the religion experienced and practiced by Archbishop Fénelon in France, Bishop Ken in England, and Bishop Bedell in Ireland?"[152] Wesley was not saying that every modernity is an improvement on every previous history, but rather that each emerging modern challenge may elicit excellent and sometimes unprecedented moral and spiritual responses.[153]

Wesley again compared the effects of the Constantinian and Reformation eras with the effects of the evangelical revival of his day. Protestants have exalted the Reformation as a former time when the quality of moral and religious life improved and durably remained. But however much the Reformation improved biblical knowledge and doctrine, it did not have spectacular successes in changing human behavior. Luther himself remarked that in most cases "their tempers and lives are the same as they were before."[154] Better doctrinal teaching did not save the magiste-

---

150"Of Former Times," B 3:447, J VII:161, sec. 9.
151"Of Former Times," B 3:447, J VII:162, sec. 10.
152"Of Former Times," B 3:448, J VII:162, sec. 11.
153"Of Former Times," B 3:449, J VII:163, sec. 13.
154"Of Former Times," B 3:449, J VII:163, sec. 14.

rial Reformation from the horrible war following it that took "forty millions within the compass of forty years!"[155]

Some hark back to Constantine for a model of a good society. Wesley thought that the age of Constantine "was productive of more evil to the church than all the ten persecutions put together.... The kingdoms of Christ and of the world were so strangely and unnaturally blended together, Christianity and heathenism were so thoroughly incorporated with each other that they will hardly ever be divided till Christ comes."[156]

What about the age before Constantine? The common opinion is that "in the age before Constantine, the Christian church was in its glory, worshipping God in the beauty of holiness. But was it so indeed? What says St. Cyprian, who lived in the midst of that century, a witness above all exception, and one that sealed the truth with his blood?"[157] "Even in the apostolic age, what account does St. John give of several of the churches which he himself had planted in Asia? How little were those congregations better than many in Europe at this day?... So early did 'the mystery of iniquity' begin to work in the Christian church! So little reason have we to appeal to the former days, as though they were 'better than these'!"[158] Working backward from modern to earlier times, Wesley punctured the illusion that the former times were better.

b. Arguments for the Revival as a Positive Change Agent for Culture

Now let's move on to Wesley's main purpose in this homily—to point realistically and experientially to the amazing work God was doing in the eighteenth-century evangelical revival: "Whoever makes a fair and candid inquiry will easily perceive that true religion has in no wise decreased, but greatly increased, in the present century."[159]

In Wesley's time, deism was a test case to show the fragile durability of untested ideas. The curse of deism had spread all over Europe, but it had been effectively resisted in the revival of evangelical religion. Contrary to its own design, deism played a major part in preparing for the revival! It made nominal Christians more ready "first, for tolerating, and, afterwards, for receiving, real Christianity."[160] Far from the common opinion that deism crippled Christianity, the revival showed that Christianity crippled deism. "O the depth both of the wisdom and knowledge of God! Causing a total disregard for all religion to pave the way for the revival of the only religion which was worthy of God!"[161] In the generation after Wesley, the

---

[155]In reference to the Thirty Years' War; "Of Former Times," B 3:449, J VII:163, sec. 14.
[156]"Of Former Times," B 3:450, J VII:164, sec. 16.
[157]"Of Former Times," B 3:450, J VII:164, sec. 17.
[158]"Of Former Times," B 3:451, J VII:164–65, sec. 18.
[159]"Of Former Times," B 3:451, J VII:165, sec. 19.
[160]Ibid.
[161]"Of Former Times," B 3:452, J VII:165, sec. 20.

evangelical revival would be credited by many for saving England from anarchic bloody revolution as happened in France.[162]

Wesley looked to the North American evangelical revival as an indicator that the old religion when challenged can rise to defeat the demoralizing aspects of the new. Moreover, it can reverse the harmful cultural effects of nascent atheism. Wesley thought this was "beyond all contradiction in North America. Look what God had done there for the revival of true religion — ironically the total indifference of the government there whether there be any religion or none leaves room for the propagation of true scriptural religion without the least let or hindrance."[163] Ironically, the end of the established religion in America opened the door for the growth of genuine faith.

In London Wesley took as his example the growth of public works of charity in London hospitals: "In proof of this we see more hospitals, infirmaries, and other places of public charity have been erected, at least in and near London, within this century, than in five hundred years before. And suppose this has been owing in part to vanity, desire of praise; yet have we cause to bless God that so much good has sprung even from this imperfect motive."[164] Today it remains an established fact that evangelicals provide works of relief and charity greater than that of the average population.

4. God Has Been at Work in Our Times

Wesley thought this reversal was a providential work of the Spirit present in all human history but especially effective at certain times of high receptivity and intense desire for repentance and faith. Amid vice of every kind, God has caused

> a grain of mustard seed to be sown near London, and it has now grown and put forth great branches, reaching from sea to sea. Two or three poor people met together in order to help each other to be real Christians. They increased to hundreds, to thousands, to myriads, still pursuing their one point, real religion, the love of God and man ruling all their tempers, and words, and actions. Now I will be bold to say such an event as this, considered in all its circumstances, has not been seen upon earth before, since the time that St. John went to Abraham's bosom.[165]

This is evidence against the romantic idealization of times past. "Shall we now say, 'The former days were better than these'? God forbid we should be so unwise and so unthankful."[166]

The revival had evidences of positive social effects. "We are not born out of due

---

[162]Élie Halévy, *A History of the English People in the Nineteenth Century* (New York: Barnes and Noble, 1961); Elissa Itzkin, "The Halévy Thesis," *Church History* 44 (March 1975).

[163]"Of Former Times," B 3:452, J VII:165, sec. 20.

[164]"Of Former Times," B 3:452, J VII:166, sec. 21.

[165]"Of Former Times," B 3:452–53, J VII:166, sec. 22.

[166]"Of Former Times," B 3:453, J VII:166, sec. 23.

time, but in the day of his power, a day of glorious salvation, wherein he is hastening to renew the whole race of mankind in righteousness and true holiness.... How many precious souls has he already gathered into his garner, as ripe shocks of corn! May we be always ready to follow them, crying in our hearts, 'Come, Lord Jesus! Come quickly!' "[167]

In this chapter, we have studied Wesley's pastoral theology on effective church leadership, tending the vineyard, protecting the vineyard, learning from failures, allowing the old religion to be made new, assessing pros and cons of the evangelical revival, tracking its social consequences and economic effects, and seeing the eighteenth-century revival in historical context. This leads directly into the final chapter on what Wesley meant by "winning souls."

Further Reading on Effective Church Leadership

Kisker, Scott. *Mainline or Methodist: Discovering Our Evangelistic Mission.* Nashville: Discipleship Resources, 2008.

Knight, Henry H., and Don E. Saliers. *The Conversation Matters: Why United Methodists Should Talk with One Another.* Nashville: Abingdon, 1999.

Luckock, Herbert Mortimer. *John Wesley's Churchmanship.* London: Longmans, Green and Co., 1891.

Stoeffler, Fred Ernest. "Tradition and Renewal in the Ecclesiology of John Wesley." In *Traditio — Krisis — Renovatio aus theologischer Sicht*, edited by B. Jaspert and R. Mohr, 298–316. Marburg: Elwert, 1976.

[167]Ibid.

CHAPTER 11

The Ministry of Evangelization

A. Winning Souls

The evangelical imperative focuses on winning souls and holy living. These are our final themes for consideration in this volume on pastoral theology.

Throughout the evangelical revival, the single-minded intention was focused on winning souls, changing guilt to forgiveness, offering eternal life. Today Protestants call it "evangelism" and Catholics call it "evangelization."

1. The Evangelical Imperative

Nothing quite like either of these terms appears prominently in Wesley. These modern terms may tend to reduce the gospel to a sales program or an organizational instrument of social change.

The spread of the gospel was Wesley's constant concern. It was neither a numbers game nor a political strategy. Every one of Wesley's writings implicitly or explicitly announced the good news of Jesus Christ. The winning of souls one by one was his central concern. But it may seem curious to modern readers why Wesley said so little about methods of evangelism.

The reason is found in the writings already set forth in volume 2 of this series on Christ and salvation. The center of the evangelical imperative is about announcing the good news of God's pardon. The driving force in evangelism is the work of the Holy Spirit to bring people to faith in Jesus Christ the Son of God. The question still remains: What part are we called to play in pointing to the work of the Spirit in our lives so as to draw others close to God?

a. Winning Souls and Holy Living

Two of Wesley's writings plunge into the depth of this evangelical imperative. They are seldom read or quoted, but they reveal much about human transformation and conversion. One of these is an early homily titled "The Wisdom of Winning Souls." The other, "On the Death of the Rev. Mr. John Fletcher," is a later-years description of a soul winner whose entire life of faith manifested this unstinting evangelical passion.

"The Wisdom of Winning Souls," an early expression of Wesley's passion for holy living, was written before Wesley had fully matured in his understanding of conversion. "On the Death of the Rev. Mr. John Fletcher" was written in 1785 when Wesley was eighty-two, upon the death of a friend who had lived out his vision. Neither work discusses "how-to" evangelism. Both deal with the intrinsic connection between conversion and holy living.

To imagine that these two works are beyond the range of issues concerning the care of souls is to limit the vision of pastoral care. The first homily shows how God is glorified through the winning of souls. The second narrates the holy life of a soul winner. It describes a life that demonstrates how the evangelical imperative is lived out in the story of an incomparable pastor, Jean Guillaume de la Fléchère (John Fletcher).

2. The Wisdom of Winning Souls

The scene for the preaching of "The Wisdom of Winning Souls" was very early in John Wesley's ministry — 1731 — at Christ Church Cathedral, built AD 1150 – 1200. Many of the scenes of the Harry Potter films were shot in these hallowed environs. And there Wesley preached this ordination sermon on winning souls [Homily #142 (September 19, 1731), B 4:305 – 17 (not in the Jackson edition)]. His text was Proverbs 11:30: "He that winneth souls is wise," and his theme was that holy living is intrinsic to winning souls. "When we have cleansed our own hearts, God will deliver others into our hands."[1]

Only the wise are prepared to deal with concerns of the soul. Only those who are on the way toward holy living are preparing to become wise. The winning of souls is the heart of evangelical preaching, and it calls for its own distinctive form of wisdom. From lives lived in complete commitment to God, the gospel is transmitted person to person.

This special form of wisdom engages in a process that brings the seeker to a conscious desire for the purification of his or her heart from its ungodly affections. It leads toward a fixed resolution to live a life pleasing to God. This is a form of wisdom that shows the soul the way from sin to grace, from vice to virtue, from rebellion to obedience, and from "the shadow of death to light and peace."[2]

a. How God Is Glorified through the Recovery of Broken Souls

The sole goal of winning souls is the glory of God.[3] God is glorified by spreading abroad news of God's goodness, nature, and attributes so that God's incomparable goodness may be seen and praised in all his works. The goodness of God's works in creation, preservation, redemption, and consummation is made clear as the soul wakes up and "comes to itself." God's purpose in all his works is that his invisible nature might be seen in them (Rom. 1:20).

When the image of God has been defaced, only God's grace can restore it. When

---

[1]"The Wisdom of Winning Souls," B 4:307, proem.
[2]Ibid.
[3]"The Wisdom of Winning Souls," B 4:307, sec. 1.

the soul has suffered incalculable losses, a wise shepherd is needed. The soul can be restored to life by the one who gave life, the incarnate Lord.[4]

The winning of souls brings good to those who are won by guiding them away from eternal separation from the joy of God's presence and by enhancing their true happiness. "He that winneth souls eminently advances the glory of God by displaying his glorious nature and attributes to the sons of men, who alone of all the visible creation are capable of contemplating them."[5]

b. The Glory of God and the Good of Man

The one who wins souls wisely shares in God's own glory in three ways:[6]

1. By becoming a partner of grace in delivering a soul from eternal misery. If it were proposed either to save the whole finite world or to save a soul "a wise man would not pause a moment." The eternal soul is greater than the temporal world.
2. By advancing the happiness of creatures. "Here is wisdom! The pursuing of such an end as this! The recovering that was just sinking into the gulf of misery to happiness incomprehensible, eternal!"
3. By doing the greatest good possible to the person — by bringing to the soul "the honor of answering the end of creation."

The unique good this process brings is twofold: the glory of God and the good of man. The human instrument with whom God cooperates in conversion is called to become "a fellow laborer" with the Spirit. God's promise: "Those who honor me I will honor" (1 Sam. 2:30 NIV).

We reflect God's incomparable happiness when we draw souls into his presence. Wesley taught, "None can resemble God in extending his mercy even to the evil and unjust, without experiencing, even at that time, some degree of his happiness whose goodness he imitates."[7] The winning of souls has to do with the increase of happiness by extending the news of God's happiness to sinners.

For Wesley the winning of souls was all about happiness. This happiness is perceived by the faithful as a foretaste of "that more ample reward." If someone becomes a means of drawing another toward a life of eternal happiness, they both "shall together enter into the joy of their Lord."[8]

Wesley recalled the "remarkable words" of James, the brother of our Lord: "Whoever turns a sinner from the error of their way will save them from death and cover over a multitude of sins" (James 5:20 NIV). The reward of the soul winner is an enlargement of the heart and a participation in the enhanced happiness of those he or she wins,[9] For these reasons, the faithful believe that it is wise to participate with God in the winning of souls.

[4]Ibid.
[5]Ibid.
[6]"The Wisdom of Winning Souls," B 4:310, sec. 1.
[7]Ibid.
[8]Ibid.
[9]"The Wisdom of Winning Souls," B 4:310–11, sec. 1.

3. The Means of Winning Souls

A comprehensive approach to the whole person is necessary for the direction of the soul to be reversed from sin to grace. The way to win a soul is set forth in Scripture at three levels — mind, will, and affection:[10]

- The *mind* must first be convicted of the truth of the gospel.
- The *will* must then become confirmed by actual decisions in which good habits of prayer and action are formed.
- The *affections* must be accompanied by a resolution to purify the heart, to give up all of one's favorite sins and lusts, and to transfer final accountability from things below to things above.

The reclaiming of the soul through intellect, volition, and affection requires good judgment.[11] To win souls is to win not their heads alone but their willing and emotive lives, so that "every inclination which is contrary to the spirit of holiness" is redirected. Then they must guard against relapse.[12]

Soul winners are those who have enlightened the understanding, tempered the will of the sinner, and won the affections so the habits of holiness are durable. They are wise who learn to convey the glory of God deep into the intellect, will, and affections.[13]

Such a transformation is far beyond the capability of any human being as such. God works with human freedom to provide converting and sanctifying grace. This commission to win souls is not for ordained clergy alone, but for the general ministry of the laity. "A general commission is given to all the servants of Christ" to exercise wisdom in the winning of souls.[14]

This very early sermon by the young Wesley at age twenty-eight is incomplete in understanding the depth of the power of converting grace that he would later discover fully at Aldersgate, but its spirit is earnest and probing and is indicative of what was to come in the revival. It is like a snapshot of his quest for the holy life, which would become maturer in due time.

B. The Holy Life as the Essence of Winning Souls

Throughout this book, we have been thinking with Wesley about the care of souls. In this final subchapter, we are talking about embodying evangelical effectiveness. In "On the Death of the Rev. Mr. John Fletcher," Wesley was painting a picture of a soul winner who was well-known to all who were well informed in Wesley's connection: John Fletcher. In this ordinary man we get a glimpse of one who knew the wisdom of winning souls.

---

[10]"The Wisdom of Winning Souls," B 4:310 – 13, sec. 2.
[11]"The Wisdom of Winning Souls," B 4:311, sec. 2.
[12]"The Wisdom of Winning Souls," B 4:310 – 13, sec. 2.
[13]"The Wisdom of Winning Souls," B 4:314, sec. 2.
[14]"The Wisdom of Winning Souls," B 4:310 – 15, sec. 2.

1. A Personal Story of One Who Embodied the Wisdom of Winning Souls

To tell this story, I will conflate two overlapping records written by Mr. Wesley. The first is the funeral sermon of 1785, "On the Death of the Rev. Mr. John Fletcher."[15] The second is another much longer later essay of 1786, "A Short Account of the Life and Death of the Reverend John Fletcher."[16] Since they meld together chronologically as if a single account, I will bring them together in a single sequence. Both of these come very late in Wesley's life. Compared to his first funeral sermon on the death of Robin Griffiths, "On Mourning for the Dead" (1726), Wesley's views had matured significantly on the possibility of living the life of perfect love under justifying grace. Fletcher helped Wesley believe in this possibility by living out a life of glorifying God.

a. Behold the Upright

Wesley took the occasion of the death of his longtime partner, John Fletcher, to honor a complete pastor and archetype of what he hoped for among Methodist pastors. For Wesley, Fletcher epitomized soul care in its most endearing way through day-by-day holy living sustained throughout an entire lifetime.

Psalm 37:37 calls the congregation to "mark the perfect man." They are to take note of and examine carefully the life of one who lives every day in full accountability to God's grace. A life of righteousness within this world is surprising, unforgettable, and inspiring. The text of the homily "On the Death of the Rev. Mr. John Fletcher" is "Mark the perfect man, and behold the upright: for the end of that man is peace" [Homily #133 (London, 1785), B 3:610–29; J #133, VII:431–49].

Wesley preached this sermon at Fletcher's funeral. It is more than a sermon; it is a moving narrative of a life of ministry and holy living that forms the only proper basis for the care of souls. If asked to point to the life of a complete pastor who thoroughly fulfilled the work of ministry, Wesley pointed to John Fletcher.

Wesley wrote in his preface to his "Short Account": "No man in England has had so long an acquaintance with Mr. Fletcher as myself.... We were of one heart and of one soul. We had no secrets between us for many years."[17] Wesley knew John Fletcher over many rough roads in Britain and over a long stretch of thirty years.

In his later years, Fletcher was Wesley's closest confidant. Wesley was moved after Fletcher's death to offer a tender reflection on Fletcher's life. He later wrote a detailed examination of Fletcher's actual life choices. His intent was to show Fletcher's mature life pattern of total responsiveness to God's grace. Wesley was convinced from experience that Fletcher was "holy in heart and life."[18]

---

15 J VII:431–52 (1785).
16 J XI:273–66.
17 J XI:375.
18 "On the Death of the Rev. Mr. John Fletcher," J VII:431–49, secs. 1–8.

b. A Life Full of Grace

To get a sense of Fletcher's extraordinary life, it is necessary to hear a story, one that begins in Switzerland. The scene is a lakeside village situated on Lake Geneva between Bern and Lausanne.

John Fletcher was born in Nyon, Switzerland, of French Huguenot descent. His given name was Jean Guillaume de la Fléchère.[19] From childhood he was a soul in search of God. Upon graduating from the University of Geneva, Fletcher sought foreign service. He settled on traveling abroad to learn languages, first to Lisbon.[20] In England he turned toward the life of a quiet scholar and tutor.[21] He served the family of Thomas Hill at Tern-Hall, Shropshire.[22]

Fletcher became a member of the Methodist Society in London in response to the simple witness of an unknown "poor old woman who talked so sweetly of Jesus Christ," testifying to the joy of the new birth.[23] After John and Charles Wesley, he was the leading interpreter of the teaching of the Methodists. His *Checks to Antinomianism* mark him as Methodism's first great theologian.

Fletcher was renowned for his holy life and complete dedication. When asked if he had any needs, he responded, "I want nothing but more grace."[24] Wesley was Fletcher's elder by twenty-six years, and he had hoped Fletcher would be his successor in giving pastoral guidance to his whole connection of spiritual formation.

2. Commending the Lives of the Saints

Wesley commended the study of the lives of the saints, for he felt that they were relevant for our spiritual formation. The Spirit did not leave the church without living models for the holy life and practitioners of the care of souls. In fact, the reason he edited his thirty volumes of the Christian Library[25] was to make accessible to a lay audience the lives and thoughts of the saints.

Wesley rejected the assumption that the Spirit is powerless to redeem human life fully. He personally qualified his report of living exemplars of perfect love with Paul's disclaimer "Not as though I had already attained" (Phil. 3:12).[26] In rightly asserting the radical corruption in human history from time immemorial, some wrongly deny the power of the Spirit to transform that corruption. They imagine that the Spirit is not omnipotent and hence unable to totally redeem the inveterate sinner. They tend prematurely to discount the power of the Spirit in enabling the higher life.

Recollections of saintly persons are often viewed by historians as worthless hagi-

---

[19]"Short Account of the Life and Death of the Reverend John Fletcher," J XI:277, sec. 1.1. Hereafter "Short Account."

[20]"Short Account," J XI:289, sec. 1.9.

[21]"On the Death of the Rev. Mr. John Fletcher," J VII:433, sec. 2.12.

[22]"Short Account," J XI:281, sec. 1.14.

[23]Ibid.

[24]W. A. Sangster, "Called to Be Saints," Proceedings of the Ninth World Methodist Conference (Nashville: Methodist Publishing House, 1956), 363; see www.victorshepherd.on.ca/Heritage/Fletcher.htm.

[25]John Wesley, ed., Christian Library, 30 vols. (London: J. Kershaw, 1827); www.ccel.org/w/Wesley.

[26]Wesley, "The Character of a Methodist," digital text in www.crivoice.org.

ography or by ethicists as simplistic romanticism. Not so with Wesley. He had carefully examined the lives of many saintly individuals. He not only studied carefully the lives of prototypical saints of the past, but of saintly people whose behavior he had actually observed. He thought he had met many people of unblemished faith and was intensely interested in those living exemplars. He could see in them persons who in fact were living out the life of total responsiveness to the grace of God.

This life which Scripture commends for all the faithful is available to all through the power of the Spirit.[27] He pointed to those narrated in Scripture, such as Abraham, whose faith justified him, and Mary, the mother of the Lord. Then there were those in Christian history, especially in the earliest Christian period, whose witness required their death. They were remembered as those who shared fully in the life of Christ. Their sins were covered by his atoning blood on the cross.

Wesley was thoroughly familiar with the extensive Anglican tradition of saints of the two centuries before him. One need only to read *Foxe's Book of Martyrs* for an Anglican view of martyrs and saints from ancient times to the seventeenth century. Foxe's *Acts and Monuments*, which is the original title of his martyrology, was abridged by Wesley for his connection of spiritual formation.[28] Wesley did not pray to the saints, but he did pray with the saints.

3. The Holy Life Lived Out amid a Quiet Parish

John Fletcher had studied divinity before he believed it. Wesley reports that the more Fletcher heard of early Methodist preaching,

> the more uneasy he grew; and, doubling his diligence, he hoped by doing much to render himself acceptable to God; till one day hearing Mr. Green, he was convinced he did not know what true faith was. This occasioned many reflections in his mind. "Is it possible," said he, "that I, who have made divinity my study, and have received the premium of piety (so called) from the University for my writings on divine subjects — that I should still be so ignorant as not to know what faith is?"[29]

That Fletcher had a mind for the study of divinity is evident from his *Checks to Antinomianism*. But it took the Methodist Societies to bring this study of God to its remarkable fulfillment.

a. The Happiness of the Holy Life

Living from grace to grace toward a life of perfect love is a scriptural command. Wesley himself had observed this holy life lived out experientially in a number of living people, one being John Fletcher, whose holy life led to a happy life.[30] Such persons actually exist, not just in our imagination. If we open our eyes, we can see

---

[27]"On the Death of the Rev. Mr. John Fletcher," J VII:431 – 49, secs. 1 – 8.
[28]*JJW* 3:507.
[29]"On the Death of the Rev. Mr. John Fletcher," J VII:437 – 48, sec. 2.12.
[30]"On the Death of the Rev. Mr. John Fletcher," J VII:431, sec. 1.3.

them in their daily walk. Those who undertake the pastoral office are called to study these people carefully.

These same habits of holy living are available to any who are ready for the fullness of grace. They do not need academic credentials or testimonials. Their behavior is sufficient testimony. They demonstrate the power of the Holy Spirit to make us holy even as God is holy. Even within the limitations of our finitude, we can reflect the glory of God's holiness.[31]

Wesley resisted publicly naming these saintly persons for good reason: naming them makes them all the more likely to be viciously attacked in attempts to destroy them, just as we see in the case of Herod seeking to destroy the holy child of the refugee holy family (Matt. 2:13). Once named, they become targets. Wesley took the occasion of Fletcher's death to speak openly about Fletcher's holy life. But only after his last breath.

b. On Taking Note of One Who Lives a Holy Life

Those who desire to be happy, both in life and in death do well to take note of a fully faithful life. Wesley thought it probable that the psalmist, "while he uttered these words ['mark the perfect man'], had a particular instance before his eyes."[32] Such lives are not so rare as to be nonexistent.

This brief funeral sermon raises two questions: "Who is the person who is here spoken of, 'the perfect, the upright man'?" The second is "How does the upright life bring peace?"

First, Wesley made clear some basic assumptions. He said that only God is holy, as only God can be holy. But creatures can participate in God's holiness by the grace he provides. The person fully matured in faith is made upright by God's grace not by his works.[33] He believes in the atoning work that God the Son has accomplished for him on the cross. His spirit is united with the Holy Spirit. He embodies the body of Christ, the risen Lord. His faith works by love.[34] He has the "same mind in him which was in Christ Jesus" (see Phil. 2:5). His conscience is void of offense. He avoids all outward sin and abstains from every appearance of evil.[35] He lives by one rule: "whether he eats or drinks, or whatever he does, to do all to the glory of God."[36] He is growing constantly from grace to grace. The holy life is not motionless, but a life of walking blameless before God and humanity in his outward behavior and in his inward life, both public and private.

c. Peace amid Adversity

Whatever the challenges or temptations, such a life is lived toward a single purpose: *shalom*, the peace that comes with life in God by faith through grace.[37] God

---

[31]"On the Death of the Rev. Mr. John Fletcher," J VII:431 – 49, secs. 1 – 8.
[32]"On the Death of the Rev. Mr. John Fletcher," J VII:432, sec. 1.1.
[33]"On the Death of the Rev. Mr. John Fletcher," J VII:432, sec. 1.2.
[34]"On the Death of the Rev. Mr. John Fletcher," J VII:432, sec. 1.3.
[35]"On the Death of the Rev. Mr. John Fletcher," J VII:432, sec. 1.4.
[36]Ibid.
[37]"On the Death of the Rev. Mr. John Fletcher," J VII:432, sec. 2.

grants this peace, certainly in an eternal future rest but also in anticipation of eternal peace in this present life within the limits of time and space. It is a peace that comes only from life with God.[38] Such a person blesses everyone he or she touches. Wesley was convinced that this psalm text was abundantly expressed and fulfilled in the ministry of John Fletcher throughout his daily life and in his triumphant death. Many besides Wesley attested the life he lived.

The peace brought by the holy life is not a peace that shields the believer from all adversity. Hence it does not refer to outward peace. Those who know inward peace may be long buffeted by adversity, as was Fletcher by illness and calumny.[39] This peace is an inward certitude and strength precisely amid adversity. This peace cannot be described in finite or human terms alone, but only as "the peace that passes all understanding."[40]

At the end of life, this peace is already so settled in the whole character that it is like a graceful river steadily and unalterably flowing toward eternal life. This "unspeakable calmness" comes from the tranquility that the soul experiences in the body of Christ. It shapes all the passions and affections "in lower or higher degree," assuming the believer continues in faith "from the time they first [find] redemption" to the last day.[41]

d. Conversion from Law to Gospel

Fletcher's conversion bore some resemblances to that of Wesley's Aldersgate experience. It was a change of heart. He had been feeling the heavy burden of his sins. Having "wandered from God," he observed that "all my endeavors availed nothing," so much so that he "almost gave up all hope" in Lisbon.[42]

In January 1755, Fletcher reported, "I cried to God, but my heart did not go with my lips." Realizing that no human power could overcome his anger, he prayed, "Give me justifying faith." By grace he found to his surprise that his besetting sin no longer had dominion over him.[43] He began to see that his deliverance was real. More so it was confirmed by others. Through prayer his entire being was "filled with joy." Having been enabled by grace to receive rightly the gospel message, he experienced a full assurance of salvation.[44] He instantly received a sense of confidence in the promise of Psalm 55:22: "Cast your cares on the LORD and he will sustain you; he will never let the righteous be shaken" (NIV). In this way, Wesley described Fletcher's evangelical transition from the bondage of sin to justifying and sanctifying grace. "From this time he walked cheerfully."[45]

In January 1754 when Fletcher was "in earnest prayer, lying prostrate on his face

---

[38]"On the Death of the Rev. Mr. John Fletcher," J VII:433, sec. 2.1.
[39]"On the Death of the Rev. Mr. John Fletcher," J VII:432, sec. 1.3–2.
[40]"On the Death of the Rev. Mr. John Fletcher," J VII:433, sec. 2.
[41]Ibid.
[42]"Short Account," J XI:282, sec. 1.9.
[43]"Short Account," J XI:285, sec. 2.6.
[44]"Short Account," J XI:286–88, sec. 2.
[45]"Short Account," J XI:286, sec. 2.

before God," he had a vision of the crucified Lord giving "his life to ransom ours," that spoke to his heart.[46] Thereafter he gained peace and assurance and cheerfulness previously unknown to him but that would remain with him throughout his days. He experienced the sustained witness of the Spirit to his own spirit within his heart.[47]

4. The Model Pastor

a. Fletcher's Ministry at Madeley

Fletcher's manner won people's hearts: "Though he was yet far from being perfect in the English tongue, particularly with regard to the pronunciation of it, yet the earnestness with which he spake, seldom to be seen in England, and the unspeakably tender affection to poor, lost sinners which breathed in every word and gesture, made so deep an impression on all that heard that very few went empty away."[48]

"About the year 1753 (being now of a sufficient age), [Fletcher] was ordained Deacon and Priest, and soon after presented to the little living of Madeley, in Shropshire. This, he had frequently said, was the only living which he ever desired to have."[49] With Holy Orders as an Anglican, he settled into the village of Madeley, where he labored untiringly during most of the next twenty-five years, until his death in 1785. He faced opposition with equanimity. He became an exemplary pastor, living what he preached, praying ceaselessly, admonishing the lapsed, often arriving home late in the night, and then arising very early in the morning to preach to miners.[50] He faced many challenges and obstacles, especially a series of chronic illnesses. "Much opposition he met with for many years, and often his life was in danger."[51]

Fletcher had a continuing ministry to the poorest of the poor — especially colliers. Through his scholarly work, he became, according to the best minds of the connection, Methodism's first theologian. He entered into an austere form of a disciplined life, walking closely with God, praying continually, giving himself wholly to walking in the Word and adoring God. "Meanwhile he lived entirely on vegetable food, and for some time on bread with milk and water."[52] "His eminent desire was ... to be a witness of all that mind which was in Christ Jesus.... His constant endeavor was to preserve a mind free and unencumbered."[53] He was ever ready to bear the weaknesses of others. "God made his way plain." He received this parish as if "from the immediate hand of God, and unweariedly labored therein."[54]

---

[46]"Short Account," J XI:286, sec. 2.9.
[47]"Short Account," J XI:286 – 88, sec. 2.9.
[48]"On the Death of the Rev. Mr. John Fletcher," J VII:435, sec. 2.3.
[49]"On the Death of the Rev. Mr. John Fletcher," J VII:436, sec. 2.4; "Short Account," J XI:282, sec. 1.9.
[50]"Short Account," J XI:292 – 96, sec. 4.
[51]"On the Death of the Rev. Mr. John Fletcher," J VII:433, sec. 2.3.
[52]"Short Account," J XI:286, sec. 2.11.
[53]"Short Account," J XI:341 – 45.
[54]"On the Death of the Rev. Mr. John Fletcher," J VII:433, sec. 2.3.

b. Fletcher's Exemplary Service as Godly Pastor-Teacher

Fletcher was called to assist the Countess of Huntingdon by teaching at the seminary at Trevecca where Joseph Benson, Methodism's leading exegete, was headmaster. Fletcher became a much-loved teacher. It was his conviction that "to be 'filled with the Holy Ghost' was far better qualification for the ministry of the gospel than any classical learning (though that too may be useful in its place)."[55] "This he did with all his power, instructing the young men both in learning and philosophy."[56]

Fletcher taught at Trevecca from 1767 to 1772, but as an act of conscience chose to withdraw when asked to renounce certain tenets of Methodism in the controversy on double predestinarian teaching.[57] Fletcher was so much admired by Lady Huntingdon that she had made him president of Trevecca College, but theological differences arose between them. When required to "renounce those eight propositions which were contained in the Minutes" of the Methodist Conference, Fletcher refused, resigned the presidency, and returned to his parish in Madeley.[58]

At this small rural parish, Fletcher proceeded to write his famous volumes of *Checks to Antinomianism*, which upheld classic Christian teaching on grace and freedom.[59] After its publication, it was clear that he stood as Methodism's premier scholar and theologian. Wesley greatly esteemed "the purity of the language (such as a foreigner scarce ever wrote before), the strength and clearness of the argument, [and] the mildness and sweetness of the spirit which breathes throughout the whole."[60]

Fletcher was, in Wesley's view, "a living comment on his own account of Christian perfection."[61] "As far as man is able to judge, from the whole tenor of his behavior, he did possess perfect humility, perfect resignation, perfect love."[62]

c. Fletcher's Relentless Overcoming of Obstacles

Fletcher relentlessly visited "his whole parish, early and late, in all weathers." He was not cowed by "heat nor cold, rain nor snow, whether he was on horseback or on foot."[63] In the parish, he continued his intense and "uninterrupted studies."[64] He limited his diet largely to "bread and cheese, or fruit."[65]

Wesley proposed the idea of Fletcher "taking a journey with me into Scotland, to which he willingly consented. We set out in spring, and after traveling eleven or twelve hundred miles, returned to London in autumn."[66]

---

[55]"Short Account," J XI:292–302, secs. 4–5.
[56]"On the Death of the Rev. Mr. John Fletcher," J VII:433, sec. 3.6.
[57]"Short Account," J XI:292–302, secs. 4–5.
[58]"On the Death of the Rev. Mr. John Fletcher," J VII:433, sec. 3.6.
[59]"On the Death of the Rev. Mr. John Fletcher," J VII:433, sec. 3.7.
[60]Ibid.
[61]"Short Account," J XI:305, sec. 5.13.
[62]Ibid.
[63]"On the Death of the Rev. Mr. John Fletcher," J VII:433, sec. 3.7.
[64]Ibid.
[65]Ibid.
[66]"On the Death of the Rev. Mr. John Fletcher," J VII:433, sec. 3.8.

During his chronic illness of pulmonary consumption (tuberculosis), Fletcher was "visited by persons of all ranks." All "marveled at the grace of God that was in him ... his every breath was spent, either in praising God or exhorting and comforting his neighbor."[67]

After recovering, Fletcher "used this health in traveling all over the kingdom, five, or six, or seven months every year." Wesley remarked that not even Mr. Whitefield himself was "more eminently qualified"[68] to preach. In Wesley's opinion, Fletcher was the complete model of the pastor. In Fletcher's small parish of Madeley, "he did abundance of good in that narrower sphere of action which he chose, and was a pattern well worthy of the imitation of all the parochial ministers in the kingdom."[69]

5. Fletcher's Holy Life Made Him an Exemplary Pastor-Teacher

Those who look for patterns in Wesley's picture of the true pastor will find them abundantly in his account of John Fletcher. It was through his holy life that he became an inspiring preacher. His attentiveness to the poor and the sick was constantly attested.[70] The dilemma of fatherless children especially touched his heart. This empathy led him to develop means "for preserving a great number of desolate children, brought up only to beg and steal," so they would be provided food and clothing.[71]

Fletcher was wholly dedicated to bringing persons not only to a condition of being "cleansed from sin" but also "filled with the Spirit."[72] His favorite subjects of preaching and pastoral care were, anticipating Phoebe Palmer, "the promise of the Father, the gift of the Holy Ghost, including that rich peculiar blessing of union with the Father and Son."[73] He was seldom seen without the Bible and the "Christian Pattern."[74] Though a gentle soul, Fletcher was a man of courage, bold enough to preach his first sermon on James 4:4: "You adulterous people, don't you know that friendship with the world means enmity against God?" (NIV).

"His whole life was now a life of prayer.... If ever misconduct of an absent person was mentioned, his usual reply was, 'Let us pray for him.'"[75] According to Wesley, he was not known to have spoken an unkind word in the last twenty years of his life.[76]

a. Wesley's Key Partner in Leadership of the Connection

From 1757 to 1760, Fletcher responded to a call by Wesley to be Wesley's deacon (helper). Fletcher told Wesley he did this "to ease you a little in your old age."

---

[67]"On the Death of the Rev. Mr. John Fletcher," J VII:433, sec. 3.9.
[68]"On the Death of the Rev. Mr. John Fletcher," J VII:433, sec. 3.11.
[69]Ibid.
[70]"Short Account," J XI:287, sec. 2.1.
[71]"Short Account," J XI:335 – 39, sec. 8.1 – 5.
[72]"Short Account," J XI:306, sec. 5.14.
[73]Joel 2; "Short Account," J XI:306, sec. 5.14.
[74]"Short Account," J XI:286, sec. 2.2.
[75]"Short Account," J XI:290, sec. 3.
[76]Ibid.

If Fletcher had outlived Wesley, he surely would have played a major if not the central role in post-Wesley Methodist leadership. In 1773 Wesley asked Fletcher to succeed him in the leadership of the society. The ministries of Wesley and Fletcher interlaced flawlessly. The deeper roots of the holiness and Pentecostal and charismatic movements in the ensuing centuries would hark back to Fletcher as much as to Wesley.

In 1776 Wesley again invited Fletcher to travel with him on his yearly trek into the north of England and Scotland.[77] In 1777, desperately ill, Fletcher was forced to seek the balm of "the Hot-Well water" at Bristol. In his recuperation, he worked on *The Plan of Reconciliation*, a work calling for ecumenical unity, "uniting together, in the bonds of peace and love, all true ministers and followers of Jesus." Only through unity in the truth of the gospel can ministers "breathe peace to Jerusalem." Fletcher struggled constantly with complications of lung disease yet lost all fear of death. After a long voyage back to Switzerland, Italy, and France (Calais, Abbeville, Dijon, Lyons, and Aix), he returned to the Madeley parish with revived determination to engage in the demanding challenges of parish life.[78]

b. A Godly Marriage

"In the year 1781, with the full approbation of all his friends, he married Miss Bosanquet." Wesley wrote that "she was the only person in England whom I judged to be worthy of Mr. Fletcher. By her tender and judicious care his health was confirmed more and more."[79] He had met the gifted Mary Bosanquet when he was only seventeen years of age (1746). He early knew that if he ever married, she would be the one. He said:

Five and twenty years ago, when I first saw my dear wife, I thought, if I ever married, she should be the person. But she was too rich for me to think of, so I banished every thought of the kind. For many years after, I had a distaste to a married life, thinking it impossible to be as much devoted to God in married life as in single life. But this objection was removed by reading, "Enoch begat sons and daughters and Enoch walked with God, and was not; for God took him."[80]

It was not until 1781 that Fletcher proposed to Mary Bosanquet.

Their marriage itself became "a perpetual covenant to the Lord" in an extremely happy, open, honest, and loving relationship.[81] With her Fletcher carried on a vibrant ministry at Madeley, where they together founded a school for the children of poor working families in Madeley-Wood, and where they contributed to the early founding of the Sunday school movement.[82] Mary wrote of her husband:

---

[77]"Short Account," J XI:300, sec. 5.
[78]"Short Account," J XI:309, sec. 6.
[79]"On the Death of the Rev. Mr. John Fletcher," J VII:433, sec. 3.11; "Short Account," J XI:326, sec. 7.1.
[80]"Short Account," J XI:331–32, sec. 7.3.
[81]Ibid.
[82]"Short Account," J XI:331–32, sec. 8.

"I never knew anyone walk so closely in the ways of God."[83] He was bold in reproof of sin and faithful amid trial and danger, and he had a "peculiar sensibility" for souls committed to his care.

c. The Testimony of the One Closest to Him: Mary Bosanquet Fletcher

Mary wrote of Fletcher:

Since the time I had the honor and happiness of living with him, every day made me more sensible of the mighty work of the Spirit upon him. The fruits of this were manifest in all his life and conversation; but in nothing more than in his meekness and humility. It was a meekness which no affront could move; an humility which loved to be unknown, forgotten, and despised.... His delight was in preferring others to himself. It appeared so natural in him, that it seemed as his meat to set everyone before himself. He spake not of the fault of an absent person but when necessary; and then with the utmost caution.[84]

Mary also said, "He had a singular love for the lambs of the flock — the children; and applied himself with the greatest diligence to their instruction, for which he had a peculiar gift."[85] Fletcher was among the first to call for Sunday school for the education of children.[86] "It was his continual endeavor to draw up his own and every other spirit to an immediate intercourse with God.... He often said, 'It is a very little thing so to hang upon God by faith as to feel no departure from him.... I want to be filled with the fullness of his Spirit.... Death has lost its sting; and, I bless God, I know not what hurry of spirits is, or unbelieving fears.'"[87] Mary said the Lord favored Fletcher with "the most firm and resolute courage. In reproving sin and daring sinners, he was a 'son of thunder.'"[88]

Though deathly ill, Fletcher persisted in his duties.

On Thursday, August 4, he was employed in the work of God from three in the afternoon till nine at night. When he came home he said, "I have taken cold." On Friday and Saturday he was not well, but seemed uncommonly drawn out in prayer. On Saturday night his fever appeared very strong. I begged him not to go to church in the morning; but he told me, "It was the will of the Lord"; in which case I never dared to persuade. In reading Prayers, he almost fainted away. I got through the crowd and entreated him to come out of the desk. But he let me and others know, in his sweet manner, that we were not to interrupt the order of God. I then retired to my pew, where all around me were in tears. When he was a little refreshed by the windows being opened, he went on; and then preached with a strength and recollection that surprised us all....

After sermon he went up to the communion-table with these words, "I am

---

[83]"On the Death of the Rev. Mr. John Fletcher," J VII:447, sec. 3.12.

[84]Mary Bosanquet Fletcher, "On the Death of the Rev. Mr. John Fletcher," J VII:437 – 48, sec. 2.12.

[85]Ibid.

[86]"The Life and Death of the Reverend John Fletcher," J XI:336, sec. 8.8.

[87]Mary Bosanquet Fletcher, "On the Death of the Rev. Mr. John Fletcher," J VII:437 – 48, sec. 2.12; "Short Account," J XI:313, sec. 6.8.

[88]Mary Bosanquet Fletcher, "On the Death of the Rev. Mr. John Fletcher," J VII:437 – 48, sec. 2.12.

going to throw myself under the wings of the cherubim, before the mercy-seat." The service held till near two. Sometimes he could scarce stand, and was often obliged to stop. The people were deeply affected; weeping was on every side.... When service was over, we hurried him to bed, where he immediately fainted away.

His speech began to fail.... To his friendly doctor he would not be silent while he had any power of speech, saying, "O sir, you take much thought for my body; give me leave to take thought for your soul."... And here I break off my mournful story: But on my bleeding heart the fair picture of his heavenly excellence will be forever drawn.

He was rigidly just, but perfectly loose from all attachment to the world. He shared his all with the poor, who lay so close to his heart that at the approach of death, when he could not speak without difficulty, he cried out: "O my poor! What will become of my poor?"... Three years, nine months, and two days, I have possessed my heavenly-minded husband; but now the sun of my earthly joy is set for ever, and my soul filled with an anguish which only finds its consolation in a total resignation to the will of God.[89]

d. Faithfulness to the End

Fletcher died prematurely at the age of fifty-six. His steady faith was described by Wesley as an "uncommon a display of the power and goodness of God in behalf of his highly-favored servant."[90] Wesley knew of no one who had such a subtle mixture of virtues: speaking skills; gentle upbringing; and training in languages, philosophy, and divinity; and who manifested a deep and constant communion with Jesus Christ.

Wesley thought that a more excellent man could not be found. Fletcher excelled in all. He was reserved in speaking of himself. He kept no secrets from his wife. He brought everything to God in prayer. "For the good of his neighbor nothing seemed hard."[91] He did not speak idle words. He never mentioned the faults of an absent person unless duty required it. He was dead to the things of this world. He did not contract debt. He had a deep commitment to the nurture of children and to the younger generation. He never wasted a penny and gave all that he had to the poor. He took pains to conceal his excellencies. Remarked Wesley, "Such hatred to sin, and such love to the sinner, I never saw joined together before."[92]

Why did I go into such detail to narrate Fletcher's life? Wesley considered him a living example of the holy life, walking in the way and going on to perfection. It is this holy life that made Fletcher a true pastor.

Wesley commented on the testimony of Mary Bosanquet Fletcher, "There is little need of adding any farther character of this man of God to the foregoing account, given by one who wrote out of the fullness of her heart. I would only observe, that

---

[89]Ibid.
[90]"Short Account," J XI:356, sec. 10.
[91]Ibid.
[92]Ibid.

for many years I despaired of finding any inhabitant of Great Britain that could stand in any degree of comparison with Gregory Lopez or Monsieur de Renty."[93]

> The writers of their lives could not have so full a knowledge of them, as both Mrs. Fletcher and I had of Mr. Fletcher; being eye and ear witnesses of his whole conduct. Consequently, we know that his life was not sullied with any mixture of either idolatry or superstition. I was intimately acquainted with him for above thirty years; I conversed with him morning, noon, and night, without the least reserve, during a journey of many hundred miles. And in all that time I never heard him speak one improper word nor saw him do an improper action. — To conclude: Many exemplary men have I known, holy in heart and life, within fourscore years, but one equal to him I have not known.[94]

Wesley had not met one so uniformly and deeply devoted to God. "So unblamable a man, in every respect, I have not found either in Europe or America; and I scarce expect to find another on this side of eternity. But it is possible we all may be such as he was. Let us, then, endeavor to follow him as he followed Christ."[95]

These last two homilies, one early, the other late, one on winning souls and the other on the model of soul-winning, constitute the best testimony I have found to Wesley's teaching of the heart of pastoral care. Wesley saw in Fletcher the living proof of the capacity of the Holy Spirit to totally transform human life.

C. Conclusion

Wesley's pastoral theology covers virtually all subjects normally examined under the topics of the doctrines of the church and ministry: calling, gifts, pastoral counseling, resisting deception, the pastoral office, visiting the sick, pastoral admonition, care for the family, spousal relationships, raising children, religious education of children, worship, the ministry of Word and sacrament, the ministry of baptism and Holy Communion, the unity of the body of Christ, effective church leadership, evangelization, and spiritual formation for holy living.

But despite this breadth and depth, it is ironic that Wesley is seldom mentioned in the literature as a pastoral counselor or pastoral theologian. That is because one must dig to find these counsels scattered throughout his extensive body of work as a preacher and writer. I have sought to excavate these insights for the reader and organize them into a systematic pastoral theology. At least, this volume should once for all end the neglect of Wesley as a major voice in the history of pastoral theology. Moreover, I hope that Wesley's vision of pastoral care will be grasped and applied by his continuing legion of followers.

---

[93]"Short Account," J VII:448, sec. 11; cf. "La Vie de Monsieur de Renty," 1651. Gregory Lopez (1542 – 96) was a Spanish hermit and missionary to America. De Renty (1611 – 49) was a French Carthusian monk who worked with the poor. Both were noted for their piety.

[94]Wesley, "On the Death of the Rev. Mr. John Fletcher," J VII:437 – 48, sec. 2.12.

[95]"Short Account," J XI:365, sec. 11.

Further Reading on the Ministry of Evangelization

Chandler, Douglas R. "John Wesley and the Uses of the Past." In *The 1972 Wilson Lectures*, 27 – 37. Washington, DC: Wesley Theological Seminary, 1972.

Coleman, Robert E. *Nothing to Do but Save Souls: John Wesley's Charge to His Preachers*. Grand Rapids: Zondervan, 1990.

Coleson, Joseph E. *Be Holy: God's Invitation to Understand, Declare, and Experience Holiness*. Indianapolis: Wesleyan Publishing House, 2008.

Collins, Kenneth J. "The Conversion of John Wesley: A Transformation to Power." In *Conversion*, edited by John S. Hong. Bucheon City, Kyungki-Do, South Korea: Seoul Theological University, 1993. Published in Korean.

Knight, Henry H., and F. Powe. *Transforming Evangelism: The Wesleyan Way of Sharing Faith*. Nashville: Discipleship Resources, 2006.

Macquiban, Tim. "Dialogue with the Wesleys: Remembering Origins." In *Unmasking Methodist Theology*, 17 – 28. New York: Continuum, 2004.

Meeks, Merrill D. "The Future of the Methodist Theological Traditions." In *The Future of the Methodist Theological Traditions*, edited by Merrill D. Meeks, 13 – 33. Nashville: Abingdon, 1985.

Outler, Albert C. "How to Run a Conservative Revolution and Get No Thanks for It." In *Albert Outler: The Churchman*, edited by Bob W. Parrott, 397 – 416. Anderson, IN: Bristol House, 1985.

Alphabetical Correlation of the Sermons in the Jackson and Bicentennial Editions

The Bicentennial edition is represented by B. The Jackson edition is represented by J. Sermon numbers are often preceded by the pound sign (#). An asterisk (*) indicates that the homily was wrongly attributed to Mr. Wesley in at least one of its early editions, with the correct author supplied, or has varying titles or numbers in different editions.

The Almost Christian (#2, B 1:131 – 41 = #2, J V:17 – 25) — Acts 26:28

Awake, Thou That Sleepest (#3, B 1:142 – 58 = #3, J V:25 – 36) — Ephesians 5:14

A Call to Backsliders (#86, B 3:201 – 26 = #86, J VI:514 – 27) — Psalm 77:7 – 8

The Case of Reason Impartially Considered (#70, B 2:587 – 600 = #70, J VI:350 – 60) — 1 Corinthians 14:20

The Catholic Spirit (#39, B 2:79 – 96 = #2, J V:492 – 504) — 2 Kings 10:15

*The Cause and Cure of Earthquakes (by Charles Wesley — #129, Jackson ed. only, VII:386 – 99) — Psalm 46:8

The Causes of the Inefficiency of Christianity (#122, B 4:85 – 96 = #122, J VII:281 – 90) — Jeremiah 8:22

A Caution against Bigotry (#38, B 2:61 – 78 = #38, J V:479 – 92) — Mark 9:38 – 39

Christian Perfection (#40, B 2:97 – 124 = #40, J VI:1 – 22) — Philippians 3:12

The Circumcision of the Heart (#17, B 1:398 – 414 = #17, J V:202 – 12) — Romans 2:29

The Cure of Evil Speaking (#49, B 2:251 – 62 = #49, J VI:114 – 24) — Matthew 18:15 – 17

The Danger of Increasing Riches (#131, B 4:177 – 86 = #131, J VII:355 – 62) — Psalm 62:10

The Danger of Riches (#87, B 3:227 – 46 = #87, J VII:1 – 15) — 1 Timothy 6:9

Death and Deliverance (#133, B 4:204 – 14; not in Jackson)

Dives and Lazarus (#115, B 4:4 – 18 = The Rich Man and Lazarus, #112, J VII:244 – 55) — Luke 16:31

The Duty of Constant Communion (#101, B 3:427 – 39 = #101, J VII:147 – 57) — Luke 22:19

The Duty of Reproving Our Neighbor (#65, B 2:511 – 20 = #65, J VI:296 – 304) — Leviticus 19:17

The End of Christ's Coming (#62,

B 2:471 – 84 = #62, J VI:267 – 77) —
1 John 3:8

The First Fruits of the Spirit (#8,
B 1:233 – 47 = #8, J V:87 – 97) —
Romans 8:1

Free Grace (#110, B 3:542 – 63 = #110,
J VII:373 – 86) — Romans 8:32

The General Deliverance (#60,
B 2:436 – 50 = #60, J VI:241 – 52) —
Romans 8:19 – 22

The General Spread of the Gospel (#63,
B 2:485 – 99 = #63, J VI:277 – 88) —
Isaiah 11:9

God's Approbation of His Works (#56,
B 2:387 – 99 = #56, J VI:206 – 15) —
Genesis 1:31

God's Love to Fallen Man (#59,
B 2:422 – 35 = #59, J VI:231 – 40) —
Romans 5:15

The Good Steward (#51, B 2:281 – 99
= #51, J VI:136 – 49) — Luke 16:2

The Great Assize (#15, B 1:354 – 75 =
#15, J V:171 – 85) — Romans 14:10

The Great Privilege of Those That Are
Born of God (#19, B 1:431 – 43 = #19,
J V:223 – 33) — 1 John 3:9

Heavenly Treasure in Earthen
Vessels (#129, B 4:161 – 67 = #129,
J VII:344 – 48) — 2 Corinthians 4:7

Heaviness through Manifold Temptations
(#47, B 2:222 – 35 = #47, J VI:91 – 103)
— 1 Peter 1:6

Hell (#73, B 3:30 – 44 = #73, J VI:381 – 91)
— Mark 9:48

Human Life a Dream (#124, B 4:108 – 19
= #124, J VII:318 – 25) — Psalm 73:20

The Imperfection of Human Knowledge
(#69, B 2:567 – 86 = #69, J VI:337 – 50)
— 1 Corinthians 13:9

The Important Question (#84,
B 3:181 – 98 = #84, J VI:493 – 505) —
Matthew 16:26

In What Sense We Are to Leave the
World (#81, B 3:141 – 55 = #81,
J VI:464 – 75) — 2 Corinthians 6:17 – 18

An Israelite Indeed (#90, B 3:278 – 89 =
#90, J VII:37 – 45) — John 1:47

Justification by Faith (#5, B 1:181 – 99 =
#5, J V:53 – 64) — Romans 4:5

The Late Work of God in North America
(#113, B 3:594 – 609 = #131,
J VII:409 – 29) — Ezekiel 1:16

The Law Established through Faith, 1
(#35, B 2:20 – 32 = #35, J V:447 – 57)
— Romans 3:31

The Law Established through Faith, 2
(#36, B 2:33 – 43 = #36, J V:458 – 66)
— Romans 3:31

Lord Our Righteousness (#20,
B 1:444 – 65 = #20, J V:234 – 46) —
Jeremiah 23:6

Marks of the New Birth (#18, B 1:415 – 30
= #18, J V:212 – 23) — John 3:8

The Means of Grace (#16, B 1:376 – 97 =
#16, J V:185 – 201) — Malachi 3:7

The Ministerial Office (#121, B 4:72 – 84
= #115, J IV:72 – 84) — Hebrews 5:4

More Excellent Way (#89, B 3:262 – 77
= #89, J VII:26 – 37) — 1 Corinthians
12:31

The Mystery of Iniquity (#61, B 2:451 – 70
= #61, J VI:253 – 67) — 2 Thessalonians
2:7

National Sins and Miseries (#111,
B 3:564 – 76 = #111, J VII:400 – 408)
— 2 Samuel 24:17

The Nature of Enthusiasm (#37,
B 2:44 – 60 = #37, J V:467 – 78) — Acts
26:24

The New Birth (#45, B 2:186 – 201 = #45,
J VI:65 – 77) — John 3:7

New Creation (#64, B 2:500 – 510 = #64,
J VI:288 – 96) — Revelation 21:5

Bicentennial Volume Titles Published to Date

Note: Volume 1 was published in 1984. Subsequently, ten more volumes have been published. As of this date of publication, nineteen Bicentennial volumes remain to be published. They are marked with an asterisk (*). Here we have used the Jackson, Sugden, Telford, Curnock, and other editions to supplement the preferred Bicentennial edition.

1. Sermons 1–33
2. Sermons 34–70
3. Sermons 71–114
4. Sermons 115–51
*5. Explanatory Notes upon the New Testament I
*6. Explanatory Notes upon the New Testament II
7. A Collection of Hymns for the Use of the People Called Methodist
*8. Forms of Worship and Prayer
9. The Methodist Societies, History, Nature, and Design
*10. The Methodist Societies: The Conference
11. Appeals to Men of Reason and Religion and Certain Related Open Letters
*12. Doctrinal Writings: Theological Treatises
*13. Doctrinal Writings: The Defense of Christianity
*14. Pastoral and Instructional Writings I

*15. Pastoral and Instructional Writings II
*16. Editorial Work
*17. Natural Philosophy and Medicine
18. Journals and Diaries I
19. Journals and Diaries II
20. Journals and Diaries III
21. Journals and Diaries IV
22. Journals and Diaries V
23. Journals and Diaries VI
24. Journals and Diaries VII
25. Letters I
*26. Letters II
*27. Letters IIIa
*28. Letters IIIb (not yet published)
*29. Letters IV
*30. Letters V
*31. Letters VI
*32. Letters VII
*33. Bibliography of the Publications of John and Charles Wesley Letters VIII
*34. Miscellanea and General Index

Subject Index

order in, 238–39
participating in, 158–59
separating from, 166–72
unity in, 160, 167, 256
church fathers, 41–42
church leadership, 243–71.
　See also leadership
Clement of Alexandria, 18,
　42, 46, 254
Clement of Rome, 42, 46,
　253–54
Communion
　"constant communion,"
　　215–20, 248, 287
　Holy Communion,
　　169–70, 174, 179,
　　215–20, 234, 288
　receiving, 167, 212,
　　219–23, 234
confirmation, status of,
　179–80
confirmation manual, 195
confirmation practice,
　212–13
conflict, mediating, 60–64.
　See also counseling
"constant communion,"
　215–20, 248, 287
corruption of human nature,
　258–59
counseling
　accountability in, 63–64
　admonitions, 69–74
　backbiting cure, 61
　being true to God, 66–68
　conflict mediation, 60–64
　confrontations and, 73–74
　evil speaking cure, 60, 64
　face-to-face visits, 59–60
　guilt and, 64
　help with, 62–63
　lay counseling, 50–51
　for life stages, 137–54
　manner of, 69–74
　mediating conflict, 60–64
　ministry of, 55–57
　resistance to, 74–77
　speaking without guile,
　　64–68

timing of, 69–70
visiting sick, 56–60
Countess of Huntingdon, 29
Cranmer, Thomas, 18, 29
Curnock, Nehemiah, 21, 295
Cyprian, 18, 42, 46, 210, 254,
　269

D
"darkness of mind," 82–83,
　91–93, 96–97. *See also*
　wilderness state
Davies, Rupert E., 192
death
　deliverance and, 148–49
　facing, 148–49
　resurrection and, 90,
　　100–102, 158, 182,
　　191, 195, 201, 204,
　　219, 223
　understanding, 148–51
deception
　dynamics of, 74–78
　"father of lies" and, 75
　love and, 77
deterioration
　causes of, 249–50
　historical degeneration,
　　266–68
　of morals, 262
　of music, 130
Dewey, John, 114
Didymus of Alexandria, 42
diligence, 262–64
discontent, 87, 90–91
dismal cycle, 263–64
dissimulation, 74–77
dying, care for, 148–51

E
education
　of children, 33, 109,
　　114–17, 131–36, 147
　discipline and, 115
　goal of, 117
　guiding, 147
　harm from, 114–16
　as preparation for ministry,
　　43–44
Edwards, Jonathan, 31

endowments, 38–42
Epiphanius, 42
eternal garden, 105–6
eternal life, 48, 97, 105–6,
　123, 149, 151, 223, 273,
　281
Eusebius, 42
evangelical effectiveness,
　243–50, 276
evangelical imperative,
　273–74
evangelical pastors, 41, 43,
　162–64, 196. *See also*
　pastors
evangelical revival
　assessing, 257–64,
　　268–71
　debate on, 168–75
　initiation of, 29–30
　lay preaching and, 240–41
　"old religion" and, 253–55
　progress of, 250–53,
　　263–66
evangelical worship, 178–79
evangelization
　holy living and, 273–74,
　　276–88
　ministry of, 273–89
evidence, search for, 266
evil-speaking cure, 60, 64

F
faith
　community of, 63–64
　counseling and, 63–64
　dismal cycle from, 263–64
　self-destructive cycle from,
　　262–64
　strengthening, 95–103
　temptations and, 95–103
Fallen man, 118, 139
false charges, resisting,
　240–41
false religion, 106–7
family. *See also* children;
　marriage
　covenant partnership,
　　137–39
　happiness of, 109–13
　intergenerational covenant
　　of, 111–12

W

Wall, William, 211
wealth, abuse of, 248–49
Weber, Max, 263
wedding feast, 223–25
wedding garment, 222–25
Wesley, Charles, 21, 30,
      130–31, 165, 195, 235,
      278
Wesley, John
   background of, 29–31
   evangelical connection
      of, 30
   intent of, 15–16
   interpretation of, 16
   opposition to, 166–67
   as pastoral guide, 29–31
   systemic ordering by, 22
   teachings of, 15–22,
      29–31
Wesley, Samuel, 42, 193–96,
      211

Wesley, Susanna, 109, 114
Wesleyan connection,
      165–68, 211, 229–33,
      236
White, James F., 187
Whitefield, George, 29, 284
Wilberforce, William, 29
wilderness state
   "darkness of mind" and,
      82–83, 91–93,
      96–97
   discontent and, 87, 90–91
   inattentiveness and, 86–88
   manifold temptations and,
      91–97
   self-examination and,
      88–90
   signs of, 85–87
   sin and, 84–85
   symptoms of, 83–84
   temptations and, 82–91

will
   breaking, 120–21
   conquering, 127
   forming, 117
winning souls
   broken souls and, 274–75
   holy living and, 273–74,
      276–88
   means of, 276
   wisdom of, 274–75,
      277–78

Y

young people. *See also* family
   appeal to, 128–29
   communicating with,
      122–29
   education of, 33, 109,
      114–17, 131–36, 147
   honoring parents, 123–25
   obedience of, 122–25,
      128–29
   selecting mate, 148

Scripture Index